OXFORD STUDIES IN EUROPEAN LAW

Legal Pluralism in European Contract Law

OXFORD STUDIES IN EUROPEAN LAW

Series Editors

Paul Craig, Professor of English Law at St John's College, Oxford and Gráinne de Búrca, Professor of Law at New York University School of Law

The aim of this series is to publish important and original research on EU law. The focus is on scholarly monographs, with a particular emphasis on those which are interdisciplinary in nature. Edited collections of essays will also be included where they are appropriate. The series is wide in scope and aims to cover studies of particular areas of substantive and of institutional law, historical works, theoretical studies, and analyses of current debates, as well as questions of perennial interest such as the relationship between national and EU law and the novel forms of governance emerging in and beyond Europe. The fact that many of the works are interdisciplinary will make the series of interest to all those concerned with the governance and operation of the EU.

OTHER TITLES IN THIS SERIES

The Horizontal Effect of Fundamental Rights in the European Union: A Constitutional Analysis
Eleni Frantziou

Frontex and Human Rights: Responsibility in 'Multi-Actor Situations' under the ECHR and EU Public Liability Law
Melanie Fink

EU Equality Law: The First Fundamental Rights Policy of the EU
Elise Muir

Subnational Authorities in EU Law
Michèle Finck

Accessing Asylum in Europe
Violeta Moreno-Lax

National Parliaments after the Lisbon Treaty and the Euro Crisis
Davor Jančić

Environmental Integration in Competition and Free-Movement Laws
Julian Nowag

EU Agencies: Legal and Political Limits to the Transformation of the EU Administration
Merijn Chamon

Coherence in EU Competition law
Wolf Sauter

Foreign Policy Objectives in European Constitutional Law
Joris Larik

Economic Governance in Europe: Comparative Paradoxes and Constitutional Challenges
Federico Fabbrini

Private Regulation and the Internal Market: Sports, Legal Services, and Standard Setting in EU Economic Law
Mislav Mataija

The EU Deep Trade Agenda: Law and Policy
Billy A. Melo Araujo

Legal Pluralism in European Contract Law

VANESSA MAK

She was a Professor of Private Law at Tilburg University from 2014-2020. From October 2020 She is a Professor of Civil Law at Leiden University

OXFORD
UNIVERSITY PRESS

OXFORD
UNIVERSITY PRESS

Great Clarendon Street, Oxford, OX2 6DP,
United Kingdom

Oxford University Press is a department of the University of Oxford.
It furthers the University's objective of excellence in research, scholarship,
and education by publishing worldwide. Oxford is a registered trade mark of
Oxford University Press in the UK and in certain other countries

First Edition published in 2020

Impression: 3

Published in the United States of America by Oxford University Press
198 Madison Avenue, New York, NY 10016, United States of America

British Library Cataloguing in Publication Data

Data available

Library of Congress Control Number: 2020937826

ISBN 978-0-19-885448-7

Printed and bound by
CPI Group (UK) Ltd, Croydon, CR0 4YY

Series Editors' Preface

Vanessa Mak's book on *Legal Pluralism in European Contract Law* is a welcome addition to this series. It is predicated on the empirical assumption that there has been a significant shift in the nature of private law relationships. The reasons underlying this are eclectic, and include the changed nature of work relationships, the possibilities that flow from the internet and the transnational dimension to private legal ordering.

The change is exemplified by the rise of the platform economy, whereby transactions between suppliers and customers are facilitated through online platforms. Individuals that had hitherto taken part in markets primarily as consumers purchasing goods and services from professional traders can now more readily, in the words of the author, 'set up shop for themselves'. The shift is further exemplified by what is known as 'servitization', connoting the shift towards service contracts enabling access to goods, such as streaming services for movies or music, and lease contracts for bicycles or cars. While there are positive aspects to these developments, viewed in terms of increased autonomy, there are also dangers in terms of protecting the vulnerable, and more generally in determining the rights that attach to such contracts. The perils of working in the gig economy are evident from the literature.

Vanessa Mak considers how the values of EU law, that are reflected in contract laws at the national and the EU level, can be safeguarded when law-making shifts from public regulation to private regulation beyond the state. She develops a theory of law-making in European private law designed to accommodate the shift from state-centred law-making, to the co-existence of sources of norms beyond the state without a formal hierarchy. The theoretical frame for the analysis is legal pluralist scholarship in transnational private law. The author does not, however, rest content with a procedural approach to law-making, but considers the substantive values that should be protected.

The subject matter of this book is important, and so too is the analysis. The book will be of interest not only to EU scholars, but also to those whose primary focus is on the nature of private legal ordering beyond the state.

Paul Craig and Gráinne de Búrca

Acknowledgements

This book is the result of a research project started during my stay as a visitor at NYU's Jean Monnet Center in 2014–2015. I have benefited immensely from discussions with colleagues in the past years, who have helped bring focus to the arguments that I present here. More pages could have been written, as the role of private regulation besides, or beyond, state law continues to be subject to debate. These are my thoughts on the topic for now, and I look forward to discussing them further.

I would like to express my gratitude to a number of people whose support has been invaluable in the course of writing the book. First, the two Hans whose work I discuss with quite a lot of detail in this book: Hans Micklitz and Hans Lindahl. Thank you both for your wisdom and your friendship. We do not always agree, and I am glad of that, because it means that there are still new things to learn. I also thank Chantal Mak, who read some of the chapters in their final stages and provided me with extremely useful comments. It is wonderful to be able to discuss new work with someone who is both kind and critical.

In the wider academic community I thank my colleagues at the Jean Monnet Center who listened to and commented on first drafts of Chapter 2. Peter Lindseth, Armin von Bogdandy, Pietro Faraguna, Kasia Granat, Dominik Steiger, Bilyana Petkova, Andrew Mitchell, Tania Voon, Áine Ryall, Mor Bakhoum, and Luc Peeperkorn. I also thank Gráinne de Búrca, who as Director of the Center was a wonderful host and who also kindly agreed to comment on my proposal for this book. Further, I am grateful for having had the opportunity to discuss chapters of the book at the Oxford Institute of European and Comparative Law, the University of Amsterdam, and most recently at the University of New South Wales.

The bulk of the book was written after my return to Tilburg. I am indebted to my head of department, Stéphanie van Gulijk. Thank you for giving me time to write and to bring this project to completion. Thank you also for always being there to bounce ideas off and for your incredible patience and tireless effort in leading our department. I also thank my Dean, Geert Vervaeke. He appointed me as Vice Dean for Research halfway through this project. That was not in itself conducive to writing, but it has been an immense pleasure working with you, Geert. Thank you for your support and for your friendship.

Finally, I would like to thank family and friends without whom this would all mean nothing: Anita Mak-van Lankeren, Elaine Mak, Chantal Mak, Joost Mak, Constant Mak, Alan Littler, Jannemieke Ouwerkerk, and Milly Freire-Archer. Thank you for your love and support.

Vanessa Mak
Utrecht, 27 April 2020

Contents

Table of Cases

ECJ CASE LAW

THE NETHERLANDS

UNITED KINGDOM

Table of Legislation

COUNCIL OF EUROPE

INTERNATIONAL LAW

INTERNATIONAL STANDARDS

FRANCE

GERMANY

ITALY

THE NETHERLANDS

UNITED KINGDOM

List of Abbreviations

ACM	Authority for Consumers and Markets (Netherlands)
ADR	alternative dispute resolution
AI	artificial intelligence
ALI	American Law Institute
ANEC	European Association for the Co-ordination of Consumer Representation in Standardisation
API	application programming interface
B2B	business-to-business
B2C	business-to-consumer
BGB	*Bürgerliches Gesetzbuch* (Germany)
CCD	Consumer Credit Directive
CEN	European Committee for Standardization
CENELEC	European Committee for Electrotechnical Standardization
CESL	Common European Sales Law
CFR	Charter of Fundamental Rights
CFR	Common Frame of Reference
CISG	Contracts for the International Sale of Goods
CJEU	Court of Justice of the European Union
CMA	Competition and Markets Authority (United Kingdom)
Cnil	*Commission nationale informatique et libertés* (France)
CPC Network	Consumer Protection Cooperation Network
CSR	corporate social responsibility
DCFR	Draft Common Frame of Reference
DGCCRF	*Direction générale de la concurrence, de la consummation et de la repression des frauds* (France)
ECC-Net	European Consumer Centres' Network
ECHR	European Convention on Human Rights
ECN	European Competition Network
EEC	European Economic Community
ELI	European Law Institute
ELSI	European Legal Studies Institute
ERPL	European Regulatory Private Law
ESO	European standard-setting organization
ESP	European Social Pillar
ETSI	European Telecommunications Standards Institute
EU	European Union
FATF	Financial Action Task Force
FDA	Food and Drug Administration (United States)

ICC	International Chamber of Commerce
IoT	Internet of Things
ISO	International Organization for Standardization
KPI	key performance indicator
NHS	National Health Service (United Kingdom)
ODR	online dispute resolution
OECD	Organisation for Economic Co-Operation and Development
OMC	Open Method of Coordination
P2B	platform-to-business
PECL	Principles of European Contract Law
PEL	Principles of European Law
PICC	Principles of International Commercial Contracts
PIP	Poly Implant Prothèse
R&D	research and development
RPM	resale price maintenance
SCENIHR	Scientific Committee on Emerging and Newly Identified Health Risks
TEU	Treaty on European Union
TFEU	Treaty on the Functioning of the European Union
UCPD	Unfair Commercial Practices Directive
UCTD	Unfair Contract Terms Directive
UNCITRAL	United Nations Commission on International Trade Law
UNIDROIT	International Institute for the Unification of Private Law
WTO	World Trade Organization

1
Introduction

This book presents a contract lawyer's perspective on lawmaking and governance. It was inspired by the observation that markets for consumer goods and services are changing. Consumer markets in the United States, Western Europe, and Asia have followed similar patterns since the 1960s. Businesses developed goods and services and offered these in a standardized format to consumers, who had little or no space to bargain for specific terms. In line with the generalization taking place in these markets, legal systems developed consumer protection rules tailored to general categories like the 'average consumer'. Consumer law, besides competition law, became an important tool in ensuring the protection of a large category of non-professional actors in markets shaped by businesses. Recently, however, this model based on balancing the interests of broad legal categories has begun to alter. Business models have emerged in which consumers obtain goods and services from peers, and in which the focus is on the access to goods (eg music, bicycles) rather than on ownership. Due to these developments, the position of consumers shifts from being part of a general category to being approached by businesses on a more individualized or personalized basis.[1]

One of the most prominent examples of this trend is the rise of the platform economy, the term used to designate transactions between suppliers and customers facilitated through online platforms. Few developments have disrupted existing market structures and power relations between market actors as platforms have in the last decade.[2] They opened the way for individuals, who until then took part in markets mostly as consumers purchasing goods and services from professional traders, to set up shop for themselves. Anyone who has something to offer, whether it concerns goods, services, or labour, can connect with a huge customer market simply by creating an account on an online platform such as Amazon, Airbnb, Uber, or Peerby.

[1] See eg C Busch and A De Franceschi, 'Granular Legal Norms: Big Data and the Personalization of Private Law' in V Mak, TFE Tjong Tjin Tai, and A Berlee (eds), *Research Handbook in Data Science and Law* (Edward Elgar 2018) 408.

[2] The term 'disruptive' is not entirely correct from an economic perspective, as platform companies have not replaced incumbents in the market. They have created alternative services that may to some extent compete with existing services (eg in the hotel or taxi services sector). See CM Christensen, ME Raynor, and R McDonald, 'What is Disruptive Innovation?', Harvard Business Review 2015 <https://hbr.org/2015/12/what-is-disruptive-innovation> accessed 28 February 2020, as are all websites in this chapter.

Legal Pluralism in European Contract Law. Vanessa Mak, Oxford University Press (2020). © Vanessa Mak.
DOI: 10.1093/oso/9780198854487.001.0001.

Whereas some have hailed this development as a new consumer era in which autonomy is almost boundless, it is not hard to see the risks that it brings too. Autonomy can indeed increase for consumers who are confident selling and buying online,[3] and who have the means to do so. But what about those who are vulnerable, either because they do not understand the terms and conditions used on platforms, cannot adequately assess the reliability of online advertisements, or have difficulty keeping track of their credit obligations? In regular business-to-consumer (B2C) transactions, this group enjoys a certain level of consumer protection, in the European Union (EU) even more than in other parts of the world. In the platform economy their rights are less straightforward. Many transactions are between consumers (peer-to-peer) and therefore not governed by rules of consumer protection. In some cases it is not even clear from the information provided on a platform whether the supplier is a professional trader or not. And with this we have not even touched upon the perils of working in the gig economy,[4] or the risk of being run over by an Uber taxi or a Deliveroo bicycle when one crosses the street.[5]

The types of questions raised here fall within the remit of private law. They concern the contractual rights that suppliers and customers have vis-à-vis each other and their potential liability. However, whereas the rights and duties of these parties would normally be governed by rules of national contract and consumer law, or perhaps also by rules of European origin if the parties are in the European Union, the platform economy has created a private sphere that operates largely through other mechanisms. In many cases, platform operators have themselves introduced rules that they deem necessary for the successful functioning of the platform,[6] for example codes of conduct or 'community standards' on safety and security. Also, online review mechanisms are used by platforms as a means to regulate the reliability of users and the monitoring of the quality of services rendered through the platform. Finally, platforms themselves provide online dispute resolution services, and many disputes between users never reach state courts because litigation is

[3] cf the 'average consumer' of EU law, who is considered to be 'reasonably well-informed, reasonably observant and circumspect'; see Case C-210/96 *Gut Springenheide GmbH v Oberkreisdirektor des Kreises Steinfurt* [1998] ECR I-4657, ECLI:EU:C:1998:369, and Directive 2005/29/EC concerning unfair business-to-consumer commercial practices in the internal market [2005] OJ L149/22 (Unfair Commercial Practices Directive), Art 5 and recital 18. The Unfair Commercial Practices Directive, however, also protects vulnerable consumers; see Art 5(3).

[4] On changing labour relations in the platform economy, see J Prassl, *Humans as a Service. The Promise and Perils of Work in the Gig Economy* (OUP 2018).

[5] Uber drivers have caused a number of fatal accidents involving cyclists in the Netherlands; see 'Dutch Road Safety Organisation Calls for Tighter Uber Regulation after Deaths' (*Dutch News*, 18 January 2019) <https://www.dutchnews.nl/news/2019/01/dutch-road-safety-organisation-calls-for-tighter-uber-regulation-after-deaths/>. The example of the Deliveroo bicycle—a meal transportation service—should be familiar to anyone who lives in Utrecht.

[6] These rules have a trust-building function between users who often do not know each other and cannot assess each other's reliability; see O Lobel, 'The Law of the Platform' (2016) 101 Minnesota Law Review 87, 146 ff.

too costly or too cumbersome.[7] In this context, the question of whether platforms comply with rules of contract or consumer law is of only relative importance. More prominent is the question regarding what substance the norms have that are designed, applied, and monitored by platform operators in this private sphere that they have created alongside or beyond the state.[8]

Other aspects of consumer markets that are increasingly subject to private governance are the terms and conditions applying to the use of new technologies—where subjective conformity requirements decided by the supplier apply in the absence of objective technical standards—and in markets in which ownership of goods is pushed aside in favour of 'servitization'. Servitization is the term used to denote a shift towards service contracts aiming to enable the use of, or access to, goods, which in some instances has decreased the purchase of goods. Examples are streaming services for movies or music; lease contracts for bicycles or cars; and construction contracts in which the ownership of components of buildings remains with the construction company or sub-contractor who supplied them, often in combination with a maintenance or other type of service contract.[9]

Parallel to the increase of private regulation and governance in consumer markets, the interaction between lawmakers at the national, European, and international level is increasingly influenced by judicial lawmaking. In particular, the Court of Justice of the European Union (CJEU) has, through judgments in preliminary reference procedures, had a significant influence on the balancing of interests in national private laws. With the justification that citizens should enjoy effective protection of rights laid down in EU law—the principle of effectiveness, now laid down also in Article 47 of the EU Charter of Fundamental Rights (CFR)—consumers have through the Court been able to find protection against eviction from their family home when invoking unfair terms in their mortgage contract.[10] The Court has, also through the interpretation of unfair terms legislation, opened up possibilities for the protection of consumers against over-indebtedness, emphasizing that transparency requires that the 'average consumer' could have understood what economic consequences a contractual term would have.[11] Taking up questions that normally would fall within the realm of the legislator, at the national

[7] This is particularly true for cross-border consumer cases, in which the stakes are considered too low to instigate proceedings or in which consumers find it difficult to determine how they can sue their foreign counterparty. See N Reich, 'Transnational Consumer Law—Reality or Fiction?' (2009) 27 Penn State International Law Review 859, 861.

[8] The term 'beyond the state' was coined by R Michaels and N Jansen, 'Private Law Beyond the State? Europeanization, Privatization, Globalization' (2006) 54 American Journal of Comparative Law 843.

[9] V Mak and E Terryn, 'Circular Economy and Consumer Protection. The Consumer as a Citizen and the Limits of Empowerment through Consumer Law' (2020) 43 Journal of Consumer Policy 227. For an evaluation, see Chapter 10, p. 237

[10] Case C-415/11 *Mohamed Aziz v Caixa d'Estalvis de Catalunya, Tarragona i Manresa (Catalunyacaixa)*, ECLI:EU:C:2013:164.

[11] Case C-26/13 *Árpád Kásler, Hujnalku Káslerné Rábai v OTP Jelzálogbank Zrt* [2014] ECLI:EU:C:2014:282, para 74.

or the EU level, the Court becomes a lawmaking actor. Moreover, its judgments blur the lines between EU law and national laws.[12] Judicial lawmaking, therefore, is a second factor besides private regulation that upsets the traditional hierarchy between legislator, courts, and other lawmakers in a monist, state-centred legal system.

I. Research Questions

This book asks what these developments in lawmaking entail for private law relationships in Europe.[13] Its main focus is on the rise of private regulation, although the relation between legislators and courts will also be touched upon.[14] The main research question is: how can the values of EU law, which are reflected in contract laws at the national and the EU level, be safeguarded when lawmaking shifts from public regulation to private regulation beyond the state? That question is of broader significance than the issues raised by the platform economy. Private regulation has been on the rise for a longer time and in contexts other than consumer markets. International trade between businesses is partly governed by public regulation, in the form of national laws and international conventions like the UN Convention on Contracts for the International Sale of Goods (CISG),[15] and partly governed by private regulation developed by trade organizations and soft law developed by international organizations.[16] There is a more general point to make, therefore, about the relations between lawmaking actors when lawmaking moves beyond the state. At a fundamental level, the questions asked in relation to lawmaking in European private law with the rise of the platform economy come back to older debates on the meaning and position of transnational private law—defined as all law which regulates actions or events that transcend national frontiers[17]—besides state law. This book's aim, therefore, is to question fundamental assumptions about who makes law in markets governed largely by private regulation and contracting beyond the state. It does so in the context of European private law, where it aims to bring a new perspective on lawmaking, based on legal pluralist theory. The

[12] In some cases, scholars have spoken of a hybridization, where national laws have to provide new remedies in private law in order to ensure the effectiveness of rules of EU law. See eg N Reich, 'Horizontal Liability in EC Law: Hybridization of Remedies for Compensation in Case of Breaches of EC Rights' (2007) 44 Common Market Law Review 705.

[13] For one of the first analyses of the field, and recognizing that it is a moving target, see V Hatzopoulos, *The Collaborative Economy and EU Law* (Hart Publishing 2018).

[14] See in particular Chapter 4, p ...

[15] UN Convention on Contracts for the International Sale of Goods (opened for signature 11 April 1980, entered into force 1 January 1988) 1489 UNTS 3 (CISG).

[16] See R Goode, H Kronke, and E McKendrick, *Transnational Commercial Law. Text, Cases and Materials* (2nd edn, OUP 2015).

[17] Following the definition coined by Jessup; PC Jessup, *Transnational Law* (Yale University Press 1956).

premises of the theory are set out below (section II), followed by a brief rumination on the special perspective that a focus on Europe can bring (section III), and an outline of the main argument presented in the book (section IV).

II. A New Perspective on Lawmaking

Private law, meaning the rules applicable to the legal relationships between citizens and businesses,[18] is firmly embedded in national legal systems. Rules concerning contracts, liability in tort, property rights, and family law are laid down primarily in national legislation and have been further developed through case law and scholarship. At the same time, private law relationships are often created without regard to state borders. The forces of consumerism bring people together across legal and geographical borders, from the traders who travelled the silk road to China to bring back spices, porcelain, and fabrics to Europe, to the modern economy in which buyers and sellers at opposite ends of the world can connect with each other online.[19] It is perhaps surprising in that light that it has taken a long time for legal scholarship to shift its focus from private law as embedded in state legal systems back to transnational private law that also takes account of other rules applicable to private law relationships, such as private regulation (ie rules made by private actors rather than public regulators or legislators) and rules of international or European law.[20] Yet, recent years have seen a revival of debates on transnational private law[21] and attempts to connect the discourse in that field to national private law discourses,[22] instigated by the perceived rise of lawmaking 'beyond the state' through international and European law, and through private regulation by standard-setting organizations and globally operating businesses.[23]

This book aims to contribute to that growing literature by developing a theory of lawmaking in European private law that can accommodate the shift from state-centred lawmaking to the co-existence of sources of norms beyond the state without a formal hierarchy. European private law is understood in a broad sense. It encompasses the rules governing private law relationships that are developed

[18] Therefore, the focus is on horizontal relationships rather than on the vertical relationship between citizens and the state. This is of course a simplification, as the government can also be subject to private law rules with regard to contractual dealings or liability.

[19] For a historical account of consumerism, see F Trentmann, *Empire of Things. How We Became a World of Consumers, from the Fifteenth Century to the Twenty-first* (Allen Lane 2016).

[20] Jessup, *Transnational Law* (n 17).

[21] Compare G-P Calliess and P Zumbansen, *Rough Consensus and Running Code* (Hart Publishing 2010).

[22] P Zumbansen, 'Defining the Space of Transnational Law: Legal Theory, Global Governance and Legal Pluralism', Comparative Research in Law & Political Economy, Research Paper No 21/2011 <http://digitalcommons.osgoode.yorku.ca/clpe/59>.

[23] Michaels and Jansen, 'Private Law Beyond the State? Europeanization, Privatization, Globalization' (n 8).

by the EU legislature and interpreted (and developed) by the CJEU, as well as the private laws of the EU Member States. 'Law' also is broadly understood, and includes legislation as well as rules created by regulators at the EU and the national levels, and rules created through private regulation by businesses and standard-setting organizations. The focus of the book is in particular on the making of contract and consumer law in the European Union, which are the areas of private law that have been most strongly affected by EU legislation. Consumer law is defined as the rules (primarily in contract) applicable to B2C relations, whereas contract law more generally applies to relationships between businesses and individuals. Where relevant, other areas of private law—eg liability in tort—will be touched upon.[24] This delimitation, however, concerns only the object of study—ie the rules themselves—and not the broader theoretical analysis presented in the book. The theoretical foundations of lawmaking in European private law are similar for all areas of private law, including contract and consumer law but also tort and property law. Each of those areas is primarily embedded in national legal systems as a reflection of economic ordering,[25] and each area is (to a greater or lesser extent) influenced by EU and international law and private regulation. For all those areas of private law, therefore, it is important to consider how lawmaking is changing under the influence of sources of norms developed beyond the state. The book's approach is to raise questions from a general private law perspective and to focus them on issues that arise in relation to contract and consumer law in order to draw more specific conclusions.

Defining the problem more closely in the light of that approach, one particular challenge for lawmakers is that the rise of private law beyond the state puts into question which lawmaker, at what level of regulation (national, EU, transnational), is responsible for safeguarding the values and objectives of private law that are otherwise observed by the state. For contract and consumer law, these concern, for example, the balancing of interests between parties in the light of (social) justice, consumer protection, or fundamental rights. While a state-centred model channels that responsibility to the state, to be monitored by legislator and courts, legal pluralist scholarship has in recent years shown that this model does not provide a good 'fit' for lawmaking in transnational private law, which includes norms developed in European and international law and through private regulation. First, the division of competences between lawmakers at the national, EU, and international level is often contested through judicial dialogues or put to the test in legislative projects aimed at the harmonization or unification of laws. For those processes, the monist, state-centred model is ill-equipped to determine where the ultimate authority

[24] That issue comes up in the case study of the platform economy in Chapters 6 and 7 of the book.

[25] On the function of private law in economic ordering, with particular focus on European contract and consumer law, see R Brownsword, 'The Theoretical Foundations of European Private Law' in R Brownsword and others (eds), *The Foundations of European Private Law* (Hart Publishing 2011) 159, 160–61.

for lawmaking lies.[26] In addition, and important for private law relationships, the increasing development of norms in private regulation takes place largely outside the reach of the state. In the private sphere, parties are largely free to determine the terms of their relationship, within the boundaries set by law, for example through mandatory rules of consumer protection that parties cannot contract out of. For norm addressees, therefore, the rules that matter are not only those laid down in legislation but also—and even primarily—those developed by parties themselves through private regulation or contracting. Such rules however can remain untested against public regulation, in particular in consumer cases where disputes are seldom taken to court due to high costs, the long duration, and the often uncertain outcome of procedures. These problems are even greater in a cross-border context than they are in the national context,[27] and are therefore exacerbated by the increase in recent years of online transactions with cross-border aspects.

To address questions of lawmaking that go beyond a monist, state-based system, the book seeks to develop a theory of lawmaking in European private law that can reconcile two aspects: it aims to ensure the safeguarding of values of EU law reflected in contract law, while recognizing that lawmaking is increasingly taking place beyond the state in a context where the hierarchy between norms is blurred or absent. In that context, the concern of norm addressees such as consumers and businesses is with the rules that are practically applicable to them. Even if norms created by private actors do not go through a process of acceptance by formal legal institutions, they may still be regarded as and used by norm addressees, as if they were binding law.[28] The book therefore focuses on the substance of norms rather than on their pedigree.[29] In support of this view, besides the analytical finding that private regulation in practice is often regarded as law by its addressees, a normative argument is developed as to why norms created outside state legislative structures should be regarded as law if they give expression to actors' public autonomy (eg the power to self-legislate).[30]

The basis for this approach to lawmaking in European private law is found in legal pluralist scholarship in the field of transnational private law. Legal pluralism, having its origin in anthropological and sociological studies of post-colonial legal

[26] N MacCormick, 'Beyond the Sovereign State' (1993) 56 Modern Law Review 1, which has inspired much legal pluralist thinking in the European context.

[27] Reich, 'Transnational Consumer Law—Reality or Fiction?' (n 7) 861.

[28] Of course, questions of legitimacy arise in relation to private regulation. For an overview of the debate in this field, see Calliess and Zumbansen, *Rough Consensus and Running Code* (n 21) 130 ff, referring in particular to the concept of 'affectedness' developed by David Held which ties any assessment of democracy to the quality by which a group has been affected by a decision. See D Held, 'Democratic Accountability and Political Effectiveness from a Cosmopolitan Perspective' (2004) 39(2) Government and Opposition 364.

[29] For the elaboration of some aspects of a qualitative approach to lawmaking in private law in a multi-level legal order see W van Gerven and S Lierman, *Algemeen Deel. 40 jaar later. Privaat- en publiekrecht in een meergelaagd kader van regelgeving, rechtsvorming en rechtstoepassing* (Kluwer 2010).

[30] See Chapter 2, p 39 ff.

systems in the 1960s and 1970s, proposes that norms created outside the framework of state lawmaking can also be regarded as 'law', or in any event as rules that have a law-like effect on societies or individuals.[31] Scholars of transnational private law, adopting an approach that can be characterized as 'new' legal pluralism,[32] in consequence regard legal norms, whether of a public of private nature and global or national, as valid.[33] The emphasis therefore is on the substance of norms rather than on their origin. The book argues that this perspective provides a better fit for understanding lawmaking in European private law than the monist, state-centred model.

The safeguarding of values of European private law—a normative objective—however requires an elaboration on existing theories of legal pluralism in transnational law. Scholarship in this field has resulted in procedural approaches to lawmaking. Adopting the view that the norms developed in other legal orders should be recognized and tolerated, under certain prescribed conditions, these approaches leave aside the question what the substance of rules *should be*, which is a normative question.[34] For example, they do not engage with the question whether minimum rules should be adhered to, for example in relation to fundamental rights, consumer protection, or more generally the protection of citizens or organizations with a weaker social or economic position. It is submitted that Europe, due to its commitment to common objectives and values laid down in the EU Treaties,[35] can provide a framework exactly for the examination of such normative questions in private law. The book uses that finding as a basis to develop an instrumental-normative approach to lawmaking (see section III below).

[31] W Twining, *General Jurisprudence* (CUP 2009) 88–121, 362–75.

[32] Compare R Michaels, 'Global Legal Pluralism' (2009) 5 Annual Review of Law and Social Sciences 243; Calliess and Zumbansen, *Rough Consensus and Running Code* (n 21). Pluralist approaches in constitutional law also often are procedural in nature; see eg P Schiff Berman, *Global Legal Pluralism. A Jurisprudence of Law Beyond Borders* (CUP 2012). Krisch's 'systemic' pluralism is procedural in its reliance on 'interface norms' to mediate conflicts; see N Krisch, *Beyond Constitutionalism: The Pluralist Structure of Postnational Law* (OUP 2010) 296. The term 'new' denotes that this is a new legal pluralism in comparison to the legal pluralist scholarship arising from legal anthropology and sociology in the 1960s. Using similar terminology N Walker, *The Intimations of Global Law* (CUP 2015) 114.

[33] Jurisprudence has dealt widely with questions concerning the validity of rules. Positivist theories generally ground the validity of rules on their pedigree, ie whether they derive from a 'rule of recognition' (Hart) or *Grundnorm* (Kelsen) postulated by a democratically chosen legislator. See HLA Hart, *The Concept of Law* (3rd edn, OUP 2012) 100 ff; H Kelsen, *Pure Theory of Law* (M Knight tr, University of California Press 1967) 8. The legal pluralist perspective, by contrast, bases the validity of norms on the persuasiveness of their substance or *ratio materiae* rather than on their pedigree. Compare Calliess and Zumbansen, *Rough Consensus and Running Code* (n 21) 125.

[34] For an earlier discussion of this argument, see V Mak, 'Globalization, Private Law and New Legal Pluralism', NYU Jean Monnet Working Paper Series, JMWP 14/15, 30–35 <http://jeanmonnetprogram.org/wp-content/uploads/JMWP-14-Mak.pdf>.

[35] See eg Consolidated version of the Treaty on European Union [2012] OJ C326/01 (TEU), Art 3(3). For an exploration of the theoretical and practical relevance of this provision, see D Ferri and F Cortese (eds), *The EU Social Market Economy and the Law. Theoretical Perspectives and Practical Challenges for the EU* (Routledge 2018).

III. Focus on Europe

The choice for the book to focus on Europe—here used as a synonym of the European Union—is inspired not only by the practical aim to address challenges in lawmaking in European private law beyond the state but also by a scientific objective to contribute to the development of theories of legal pluralism in transnational (private) law. The normative basis that EU law provides for lawmaking in European private law, as exemplified by contract and consumer law, means that a theory for legal pluralism in this field can potentially go beyond the procedural approaches adopted in transnational law that have not addressed the protection of values.

The proposed perspective on lawmaking has not been explored in legal pluralist scholarship in European private law until now. While theories of legal pluralism in European private law that emerged in the last decade have established a greater recognition at least for a plurality of lawmaking actors in the field, they have not completely shrugged off the ordering imposed by state-centred perspectives on lawmaking. In particular, these theories appear to relate normative questions to the national, doctrinal private law systems of the EU Member States. For example, issues of social justice are considered to fall mostly within the realm of national laws,[36] and norms developed by private actors are often regarded as ultimately subject to national laws in order to ensure their compliance with mandatory rules.[37] The book aims to challenge these positions and show that it is possible to adopt a strong legal pluralist perspective for lawmaking beyond the state that at the same time can safeguard values that would otherwise be monitored through state laws and institutions.

Apart from the potential advances in legal pluralist scholarship that can be made by studying Europe, there is another reason to focus on this region. Europe is in a special position in the race for technological development and the creation of new products, services, and business models. The power players in this race, on a geopolitical level, are China and the United States. In the last decade, both countries have been the breeding ground for private companies developing new technologies and innovative business models. They are the main homes of so-called unicorn companies, that is, start-up companies with a value over US$1 billion, which have emerged as developers of digital media, artificial intelligence (AI) technologies, blockchain, fintech, on-demand services, gaming, consumer electronics, and e-commerce services.[38] While potential unicorn companies can be identified in

[36] H-W Micklitz, *The Politics of Justice in European Private Law. Social Justice, Access Justice, Societal Justice* (CUP 2018) 27.

[37] I have explored these issues in earlier work. See V Mak, 'Pluralism in European Private Law' (2018) 20 Cambridge Yearbook of European Legal Studies 202.

[38] A list of unicorn companies is maintained and regularly updated by CB Insights. See <https://www.cbinsights.com/research/unicorn-startup-market-map/> (14 March 2019) and <https://www.cbinsights.com/research-unicorn-companies>.

India, Singapore, and Brazil,[39] the majority of technology start-ups originate from China and the United States.

Europe is on the receiving end and houses few large tech companies itself. The dangers of that lack of home-grown technologies have been pointed out by experts who fear that Europe will become dependent upon technologies over which it has no power, such as Chinese 5G technology.[40] That risk is all but real, seeing for example that the Chinese government exercises significant control over companies in its jurisdiction and that it therefore has the tools for cutting off access to technologies used in Europe. While the relation to US companies is different, Europe also puts itself on the receiving side there, as California-based tech companies have gained strong footholds in European consumer markets in recent years. Examples are the big five: Facebook, Microsoft, Apple, Airbnb, and Alphabet (Google's mother company). Also in relation to these, the question has been asked whether the power of large tech companies should be curbed. Concerns with regard to these companies are data protection and (the lack of) competition.[41]

For the enquiry into lawmaking in European contract and consumer law the relevance of this geopolitical framework lies in the regulatory response that was chosen in the European Union. When US tech companies started gaining ground in foreign markets, China's response was to 'exclude and compete'.[42] In other words, US companies were kept out of markets where possible and the government stimulated the development of local technologies through funding schemes. This meant that Uber, for example, had a hard time getting into the Chinese market, as a local competitor was developed (Didi Chuxing) that became the preferred choice of local consumers. For its operations in China, Uber merged with its Chinese rival in 2016.[43] In the European Union, on the other hand, the entry of US companies in consumer markets was not barred or competed with. Instead, Europe has chosen to 'capitulate and regulate'.[44] That means that, through regulation, the European Union seeks to safeguard the values and objectives on which the Union is founded, such as the pursuit of an EU social market economy and, more specifically, a high level of worker and consumer protection.[45] Areas of law through which these values and objectives are pursued include competition law, labour law,

[39] E Griffith, 'The Next Wave of "Unicorn" Start-Ups' *New York Times* (New York, 10 February 2019) <https://www.nytimes.com/2019/02/10/technology/new-wave-unicorn-start-ups.html>.

[40] R Dobbe and M Stikker, 'Vergeet China en Silicon Valley' *NRC* (Amsterdam, 13 April 2019). See also 'How to Handle Huawei. Banning One of China's Leading Firms from Operating in the West Should be a Last Resort' *The Economist* (London, 31 January 2019).

[41] 'Why Big Tech Should Fear Europe' *The Economist* (London, 23 March 2019) https://www.economist.com/leaders/2019/03/23/why-big-tech-should-fear-europe.

[42] N Ferguson, *The Tower and the Square* (Penguin Books 2017) 413.

[43] 'Uber to Merge with Chinese Rival Didi in $35 Billion Deal' *Business Insider* (New York, 1 August 2016).

[44] Ferguson, *The Tower and the Square* (n 42) 413.

[45] Compare Art 3(3) TEU; Consolidated version of the Treaty on the Functioning of the European Union [2012] OJ C326/47 (TFEU), Arts 9 and 12.

data protection law, and consumer law. The focus of this book is on that last field, consumer law, and on contract law, which more generally regulates business-to-business (B2B), B2C, and peer-to-peer relations. Interestingly, public regulation in that field has been relatively sparse until now, leaving much space for private governance through contracts and forms of private regulation (eg codes of conduct). The extent to which the EU's values and objectives are realized in consumer markets dominated by large tech companies therefore becomes a question of how lawmaking is monitored and balanced in a legal pluralist constellation.

IV. Outline

The central question of the book is under what conditions a theory of lawmaking in European private law can be developed that can accommodate the shift from state-centred lawmaking to the co-existence of sources of norms beyond the state without a formal hierarchy. The book adopts a legal pluralist perspective as a basis for developing that theory. The theoretical basis for choosing that perspective, and its implications, are fleshed out as follows.

First, starting at a general level, Chapter 2 analyses the theoretical foundations of lawmaking in European private law and shows that they can be traced to transnational and constitutional pluralist theories. The main question for this part of the book is in which respects legal pluralism should replace the monist, state-centred perspective on lawmaking that prevailed in Western Europe since the creation of the Westphalian nation state. It will be argued that, even though the state remains the primary locus for lawmaking in private law in the European Union, the rise of private regulation and the interaction between courts through judicial dialogues plead in favour of adopting a strong legal pluralist perspective. 'Strong' or 'radical' legal pluralism, other than monism or 'ordered' legal pluralism, holds that norms can co-exist without a formal hierarchy.[46] Both a descriptive case and a normative case are put forward in support of adopting this perspective. Descriptively, the case for a strong legal pluralist perspective in transnational private law—which concerns lawmaking at multiple levels of regulation, and therefore includes European private law—emerges from the observation that the hierarchy between these sources of law is changing and perhaps even tilting away from the nation state.[47]

[46] W Twining, 'Normative and Legal Pluralism: A Global Perspective' (2010) 20 Duke Journal of International and Comparative Law 473, 501–02.

[47] A trend noted by H-W Micklitz, 'The Visible Hand of European Regulatory Private Law—The Transformation of European Private Law from Autonomy to Functionalism in Competition and Regulation' (2009) 28 (1) Yearbook of European Law 3, who sees this as part of a process of 'politicization' of European private law in which new forms of governance are emerging. See also JM Smits, 'Plurality of Sources in European Private Law, or: How to Live with Legal Diversity?' in R Brownsword and others (eds), *The Foundations of European Private Law* (Hart Publishing 2011) 323; JM Smits, 'Het privaatrecht van de toekomst' (2015) 52(2) Tijdschrift voor Privaatrecht 517.

This means that analytically, in describing what perspective can best capture all relevant sources of law in transnational private law, it seems to be more correct to consider norms on the basis of their substance or rationale[48] rather than on the basis of their absorbance into official legal systems. Normatively, strong legal pluralism is appealing as it promotes a framework for lawmaking in which multiple viewpoints and values can be taken into account. Other than a monist system, it therefore opens up space for the realization of public autonomy—the ability to self-legislate through democratic mechanisms—of different groups or communities. This includes lawmaking by formal, public legislators and regulators, but it can also apply to informal lawmaking by private actors when rules extend beyond individual relationships and are meant to regulate an entire sector of industry, for example.[49]

As an important aside: this theoretical argument in favour of public autonomy would also apply to online platform operators. From a theoretical point of view, there is no reason to diverge from the fundamental idea that groups or communities should be enabled to self-legislate.[50] That may to some be an uncomfortable conclusion. In consumer markets, with an eye to safeguarding the interests of consumers and small business, calls have been made to limit the power of large tech companies. Regulation is needed to ensure consumer protection, fair use of data, and competition. What this book aims to show, however, is that one conclusion does not have to forego the other. Private actors operating beyond the state, such as platform operators, have the power to self-legislate. Yet, their power can be curbed, either through regulation or—where that fails or remains absent—through alternative mechanisms. Seeing that lawmaking beyond the state often occurs outside the reach of state regulation, the book focuses on examining alternative private governance mechanisms.

Picking up the examination of pluralist theories in transnational and constitutional law, Chapter 3 takes the enquiry one step further by examining another type of normativity, namely the normative *substance* of rules of European private law.

[48] Callies and Zumbansen refer to the 'inherent, rational content' of norms. See, with reference to the UNIDROIT Principles of International Commercial Contracts, Calliess and Zumbansen, *Rough Consensus and Running Code* (n 21) 125.

[49] Private autonomy, by contrast, is the ability to freely give shape to individual relationships between private parties. Individual autonomy can also be regulated so as to contribute to the pursuit of societal goals See H Dagan, 'Between Regulatory and Autonomy-Based Private Law' (2016) 22 European Law Journal 644, 647 ff. Moreover, it can morph into public autonomy when rules adopted in individual private law relationships become a template for regulation.

[50] Moreover, the application of public autonomy arguments to large tech companies finds support in regulatory theory: autonomy can be a factor that stimulates innovation. See OECD, 'Hearing on Disruptive Innovation', DAF/COMP(2015)3, p 7 points out that in certain circumstances regulation may be unnecessarily harmful to competition. See also A De Streel and P Larouche, 'Disruptive Innovation and Competition Policy Enforcement', Background Note for the OECD Global Forum on Competition (OECD 2015) <https://ssrn.com/abstract=2678890>, examining how antitrust agencies can ensure that the process of disruptive innovation is not affected or prevented through the actions of incumbent firms.

It was said above that lawmaking in this field stands apart from transnational law due to its commitment to the objectives and values of European contract and consumer law. That characteristic means that, in theory, legal pluralism in European private law could go beyond a procedural approach—in which mechanisms of recognition and toleration determine how norm conflicts are mediated between legal orders—to a normative approach that prescribes to which values outcomes should adhere. It is submitted, therefore, that European private law contains elements that allow for a 'substantive deliberation' of rules, values, and objectives.[51] By this I mean a recursive process between lawmaking actors in which the substance of rules—laid down in public and private regulation—is examined and adjusted if it falls below the threshold that EU law prescribes. Whilst the reference to objectives and values seems to imply an ordering of some sort, it is argued that a strong legal pluralist framework can still be maintained. The coordination of lawmaking can occur through an instrumental-normative approach: an approach that requires that a result is achieved through law (hence: instrumental),[52] and in which this result amounts to the safeguarding of objectives and values of EU law, such as consumer protection (and in that way is normative).

The idea of substantive deliberation, which is operationalized as an instrumental-normative approach, is fleshed out in the following chapters of the book. Chapter 4 delves into the substantive values that underlie contract and consumer law in the European Union. Which are they? The chapter shows that lawmaking in European contract and consumer law is embedded within the ordoliberal ideology on which the EU internal market was founded, yet is shaped not only by economic rights but also by social rights. Those rights have a basis in Articles 2 and 3 of the Treaty on European Union (TEU), which ground European cooperation in the common pursuit of a 'highly competitive social market economy', social justice, and equality, amongst other values and objectives. While the balance between economic and social rights in this area is in flux, the EU Treaties in combination with secondary legislation, case law, and the EU CFR circumscribe a framework of shared values and objectives within which a substantive deliberation between lawmaking actors can take place. It can be argued, therefore, that the EU legal order has a normative basis that enables legal pluralist perspectives on lawmaking to go beyond procedural approaches.

Chapter 5 examines the further contours of an instrumental-normative approach, focusing on how the question 'who does what, and at what level of

[51] The term 'substantive deliberation' is a modification of Habermas' deliberative democracy; J Habermas, *Between Facts and Norms* (W Rehg tr, MIT Press 1998) 287 ff.

[52] Instrumentalism can be defined as the pursuit of policy goals through law. The book takes note of potential risks of that approach. Some of its darker sides have been subject to discussion in other contexts; see eg on US law B Tamanaha, *The Perils of Pervasive Legal Instrumentalism* (Wolf Legal Publishing 2008), arguing that 'in situations of sharp disagreement over the social good, if law is perceived as an instrument, individuals and groups within society will endeavor to seize the law, and fill in, interpret, and apply the law, to serve their own ends'.

regulation' is answered by existing theories of legal pluralism in European private law. (As an aside: the term European private law is used here in continuance of the theoretical framework set out in Chapters 2 and 3. Practically, examples mainly concern rules of contract and consumer law.) It has been said that most theories of legal pluralism in European private law, even if they proclaim to adopt a strong legal pluralist perspective, still fall back on an ordering of some sort.[53] Chapter 5 tests that assumption by analysing how the market rationality of EU law interacts with the juridical rationality of national private laws in relation to three aspects of lawmaking: actors, norms, and processes.[54] The chapter concludes that many theories of legal pluralism in European private law lean towards an ordering of some kind. Yet, at the same time the chapter reveals several instances in which inroads are made on the ordered conception of legal pluralism which could provide the premises for the further development of a strong legal pluralist theory for European private law. The primary observation that I make in this regard is that each of the existing theories in some way confirms that the conception of 'who makes law' is in flux. The rise of private actors as lawmakers has been noted and has, for example for Smits, been a ground for developing a bottom-up perspective on lawmaking.[55] Further, the emergence of 'prosumers' as a potential new category of legal subjects, but also as lawmakers, raises new doctrinal questions. Micklitz's European Regulatory Private Law (ERPL) project, finally, has paid particular attention to the emergence of standardization and co-regulation in lawmaking processes.[56]

With this, the theoretical framework for a strong legal pluralist theory of lawmaking in European private law has been defined. Chapters 6, 7, and 8 turn to the practical ramifications of the theory. Does the instrumental-normative approach proposed in the book resonate with practical experiences with lawmaking in European contract and consumer law? The book uses two case studies to gain insights on this question. The first focuses on the platform economy. It examines the question how much space for deliberation formal and informal lawmaking actors in the platform economy have, focusing on two strands. First, Chapter 6 charts which rules concerning contracts and consumer protection have until now emerged in public and private regulation. These contain a mix of public regulation,

[53] R Michaels, 'Why We Have No Theory of European Private Law Pluralism' in L Niglia (ed), *Pluralism and European Private Law* (Hart Publishing 2013) 139.

[54] This three-way division approximately overlaps with Zumbansen's 'methodological lens' for the study of transnational private law. That three-pronged framework is developed by Zumbansen as a methodology for studying the transnational legal sphere and makes it possible to consider norms from a perspective that is neutral on whether norms are part of an official legal system, and also independent from the territorial grounding of law in a particular jurisdiction. See Zumbansen, 'Defining the Space of Transnational Law' (n 22).

[55] JM Smits, 'A Radical View of Legal Pluralism' in L Niglia, *Pluralism and European Private Law* (Hart Publishing 2013) 161. See in detail Chapter 5.

[56] Compare H-W Micklitz and Y Svetiev (eds), 'A Self-Sufficient European Private Law—A Viable Concept?', EUI Working Papers LAW 2012/31. See in detail Chapter 5.

co-regulation, codes of conduct, soft law projects to develop model rules, and reputational feedback systems. Also, online dispute resolution can in practice be a source of norms as norms developed in this context are often through a feedback loop used to improve the quality of services offered by platform operators.

Chapter 7, subsequently, analyses the relations between these various sources of norms to assess the space for deliberation between lawmaking actors. To that end, the substance of norms developed in private regulation by platforms and through contracting is tested against the objectives and values of existing rules of EU and national contract and consumer laws to establish whether these are adhered to, or not. In terms of substance, the case study focuses in particular on transparency in contracting, that is, the question whether terms and conditions are clear and comprehensible to parties entering into contracts. The focus on transparency delimits the enquiry—in other words it defines its scope—but that does not mean that it also limits its relevance. Transparency is required in all contractual relationships in the platform economy, be it B2C and B2B relations between the platform and its users, or peer-to-peer contracts concluded through a platform. Moreover, it is of fundamental importance at all stages of these contractual relationships: formation, interpretation, execution of the contract, and the availability of remedies in case of non-performance or non-satisfactory performance. The choice to focus on transparency, further, can be justified on the ground that it is one of the first topics concerning online platforms that lawmakers at various levels of regulation have picked up as a focus for rulemaking. This topic therefore provides sufficient material for analysis. Practically, two platforms are selected for the case study, one aimed at connecting users for the exchange of services (Airbnb) and one for the exchange of goods (Amazon).

One hypothesis that Chapter 7 puts to the test is whether private regulation, as is often assumed, results in lower levels of consumer protection. When businesses introduce rules of private regulation, for example through mandatory terms and conditions in B2C contracts or through codes of conduct, it is often thought that they opt for rules that on balance are more favourable to their own interests than those of consumers. Interestingly, as Chapter 7 reveals, that outcome is not a given. At least for transparency, similar outcomes can be achieved as one would expect to find in rules of European consumer law. An explanation, which will be explored in detail, is that the trade-offs in the platform economy are different, as they often involve triangular relationships between platforms, third-party suppliers, and final consumers. With trust-building and customer satisfaction being key drivers for online platforms' operational choices, consumers enjoy higher levels of protection, whilst third-party traders are trapped in onerous relationships with platform operators. Further, an important caveat to the empirical study is that it focuses only on one aspect of consumer protection. Other aspects, such as product safety, are not influenced by exactly the same drivers as transparency—for example, the (low) price of products in that case adds an important factor to the mix—and the outcomes may therefore well be different. Chapter 9 considers the boundaries of the space governed by private regulation in more detail.

Chapter 8 presents a second case study, focusing on standardization. This is defined as a process of private regulation whereby private actors engage in the development of standardized norms for particular sectors of industry or for particular types of contract. Standards, which are widely used in European markets, can also serve as a case study for determining whether the substance of norms created through private regulation can fulfil the instrumental-normative aims of a legal pluralist theory of lawmaking in European contract and consumer law. Noting that such a case study, especially if it includes empirical research on the substance of standards, could take up an entire book,[57] I have chosen to delimit the enquiry to harmonized standards in EU law. Harmonized standards are developed by European standard-setting organizations (ESOs) at the instigation of the European legislator.[58] The choice to focus on these is grounded on the idea that relevant conclusions on the role of standards in European private law can be drawn from an analysis of the legislation, case law, and scholarship relating to harmonized standards. In recent years, through the influence of CJEU case law, debates have arisen on the quality of these standards, focusing on the potential of norms to prevent harm or to compensate for harm when it has occurred. The choices made by lawmaking actors with regard to the liability of certification bodies and of users of certified products that caused harm are illustrative of whether these two quality aspects are achieved in European private law, and at which level of regulation they are being pursued.

The final aspect of the instrumental-normative theory for lawmaking in European private law that requires attention, then, is which instruments are available for ensuring that the objectives and values of EU law are safeguarded. Chapter 9 examines which mechanisms can provide 'checks and balances' for the rules created by different lawmakers in a legal pluralist constellation. The question here is which space exists for the creation and maintenance of private governance mechanisms based on voluntary participation. These mechanisms are, by definition, an expression of the public and private autonomy of lawmaking actors, that is, of the ability to self-legislate and to choose the design of contractual relations freely. The important mechanisms in European contract law are standardization, optional instruments, and online dispute resolution (ODR).

Rounding up, Chapter 10 concludes that a case can be made for a strong legal pluralist theory of lawmaking in European private law. At the same time, the conclusions from the foregoing chapters should be seen in context. Chapter 10, taking

[57] Compare eg H Schepel, *The Constitution of Private Governance: Product Standards in the Regulation of Integrating Markets* (Hart Publishing 2005); BJ van Leeuwen, *European Standardisation of Services and Its Impact on Private Law. Paradoxes of Convergence* (Hart Publishing 2017).

[58] See <https://www.cen.eu/you/EuropeanStandardization/Pages/default.aspx>.

a discursive approach, focuses on some aspects that require further consideration. First, one may wonder how generally applicable the conclusions reached in the book are. Seeing that the analysis of European contract and consumer law in the book only covered part of the EU market for goods and services—taking account of online but not offline transactions—some weighing of the findings is in order. The analysis in the final chapter considers how, and to what extent, the regulation of offline transactions is affected by the perceived shift towards legal pluralism. It seems likely that this part of the market is less affected by legal pluralism, since many transactions will not be of a cross-border nature and therefore less vulnerable than online, cross-border transactions to uncertainties concerning the reliability of the other party, the applicable law, and the probable outcomes of disputes. Still, these transactions can also be subject to rules emanating from various legal sources, for example from EU harmonized legislation or from private regulation. The chapter will therefore consider under what conditions an instrumental-normative approach would, at least in theory, work for the offline part of the market. Second, the 'European project' has been under pressure recently, for instance because of the Greek debt crisis, immigration, Poland's judicial reforms, Brexit, and the Covid-19 crisis. These events have rekindled debates on the basis of EU cooperation and integration, and have emphasized differences between Member States rather than commonalities. The instrumental-normative approach proposed in this book, at the same time, rests upon the EU's allegiance to common objectives and values. This chapter will assess which risks are posed to this framework by political, economic, and social divides in the European Union. Finally, lawmaking in European contract and consumer law only focuses on selective aspects of citizens' lives. Connections could also be made to citizens' rights as workers or in relation to environmental protection, which like consumer law are part of the EU's objectives and values in the pursuit of a social market economy. The book closes with a reflection on the connections that could be made between these fields, opening up vistas for further research on lawmaking in European private law.

2

New Legal Pluralism and Transnational Private Law

Globalization has been hailed as the main paradigm of our time by legal scholars, yet its relation to law remains complicated.[*,1] For one, can we say that globalization is a new phenomenon that law does not know how to handle? New, in any case, globalization is not if we look for example at cross-border trading. The golden age of commerce for a number of European trading nations lay much earlier, in the seventeenth and eighteenth centuries. The musings of a British captain, as imagined by David Mitchell in his novel *The Thousand Autumns of Jacob de Zoet*, express the sentiment of the time:[2]

> What prophet of commerce in, let us say, the Year 1700 could have foreseen a time when commoners consume tea by the bucket and sugar by the sack? What subject of William and Mary could have predicted the 'need' of today's middling multitudes for cotton sheets, coffee and chocolate? Human requisites are prone to fashion; and, as clamoring new needs replace old ones, the face of the world itself changes.

The British in this particular instance had to give way to the Dutch, whom from the seventeenth century until well into the nineteenth century were the only nation besides China to maintain trade relations with Japan, operating through a small settlement on the artificial island of Dejima, just off the coast of Nagasaki. Nevertheless, the expansion of trade across the globe was indeed the paradigm of that time, and if we extrapolate the needs of consumers to today's 'middling multitudes', not much seems to have changed in the way that fashions crop up and global trade seeks to respond—apart from that those needs may now relate to iPhones rather than cotton sheets.

[*] An earlier version of this chapter was published as a working paper during my stay as an Emile Noël fellow at NYU. See V Mak, 'Globalization, Private Law and New Legal Pluralism', NYU Jean Monnet Working Paper Series, JMWP 14/15 <http://jeanmonnetprogram.org/wp-content/uploads/JMWP-14-Mak.pdf> accessed 28 February 2020, as are all websites in this chapter.

[1] R Michaels, 'Globalization and Law: Law Beyond the State' in R Banakar and M Travers (eds), *Law and Social Theory* (Hart Publishing 2013) 287. Online version available at SSRN <http://ssrn.com/abstract=2240898>.

[2] D Mitchell, *The Thousand Autumns of Jacob de Zoet* (Random House 2011) 328.

Legal Pluralism in European Contract Law. Vanessa Mak, Oxford University Press (2020). © Vanessa Mak.
DOI: 10.1093/oso/9780198854487.001.0001.

The question for legal scholarship is to determine if, when 'the face of the world itself changes', it is also necessary for laws to change. Trade and consumer relationships, on which this book focuses, would normally be governed, or facilitated, by rules of private law, in particular contract law. Depending on whom one asks, contract law as it stands today is, or is not, able to respond adequately to the challenges posed by globalization. Two main viewpoints exist. On the one hand, there is the monist, state-centred perspective of private lawyers who consider contracts valid only if they are governed by the law of a state,[3] the applicable law to be determined in accordance with the rules of private international law. Proponents of this view believe that contracts should be governed by state or state-like rules,[4] mainly because the legitimacy of rules developed through democratic channels is given but also because national private law systems are substantively valued for their ordered framework of rules, values, and practices. At the same time, those subscribing to a monist, state-centred perspective on lawmaking tend to be reluctant to acknowledge external sources of rules—such as private regulation—as 'law', unless these have received some sort of official recognition, which simultaneously lends legitimacy to the operation of such a formerly 'unofficial' norm into the 'official' legal system.[5] This focus on national laws has remained predominant in private law discourses, even if transactions have become more international and rules of national laws often fall short of providing appropriate solutions.

On the other hand, a transnational perspective has emerged. Finding that the monist, state-centred framework ignores the increasing body of transactions that take place altogether outside the state legislative framework—for example on global marketplaces such as eBay, or in commercial networks—transnational law goes beyond questions of validity to search for a framework that encompasses formal and informal rules, at the national and at the international or global level.[6] The aim of such transnational approaches to private law is to provide a new empirical understanding of law beyond the state, describing which sources of norms exist outside state regulation, and a theoretical conceptualization of how these rules relate, or should relate, to state law in a world less marked by state-centred views.[7] How this conceptualization works out, nevertheless, is an open question.

3 Although legal positivism exists in various forms, its main premise is always to determine which social facts lend validity to the existence and content of law in a given society. The most influential theory in our time is HLA Hart, *The Concept of Law* (3rd edn, OUP 2012).

4 See for the elaboration of the idea of the European Union as a (market) state H-W Micklitz and D Patterson, 'From the Nation State to the Market: The Evolution of EU Private Law as Regulation of the Economy Beyond the Boundaries of the Union?' in B Van Vooren, S Blockmans, and J Wouters, *The EU's Role in Global Governance. The Legal Dimension* (OUP 2013) 78.

5 G-P Calliess and P Zumbansen, *Rough Consensus and Running Code* (Hart Publishing 2010).

6 P Zumbansen, 'Defining the Space of Transnational Law: Legal Theory, Global Governance and Legal Pluralism' (2011) Comparative Research in Law & Political Economy, Research Paper No 21/2011 <http://digitalcommons.osgoode.yorku.ca/clpe/59>.

7 Michaels (n 1) 303 speaks of 'a theoretical conceptualization of law after the breakdown of methodological nationalism', which amounts to the same thing in this context.

Some use the terminology of 'new legal pluralism',[8] blurring the lines between legal and social norms, whereas others adopt more narrowly defined notions of 'law beyond the state'.[9]

This chapter adopts a transnational perspective and seeks to lay the basis of a legal pluralist theory for lawmaking in European private law, primarily contract law, in times of globalization. In doing so, it joins a growing literature on legal pluralism in transnational law.[10] Yet, whereas the new pluralist discourse in other areas of law—that is, constitutional law, international law, and administrative law—has been ongoing for approximately two decades, the private law debate is lagging behind. That seems somewhat surprising since private law has traditionally always been familiar with pluralist perspectives, in particular in relation to trade relations for which a law of merchants developed that encompassed transnational rules, the *lex mercatoria*.[11] The discourse in that area, nonetheless, has only more recently taken off[12] and will need more time to develop the various viewpoints that may be taken on private law in times of globalization.

The aim of this chapter, as part of this inquiry, is to seek to define a more narrow reading of legal pluralism in private law that can practically be of help in finding ways to manage the divergence of norms between formal and informal lawmaking actors. Part of the difficulty of getting a grip on the current debate seems to be due to the very general approaches taken in the literature, spanning global and local manifestations of private law—albeit discerning between the role of law in the Westphalian model of western capitalist societies and the contrasting context of the global South[13]—and considering private law relations in general, rather than focusing on specific areas (eg contract law, corporate law,[14] labour law, or tort

[8] The term 'new' denotes that this is a new legal pluralism in comparison to the legal pluralist scholarship arising from legal anthropology and sociology in the 1960s, discussed below in section I. Using similar terminology, N Walker, *The Intimations of Global Law* (CUP 2015) 114.

[9] Michaels, 'Globalization and Law: Law Beyond the State' (n 1), and R Michaels, 'Global Legal Pluralism' (2009) 5 Annual Review of Law and Social Sciences 243.

[10] Beside references to transnational legal scholarship throughout this chapter, for or a recent overview of the field see the collection of papers in MA Helfand (ed), *Negotiating State and Non-State Law. The Challenge of Global and Local Legal Pluralism* (CUP 2015).

[11] See examples cited by G Teubner, 'Global Bukowina: Legal Pluralism in the World Society' in G Teubner (ed), *Global Law without a State* (Dartmouth 1997) 3; B Tamanaha, 'Understanding Legal Pluralism: Past to Present, Local to Global' (2008) 30 Sydney Law Review 375, 388.

[12] See the references to the work of Michaels and Zumbansen in the preceding footnotes.

[13] See eg P Zumbansen, 'The Constitutional Itch: Transnational Private Regulatory Governance and the Woes of Legitimacy' in MA Helfand, *Negotiating State and Non-State Law. The Challenge of Global and Local Legal Pluralism* (CUP 2015) 83, 90, stating quite rightly that in the search for a reconceptualization of the role of private law in global governance '[t]he postcolonial challenge in legal and political theory makes more than clear today that a reinvigoration of private law's abilities to "pierce the legal veil" in an attempt to render visible the social and economic inequalities that pervade the realities underneath the floorboard of rules and principles in legal argument can no longer take the troubled regulatory history of the Western welfare state as its obvious starting point and as its all determining frame of reference'.

[14] Although some work engages with case studies; eg Calliess and Zumbansen, *Rough Consensus and Running Code* (n 5) chs 3 and 4.

law).[15] Whereas a global pluralist account is helpful for obtaining a better understanding of the role of law in society and its relation to social and economic policies, the discussion of legal pluralism across such a broad spectrum and with such a broad, global span makes it difficult to explore ways of 'managing pluralism'. This idea, of managing pluralism, holds that even if legal pluralism offers the most appropriate framework for understanding law, it will still need to be coordinated in such a way that conflicts in legal orders are channelled, either into a process in which values may be weighed and conflicts may be resolved, or in a way that upholds core values of a legal system.[16] The latter aspect is difficult at the global level due to the wide divergence of values observed in private law systems throughout the world. It may nonetheless be more manageable at the regional level of the European Union.

The book therefore focuses on European contract and consumer law as a case study for lawmaking in private law beyond the state. It should be noted, however, that the current chapter starts from a perspective of private law that is broader than contract and consumer law alone. The theoretical foundations of lawmaking in European private law are similar for all areas of private law, including contract and consumer law but also tort and property law. Each of those areas is primarily embedded in national legal systems as a reflection of economic ordering,[17] and each area is (to a greater or lesser extent) influenced by EU and international law, and private regulation. For all those areas of private law, therefore, it is important to consider how lawmaking is changing under the influence of sources of norms developed beyond the state. The approach taken in this chapter is to raise questions from a general private law perspective, and to focus them on issues that arise in relation to contract and consumer law in order to draw more specific conclusions.

As to core values, private law systems in Europe are relatively consistent in defining which ones they find should be secured through private law mechanisms. Legal certainty is regarded as a core value, expressing good lawmaking but also doing justice to the interests of private parties in consistency and predictability of outcomes.[18] In contract law, fairness is regarded as a general value or principle,

[15] The same problem arises for other areas of law. Compare Jennifer Hendry's observation that '[t]he potential and scope of the concept of legal pluralism lend it a malleability that operates as a double-edged sword: on the one hand it is flexible enough to be discussed from many different perspectives, while on the other it appears to lack any real defining contours, other than being premised upon con testability'. J Hendry, 'Legal Pluralism and Normative Transfer' in G Frankenberg (ed), *Order from Transfer. Comparative Constitutional Design and Legal Culture* (Edward Elgar 2013) 153, 156.

[16] cf P Schiff Berman, *Global Legal Pluralism. A Jurisprudence of Law Beyond Borders* (CUP 2012) 151, although Schiff Berman himself does not specify values that should be safeguarded and focuses primarily on conflicts between legal orders.

[17] On the function of private law in economic ordering, with particular focus on European contract and consumer law, see R Brownsword, 'The Theoretical Foundations of European Private Law' in R Brownsword and others (eds), *The Foundations of European Private Law* (Hart Publishing 2011) 159, 160–61.

[18] On good lawmaking, see LL Fuller, *The Morality of Law* (9th edn, Yale University Press 1973) 33 ff and the analysis by Esther van Schagen for European private law in *The Development of European Private Law in a Multilevel Legal Order* (dissertation Tilburg 2013, unpublished) 26–27. See also MW

although legal systems differ in the ways in which it is expressed in specific rules, for example concerning good faith or transparency at the precontractual stage.[19] Another value that systems mostly adhere to, albeit it to differing degrees, is the protection of weaker parties such as consumers, tenants, or employees. Although it is a debated question whether private law should be used as a mechanism for pursuing redistributive goals when alternatives are available, eg taxation, it is well recognized in Europe that private law systems in many instances reflect political, redistributive aims.[20] In the case of the European Union a primary regulatory aim that has been pursued through contract and sometimes tort law is consumer protection.[21] These values could provide the foundations for a theory of lawmaking that goes beyond procedural mechanisms for managing conflicts between legal orders and that can safeguard values and objectives of European private law, or more specifically contract and consumer law.

Europe has another advantage. A particular challenge for transnational private law is that the mechanisms for managing pluralism tend to be context-specific. The coordination of lawmaking between different lawmakers—such as legislators, courts, and private regulatory bodies—is dependent upon which institutions are actually active as lawmakers in a given society, and on how interactions and power relationships play out between them.[22] Coordination of lawmaking may, for example, be more readily achieved within the EU's institutional context, in which legislators and policy-makers at national and EU level coordinate their lawmaking and in which also often note is taken of comparative legal solutions adopted by other Member States, than in legal orders with a lesser degree of regional cooperation between states or other lawmakers.[23] The question of how to manage pluralism, however, goes beyond the scope of this chapter,[24] which first seeks to clarify

Hesselink, 'How Many Systems of Private Law are there in Europe? On Plural Legal Sources, Multiple Identities and the Unity of Law' in L Niglia (ed), *Pluralism and European Private Law* (Hart Publishing 2013) 199, 231–33.

[19] Compare S Whittaker and R Zimmermann, *Good Faith in European Contract Law* (CUP 2000); C Willett, *Fairness in Consumer Contracts: The Case of Unfair Terms* (Ashgate 2007).

[20] For example, AT Kronman, 'Contract Law and Distributive Justice' (1980) 89 Yale Law Journal 472; R Michaels and N Jansen, 'Private Law Beyond the State? Europeanization, Privatization, Globalization' (2006) 54 American Journal of Comparative Law 843, 848.

[21] Consolidated version of the Treaty on the Functioning of the European Union [2012] OJ C326/47 (TFEU), Arts 114(3) and 169(2).

[22] The importance of institutional context has been highlighted in particular in the work of Neil Komesar, who has shown that the pursuit of policy goals is shaped and determined by institutional processes. See N Komesar, *Imperfect Alternatives: Choosing Institutions in Law, Economics and Public Policy* (University of Chicago Press 1997).

[23] Even within the European Union this may be more realistic in contract law or other aspects of economic ordering than in relation to aspects of social policy, in relation to which the Union only has limited competences. See eg F De Witte, 'The Architecture of a Social Market Economy' in P Koutrakos and J Snell (eds), *Research Handbook on the EU's Internal Market* (Edward Elgar 2016) 117.

[24] I save a further exploration of that question for discussion in later chapters, in particular Chapter 9, although I do where relevant in this chapter refer to the work of others who engage in questions of pluralism in European contract law—eg Micklitz, Hesselink, and Smits. It should also be noted that since the chapter is concerned with lawmaking in private law, which results in relatively specific

the theoretical foundations of lawmaking in European private law. To that end, it seeks inspiration from more developed theories of legal pluralism in transnational private law.

The chapter is structured as follows. Objections to the prevailing monist, state-centred framework for lawmaking in private law are briefly summarized in section I. The chapter then moves on to the main question: can a theoretical framework based on new legal pluralism do better? Answering this question requires two steps, an analytical and a normative one. Analytically speaking—that is, asking whether a legal pluralist framework fits the descriptive reality of norm-creation in contract law today—the chapter suggests that it is not hard to make a case for legal pluralism as a conceptual framework, and that there is some evidence that legal pluralism has established itself as a valid, albeit still 'alternative' view in the private law discourse. To flesh out this argument, the chapter will provide some background on the origins of legal pluralism in 1960s and 1970s scholarship and the reasons for its re-emergence in current legal scholarship (section I.A). Further, it will discuss the analytical question arises as to whether norms created by non-state actors can be considered 'law' for the purposes of a theory of transnational private regulation (section I.B).

After exploring legal pluralism as a descriptive framework, a normative question remains. Ralf Michaels has raised doubts concerning the usefulness of 'global legal pluralist' approaches. In his view, such theories mesh empirical findings about the existence of law beyond the state with theoretical conceptions of non-state norms as 'law' and ideological positions holding that greater deference must be granted to non-state orders.[25] Although I share his caution to some degree—it is important not to romanticize notions of private law relations as existing purely beyond state law, subject to customary rules only—we should not outright reject using a pluralist framework to develop a better understanding of transnational lawmaking. In particular, it would seem that a legal pluralist perspective can have advantages for a reconceptualization of lawmaking in relation to transnational trade and consumer contracts,[26] provided that the institutional context supports it. To explore the merit of this claim, the second part of the question focuses on the normative case for adopting a legal pluralist perspective for lawmaking in European private law. Why should we prefer it over a monist, state-centred framework, or over more modest transnational approaches to law beyond the state? Section III explores this question with reference to theories of cosmopolitan, constitutional, and transnational

rules, the coordination aimed for is much more rule-oriented than the existing framework for policy-coordination in Europe: the Open Method of Coordination (OMC).

[25] Michaels, 'Globalization and Law: Law Beyond the State' (n 1) 299.

[26] The limited scope of this chapter, focusing on trade and consumer contracts, perhaps overcomes some problems that Michaels signals in relation to a broader treatment of pluralism relating also eg to Islamic law or corporate governance.

pluralism—fields in which the debate on new legal pluralism is ahead of private law. Section IV concludes.

I. Positivism in Crisis?

The monist, state-centred perspective on lawmaking is grounded in modern positivist thinking, which started to emerge around the time that the Westphalian nation state was established. As political order became tied to a population and a territory, governed by a sovereign on the basis of a social contract,[27] the focus of lawyers became oriented towards the formal requirements for legal validity in this particular context. Positivist views of law require a grounding rule from which the authority of law is derived—according to Hart a social convention which is actually practised by officials, a *rule of recognition*[28]—and which is almost invariably linked to the state.[29] Norms created 'unofficially', outside the sphere of state influence and without being adopted into the official system, are regarded as non-law—they are social norms only. That is relevant in particular because it means that these norms are not enforceable in state courts, that is, they are not considered binding.[30] Methodological nationalism, directing the focus of lawyers to state law as the only valid existing law, was born.

Globalization is said to pose challenges to this framework. But why would legal positivism in a monist, state-centred form not be an appropriate lens through which to consider the creation of rules of private law in our times?

The first, and often mentioned reason, is that an increase in self-regulation or private regulation—in other words the creation of norms by private actors such as businesses or private standard-setting bodies—has diminished the importance of the state as a regulator. That point seems to hold some merit, even if this is by no means the first time in history that private regulation has gained importance. Arguably, private law has traditionally always been familiar with non-state law, in particular in relation to trade relations for which a transnational 'law of merchants' developed—largely made up by private lawmaking activities—the *lex mercatoria*. What makes it a relevant argument today is that for the first time all the characteristics of globalization seem to be highly present in our society and are having a direct impact on the increase of cross-border, private law transactions. These four characteristics have been defined as *extent*, *intensity*, and *velocity* of

[27] A state is constituted by four elements: territory, population, government, and the ability to enter into relations with other states. cf Art 1 of the Montevideo Convention on Rights and Duties of States (opened for signature 26 December 1933, entered into force 26 December 1934).

[28] Hart, *The Concept of Law* (n 3).

[29] cf Michaels, 'Globalization and Law: Law Beyond the State' (n 1) 302.

[30] ibid, noting further that only decisions on law have the force of precedent, and that questions of law are allocated to judges whereas questions of fact can sometimes be decided by judged.

global transactions—referring to the stretching of activities across borders, their interconnectedness, and the speed at which they take place—and the *enmeshing between the global and the local*, reflected in the blurring of lines between domestic and international laws.[31] Not only can an increase in global transactions be observed, it is accompanied by a growing body of informally developed rules, such as terms and conditions and rules of dispute resolution developed by global market platforms (such as eBay or Airbnb), rules developed by private standard-setting bodies,[32] or corporate codes with a transnational reach.

That by itself is not the only reason why the positivist, state-centred perspective in private law may need to be reconsidered. As Michaels notes, the distinction between law and non-law also 'begins to collapse because the criteria used in legal positivism to define what should count as law are becoming questionable'.[33] If the state is no longer the only source of regulation, it follows that the premise of legal positivism that the validity of rules should be channelled back to an absolute starting point—in most cases related to the state—comes under pressure. At the very least, proponents of the positivist view will be required to justify why this point is vital for establishing the validity of rules.[34] That may be a daunting task if we take, for instance, Hart's rule of recognition as our starting point. While it may be possible to identify within a nation state which criteria deriving from the rule are regarded by officials as standards that govern their actions,[35] the same exercise seems harder to apply on the transnational plane. Who are the relevant officials in that case, and is it in any event possible to identify a meta-rule for the validity of legal norms if the transnational order itself lacks any kind of discernible system?

A third point concerns non-state law in another sense: the rules espoused by supranational or international lawmaking actors. Their rule-making powers are often regarded as a derivative of the state's lawmaking powers. The state has transferred part of its sovereignty to them, giving them competence to lay down new rules that may legally bind the state and its subjects. Although this interaction between lawmakers at the national and international level may still be couched in positivist language, seeing that the final authority rests with and is derived from the state, that does not mean that no new challenges lie ahead when lawmaking is increasingly taking place at the supranational or international level. Legitimacy can be a concern too, in various ways. First, the validity of laws emanating from a supranational or international lawmaker may be questioned. Did they have competence to promulgate new laws, or not? The answer to that question has in the

[31] cf D Held and others, *Global Transformations: Politics, Economics, and Culture* (Stanford 1999) 14, 14–16.

[32] On standardization in services contracts, see P Delimatsis, 'Standard-Setting in Services: New Frontiers in Rule-Making and the Role of the EU' in P Sauvé and M Roy (ed), *Research Handbook on Trade in Services* (Edward Elgar 2016) 268.

[33] Michaels, 'Globalization and Law: Law Beyond the State' (n 1) 302.

[34] ibid.

[35] Hart, *The Concept of Law* (n 3) 100 ff.

EU context proven to be quite fluid, with the European Union subtly extending its competences through open-ended legislative provisions or through general principles.[36] Second, the lawmaker can be seen as too distant from the polity to have a proper mandate. In the European Union, for example, concerns continue to exist about a 'democratic deficit', meaning that the institutions are insufficiently accessible to citizens and therefore unable to ensure democratic legitimacy.[37]

Another problem is whether supranational or international lawmakers are positioned in an appropriate place in the political order to make laws that affect the interests of private actors or of states. That is a contextual question. Lawmaking at the supranational or international level is often justified on the basis of economic policy goals, such as market integration, yet it may not be the place to deal with social policy particular to individual states.[38]

My aim is not to engage in more detail with all these questions. To make a full inquiry of the merits and non-merits of legal positivism in transnational law would require a philosophical and political theory analysis going far beyond the scope of this chapter. What is important, however, is to raise these questions in order to make us reconsider the position of state law in the changing constellation of norm-creation in a globalized world. To say that positivism is in crisis is probably too strong a way to put it—in particular in such a general way. In many cases, the state is still the primary entity to take care of the legal interests of its citizens.[39] Nonetheless, the challenges that globalization of private law transactions pose to the theory at least demand a consideration of alternative frameworks. As set out in the introduction, this chapter will consider the merits of a legal pluralist framework for transnational private law, in particular in relation to contracting in the European Union. The first step to consider, then, is to what extent legal pluralism is fitting as a descriptive framework for transnational lawmaking in contract law.

[36] See eg S Weatherill, 'Competence Creep and Competence Control' (2004) 23 Yearbook of European Law 1; S Prechal, 'Competence Creep and General Principles of Law' (2010) 3 Review of European Administrative Law 5.

[37] For an insightful analysis, see FW Scharpf, 'Legitimacy in the Multilevel European Polity' (2009) 1 European Political Science Review 173. Also published as MPIfG Working Paper 09/1 <http://www.mpifg.de/pu/workpap/wp09-1.pdf>.

[38] Hans Micklitz's argument that the European Union, through its legislative actions, can only create 'access justice', ie access for all participants to the European market, fits with this understanding. Social policy is still primarily within the realm of the Member States. See H-W Micklitz, 'Social Justice and Access Justice in Private Law', EUI Working Papers LAW 2011/02, 21–23.

[39] Although even within a state clashes between sub-groups may occur for which a pluralist framework would provide a more helpful context; compare eg E Darian-Smith, *Law and Societies in Global Contexts* (CUP 2013).

II. Legal Pluralism as a Descriptive Framework for Transnational Lawmaking

Neil Walker has contributed the emergence of a 'new legal pluralism' to a double deformalization in law: first, the focus is no longer exclusively or mainly upon state parties as the subject of (international) law; and second, the context in which choice of law questions arise is now as likely to be horizontally (between state laws) as vertically shaped (state law increasingly overlaps with other, substantive jurisdictions).[40] Whereas this characterization focuses primarily on the position of states and state law in international law, this process of deformalization has similar effects in private law. There too, as discussed in the previous part, the focus is moving from state law to other sources of norms. Also, established hierarchies between state law and other sources of law—whether supranational or international, or non-state law—are becoming less clear.

The term 'new legal pluralism' indicates that what we are talking about is not the legal pluralism that emerged in colonial and post-colonial legal anthropology after the 1960s. But what then are its characteristics and why does it fit the new constellation of sources of lawmaking in transnational contract law? This part explores those questions in more detail, starting with a brief overview of classical conceptions of legal pluralism.

A. Legal Pluralism: Origins and Development

Legal pluralism became popular in the wake of anthropological studies of post-colonial societies in the 1960s.[41] Although its origins go much further back,[42] legal anthropologists in the 1970s and 1980s became interested in the ways in which state laws had taken hold—or not taken hold—in colonial and post-colonial societies. Research on these questions resulted in seminal works on legal pluralism, inter alia by Sally Engle Merry, John Griffiths, and by Sally Falk Moore on 'semi-autonomous fields'.[43]

[40] Walker, *The Intimations of Global Law* (n 8) 114.

[41] The literature on legal pluralism has rapidly expanded since the earliest studies and is almost becoming too vast to survey fully. In this part, I will give an overview of some of the main works, many of which are also cited in the footnotes. It should be noted that the enquiry encompasses lawmaking within and beyond the state and is therefore not limited to the emergence of 'global law'. On that topic, see Teubner, 'Global Bukowina: Legal Pluralism in the World Society' (n 11).

[42] Tamanaha, Understanding Legal Pluralism: Past to Present, Local to Global' (n 11); L Benton, 'Historical Perspectives on Legal Pluralism' (2011) 3 Hague Journal on the Rule of Law 57.

[43] S Engle Merry, 'Legal Pluralism' (1988) 22 Law and Society Review 869; J Griffiths, 'What is Legal Pluralism?' (1986) 24 Journal of Legal Pluralism and Unofficial Law 1; S Falk Moore, 'Law and Social Change: the Semi-Autonomous Social Field as an Appropriate Object of Study' (1973) 7 Law and Society Review 719.

Central to these works is the realization that most state legal systems, even if they can be perceived as a coherent whole from the outside, in fact host various sets of norms that can overlap but also conflict. Taking the description from legal anthropology, legal pluralism denotes the 'situation in which two or more laws (or legal systems) co-exist in (or are obeyed by) one social field (or a population or an individual)'.[44] In the colonial and post-colonial societies that researchers in this field became interested in, the focus was mostly on the existence of norms other than state law, often rules developed by local communities and by Western researchers branded as tribal or customary law, that governed the relationships of legal subjects in those communities. Such rules would operate alongside state law—or perhaps better said, independent from state law—and could also come into conflict with rules of state law, although the perspective mostly tended to be state-centred.[45]

The distinction between state law and other sources of norms is what strongly characterizes these approaches. The suggestion of legal pluralism is that norms created outside the framework of state lawmaking can also be regarded as 'law', or in any event as rules that have a law-like effect on societies or individuals.[46] That perspective opens up space for taking account of non-state norms, such as customs or—of particular importance in modern enterprises or industries—rules developed through private regulation. It should be noted, however, that whilst legal pluralism as a theoretical perspective gives room to adopting a factual view on what norms govern a particular community or society, it does not prescribe how the validity of norms as 'law' should be assessed or how the interaction between different (state and non-state) norms should be given shape. At the same time, these are questions that have come up in pluralist debates and some grouping of theories is possible, painting with a broad brush, along the lines of 'weak' or 'strong' legal pluralism.[47]

Weak legal pluralism, in early legal literature on pluralism, followed the observations of anthropologists made in their studies of colonial and post-colonial societies. Lawyers studying legal systems in Asia and Africa described patterns that were similar to most colonies, where the colonizing power would introduce its own law as an overarching systems whilst leaving some room for the customary laws that it found.[48] These descriptions focused on the co-existence or plurality of rules,

[44] R Michaels, 'Why We Have No Theory of European Private Law Pluralism' in L Niglia (ed), *Pluralism and European Private Law* (Hart Publishing 2013) 139, 140–41; Griffiths (n 43) 2; and compare Engle Merry (n 43) 870.

[45] W Twining, 'Normative and Legal Pluralism: A Global Perspective' (2010) 20 Duke Journal of International and Comparative Law 473, 500.

[46] W Twining, *General Jurisprudence* (CUP 2009) 88–121, 362–75; and compare at 63–64, where Twining advocates an approach in which law regarded from a global perspective is used as an analytical tool to capture the norms created at various levels of regulation.

[47] Also referred to as 'state law pluralism' and 'deep legal pluralism'; see GR Woodman, 'Ideological Combat and Social Observation. Recent Debate about Legal Pluralism' (1998) 42 Journal of Legal Pluralism 21, 34.

[48] Michaels, 'Why We Have No Theory of European Private Law Pluralism' (n 44); MB Hooker, *Legal Pluralism: An Introduction to Colonial and Neo-Colonial Laws* (Clarendon Press 1975).

but in looking at the interaction between them came back to particular legal means such as hierarchically superior rules or conflict of laws mechanisms.[49] Legal pluralism in this sense was therefore a 'juridical' pluralism in which the element of plurality related mainly to the co-existence of legal orders. However, whereas the existence of non-state 'law' was acknowledged, the state was still regarded as superior to other legal orders. Weak legal pluralism, therefore, does not relinquish the hierarchical ordering mechanism of state centralism.

Criticism of the state-centred view pertinent to these early legal works on pluralism gave rise to the development of views of so-called strong, or radical legal pluralism.[50] Whereas juridical pluralism adopts a very much internal perspective on law—looking at it through a lawyer's eyes and falling back on legal mechanisms—strong legal pluralism takes an external or sociological view.[51] Scholarship in this field regards legal pluralism as a sociological fact.[52] Its focus is therefore on how norms function in 'reality', such as the effects that norms have in society and the expectations that those who are addressed by them have of the content of norms.[53] In relation to legal ordering, this poses new challenges. Strong legal pluralism rejects hierarchy both on normative and empirical grounds. Normatively because it is undesirable to subordinate legal orders to state law—which can be regarded as pejorative, treating non-state law as inferior[54]—and empirically because (state) hierarchy is not a given but the relation between different legal orders is under constant negotiation.[55] What can come in the place of a hierarchical ordering, however, is unclear. Classical legal mechanisms, such as conflict of laws rules, are sometimes rejected, though a renewed interest in their usefulness as a mechanism for managing pluralism is apparent in the work of Schiff Berman and Michaels.[56] It is important to realize that the more open framework presented by strong legal pluralism has been subject to criticism itself, in particular because of the perceived indeterminacy or vagueness that it invokes.[57] Similar criticism has been levied against the idea of inter-legality or hybridity.[58]

[49] Michaels, 'Why We Have No Theory of European Private Law Pluralism' (n 44) 142, with sources there cited.

[50] In particular Griffiths, 'What is Legal Pluralism?' (n 43).

[51] AAH van Hoek, 'Managing Legal Diversity—New Challenges for Private International Law' (2012) 30 Nederlands Internationaal Privaatrecht 362.

[52] cf Griffiths, 'What is Legal Pluralism?' (n 43) 4.

[53] Van Hoek, 'Managing Legal Diversity—New Challenges for Private International Law' (n 51) 367.

[54] Twining, 'Normative and Legal Pluralism: A Global Perspective' (n 45) 501–02.

[55] Michaels, 'Why We Have No Theory of European Private Law Pluralism' (n 44) 142.

[56] Schiff Berman, *Global Legal Pluralism* (n 16) Part IV; Ralf Michaels (n 9) 256.

[57] See eg Woodman, 'Ideological Combat and Social Observation. Recent Debate about Legal Pluralism' (n 47) 40 ff.

[58] Michaels, 'Global Legal Pluralism' (n 9) 254.

B. Strong or Weak Legal Pluralism, and the Relevance of the Question 'But is it Law?'

In what way does a new legal pluralist framework then fit with the sources of law that exist in our current era of globalization? From an ontological perspective it is hard to deny that lawmaking in private law has over the years broadened into a wider amalgam of rules than those laid down by a state legislator.[59] The European Union has become an important norm-setter in private law through Directives and Regulations, as well as through soft law instruments like the Draft Common Frame of Reference (DCFR).[60] Apart from rules created in this supranational sphere, both transnational rulemaking (eg by the United Nations Commission on International Trade Law (UNCITRAL) or the International Institute for the Unification of Private Law (UNIDROIT))[61] and private regulation by specific industries have added a significant body of non-state rules to the picture. That in itself, however, does not require us to move away from a model in which the state is regarded as the primary lawmaker.

The case for a legal pluralist perspective in transnational private law emerges from the observation that the hierarchy between these sources of law is changing, and perhaps even tilting away from the nation-state. Thus, analytically, in describing what perspective can best capture all relevant sources of law in transnational private law, it seems to be more correct to consider norms on the basis of their substance or rationale[62] rather than on the basis of their absorbance into official legal systems. I will elaborate on each point and will then set out how they lend support to adopting a strong legal pluralist view as an analytical framework for transnational private law. This part wraps up with a few observations on how such a strong legal pluralist framework can accommodate questions of legitimacy of rulemaking 'beyond the state'—or in other words, how important the question 'But is it Law?' is in this view.

[59] Compare H Schepel, *The Constitution of Private Governance: Product Standards in the Regulation of Integrating Markets* (Hart Publishing 2005) 35, who in relation to standards developed by private standardization bodies states that '[s]tandard bodies link . . . social custom to law. They should at least be taken seriously as sites of modern governance.'

[60] Study Group on a European Civil Code, Research Group on the Existing EC Private Law (Acquis Group), *Draft Common Frame of Reference (DCFR). Principles, Definitions and Model Rules of European Private Law. Full Edition* (Sellier 2009).

[61] UNCITRAL, the core legal body of the UN system in international trade law, is responsible for the UN Convention on Contracts for the International Sale of Goods (opened for signature 11 April 1980, entered into force 1 January 1988) 1489 UNTS 3 (CISG). Under the aegis of UNIDROIT a set of non-binding principles for international commercial contracting was created, the UNIDROIT Principles of International Commercial Contracts (PICC).

[62] Callies and Zumbansen refer to the 'inherent, rational content' of norms. See, with reference to the UNIDROIT Principles of International Commercial Contracts, Calliess and Zumbansen, *Rough Consensus and Running Code* (n 5) 125.

1. Blurring hierarchies between state and non-state norms

The first point that must be observed is that the state, although it still has a central position as a lawmaking entity in transnational private law, is gradually losing ground to other lawmakers. An area in which this is becoming apparent is consumer contract law. A growing part of consumer transactions are conducted in environments regulated by private regulation, and therefore largely outside the reach of formal, state-originated private law. One can think of eBay, or its spin-off company PayPal. Each offers a global platform through which buyers and sellers can connect. Disputes can be resolved through the platform's own dispute resolution mechanisms, and according to the rules written up by the operators of the platform.[63] Even if, theoretically, a consumer could opt for litigation in a domestic court, the likelihood of that is slim, seeing that the costs at stake in consumer contracts are usually too low to justify that, plus that such a procedure would undoubtedly take much longer to complete than arbitration or other forms of alternative dispute resolution through eBay or PayPal.

Legal scholars who say that for these types of marketplaces or platforms—other examples can be Airbnb or Uber—the state should guarantee the effective enforcement of consumer rights may have a point,[64] seeing that it can be hard to guarantee a minimum level of consumer protection without the involvement of a public regulator like the state.[65] Yet, that observation does not solve the problem that many disputes between consumers and businesses never reach the courts, for the reasons stated in the previous paragraph, and that therefore in practice the rules set by online platforms determine how relationships between users, or between the platform itself and the users, are regulated. Also, it does not diminish the observation that there is a trend for more consumer contracts to be concluded in a cross-border context, even if cross-border contracts for now only make up a minor part of the market.[66] Coupling that back to the question what framework would provide the best fit, a transnational, legal pluralist perspective has the advantage over a monist, state-centred view in that it includes all relevant sources of norms in its analysis—including non-state law—and therefore can perhaps do more justice to the real interests of consumers in the global marketplace. Importantly, a transnational view does not say that state law has lost its relevance. It merely opens up the debate to a more realistic analysis of consumer contracting in a globalized world, in which

[63] Calliess and Zumbansen, *Rough Consensus and Running Code* (n 5) 165.

[64] For example, N Reich, 'Transnational Consumer Law—Reality or Fiction?' (2009) 27 Penn State International Law Review 859, 867–68.

[65] This question forms part of a wider debate on social justice in private law. On the situation in Europe, see eg H-W Micklitz, 'Introduction' in H-W Micklitz (ed), *The Many Concepts of Social Justice in European Private Law* (Edward Elgar 2011) 3, 34–36. Micklitz proposes the concept of 'access justice', meaning that the EU legislator should ensure that those for whom mandatory rules are written—such as consumers—actually have access to the market so that they can benefit from these rules.

[66] The volume has steadily increased over recent years and has been estimated at 10 to 15 per cent of total e-commerce volume (incl. domestic); see <https://www.bcg.com/publications/2014/post-parcel-sales-channel-transformation-cross-border-e-commerce.aspx>.

many contracts are still concluded within national borders and under state law,[67] but in which an increasing number are concluded across state borders and have special characteristics to which state law cannot always cater but to which other (non-state) norms may.

In sum, what examples in transnational contracting show is that many transactions are conducted outside the reach of state law and instead are governed by private regulation. If that is increasingly the case in consumer contracts, it has since much longer been apparent in commercial contracting.[68] Commercial parties are of course under formal, state law already more free to decide upon the terms and conditions of their contracts, seeing that they are not bound by mandatory rules in the same way as businesses are who contract with consumers. In many cases, in particular in cross-border transactions, they moreover prefer to refer disputes to non-state dispute resolution bodies, who are often not bound to decide on the basis of state law. Arbitration is a popular form of dispute resolution, for example through the International Chamber of Commerce (ICC).[69]

The hierarchy of sources of law in private law transactions therefore does not per se put state law at the top. Practice shows that private regulation is of equal or greater importance in some areas of trade and commerce.[70] A framework for law-making in private law in times of globalization from this viewpoint character-wise fits with the idea of new legal pluralism. Whether a 'weak' or a 'strong' legal pluralist approach fits best is another question.

2. Weak or strong legal pluralism and the relative importance of norms as 'law'

Let me say at the outset that the labels 'weak' or 'strong' legal pluralism to my mind do not do justice to the sources of law that we can observe in transnational private law and their interrelation. Weak legal pluralism seems unfitting because it considers the relationship between norms from a purely juridical standpoint. It

[67] It should be noted that globalization does not impact only upon cross-border contracting, but that it can also increase the availability of foreign products in markets all over the world. Tilburg University, for example, has had a Starbucks on campus since the autumn of 2014. To purchases concluded on their premises, normally the rules of domestic law would apply without problem, since consumer transactions take place completely in the domestic realm. Transactions costs may of course still arise earlier, at the time that the company assesses whether it wants to establish itself in a foreign market.

[68] On the evolution of the transnational *law merchant*, and its political significance, see CA Cutler, *Private Power and Global Authority* (CUP 2003).

[69] The ICC is the most preferred and widely used arbitration institution; see Queen Mary University of London, '2010 International Arbitration Survey: Choices in International Arbitration', 3 <http://www.arbitration.qmul.ac.uk/media/arbitration/docs/2010_InternationalArbitrationSurveyReport.pdf>.

[70] The discussion in this chapter primarily focuses on consumer contract law. For a further exploration of legal pluralism and international trade see J Linarelli, 'Global Legal Pluralism and Commercial Law' in P Schiff Berman (ed), *Oxford Handbook on Global Legal Pluralism* (OUP, forthcoming 2020) <https://www.researchgate.net/publication/329024616_GLOBAL_LEGAL_PLURALISM_AND_COMMERCIAL_LAW>.

presumes a hierarchy between sources, usually with the state designated as the primary lawmaker. Even if alternative frameworks can be conceived within this view, for example with a supranational lawmaker rather than a state in the role of primary lawmaker, it in any event requires some sort of juridical ordering. As explained in the previous section, that view does not correspond to the realities of contracting in a globalized world. Businesses as well as consumers increasingly conclude contracts, and resolve disputes, through legal mechanisms operating outside the reach of state law.

Strong legal pluralism would at first blush seem to be a better label to place upon this constellation of sources of law. It would include all norms, whether they are created by formal lawmakers—the state, or European or international legislators—or through informal, private regulation. Moreover, questions of legitimacy of norms can be addressed by focusing on the substance of norms rather than on their pedigree. In the words of Calliess and Zumbansen, the governing validity of norms is derived from their 'inherent, rational content' (or *imperio rationis*).[71] The UNIDROIT Principles, for example, are generally accepted by the international trading community on the basis of their substantive suitability for commercial contracting.[72]

Still, this remains a difficult point. An objection often heard in relation to private regulation is that it lacks the legitimacy of rules that have been created through a legislative process in which a democratically chosen body—for example, a national or supranational parliament—has been able to assess and possibly amend the rules before they are adopted as law. The question 'But is it law?' reflects the sentiments of most positivist lawyers, who would not put private regulation on par with state legislation in particular for this lack of legitimacy. It continues to be a challenge for lawyers and for legal sociologists with an interest in transnational law to articulate a framework in which norms can be grounded in democratic legitimacy.[73] They may be able to look to the work of political philosophers, who have been engaged in a similar search to combine democratic theory with a programme of deliberation. Their studies seek to identify how one can identify communities of stakeholders beyond the state based on the degree of 'affectedness' of a group or community.[74] The idea is that those who are affected by decisions should also

[71] Calliess and Zumbansen, *Rough Consensus and Running Code* (n 5) 125.

[72] cf U Drobnig, 'Ein Vertragsrecht für Europa' in JF Baur, KJ Hopt, and KP Mailänder (eds), *Festschrift für Ersnt Steindorff zum 70. Geburtstag am 13 März 1990* (De Gruyter 1990) 1141, 1151.

[73] Another approach is to determine under what conditions social norms develop into something that can be called 'law'. Calliess and Renner have proposed a functionalist approach based on systems theory, which provides a promising start to that debate. See G-P Calliess and M Renner, 'Between Law and Social Norms: The Evolution of Global Governance' (2009) 22 Ratio Juris 260.

[74] For an overview of the debate in this field, see Calliess and Zumbansen, *Rough Consensus and Running Code* (n 5) 130 ff, referring in particular to the concept of 'affectedness' developed by David Held which ties any assessment of democracy to the quality by which a group has been affected by a decision. See D Held, 'Democratic Accountability and Political Effectiveness from a Cosmopolitan Perspective' (2004) 39 Government and Opposition 364.

be involved in their development. That principle is still quite vague and further work has tried to make it more concrete by focusing on *institutions* and their ability to give access to essential resources.[75] Translated to private law, that means that a nexus for legitimacy should be created by enabling individuals or communities to take part in lawmaking processes of institutions that affect them.

Here lies a significant challenge. While democratic deficiencies are hard to avoid if we move from a national to a supranational legislator,[76] it is perhaps even harder to see how those affected would have a role in lawmaking by private actors. Here, ultimately, the legitimacy of norms may only follow from them being used and accepted by the community at which they are aimed.[77] On the flipside, should the addressees of the norms not wish to be bound by them, they have the option to challenge them in a state court—which in practice seldom happens. Private regulation therefore may often obtain legitimacy by being adopted, or in practice, not challenged, by those affected by it.

The latter point raises a concern, namely that if norms go unchallenged industry bias might colour rules of private regulation in favour of businesses. Self-regulation is said to be an example of 'modern corporatism'.[78] While private regulation may extend also to an entire branch of industry, even in that context bias is hard to rule out, since not every stakeholder may be equally represented. To ensure consumer protection, therefore, some sort of coordination is likely to be needed.[79]

Hence, even if strong legal pluralism can find favour as an analytical lens through which to examine transnational private law, a caveat is in order. A strong legal pluralist view may be appropriate as an analytical description of the status of sources of law in this field, yet it cannot answer questions such as how rules of private law created by different lawmakers can be attuned to one another, or how the interests of weaker parties in private law—such as consumers—should be protected. Nor does it answer the question whether legal pluralism *should be* the preferred perspective for understanding lawmaking in transnational private law. These are normative questions, and answering them requires further scrutiny of pluralist theories. I will now turn to these issues, focusing on the question on what grounds legal pluralism should be preferred over state-centred perspectives on lawmaking beyond the state.

[75] R Kreide, 'The Ambivalence of Juridification. On Legitimate Governance in the International Context' (2009) 2 Global Justice: Theory Practice Rhetoric 18, 28.

[76] M Bartl, *Legitimacy and European Private Law* (doctoral thesis, EUI 2012) <http://cadmus.eui.eu/bitstream/handle/1814/22455/2012_Bartl.pdf?sequence=2>.

[77] Compare Calliess and Zumbansen (n 5) 129, collapsing the distinction between norms that become law at the moment an official authority recognizes them as law, and norms that are recognized as law by the relevant community.

[78] A Ogus, 'Rethinking Self-Regulation' (1995) 15 Oxford Journal of Legal Studies 97, 98.

[79] See further Chapter 9.

III. A Normative Case for Legal Pluralism in Transnational Lawmaking

In private law, normative aspects of legal pluralism are relatively unexplored. Theories that could qualify as pluralist often contain normative choices, but these are mostly not explicitly acknowledged, in part because (European) private law has in many cases not directly engaged with the pluralist discourse or sought to rephrase its questions in pluralist terminology.[80] In this part, I consider why a case should be made for legal pluralism in private law, in particular contract law, taking account of insights emerging from theories of pluralism in constitutional law and international public law.[81] Here we reach the core of the submission that was made at the outset of this chapter, namely whether a theory of transnational contract law should be reconstructed along the lines of legal pluralism because it offers the best framework for transnational lawmaking in this field. And, what limitations should be observed in relation to this proposition?

The normative question is dealt with by assessing which moral principles lend support to the idea that a legal pluralist framework should be adopted for transnational contract law. It takes its lead from studies in the field of constitutional and international public law, including human rights law. Jurisprudential viewpoints put forward in these fields tend to focus on two principles that, albeit it with modification, may also be regarded as fundamental to a pluralist perspective on contract law. The legal framework should create or maintain a space for deliberation between different communities. It should do that first, by giving voice to *public autonomy*, and in contract law—as will be submitted—private autonomy. Second, the interaction between different communities should be based on *toleration* of other values or viewpoints.

Cosmopolitan pluralism and postnational pluralism, as developed by Paul Schiff Berman and by Nico Krisch, are theories that aim to offer frameworks for understanding the transnational pluralist workings of (primarily) public international law, human rights law, constitutional law, and administrative law. Although their theories start from different premises—Schiff Berman's as a means of finding a compromise between sovereigntist and universalist approaches, and Krisch's as a denunciation of monist views of constitutional pluralism[82]—they appear to have much in common in their outlook. Both look at modern transnational law through a—at least partly—strong or radical legal pluralist lens. Moreover, the theories

[80] cf L Niglia, 'Prologue: Of Pluralism and European Private Law' in L Niglia (ed), *Pluralism and European Private Law* (Hart Publishing 2013) 1.

[81] Niglia has proposed a similar case but has focused on rulemaking of a (semi-)legislative kind, such as the DCFR, rather than on private regulation. See L Niglia, 'The Double Life of Pluralism in Europe: Between Constitutionalism and Private Law—Arguments for a Post-Formalist Paradigm' in L Niglia (ed), *Pluralism and European Private Law* (Hart Publishing 2013) 13.

[82] Both positions are explained in more detail below. See 36 and 38.

share common ground in their underlying principles and in their proposed ways for 'managing' pluralism.[83] Before looking at these principles the theories will be briefly described, with a few words on the mechanisms that they envisage for managing pluralism. For the question of managing pluralism, notably, recourse can be had to methodologies borrowed from the conflict of laws.[84]

A. Schiff Berman's Cosmopolitan Pluralism

The moniker that Paul Schiff Berman attaches to his normative vision of a global jurisprudence is 'cosmopolitan pluralism'.[85] This notion encapsulates two concepts, that of cosmopolitanism and that of pluralism. With cosmopolitanism, Schiff Berman means to invoke a framework that regards individuals as all being part of multiple communities, both local and global, territorial and epistemic.[86] It is important to note that this definition does not identify one global community, either as a descriptive status quo or as a normative future for post-national law, but rather recognizes the existence of multiple communities. In that sense, Schiff Berman's view may be seen as a variation from other definitions of cosmopolitanism that identify the 'world community' as the relevant community and that seek to move forward towards one global legal order.[87] Those frameworks rely on a global constitutional framework of principles that have ultimate authority.[88] Schiff Berman on the other hand notes explicitly that his cosmopolitan jurisprudence should not be conflated with universalism: it does not 'require a belief in a single global welfare or even a single universal set of governing norms; nor does it necessarily require that global welfare trump state or local welfare'.[89]

Against this backdrop, Schiff Berman develops a pluralist view based in hybridity. His aim is to provide a middle ground between sovereigntist territorialism—a

[83] Compare A Galán and D Patterson, 'The Limits of Normative Legal Pluralism: Review of Paul Schiff Berman, *Global Legal Pluralism: A Jurisprudence of Law beyond Borders*' (2013) 11 International Journal of Constitutional Law 783, who criticize both authors for not engaging more explicitly with each other's work.

[84] I will refer to such methodologies in the section on 'toleration' below. Ralf Michaels and Horatia Muir Watt have both explored the ways in which the conflict of laws can be integrated with ideas of legal pluralism. See eg Michaels (n 9), and H Muir Watt, 'Conflicts of Law Unbounded: The Case for a Legal-Pluralist Revival' (2016) 7 Transnational Legal Theory 313.

[85] Schiff Berman, *Global Legal Pluralism* (n 16) 11 ff.

[86] ibid.

[87] See Hesselink, 'How Many Systems of Private Law are there in Europe?' (n 18) 218–19, who finds cosmopolitan theory useful for highlighting the importance of monist perspectives, which in European private law would be translated in a need to ensure legal certainty for private parties. He for now leaves open how this monist ideal can be given practical substance in a composite legal order in which the relationships between national, European, and international law are a matter of political deliberation.

[88] M Kumm, 'The Cosmopolitan Turn in Constitutionalism: on the Relationship between Constitutionalism in and beyond the State' in JL Dunoff and JP Trachtman (eds), *Ruling the World? Constitutionalism, International Law and Global Governance* (CUP 2009) 258.

[89] Schiff Berman, *Global Legal Pluralism* (n 16) 11.

state-centred view—and universalist harmonization—a vision that seeks to erase normative difference altogether. The alternative view that he proposes considers overlapping juridical assertions as 'hybrid legal spaces'.[90] By this he means spaces in which multiple, legal and quasi-legal, actors assert authority. The challenge for legal theorists is to determine how conflicts of norms within these hybrid legal spaces are, and should be dealt with.

Concretely, Schiff Berman's view proposes that ports of entry into decision-making should be created for more, alternative lawmaking communities through procedural mechanisms, institutions, and discursive practices.[91] This, what he calls 'juris-generative' approach,[92] or procedural pluralism,[93] is justified on two grounds. First, it should sometimes produce better substantive outcomes. Further, Berman suggests that it is likely to make decision-makers take a restrained view of their own power, which could lead to 'greater tolerance, inclusion, and the development of harmonious processes because even losing parties feel that their voices were heard and taken seriously'.[94] To give shape to this ideal, Schiff Berman opts for a conflict of laws framework as a procedural mechanism that aims to instantiate a social space in which conflicting viewpoints can be deliberated.[95]

B. Krisch's Postnational Pluralism

Krisch developed his theory of postnational pluralism in international law as a response—and denunciation—of the debate in constitutional pluralism. The discourse in this area started out from a 'strong' legal pluralist perspective but has since evolved into more nuanced, 'weak' versions of pluralism. Another typification, following Krisch, would be to discern between 'systemic' and 'institutional' pluralism.[96] In the European context, the first focuses on the European Union and the national systems of the Member States as separate orders that run in parallel without subordination or coordination. Both levels, as systemic units, have internally plausible claims to ultimate authority.[97] The institutional view regards both levels as part of a monist international order, in which the EU and domestic constitutional laws have equal positions. Pluralism exists in this view not between

[90] Schiff Berman, *Global Legal Pluralism* (n 16) 14.

[91] Schiff Berman, *Global Legal Pluralism* (n 16) chapter 6. See also P Schiff Berman, 'How legal pluralism is and is not distinct from liberalism: A response to Galán and Patterson' (2013) 11 International Journal of Constitutional Law 801.

[92] Schiff Berman, 'Response to Galán and Patterson' (n 91) 801, with reference to R Cover, 'Foreword: Nomos and Narrative, The Supreme Court 1982 Term' (1983) 97 Harvard Law Review 4, 11–15.

[93] ibid 803.

[94] Schiff Berman, 'Response to Galán and Patterson' (n 91) 801.

[95] Schiff Berman, *Global Legal Pluralism* (n 16) 327.

[96] N Krisch, *Beyond Constitutionalism: The Pluralist Structure of Postnational Law* (OUP 2010) 71.

[97] Compare N MacCormick, 'Beyond the Sovereign State' (1993) 56 Modern Law Review 1.

systems but within one (international) system on the basis of a lack of hierarchy or coordination in its institutional structure.[98] A large part of the early literature, which centred on constitutional pluralism, could be characterized as institutional pluralism. Authors like Walker, Maduro, Kumm, and Delmas-Marty all sought to instil some sort of institutionalized harmony in order to contain the perceived 'messy' nature of a stronger pluralist perspective.[99]

An alternative to constitutional theories originating from state-centred views is according to Krisch, however, only given by systemic pluralism.[100] Although both perspectives are based on the idea that everyone who is affected by lawmaking action should be included—the idea of political deliberation is echoed here—the systemic pluralist perspective lets go of the idea that different legal orders should be coordinated *within* one overarching system. Rather, it accepts that pluralism can exist *between* different orders. The systemic pluralist perspective emphasizes decentralist management of diversity. The theoretical starting point is that different legal orders can co-exist without subordination or hierarchy. Systemic pluralism therefore at first sight resembles strong, or radical legal pluralism.

Weighing alternative views on pluralism, Krisch identifies perhaps mostly with the work of Teubner and Fischer-Lescano on networks, favouring a conflict-of-laws approach based in systemic pluralism.[101] That similarity is also reflected in the ordering mechanism that he proposes. It is based on what he calls 'interface norms'.[102] Interface norms are defined as the norms that regulate to what extent norms and decisions in one sub-order have effect in another legal order.[103] Or in other words, they are the rules that determine in which instances rules originating outside the legal order can be recognized. In essence, this regime therefore relies on toleration of other legal orders.[104]

[98] A view taken by Neil MacCormick in later work. See MacCormick, 'Risking Constitutional Collision in Europe' (1998) 18 Oxford Journal of Legal Studies 517, 527.

[99] cf Krisch, *Beyond Constitutionalism* (n 96) 75.

[100] ibid. One may wonder, nonetheless, whether Krisch's concept of systemic legal pluralism fundamentally qualifies as a 'strong' legal pluralist perspective. Interface norms—the norms which in his theory provide an organizing mechanism for deciding what norm ultimately prevails in a given situation—resemble rules of private international law, and would therefore be promulgated by a state or an international organization. These norms would therefore, after all, impose a state-centric hierarchy on sources of law.

[101] Krisch, *Beyond Constitutionalism* (n 96) 77. And see A Fischer-Lescano and G Teubner, *Regime-Kollisionen: Zur Fragmentierung des globalen Rechts* (Suhrkamp Verlag 2006). Although Krisch presents his view as distinct from the conflicts of laws approach arguably his view falls within that category; compare Galán and Patterson, 'The Limits of Normative Legal Pluralism' (n 83) 791.

[102] Krisch, *Beyond Constitutionalism* (n 96) 296.

[103] ibid 285.

[104] Krisch, *Beyond Constitutionalism* (n 96) 285–96. cf Galán and Patterson, 'The Limits of Normative Legal Pluralism' (n 83) 797.

C. Principles Supporting a Normative Case for Legal Pluralism

Although there are differences, Schiff Berman's theory has conceptual links with Nico Krisch's work on pluralism. Krisch likewise eschews universalism in favour of an approach that leaves room for the inclusion of multiple viewpoints, values, and preferences in society. Therefore, both propose views that, normatively, promote legal pluralism on the ground that it creates (or maintains) a space for contestation or *deliberation*. The justification for that goal is based on a two-pronged argument that can be useful, with modification, for making a normative case for pluralism in transnational private law.

1. Public autonomy/private autonomy

First, a space for deliberation should be maintained because it enables individuals to realize their public autonomy, that is, to be involved in democratic lawmaking processes. Krisch places his argument in the context of political theory, albeit that the precise justification for his view on public autonomy remains somewhat opaque.[105] Briefly restated, he elaborates the point on deliberation by putting forward that pluralism provides adaptability, it creates space for contestation, and it offers a possibility of keeping 'checks and balances' between different levels with competing claims to supremacy.[106] Suggesting that these three elements can apply in the European Union but may fall short for maintaining a global pluralist order, he adds that ultimately the normative argument in support of legal pluralism rests on the foundational ideals of political order, in particular on public autonomy.[107] Specifying when those foundational ideals are met, he defers to Habermas: '[i]n a Habermasian interpretation, social practices deserve the attribute "public autonomy" when they concretise the discursive requirements that allow all to be the authors of the rules to which they are subject'.[108] Krisch emphasizes the need for inclusion through procedural mechanisms and discursive practices. Ultimately, this kind of pluralist conception should provide the best fit for managing the tension between the inclusion of all those affected and the insistence on self-determination by groups with particular commonalities and common goals.[109]

Schiff Berman appears more hesitant to pursue an argument based in political philosophy,[110] but he also acknowledges that his cosmopolitan pluralist view is

[105] A particular criticism that has been raised is that he groups together, and treats as similar, groups of philosophers with very different views: Waldron (a Lockean liberal), Habermas (a discourse theorist), Rawls (a Kantian liberal), Pettit (a republican), and political pluralists like Laski. See P Capps and D Machin, 'The Problem of Global Law' (2011) 74 Modern Law Review 794, 803.

[106] Krisch, *Beyond Consitutionalism* (n 96) 70 and 78 ff.

[107] ibid 99 and 103.

[108] ibid 103.

[109] Krisch, *Beyond Consitutionalism* (n 96) 100.

[110] Schiff Berman, 'Response to Galán and Patterson' (n 91) at 803 notes that 'my book is not, and does not attempt to be, a work of political philosophy'.

at least partially indebted to the proceduralist vision of Habermas.[111] Leaving his political commitment somewhat open—he concedes a liberal core in his theory of cosmopolitan pluralism but is unwilling to commit to a particular vision of liberalism[112]—Schiff Berman defends his proceduralist approach to pluralism on the basis of four normative arguments.[113] First, pluralists acknowledge the reality that people hold multiple community affiliations rather than—like the universalists or territorial sovereigntist against whom his theory argues—dissolving that multiplicity into either universality or separatism. Second, Schiff Berman argues that pluralism creates a situation in which decision makers are encouraged to take 'a restrained approach to their own potentially jurispathic power', in particular by asking whether deference to other norms might potentially be possible. Third, there is a substantive argument that says that outcomes might be better because there is, in this procedural pluralist view, more opportunity for variations and experimentation. Finally, four, the inclusion of multiple communities may make it more likely that they will at least acquiesce in the ultimate decision, even if they do not agree with the result. From a normative perspective, therefore, a legal pluralist view can be regarded as preferable to alternative approaches—such as sovereignty or universalism—because it creates spaces within which the voices of individuals or groups can be heard. That enables actors to be at least partially—to the extent that they do not defer to others—in charge of their own autonomy.[114]

The argument that a pluralist perspective enables actors to be in charge of their own autonomy carries weight also in private law, in particular in contract law. Different kinds of autonomy are at stake there: not just public autonomy—the authority of groups to self-legislate through democratic mechanisms—but also private autonomy. The value of private autonomy requires that contract law enables contracting parties to give effect to their will.[115] It is often exemplified by the

[111] Schiff Berman, *Global Legal Pluralism* (n 16) 18.

[112] Schiff Berman, 'Response to Galán and Patterson' (n 91) 805, where he contrasts his work with that of Will Kymlicka, in particular *Multicultural Citizenship. A Liberal Theory of Minority Rights* (OUP 1995). Whereas Kymlicka seeks a structural representation of minority groups, Schiff Berman only goes as far as saying that the inclusion of multiple groups in society is *preferable*, but not that it is a requirement for legitimacy.

[113] For a 'restatement' based on the theory put forward in his book on *Global Legal Pluralism*, see more recently P Schiff Berman, 'Non-State Lawmaking through the Lens of Global Legal Pluralism' in MA Helfand (ed), *Negotiating State and Non-State Law. The Challenge of Global and Local Legal Pluralism* (CUP 2015) 15, 27.

[114] But note that Schiff Berman leaves it open in which circumstances such deference should take place. His view is procedural and therefore focuses on inclusion, recognizing that many normative conflicts remain unsettled. See Schiff Berman, *Global Legal Pluralism* (n 16) 15.

[115] This is the most commonly recognized foundation of autonomy in private law; see eg J Gordley, *The Philosophical Origins of Modern Contract Doctrine* (OUP 1991) 161 ff and compare Art II.-1:102 of the DCFR. Some arguments have been put forward in support of a broader notion of party autonomy in contract law, encompassing not just the freedom of contract but also extending to goals of self-realization and fairness; see eg SA Smith, 'In Defence of Substantive Fairness' (1996) 112 Law Quarterly Review 138 and further back L Raiser, 'Vertragsfunktion und Vertragsfreiheit' (1960) part IV, reprinted and online <http://www.european-law-school.eu/media/ReaderGrundmann.pdf>.

freedom of contract, which requires that parties are free to decide with whom to contract and on what terms. Against this backdrop, legal pluralism can add a new element to the realization of private autonomy by establishing that parties are free to decide also *under what law* to contract. That is of particular relevance in transnational contracting, where parties deal with counterparties in other jurisdictions. Whereas a monist system may curb the possibilities that parties have in relation to choice of law, a legal pluralist framework allows parties to opt out from systems that they do not like and to opt in to systems that they find more favourable.[116] Normatively, this supports the case for legal pluralism in contract law—even if it should be noted that in reality autonomy in contract law is hardly ever absolute, since mandatory rules often set limits to the freedom of contract.[117]

2. Toleration

Second, the interaction between different legal orders or communities is mediated through a principle of *toleration*. Toleration is an element more often encountered in 'strong' pluralist theories, apparently as a counter-argument to the way in which conflicts are resolved in monist (or even in weak pluralist) systems, where the authority of the state often decides conflicts. Non-state-centred, strong pluralist views instead focus on mechanisms that enable lawmaking actors to engage in norm conflicts in a non-hierarchical way. Such approaches thereby support the inclusion of multiple values and viewpoints for the sake of public autonomy—making toleration a secondary argument in favour of a strong pluralist perspective.

The normative argument seems at first blush persuasive. How a principle of toleration is applied in practice to manage conflicts between different normative orders, and how it relates to public or private autonomy, however, are questions that require further work. At this point, existing theories are only partially able to provide grounds for a pluralist theory for transnational private law, which is in part due to the diverging meanings that are given to ideas of toleration.

According to Krisch, toleration means that the value choice made by a community are tolerated, or given deference, by another community even if that choice does not fit the normative commitment of the other community.[118] More concretely, in the context of Krisch's inquiry into international public law, regulatory bodies should tolerate and respect the standards and decisions of other bodies.[119] According to Krisch, this approach will be straightforward within the European Union, where the national and European polities and their respective institutions

[116] cfJM Smits, 'A Radical View of Legal Pluralism' in L Niglia (ed), *Pluralism in European Private Law* (Hart Publishing 2013) 161.

[117] This is an important reason why theories of European contract law, even if they claim to take a radical legal pluralist view—such as the one espoused by Jan Smits—in reality cannot be deemed 'strong' pluralist approaches. See Chapter 4 in more detail.

[118] cf Schiff Berman, *Global Legal Pluralism* (n 16) 193.

[119] Krisch, *Beyond Constitutionalism* (n 96) 100–01.

can be characterized as polities that deserve such respect, but harder outside the European Union, where 'the candidates are many and their credentials often unclear; moreover, the link between polities and institutions will often be tenuous'.[120] The solution in those cases is that not every alternative view should be deferred to: only those of bodies which instantiate public autonomy, in which the level of toleration is directly proportionate to the way in which it is internally structured so as to give effect to public autonomy. Examples where this might work are, according to Krisch, cases such as the Organisation for Economic Co-Operation and Development (OECD) negotiating foreign investment rules mainly targeted at outsiders, the Basel Committee drawing up financial regulation for the rest of the world, or the Financial Action Task Force (FATF) enforcing money-laundering standards against recalcitrant third parties.[121]

This view, in particular in the field of public international law, seems attractive since it envisages a space for political deliberation in which actors with the greatest commitment to public autonomy prevail in cases of conflict. Yet, there are concerns as to how this would work in practice that make the theory open to vulnerability. First, it is hard to see how the 'win' in each conflict would not go to the most powerful regulatory body, in effect lending support to extant inequalities.[122] Second, if a regulatory body must respect or defer to another normative system, it is hard to uphold that 'toleration' supports public autonomy—at least not the public autonomy of that body. It has been suggested that the only solution to this conundrum is to decide conflicts on the basis of general international legal norms or general principles of justice and legitimacy, such as applied by institutional pluralists like MacCormick, Kumm, or Maduro.[123] That would then of course result in a 'weak' form of legal pluralism, as discussed above,[124] and moreover demands a consensus on public autonomy at the global level that is unlikely to be established.[125]

Other authors plead for a principle of toleration in another way, resembling mechanisms of private international law, or conflict of laws as it is referred to in the United States and in the United Kingdom. Schiff Berman opts for a conflict of

[120] ibid 101.

[121] ibid. Krisch also notes that private regulation may easily fail to satisfy public autonomy demands. That is a valid point, and it would suggest that in case of conflict, public regulation is likely to trump private regulation. Seeing that many cases governed (in the first instance) by private regulation are never brought before a court or tribunal in which this relationship between sources of law is put to the test, alternative ways of managing pluralism will however need to be considered.

[122] Capps and Machin, 'The Problem of Global Law' (n 105) 808.

[123] ibid 809.

[124] See pp 28.

[125] Neil Walker discusses a number of 'convergent' theories that work towards that kind of consensus, yet they relate primarily to international law and human rights law; see Walker, *The Intimations of Global Law* (n 8) 58 ff. In private law, with its variety of lawmaking actors and substantive norms, such consensus seems harder to find the further one gets away from national polities. Compare also G Comparato, *Nationalism and Private Law in Europe* (Hart Publishing 2014) chapter 3.

laws approach that—other than existing regimes of private international law—not only includes state law but also norms created by non-state actors. The aim is to create a space for negotiation between normative systems: '[t]his vision of conflict of laws may help to better negotiate the inevitable divide between self and other by requiring communities both to acknowledge competing community norms and to wrestle explicitly with the question how much to assimilate or give deference to those competing norms'.[126] This view seems attractive in its attempt to create a (hybrid) space for deliberation, yet it has been criticized for remaining vague in relation to its normative underpinnings. For it to constitute a normative view, it has been said, there should be some moral guidance on how legal conflicts between different communities should be resolved. For example, on what ground can jurisprudential practices that are considered 'beyond the pale' (eg certain practices of *Shari'ah* law such as stoning) be set aside by other legal communities (eg a Western legal system)? Although Schiff Berman indicates that the possibility exists to overcome the deference that would normally be owed to a non-state jurisdiction,[127] he does not specify the basis of that outcome. One would however expect that there was some normative (or moral) basis to reach this conclusion, indicating within which reasonable boundaries solutions can be regarded as acceptable. The recognition of such boundaries would, however, be likely to restrict contestation of claims and thereby mute real discussion.[128] Schiff Berman's theory may be criticized for remaining vague on this issue.

A similar approach is put forward by Ralf Michaels. Finding that a pluralist perspective—or a view based in inter-legality—is the most appropriate framework for law in times of globalization, he suggests that ordering of some sort is still a requirement of most legal systems, and that it should be achieved through the concept of recognition: 'recognition among legal systems ... creates stability (or the illusion of it)'.[129] Legal systems, or if one prefers: legal orders, can in this view create ordering by giving mutual recognition to solutions found in other systems. This is a view very close to conflict-of-laws positions on comity.[130] Recognition by a legal system is not regarded as a constitutive element for the validity of rules developed within another legal system, as might have been the case in traditional studies of legal pluralism, in which customary law needed the recognition of the state in order to be enforceable. Instead, the focus is on 'recognition as a practice of the recognizing law'.[131] Put differently, the problem is one of perspective. In the eyes of

126 Schiff Berman, *Global Legal Pluralism* (n 16) 194.
127 Schiff Berman, *Global Legal Pluralism* (n 16) 225.
128 Galán and Patterson, 'The Limits of Normative Legal Pluralism' (n 83) 796–97.
129 Michaels, 'Global Legal Pluralism' (n 9) 256.
130 The toolbox provided by the conflict of laws is closely related to discussions of transnational legal pluralism. See also Muir Watt (n 84). Note that Muir Watt's perspective on pluralism is also based on constitutional perspectives, in particular on Teubner's 'societal constitutionalism'. See G Teubner, *Constitutional Fragments: Societal Constitutionalism and Globalization* (OUP 2012).
131 ibid.

the state, all other legal orders depend on recognition by the state, but in the view of Islam even state law is subject to recognition by *Shari'ah* law.[132] In accordance with strong legal pluralist views, no system takes hierarchy over another in a more absolute manner. Practically, however, it would seem that this approach makes it possible for a state to deny recognition to religious law, since each normative system—in this case the state—decides for itself which rules it regards as law.[133]

While Krisch's view raises questions by seemingly creating a loophole for more powerful actors to impose their norms on weaker regulatory bodies, Schiff Berman's approach may be criticized for remaining vague. Without minimum values or other guiding principles to steer choices in hybrid regulatory spaces, almost any move is possible. Michaels' solution, also based in private international law, seems more straightforward and offers some useful contours for a practical application of a principle of toleration. How it applies in private law—in particular how it can safeguard private law values such as legal certainty and consumer protection—is however also not immediately clear. Michaels has expressed a preference for a private international law approach to European private law, primarily because he finds it better matched with a strong pluralist or inter-legal approach than mechanisms suggested by other scholars in that field,[134] but while that view carries some normative weight by paying heed to public and private autonomy, it is not clear how it can safeguard private law values. An explanation for that may be that private international law is a technical field and that it takes an abstract approach to political issues that underlie conflicts.[135] As Michaels states:[136]

> Private international law as technique is not an alternative to a political understanding of conflicts; instead, it becomes the language with which these political conflicts are not only expressed but also made soluble, if only for the concrete case, and if only in an always preliminary, incomplete manner... private international law operates in an 'as if' mode—it operates *as if* the politics could be ignored, as if insoluble conflicts were soluble. This is a fiction. And a fiction is not the denial of reality—the fiction is a tool formulated in full awareness of its incompatibility with reality, a tool in order to reach results despite that reality.

[132] ibid 252.

[133] For an application of this approach to a German case on circumcision of boys on religious grounds, see R Michaels, 'What is Non-State Law? A Primer' in MA Helfand, *Negotiating State and Non-State Law. The Challenge of Global and Local Legal Pluralism* (CUP 2015) 41.

[134] For example, Jan Smits or Thomas Wilhelmsson. See Michaels, 'Why We Have No Theory of European Private Law Pluralism' (n 44) 142–43, 159.

[135] Although Muir Watt's reconceptualization of the conflict of laws could provide a starting point for 'unbounding' the conflict of laws so that it can connect claims based on individual rights to the underlying rationalities of social systems. See Muir Watt (n 84) 338–40.

[136] R Michaels, 'A Symmetry of Asymmetries? A Private-International-Law Reconstruction of Lindahl's Work on Boundaries' (2019) 29 Duke Journal of Comparative & International Law 405, 417.

In sum, the theories put forward by Schiff Berman and by Krisch, and on this point also by Michaels, provide useful guidance on the normative reasons that may support a legal pluralist perspective on transnational private law, yet they waver when it comes to defending a 'strong' pluralist perspective, either by leaving quite a bit of leeway for the theory to lend support to extant inequalities, by remaining vague on how conflicts can actually be resolved, or on how minimum values of private law can be safeguarded. Nonetheless, that does not automatically lead to the conclusion that it is impossible to normatively defend a strong or radical pluralist theory for transnational private law. If it is accepted that the realization of public and of private autonomy should be a core value, the only question is how the second value, the principle of toleration, can practically lend support to it in a way that does not impose a hierarchy upon lawmaking actors, whilst at the same time safeguarding core values of private law such as legal certainty, fairness, and consumer protection.

D. Towards an Instrumental-Normative Approach

The question then remains how minimum values of private law can be safeguarded in a legal pluralist context. The hypothesis put forward in this book is that Europe, due to its commitment to common objectives and values laid down in the EU Treaties,[137] can provide a framework for the examination of such normative questions that transnational private law cannot. The theoretical basis for that standpoint, which will be further developed in the next chapter, rests on the idea that the European Union can be conceived of as a legal order based on common values, even if those values have in the current time and space not found full expression in the rules, principles, and practices of private law in Europe. The perceived unity of values can have different expressions over time: it can be related to the past—for example, the hope expressed in the Treaty of Rome to create an 'ever closer union between the peoples of Europe'—and to the future, in the form of a putative unity that may be reached at a later time between the EU Member States and their citizens.[138]

While the reference to unity may seem contradictory in a legal pluralist context, it is not if one bears in mind this temporal aspect. In that sense, it seems that pluralism cannot be discussed without also taking account of unity. Where multiple lawmaking actors currently operate autonomously and without a clear hierarchy (hence in a pluralist constellation), they may in the future, for example through

[137] See eg Consolidated version of the Treaty on European Union [2012] OJ C326/01 (TEU), Art 3(3). For an exploration of the theoretical and practical relevance of this provision, see D Ferri and F Cortese (eds), *The EU Social Market Economy and the Law. Theoretical Perspectives and Practical Challenges for the EU* (Routledge 2018).

[138] This argument is based on H Lindahl, *Authority and the Globalisation of Inclusion and Exclusion* (CUP 2018) 200.

deliberative lawmaking processes, adapt their rules and practices to one another and therefore converge towards common values and objectives (or towards unity). It is not a given that they will, but the conception of legal orders based on time, space, subjects, and act-types[139] nonetheless veers between these two sides of the spectrum.

By shifting the focus to the common values and objectives laid down in the EU Treaties, and hence to a putative unity, one step is taken towards a theory for lawmaking in European private law that can safeguard minimum values of contract and consumer law.[140] The values and objectives of the EU Treaties can provide the framework within which more specific rules on contract and consumer law are created by public and private lawmaking actors.[141] That step provides a basis for a theory of lawmaking in European private law that goes beyond the proceduralist theories of transnational legal pluralism discussed above and that therefore can become a normative theory of legal pluralism. Moreover, other than those theories, the focus is not per se on conflicts between legal orders but rather on the question of how—considering the spectrum between plurality and unity of values—processes between lawmaking actors can be designed in a way that supports the safeguarding of those common values.

IV. Conclusion

The argument put forward in this chapter has sought to establish that a legal pluralist framework for transnational private law is indeed preferable to a monist, state-centred perspective. Two strands of argumentation lend substance to this view.

First, legal pluralism is in tune with the ways in which private law works today. It is descriptively more accurate than a state-centred view that focuses on the positive laws of states as the ultimate source of lawmaking, as it takes due account of alternative sources of private law that are of growing importance to transnational contracting: supranational law, international law, and in particular private regulation.

Second, a normative case can be made for a legal pluralist perspective. This aspect of the inquiry has had surprisingly scarce attention until now, even if private law scholars are increasingly interested in legal pluralism as a framework for understanding transnational lawmaking. The work of Ralf Michaels has highlighted the enduring importance of state law as a primary source of private law and the need

[139] Lindahl bases his conception of legal order on these four aspects. See Lindahl (n 138) 51 and further Chapter 3.

[140] This view implies that the common values laid down in the EU Treaties are *minimum* values. Whether they are, or whether they could be conceived as more ambitious goals, eg for the European Union to take over certain responsibilities from the Member States with regard to social rights or the environment, is a different question. I will return to it in the final chapter.

[141] On which in detail Chapter 5.

to be careful with adopting a 'global pluralist' framework that might romanticise private law relationships as taking place entirely beyond state law. Taking a nuanced approach that seeks to take account of the co-existence of public and private regulation in transnational private law, this chapter has explored arguments that can sustain a pluralist view on lawmaking in this field. Its key elements are that legal pluralism creates a space for deliberation between lawmaking actors, giving an outlet to the public autonomy of groups to self-legislate, but also to the private autonomy of contracting parties in their choice of law options. As a secondary argument, mechanisms of toleration are needed to ensure that lawmakers can engage in norm conflicts in a non-hierarchical way, thereby including multiple values and viewpoints for the sake of public autonomy.

The chapter adds an important caveat to this second element of toleration. Namely, it submits that legal pluralism does not have to revolve around conflicts between legal orders. In the context of European private law, the balance is rather one between plurality and unity of values as the EU legal order evolves over time. Mechanisms for 'managing pluralism' in European private law will therefore have to consider how a space for deliberation between lawmaking actors can be created that gives room to pluralism, whilst it supports the pursuit of values and objectives of EU law through private law. The following chapter will examine how such an instrumental-normative approach can be further developed.

3

A Theory of Substantive Deliberation

Legal pluralist theories in transnational law generally have a difficult relationship to normative issues. Transnational pluralist theories are mostly procedural in nature since they find it hard, even if they focus on specific sectors of transnational cooperation,[1] to agree on minimum values or norms that should be adhered to. They therefore focus on the question who has ultimate authority to decide a conflict between legal orders, for example between EU law and national laws. These theories veer between no solution (or, in other words, a case-by-case decision),[2] and procedural views in which either a legal order defers to the norm of another order if it is sufficiently grounded in public autonomy,[3] or in which a legal order recognizes norms only if they fulfil the criteria of its own recognizing law.[4]

The previous chapter argued that the situation in the EU is different. The EU framework recognizes a number of common objectives and values, such as certainty, fairness, and the protection of weaker parties,[5] that give normative substance to the legal framework. For private law relationships, that finding would entail that the rules developed by lawmaking actors at various levels of regulation—national, EU, or in private regulation—should never fall below a certain level of, for example, consumer or environmental protection. The development of European private law over the last decades appears to have resulted in a body of law that pays heed to such interests and that, arguably, reflects political choices with regard to redistribution and inclusion that go beyond the economic organization of the European market.[6]

[1] Compare eg Zumbansen's finding that for several areas in international economic law 'we can witness a growing number of efforts to initiate and consolidate processes of political and legal advocacy—all of which seem to be characterized by a focus on process, facilitation of discourse and contestation, but not on a narrowly defined set of principles or values.' See P Zumbansen, 'The Constitutional Itch: Transnational Private Regulatory Governance and the Woes of Legitimacy' in MA Helfand (ed), *Negotiating State and Non-State Law. The Challenge of Global and Local Legal Pluralism* (CUP 2015) 83, 106.

[2] P Schiff Berman, *Global Legal Pluralism. A Jurisprudence of Law Beyond Borders* (CUP 2012) 194.

[3] N Krisch, *Beyond Constitutionalism: The Pluralist Structure of Postnational Law* (OUP 2010) 100–01.

[4] R Michaels, 'Global Legal Pluralism' (2009) 5 Annual Review of Law and Social Sciences 243, 256.

[5] Chapter 2, p . . . The protection of weaker parties can be seen as part of the pursuit of a social market economy; Art 3(3) of the Treaty on European Union (TEU). See in more detail Chapter 5.

[6] See eg T Wilhelmsson, 'Varieties of Welfarism in European Contract Law' (2004) 10 European Law Journal 712; N Reich, *General Principles of EU Civil Law* (Intersentia 2013) 38–40 (highlighting the protection of the weaker party in employment and consumer law in the pursuit of a social market economy) and 60–61 (on the transformative force of the principle of non-discrimination also in social policy); MW Hesselink, 'Private Law, Regulation, and Justice' (2016) 22 European Law Journal 681.

Legal Pluralism in European Contract Law. Vanessa Mak, Oxford University Press (2020). © Vanessa Mak.
DOI: 10.1093/oso/9780198854487.001.0001.

None of this, however, is uncontroversial. To substantiate the claim that its normative substance sets legal pluralism in European private law apart from pluralist theories in transnational private law, that claim will have to be assessed in the light of several contemporary narratives of European private law and EU market rationality. An important contestation is Marija Bartl's claim that the EU's internal market rationality has transformed or distorted private law's internal normativity, restricting the space of democratic politics.[7] It is undoubtedly true that the private law rules at EU level have sprung from a different well than the private laws of the Member States. They have been created as part of the EU's internal market project, and with a particular economic function, which is the facilitation of cross-border transactions by taking away legal barriers to trade and commerce.[8] Yet, whether the internal market project has hollowed out the traditional normative values of (national) private laws is a question that, considering also other, more generous viewpoints on European private law's internal normativity, requires further investigation. One contrasting perspective is for example presented by Martijn Hesselink's exposition of the 'transformative force' of the European consumer *acquis*.[9] The consumer *acquis* in private law builds on a set of constructs or 'pillars'—such as withdrawal rights, unfair terms control, and remedies—that could be regarded as a starting point for a loosely coherent body of European private law, with a matching notion of justice.[10] As observed by Hesselink in relation to a potential common European sales law, '[t]hese rules also express the fundamental idea that the Internal Market is not a jungle where might is right. In other words, the European model of justice between the parties is a concrete expression and implementation of the idea of a social market economy (Art 3, Para 3 TEU).'[11]

Chapter 5 will explore this dichotomy of normative claims—the internal market rationality versus the emergence of a loosely coherent European private law ascribing to broader values and objectives—and how it plays out in different theories of pluralism in European private law.[12]

One preliminary step in the development of the theoretical framework for law-making in European private law is to identify in more detail how the claim that Europe adheres to common values and objectives can be developed within, and reconciled with, a legal pluralist perspective. To that end, this chapter discusses three elements that can provide a basis to the claim that a normative theory of legal

[7] M Bartl, 'Internal Market Rationality, Private Law and the Direction of the Union: Resuscitating the Market as the Object of the Political' (2015) 21 European Law Journal 572.

[8] The legal basis for private law regulation in the European Union is primarily Art 114 of the Consolidated version of the Treaty on the Functioning of the European Union [2012] OJ C326/47 (TFEU), ie the internal market provision.

[9] Hesselink, 'Private Law, Regulation, and Justice' (n 6).

[10] ibid 686.

[11] MW Hesselink, 'The Case for a Common European Sales Law in an Age of Rising Nationalism' (2012) 8 European Review of Contract Law 342, 361. TEU refers to the Consolidated version of the Treaty on European Union [2012] OJ C326/01 (TEU).

[12] See Chapter 4.

pluralism can be developed for European private law—with normativity here relating to the substance of norms, framed by the objectives and values of EU law.[13]

First, greater definition needs to be given to the position of the objectives and values of EU law. Where are these objectives and values found and how do they inspire lawmaking in private law, in particular in European contract and consumer law? This question comes back to some of the issues concerning the demarcation of legal orders which were raised in Chapter 2.[14] In the absence of a set idea of a legal order, as exemplified by monist, state-centred perspectives on law, legal pluralism has to define other criteria for determining which norms count as 'law' and by whom they should be observed. In particular in relation to emergent legal orders—of which online platforms in consumer markets can be an example—these criteria can be more fluid than they are in a monist perspective. I draw on the work of Hans Lindahl to define in more detail on what grounds a legal order can be defined, identifying criteria that are capable of demarcating legal orders even when they are emergent, in flux, or otherwise lacking a clear hierarchy between lawmaking actors and between norms.

Second, the case for a legal pluralist perspective on lawmaking in European private law can be given further depth. To that end, the chapter returns to the structural elements of legal pluralist theories. These elements are, primarily, public autonomy and toleration. They are derived from Habermas' theory of deliberative democracy, as was explained in Chapter 2 for several prominent theories of legal pluralism in constitutional and transnational law.[15] In this chapter, my aim is to analyse how that same framework applies to European private law. Although viewpoints can differ, the overall conclusion that emerges from this analysis is that political, economic, social, and cultural arguments support the idea that legal pluralism, normatively, should be preferred over a top-down harmonization strategy in European private law fitting with a monist perspective.

Third, the chapter turns to the question how the common objectives and values of EU law can be safeguarded in this context. It will be submitted that an instrumental-normative approach to lawmaking is required, meaning an approach that does not interfere with rule-making by different actors *unless* their rules fall below a certain level of consumer protection. In other words, an approach that requires that a result is achieved through law (hence instrumental),[16] and in which

[13] In contrast to the normative question whether strong legal pluralism should be preferred over other perspectives on lawmaking, discussed in Chapter 2.

[14] See pp 33 ff.

[15] In particular the work of Krisch, Schiff Berman, and Michaels. See in detail Chapter 2.

[16] Instrumentalism can be defined as the pursuit of policy goals through law. The book takes note of potential risks of that approach. Some of its darker sides have been subject to discussion in other contexts; see eg on US law Brian Tamanaha, *The Perils of Pervasive Legal Instrumentalism* (Wolf Legal Publishing 2008), arguing that 'in situations of sharp disagreement over the social good, if law is perceived as an instrument, individuals and groups within society will endeavor to seize the law, and fill in, interpret, and apply the law, to serve their own ends'.

this result amounts to the safeguarding of values of EU law, such as consumer protection (and in that way is normative). The envisaged approach therefore requires only a limited extension of proceduralist theories of legal pluralism, as it does not prescribe beforehand *what* the normative content of European private law should be. It is therefore a legal pluralist approach that respects the space within lawmaking actors to develop, propose, criticize, review, and finally adopt new rules, and only intervenes when no alternative is conceivable. One may call this a 'substantive deliberation' of rules, values, and objectives.[17] By this I mean a recursive process between lawmaking actors in which the substance of rules—laid down in legislation, (co-)regulation, or self-regulation—is examined, and adjusted if it falls below the threshold that EU law prescribes.

The invocation of values of EU law nevertheless can create the impression that the envisaged lawmaking process in European private law is governed by norms of a higher or ultimate authority. Does this perspective then offer anything new in relation to existing theories, and is it not also in effect an 'ordered' legal pluralism? That question will be considered in the final part of this chapter. It should be read as a prelude to Chapter 5, which considers whether and in which respects the proposed theory of substantive deliberation improves upon existing theories of legal pluralism in European private law. Many of those theories have elements that place them within the category of ordered legal pluralism, and it remains to be seen whether the strong legal pluralist approach advocated here can overcome the perceived European preference for ordering.[18] First, however, in this chapter we turn to the question what it means to focus on a Europeanist legal order.

I. A Europeanist Legal Order

First, what does it mean that we focus on a Europeanist legal order? While the concept 'legal order' was used in the previous chapter in a general way to refer to systems of rules, principles, and practices, the turn that we now make towards the analysis of a Europeanist legal order requires a deeper analysis of the concept. To go beyond a proceduralist approach to legal pluralism in private law and to develop a view on lawmaking that presupposes the existence of a framework that safeguards common objectives and values requires that the boundaries of that framework are somehow demarcated. What then is a 'legal order', and on what basis can we say that there is a 'Europeanist' legal order?

[17] The term 'substantive deliberation' is a modification of Habermas' deliberative democracy; J Habermas, *Between Facts and Norms* (W Rehg tr, MIT Press 1998) 287 ff.

[18] R Michaels, 'Why We Have No Theory of European Private Law Pluralism' in L Niglia (ed), *Pluralism and European Private Law* (Hart Publishing 2013) 139, 158.

A. Demarcating Legal Orders

The first question is complicated by shifting views on the definition of a legal order, as the criteria by which to define it continue to be in flux under the influence of the globalization not just of markets but also of lawmaking.[19] The central position of the state as the locus of authority is, in many ways, hollowed out by the emergence of lawmakers at other levels of regulation such as international and European levels, but also in private regulation. Whereas a positivist lawyer in a national legal system may regard the state as the primary legal order to which all other forms of lawmaking should in some way be related, with the state having ultimate authority, socio-legal perspectives on lawmaking provide different lenses through which to view the changing roles of lawmaking actors. To begin with, they acknowledge the role of non-state lawmakers as actors that are sometimes better placed to make lawmaking decisions. Besides this legal pluralist perspective, another important element is that emergent legal orders are not reduced to their new actors and regulatory instruments.[20] Taking stock of current positions in socio-legal research, the following observation made by Hans Lindahl is insightful:[21]

> the concept of legal pluralism must be revised. A first step would be to note that each legal order is a distinct time-space, hence that there are as many time-spaces as there are legal orders. I am happy, here, to join forces with (legal) sociology and socio-legal studies, which acknowledge the insufficiency of approaches to globalization processes that focus exclusively on space. Santos, for example, refers to legal 'time-spaces'. So also Sassen, who has been concerned to describe the 'spatialities and temporalities' of globalisation processes. A third leading contributor to the sociology of globalization, Manuel Castells, has described the internal connection between the space and time of the global in terms of a 'space of flows' and a 'timeless time'.

The connection of legal orders as tied to time and space is important because it offers an opening for construing a concept of legal orders that goes beyond territorialist, positivist accounts of law.[22] A legal order can also emerge where rules

[19] The work of Hans Lindahl is inspiring in this regard. He examines the continuities and discontinuities between state law and emergent global legal orders, and posits a framework for determining the boundaries of legal orders based on 'institutionalised and authoritatively mediated collective action'. See H Lindahl, *Authority and the Globalisation of Inclusion and Exclusion* (CUP 2018).

[20] Lindahl, *Authority and the Globalisation of Inclusion and Exclusion* (n 19) 69.

[21] Lindahl, *Authority and the Globalisation of Inclusion and Exclusion* (n 19) 70. The scholarship that Lindahl builds on includes S Sassen, *A Sociology of Globalization* (WW Norton 2007) (a study aiming to expand the analytical terrain of sociology within which to examine globalization); B de Sousa Santos, *Toward a New Legal Common Sense* (2nd edn, CUP 2002) (reconstructing the notion of legality based on locality, nationality, and globality); M Castells, *The Rise of the Network Society* (2nd edn, OUP 2010) 407–99.

[22] See already Lindahl's earlier work: H Lindahl, *Fault Lines of Globalization* (OUP 2013) 191 ff.

are created through the work of various actors in the global sphere—for example through the World Trade Organization (WTO)—and therefore in a space that is not bound to a particular territory. Further, in relation to the dimension of time, the characterization of legal orders as 'temporalities' gives expression to the idea that legal orders are not fixed, but that they continually evolve. The concept of legal order can therefore apply to legal orders at various stages of development, either as emergent systems of rules or as more developed, settled legal systems. At the same time, it is broad enough to include the positivist, state-centric view of legal systems, namely as the law applicable at a particular time (and within a defined territory).[23] This flexibility is useful because it enables analytical approaches to legal pluralism—how many legal orders are there?—whilst leaving open the possibility that legal orders exist within state borders, that they may overlap, and that legal orders exist beyond state territories.

Time and space, however, are but two dimensions of legal orders. At least two other elements are relevant: the subjects or participants in a legal order, and the substance of norms created within a legal order.[24] The first element concerns questions such as who makes law, what roles do participants have in lawmaking processes, and to whom do rules apply?[25] In jurisprudence these questions are often connected to legitimacy, and answers are sought by considering the various communities to which legal subjects or participants belong.[26] As to norms, the primary connection to legal orders is in relation to legality. Norms that are formally integrated into a legal order along certain predetermined lines—such as democratic lawmaking procedures—are regarded as legally valid, or in other words, as having authority.[27] In case of emergent legal orders, the lines between what is allowed and what is not will often be more fluid.

The contribution of (legal) sociology or socio-legal scholarship to determining what counts as a legal order is, in a legal pluralist constellation, that it gives direction to when—or under what conditions—emergent rules can be considered part of a broader, institutionalized system. The question when norms become law

[23] See also Lindahl, *Authority and the Globalisation of Inclusion and Exclusion* (n 19) 63.

[24] cf Lindahl, *Authority and the Globalisation of Inclusion and Exclusion* (n 19) 54–56. These elements coincide with Zumbansen's actors and norms in a proceduralist perspective of legal pluralism; see P Zumbansen, 'Defining the Space of Transnational Law: Legal Theory, Global Governance and Legal Pluralism', Comparative Research in Law & Political Economy, Research Paper No 21/2011 <http://digitalcommons.osgoode.yorku.ca/clpe/59> accessed 28 February 2020, as are all websites in this chapter.

[25] Lindahl puts subjects at the centre, arguing that authority emerges from a first-person collective, a 'we'. See Lindahl, *Fault Lines of Globalization* (n 22) 81. This idea is developed further in Lindahl, *Authority and the Globalisation of Inclusion and Exclusion* (n 19) 48 ff.

[26] See further below, p 57.

[27] Jurisprudence has dealt widely with questions concerning the validity of rules. Positivist theories generally ground the validity of rules on their pedigree, ie whether they derive from a 'rule of recognition' (Hart) or *Grundnorm* (Kelsen) postulated by a democratically chosen legislator. See HLA Hart, *The Concept of Law* (3rd edn, OUP 2012) 100 ff; H Kelsen, *Pure Theory of Law* (M Knight tr, University of California Press 1967) 8.

is thereby made more concrete. In terms of making the transition from norms in the sociological sense to legal rules, however, the theories leave room for interpretation. If applied to actual rule-making, can we tell which situations count as (emergent) legal orders and which do not? It is helpful in this regard to refer again to the work of Hans Lindahl, who provides a stepping stone by identifying three dimensions or facets of legal order: a legal collective, a legal system, and a pragmatic order.[28] The first, a legal collective, starts from the first-person plural (the 'we') perspective of a group and 'captures the idea that a legal order involves a putative unity in the form of a manifold of participant agents that are deemed to refer to themselves as a unit in action'.[29] The notion of a legal system goes further by adding that a legal order is approached as a 'putative unity of rules' or, in other words, what in legal doctrine and in legal theory would often be called 'law'.[30] Third, a pragmatic order is built from similar elements as a legal system—places, times, subjects, and act contents—[31] but instead of a fixed delineation focuses on 'those whose behaviour is ordered by law by dint of setting up certain ought-relations' between these elements.[32] The focus on the behaviour of legal subjects or participants means that the boundaries of a legal order are considered fluid. In the words of Lindahl:

> certain acts by certain persons are allowed or disallowed at certain times and in certain places. Importantly, this need not entail that the boundaries of a pragmatic order must be sharply delineated in each case; it suffices that the boundaries can be determined in individual cases, and when the need so arises. The fixed jurisdictional boundaries of states are but one of the ways in which the putative unity of pragmatic orders can be organised.[33]

Of the three dimensions of legal order, the conception of the European Union as a pragmatic legal order is important if a strong legal pluralist perspective is adopted for lawmaking. It can help us determine when norms in the sociological sense become rules in a formal, legal sense and, importantly, can do so without imposing a hierarchy between legal sources. While that may sound abstract, a study of lawmaking in the platform economy reveals that lawmaking can in practice take place through a mix of public and private regulation, in which norms developed

[28] Lindahl, *Authority and the Globalisation of Inclusion and Exclusion* (n 19) 34–35.

[29] Lindahl, *Authority and the Globalisation of Inclusion and Exclusion* (n 19) 34. Lindahl refers to the idea of collective self-identification as a means for setting legal boundaries in Lindahl, *Fault Lines of Globalization* (n 22), chapter 6, building on PF Strawson, *Individuals* (1959, reprint Routledge 1991).

[30] ibid.

[31] These four aspects translate into the question *who ought to do what, where, and when*; see Lindahl, *Authority and the Globalisation of Inclusion and Exclusion* (n 19) 51.

[32] ibid. This notion of pragmatism is more complex than the one discussed later on—in a juxtaposition of pragmatic solutions vs doctrinal law—as it contains a normative element in the form of 'ought-relations' whereas the other form of pragmatism is concerned with instrumentalist solutions to legal problems. See further Chapter 4.

[33] Lindahl, *Authority and the Globalisation of Inclusion and Exclusion* (n 19) 61.

by online platforms can be seen as part of lawmaking within the European legal order. They fulfil a particular function—trust-building between users of online platforms—that legislators and regulators have for now left untouched, either because they do not wish to stifle innovation in the platform economy or because they are lagging behind in realizing the need for regulation of this kind.[34] The validity of these norms as 'law' is derived from their acceptance and application by the addressees of the norms, that is, the users of online platforms.[35] Those users, moreover, have their own regulatory role through the monitoring of quality by means of online reviews and other reputational feedback systems.[36] Thus, as this example shows, the idea of pragmatism is normatively appealing. It gives an opening for legal orders to be responsive to changing viewpoints and values rather than to get fixated within the framework of rules established at one point in time. In some respect, that perspective corresponds with the Habermasian idea of deliberative democracy.[37]

The idea of pragmatism is also of analytical significance in relation to lawmaking in European private law. The idea of a pragmatist legal order seems in several ways to fit well with the conceptualization of the European Union as a legal order with two faces: on the one hand a legal pluralist constellation, but on the other hand a legal order centred towards common values and objectives. The European Union can be regarded as a legal system that applies in a delineated territory and that is based on a 'putative unity of rules'. Yet, at the same time studies of EU law, including European private law, have revealed a great diversity of legal rules at different levels of regulation, and an uncertainty as to where ultimate authority rests. This legal pluralist view can be merged with the idea of a legal order if we assume that it is a pragmatic legal order in which boundaries between what is allowed and what is not allowed may be fluid. At the same time, it is a legal order that is aimed at putative unity that may come about at some point in the future.

The idea of a pragmatic European legal order based on pluralism is supported, furthermore, by the text of the EU Treaties. At the time of creation of the European Economic Community, the Treaty of Rome already declared that its signatories were 'determined to lay the foundations of an ever closer union among the peoples

[34] cf O Lobel, 'The Law of the Platform' (2016) 101 Minnesota Law Review 87, 146 ff. See further Chapter 7.

[35] These two elements—recognition and use—are generally required for norms to be considered 'customary law'. See DJ Bederman, *Custom as a Source of Law* (CUP 2010) 171–72.

[36] While this gives users the ability to influence other users' behaviour, their relation to the platform is regulated through contract. In practice that leaves third-party suppliers in a vulnerable position; see Chapter 7. Therefore, while the 'acceptance argument' can be applied, it should be realized that power relations are at play and that co-regulation may in some cases be needed to ensure the protection of collective or fundamental values. See in detail Chapter 9, p 221 ff.

[37] Habermas, *Between Facts and Norms* (n 17). See in detail below, p 65 ff. The scope of this chapter does not allow for an in-depth discussion of the relation between Habermas' social theory and pragmatism. On this topic see eg M Aboulafia (ed), *Habermas and Pragmatism* (Routledge 2002); DN Shalin, 'Introduction: Habermas, Pragmatism, Interactionism' (1992) 15 Symbolic Interaction 251.

of Europe',[38] a statement repeated in all subsequent versions of the Treaty. As Lindahl observes,[39] that statement can be read as a confirmation that the European Union is not a federal unity—as it refers to 'peoples' in the plural—but the more interesting part may be the declaration to aspire to 'an *ever closer union*'. By using those terms, the signatories implied that the existence of a union was not the hope of a distant future, but rather that there already was a collective spatio-temporal unity at the time that the Treaty of Rome was concluded.[40] In other words, the European Union can be defined as a legal order, bounded in space and time, containing 'a community of peoples that, by virtue of their shared values and interests, can engage in a process of legal and economic integration'.[41]

Those shared values and interests can be what sets Europe apart from global legal pluralist orders when we consider the possibilities for safeguarding values and objectives in private law. It deserves further consideration in relation to the analysis of European private law in this chapter.

B. Which Legal Order? Europeanism versus Nationalism and Cosmopolitanism

Of the four parameters for the identification of legal orders referred to in the previous section—space, time, subjects, and act contents—the latter two require further refinement in order to substantiate the claim in favour of a Europeanist legal order. The idea that regional cooperation on lawmaking is feasible, whereas the coordination of lawmaking in transnational private law largely fails, is a claim relating to substance. It is based on the presumption that it is possible on this smaller scale to agree on a minimum set of values and objectives concerning difficult issues, such as redistribution. Further, it assumes that a community can be identified—a community of 'Europeans'—that will regard Europe as a legal order based on political authority.[42] Both aspects require further scrutiny.

The first claim, concerning the coordination of substantive legal issues at regional level, taken at face value has analytical merit, although substantiating it

[38] Consolidated versions of the Treaty on European Union and the Treaty on the Functioning of the European Union [2012] OJ C326/1, preamble.

[39] Lindahl, *Fault Lines of Globalization* (n 22) 200.

[40] As part of his theoretical framework for determining boundaries of legal orders, Lindahl points out the paradox in this statement: it creates a legal collective by reidentification with a past which is held to function as the origin of the new legal collective. See Lindahl, *Fault Lines of Globalization* (n 22) 201.

[41] Lindahl, *Fault Lines of Globalization* (n 22) 200.

[42] This is a validity claim. However, although it does not automatically extend to the legitimacy of rules emanating from lawmakers in Europe, that is a related issue. See on the relationship between authority and legitimacy, arguing that the right to rule should be determined by substantive criteria related to the specifics of the issue to be dealt with and should include non-state actors, B Krehoff, 'Legitimate Political Authority and Sovereignty: Why States Cannot be the Whole Story' (2008) 14 Res Publica 283.

would require further empirical work.[43] The claim derives sustenance from the recognition that it is more feasible at regional level to define common values and objectives to which to direct lawmaking than it is at global level. For example, it would seem possible to identify common standards of social justice in the European Union where, in comparison to non-European countries, the differences in people's welfare are less considerable (albeit that inequality is growing).[44] Habermas has argued that the best that can be achieved, on the global level, are peace and fundamental rights, whereas for further integration, especially when it comes to the solidarity required for distributive justice, we will have to limit ourselves to regional solutions such as the European Union.[45] That argument comes not only from a pessimistic reading of the potential for developing transnational or global cooperation on social policies but it is also based on a positive assessment of the EU's capacity for integration. Europe is thought to have gone through a series of specifically European experiences that together provide a 'learning process that can lead toward a European civil solidarity',[46] which include conflicts between political powers, conflicts between secular and ecclesiastical powers and between faith and knowledge, and wars between countries. According to Habermas, these conflicts have 'acted as a spur toward the decentring of perspectives; as an impulse toward critical reflection on, and distancing from, prejudices and biases; as a motive for the overcoming of particularisms, toward tolerance and the institutionalization of disputes'.[47] While Eurosceptics might perceive Habermas' view on Europe as too optimistic, in particular in relation to the hope of developing a European civil solidarity, the idea that regional integration is more feasible than transnational or global cooperation in relation to social policies would seem plausible.

At the same time, the claim about regional cooperation also requires that a relevant community can be identified to which lawmaking is addressed. As will be recalled, an argument concerning the legitimacy of rules can, to some extent, be derived from their acceptance by the community to which they are addressed.[48] If we limit the potential coordination of lawmaking in a legal pluralist context to Europe, based on the idea that the density of shared values and objectives is great enough to make such coordination feasible, we will also have to identify to *whom* those shared values and objectives belong. In other words, who are the ones 'affected' by lawmaking in European private law? To what community do they belong?

[43] For an exploration of the objectives and values of European private law, see Chapter 5.

[44] G Comparato, *Nationalism and Private Law in Europe* (Hart Publishing 2014) 181. Within the European Union also, however, different views on welfare and redistribution may coexist. See for a comprehensive analysis H-W Micklitz, *The Politics of Justice in European Private Law. Social Justice, Access Justice, Societal Justice* (CUP 2018). For further discussion, see Chapter 4, pp 80 and Chapter 5, pp 105.

[45] As summarized by MW Hesselink, 'How Many Systems of Private Law are there in Europe?' in L Niglia (ed), *Pluralism and European Private Law* (Hart Publishing 2013) 199, 221.

[46] J Habermas, *The Postnational Constellation. Political Essays* (M Pensky tr, Polity Press 2001) 103.

[47] ibid.

[48] See the discussion on the concept of 'affectedness', developed by David Held, in Chapter 2.

The answer to that question—of community—is often approached as one of identity by political philosophers.[49] Distinctions can be made, for example, between nationalist, European, and cosmopolitan worldviews, in which the social, political, and otherwise collective identity of norm addressees is tied to the national, European, or global community to which they are considered to belong.[50] The identity of individuals is therefore tied to a territory.[51] The claim in favour of Europeanism, in this comparison, can be read as a counter-perspective to nationalist or to cosmopolitan worldviews.[52] Whereas nationalists regard the nation state as central to their identity, and cosmopolitans consider people not as Europeans or nationals but rather as persons,[53] Europeans turn to Europe as the community to which they feel they belong. In other words, identity, and thereby the question of which national, social, or other collective categories one ascribes to, for most of us is closely connected to the community to which we consider ourselves to belong.

This perspective does not overlap one-on-one with a communitarian worldview which, centred towards a community, could collapse into an imposed idea of the common good.[54] It is possible for several identities to coexist as people will often consider themselves to belong to various groups, sometimes with shifting allegiances. They may be Europeans, Italians, women, consumers, climate activists, and so on. Moreover, although there may be overlaps—for example, a person can belong to a national, for example Dutch, German, or French community, and at the same time consider herself to be European—the interaction of these different identities does not have to be a 'zero sum' game. Being Dutch, German, or French

[49] See eg Lindahl, *Authority and the Globalisation of Inclusion and Exclusion* (n 19) who develops a theory of collective identity partly based on the work of Ricoeur; M Sandel, *Liberalism and the Limits of Justice* (2nd edn, CUP 1998) who puts forward a communitarian critique of liberalism; C Taylor, *Sources of the Self* (Harvard University Press 1989) who explores the pursuit of social, religious, and political ideals of individuals as part of a common good of their community; or contra, J Rawls, *A Theory of Justice* (Belknap 1971), who justifies the cooperation between individuals towards common goals if it is to the mutual benefit of both parties.

[50] Hesselink, 'How Many Systems of Private Law are there in Europe?' (n 45) 211 ff, who discusses these viewpoints in relation to European private law under the heading of 'senses of belonging'. By comparison, Brugger situates the local and national governmental levels, the European and the international community on the spectrum between personal relations (the single individual and his or her near horizon of partner and family) and the relations between all human beings. The communities envelop each other like concentric circles in which, in a liberal communitarian view, diverse conceptions and spheres of morality and justice gradually grow outwards from the personal to the global level. See W Brugger, 'Communitarianism as the Social and Legal Theory behind the German Constitution' (2004) 2 International Journal of Constitutional Law 431, 440–41.

[51] Hesselink, 'How Many Systems of Private Law are there in Europe?' (n 45) 211.

[52] Hesselink, 'How Many Systems of Private Law are there in Europe?' (n 45) 221.

[53] Comparato, *Nationalism and Private Law in Europe* (n 44) 180, with reference to CR Beitz, 'Rawls's Law of Peoples' (2000) 110 Ethics 669, 677.

[54] Comparato highlights this problem of communitarianism by applying it to European private law debates, stating that 'if we were to take communitarians "seriously" we should admit that not only a supranational but even a national system of social justice is unjust, as it overrides the understanding of justice which is spread among the different communities (not to be intended in a merely geographical sense) within the nation'. See Comparato, *Nationalism and Private Law in Europe* (n 44) 176.

does not necessarily take something away from being European, and vice versa.[55] It might even be that belonging to two different groups enhances a person's possibilities, for example to realize his or her autonomy.

The identification of a relevant community for determining values and objectives of a legal order, therefore, can be complex in the European context. Nonetheless, perhaps it is already sufficient, in terms of defining who the addressees of lawmaking in the field are, to establish that there is a group of addressees that can be regarded as European, that is as belonging to the EU territory. Regardless of whether these people consider themselves to belong to a national, European, or global community, or a mix, the reality for them is that they are addressees of rules developed in the European Union. Those rules can be of national origin, or they can emanate from the EU legislator or from private regulators. As long as they apply within the EU territory they can be considered 'European' and therefore as being addressed to the community of Europeans. That perspective, moreover, could go beyond a territorial approach. Communities can also be constructed on other grounds, for example on the basis of a shared epistemological or political framework.[56] The concept of Europeanism could therefore include not only the community within a certain geographical area (the European Union) but also the epistemic, political, or other kind of community to which the addressees of rules belong. For European private law, the conceptualization of Europeanism in this sense can add something to positivist readings of lawmaking. Whereas positivist law of national or EU origin is considered valid, binding, and established through democratically legitimate procedures,[57] the broader perspective of Europeanism can achieve the same result for rules that are established outside the state or EU legislative context, such as private regulation.

Arguably, therefore, there appears to be a Europeanist perspective that lends support to the claim that regional coordination of legal pluralism is feasible.[58] It

[55] Hesselink, 'How Many Systems of Private Law are there in Europe?' (n 45) 224. Schiff Berman has argued that the inclusion of multiple communities in decision-making processes makes it more likely that norms emanating from other actors are accepted even if not all addressees agree with them. See P Schiff Berman, 'Non-State Lawmaking through the Lens of Global Legal Pluralism' in MA Helfand (ed), *Negotiating State and Non-State Law. The Challenge of Global and Local Legal Pluralism* (CUP 2015) 15, 27.

[56] Compare PM Haas, 'Policy Knowledge: Epistemic Communities' in NJ Smelser and PB Baltes (eds), *International Encyclopedia of the Social and Behavioral Sciences* (Elsevier 2001) 11578. Note also that Schiff Berman's global legal pluralism explicitly rejects territorial approaches on the basis that they define the relevant community in a way that, from a global legal pluralist perspective, is too narrow, namely as connected only to the nation state. Schiff Berman, *Global Legal Pluralism* (n 2) 14. The same critique might be applied in the European context, where an approach tied to the nation state is also outdated.

[57] This statement is generally true for political systems in Europe, although debates about the so-called democratic deficit in EU law have not yet abated. See eg Comparato, *Nationalism and Private Law in Europe* (n 44) 143–45. See also MW Hesselink, 'Democratic Contract Law' (2015) 11 European Review of Contract Law 123.

[58] Notably, coordination is bound to be harder in some areas than in others. More contested areas, or fields in which the European Union does not have legislative competence, such as fiscal

rests on the finding that European private law is part of a putative legal order based on common values and objectives of EU law that should be observed by lawmaking actors in the field. Further, those lawmaking actors and the addressees of the rules are part of the same community which, in this context, can also be defined as European. If these basic premises are accepted, another issue that arises in the extension of proceduralist theories of legal pluralism from transnational private law to European private law is whether the latter can fulfil the normative requirements of legal pluralism.

II. Normative Underpinnings of Legal Pluralism: Autonomy and Toleration

At this point, it is helpful to recall the main tenets of the legal pluralist perspectives discussed in Chapter 2 of the book. Painting with a broad brush, the normative argument for legal pluralist perspectives is that legal pluralism should be supported because it creates (or maintains) a space for contestation or deliberation.[59] The justification of that goal—the creation or maintenance of such a space—is based on a two-pronged argument. First, a space for deliberation should be maintained because it enables individuals to realize their public *autonomy*, that is it allows them to be involved in democratic lawmaking processes. The argument may even be extended to private autonomy since a legal pluralist framework, other than a monist framework, allows parties to opt out of systems that they do not like and to opt in to systems that they find more favourable.[60] Second, the interaction between different legal orders or communities is mediated through a principle of *toleration*. Toleration is an element more often encountered in 'strong' pluralist theories, apparently as a counter-argument to the way in which conflicts are resolved in monist (or even in weak pluralist) systems, where the authority of the state often decides conflicts. Non-state-centric, strong pluralist views instead focus on mechanisms that enable lawmaking actors to engage in norm conflicts in a non-hierarchical way. Such approaches thereby support the inclusion of multiple values and viewpoints for the sake of public autonomy—making toleration a secondary argument in favour of a strong pluralist perspective.[61]

policy or education, are difficult to conceptualize as community issues. See A Etzioni, 'The EU: the Communitarian Deficit' (2013) 15 European Societies 312.

[59] This section therefore returns to the normative question of Chapter 2, namely whether legal pluralism as such should be supported.

[60] V Mak, 'Globalization, Private Law and New Legal Pluralism' NYU Jean Monnet Working Paper Series, JMWP 14/15 <http://jeanmonnetprogram.org/wp-content/uploads/JMWP-14-Mak.pdf>, 30.

[61] ibid 31.

Transposed to lawmaking in European private law, it seems that a normative case in favour of legal pluralism can be made. Scholarship of recent years, in particular the work of Hans Micklitz, supports the view that lawmaking in this field is moving away from a top-down approach in which rules are imposed upon the EU Member States by the European legislature.[62] The reason why it *should* move away from this top-down approach is that legal harmonization of this kind insufficiently pays heed to the public autonomy of national or local legislatures, or of private entities affected by the rules. Arguments to this effect have come up often in debates on the harmonization of European private law and relate to political, economic, social, and cultural barriers to integration through law.

First, in relation to the political framework, the legislative process in EU law has been criticized for its 'democratic deficit', meaning that the European legislature is too far removed from the citizens who will be affected by the rules to take account of their interests. While citizens have influence on the political process, of which lawmaking is a part, that influence is considered weak in the European Union, where many either do not make use of their right to vote for the European Parliament or, even if they do, do not feel that the Parliament acts to the best representation of their interests.[63]

The second argument, from the economic angle, rests on a similar basis. It holds that the European legislature is often considered to be too far removed from the citizens to assess their (economic) preferences.[64] While that still sounds rather vague—what does it mean that a legislature is too 'distant' to ascertain the preferences of citizens?—it has been argued that 'it is reasonably more difficult to guess the preferences of a large number of people than those of a more limited group'.[65] Based on that premise, a nationalist approach to lawmaking would be more favourable than a Europeanist model. Extended to the legal pluralist perspective put forward here, the same argument would probably work in relation to private regulation since private actors are in an ideal position to determine their own preferences or those of a (small) group of users. Online platforms, such as Airbnb and Uber, moreover obtain vast amount of data from their users that can be analysed and processed with a view to learning more about user preferences.[66] Notably, the

[62] Micklitz was one of the first authors to predict the failure of the ambitious projects on harmonization of European private law eg through a Common Frame of Reference (CFR) or a Common European Sales Law (CESL). See H-W Micklitz, 'Failure or Ideological Preconceptions? Thoughts on Two Grand Projects: the European Constitution and the European Civil Code' in K Tuori and S Sankari (eds), *The Many Constitutions of Europe* (Ashgate 2010) 109.

[63] See Comparato, *Nationalism and Private Law in Europe* (n 44) 135 ff.

[64] Comparato, *Nationalism and Private Law in Europe* (n 44) 140–41. See also A Ogus, 'Compe tition between National Legal Systems: A Contribution of Economic Analysis of Comparative Law' (1999) 48 International and Comparative Law Quarterly 405; MG Faure, 'Economic Analysis of Tort Law and the European Civil Code' in A Hartkamp and others (eds), *Towards a European Civil Code* (4th and expanded edn, Kluwer Law International 2011) 985.

[65] Comparato, *Nationalism and Private Law in Europe* (n 44) 135.

[66] Compare V Mayer-Schönberger and T Ramge, *Reinventing Capitalism in the Age of Big Data* (Basic Books 2018), Chapter 5.

weight of the economic argument against top-down harmonization could be downplayed once a new factor is added to the mix: the possibility of determining the preferences of citizens through empirical research or impact assessments.[67] Rather than guessing citizens' preferences, the question would then rather be whether this would be a justifiable regulatory choice from a cost/benefit perspective. Still, it may well be the case that empirical studies or impact assessments are deemed too costly in individual instances, and besides that it remains practically difficult to include private regulation in this process. Private actors will carry out their own data analyses but are unlikely to share these with external parties, let alone legislators.[68]

Third, social considerations can lend support to a normative argument in favour of a legal pluralist framework for lawmaking over a top-down approach. While the European Treaties contain provisions establishing social values and objectives as part of the EU's integration project, the reality is that social policy is mostly still the prerogative of national legislatures. Redistributive choices are difficult to make at a supranational level, due to the widely divergent welfare policies and underlying political beliefs prevailing in the EU Member States. Lacking fiscal powers,[69] the European legislature has little elbow room to introduce its own social policies. In private law, that limitation is reflected also, with much emphasis in legislative projects placed on the autonomy of private actors rather than on policies aimed at the pursuit of social justice.[70] Although a decentralized approach to lawmaking also does not immediately provide a framework for the concerted pursuit of social policies—in fact, this touches upon the concern that a legal pluralist approach cannot safeguard minimum values or objectives—there is at least space in that framework for individual actors to develop social policies and accompanying rules. In that respect, a legal pluralist framework is preferable over a top-down approach. It creates space for deliberation and debate, and for lawmaking actors to realize their public autonomy.

Fourth, and finally, differences in (legal) cultures may support the case of legal pluralism over a monist approach of top-down harmonization. This is an aspect on which much more can be said than the space within this book allows. The ardent

[67] That perspective, it should be noted, was researched in detail in a twin PhD project by Gary Low in the same HiiL-funded project; see G Low, 'The (Ir)relevance of Harmonisation and Legal Diversity to European Contract Law: A Perspective from Psychology' (2010) 18 European Review of Contract Law 285.

[68] They may even be barred from sharing user data by data protection regulation; see eg Art 5 of Regulation (EU) 2016/679 on the protection of natural persons with regard to the processing of personal data and on the free movement of such data [2016] OJ L119/1 (General Data Protection Regulation), which replaces Directive 95/46/EC as of 24 May 2016.

[69] Peter Lindseth has, correctly, raised the criticism that the EU's integration is held back by the absence of a fiscal union; see eg P Lindseth, 'The Eurozone Crisis, Institutional Change, and "Political Union"' in F Allan, E Carletti, and J Gray (eds), *Political, Fiscal, and Banking Union in the Eurozone?* (Wharton Financial Institutions Center Press 2013), SSRN <https://ssrn.com/abstract=2495818>.

[70] Compare Study Group on Social Justice in European Private Law, 'Social Justice in European Contract Law: A Manifesto' (2004) 10 European Law Journal 653.

criticism of Pierre Legrand in the early days of harmonization debates in European private law rested precisely on this argument: cultural identities of nation states and their legal systems are deeply engrained and, according to Legrand, can hardly be overcome by harmonized legal rules.[71] Nevertheless, counter-arguments have also been made. In the private sphere, for example, contract clauses could be regarded as representative of legal culture and it could therefore be envisaged that a practical European legal culture can be built based on contract clauses.[72] The answer is likely to be somewhere in the middle. While cultural differences undoubtedly exist between EU Member States, and between the Member States and the Union, these do not have to stand in the way of lawmaking approaches based on common values and objectives. At the same time, the way in which these values are pursued is likely to be open, leaving room for different cultures. The pendulum will swing between such open, more substance-based approaches and attempts at neo-formalist lawmaking.[73] Overall, that means that a legal pluralist approach is at work.

The case for a legal pluralist perspective on European private law, therefore, seems strong. The pluralist perspective outperforms a monist, top-down approach to legal harmonization in its ability to create a space for the deliberation of political, economic, social, and cultural factors. In that respect, it enables lawmaking actors and rule addressees to realize their public autonomy, that is their authority to self-legislate through democratic means. That at least is the theory. Another question is under what conditions lawmaking actors can effectively make use of this potential. In that light, it is relevant also to consider the second element of the normative case for legal pluralism: toleration. Public autonomy can only be fully realized if norm conflicts between lawmaking actors are moderated through a process that is non-hierarchical and that leaves room for different viewpoints. The mechanisms for 'managing' toleration, however, are ambivalent, as was seen in the discussion of transnational legal pluralist theories.[74] One advantage that the European Union nonetheless has over the transnational sphere is that it would seem that toleration can more easily be achieved within the European context. Lawmakers are likely to have greater trust in other polities and institutions in Europe—often national polities and their respective institutions—than they would have in relation to institutions outside Europe, which vary greatly in terms of stability and representation.[75]

[71] P Legrand, 'Against a European Civil Code' (1997) 60 Modern Law Review 44.

[72] For an argument to this effect, see G Helleringer, 'The Potential for Contract Clauses to Build a European Legal Culture' in G Helleringer and K Purnhagen (eds), *Towards a European Legal Culture* (Beck/Hart Publishing/Nomos 2014) 243.

[73] Compare MW Hesselink, 'The New European Legal Culture—Ten Years On' in G Helleringer and K Purnhagen (eds), *Towards a European Legal Culture* (Beck/Hart Publishing/Nomos 2014) 17. Hesselink's chapter was written before the demise of the CESL. For a current reappraisal, see Chapter 9, p 213 ff.

[74] Chapter 2.

[75] Compare Krisch, *Beyond Constitutionalism* (n 3) 101.

There is then of course still the question *how* the deliberation between different lawmaking actors can be constructed so that the values and objectives of EU law are safeguarded. The final step in the construction of European private law as a strong legal pluralist order turns to that question.

III. Coordinated Pluralism: A Paradox and a New Approach

How can legal pluralism in European private law be coordinated in such a way that values and objectives of EU law—for example, those laid down in Article 3(3) of the Treaty on European Union (TEU) or in the EU Charter of Fundamental Rights—can be safeguarded? The proposition was made that this is an achievable goal in the European context, other than at the transnational or global level, even if some uncertainty remains. Lawmaking, after all, is a continuous process and it can be envisaged that some issues remain unresolved as various actors are working out whether new rules are needed, if so in what form, and how they relate to rules made by others.

'Coordinating' legal pluralism can be seen as a puzzle. Smits has suggested that there are two or, depending on how one distinguishes them, three categories of strategies for dealing with it: there are strategies that attempt to eliminate pluralism, and those that try to accommodate or even encourage it.[76] Within the second category, approaches can be discerned that aim to manage or 'coordinate' legal pluralism to achieve certain policy goals—such as consumer protection—and those that adopt normative debate as a goal in itself. The latter, 'encouraging' form of legal pluralism holds that the answer to a normative question is always subject to debate, and that it should be left to a competition between different communities to determine which norm prevails in given situations.[77] Of course these are ideal types and, whilst one can agree with Smits that this is a logical starting point for examining legal pluralism in European private law, the picture may be more complex than this (tri-)division suggests. Even in a context of coordinated legal pluralism, lawmaking strategies might well be used that seek to eliminate pluralism.[78]

Notwithstanding the potential spillovers of one perspective into another, it would seem that the most fitting approach to lawmaking in European private law should be to explore the ways in which legal pluralism can be coordinated. The main argument for taking that approach is that it is needed to ensure that values of EU law (such as consumer protection) are safeguarded, whilst at the same time

[76] JM Smits, 'Plurality of Sources in European Private Law, or: How to Live With Legal Diversity?' in R Brownsword and others (eds), *The Foundations of European Private Law* (Hart Publishing 2011) 323, 330 ff.

[77] ibid 333.

[78] For example, even in a legal pluralist perspective of EU law, one form of lawmaking may be the harmonization of consumer contract law, sometimes to a degree of full harmonization.

it takes account of the pluralist reality of lawmaking in European private law. The theoretical underpinnings of a model of 'coordinated legal pluralism', however, require further elaboration. Where most existing pluralist theories tend to be of a proceduralist nature, tracing the lines along which legal orders communicate but not answering which normative outcomes should be reached, something more is needed. Building on Habermas' proceduralist theory of deliberative democracy, I will aim to establish that a substantive element can be included in a pluralist theory of lawmaking in European private law in a way that coordinates legal pluralism whilst it does not eliminate it. The argument will be put forward in two steps: first, a move from proceduralism to substance and second, the operationalization of this idea into an instrumental-normative approach to lawmaking in European private law.

A. From Proceduralism to Substance

Given the premises set out above—a Europeanist legal order based on shared values and objectives, but in which public autonomy and toleration provide the reasons why legal pluralism should be preserved—the coordination of legal pluralism in European private law fits within the proceduralist approaches of transnational theories, but with a modification concerning the substantive norms that require safeguarding. I refer to this combination of deliberation and substance as a theory of 'substantive deliberation'. The term is a variation on Habermas' idea of democratic deliberation or 'deliberative democracy', which also underlies proceduralist theories of transnational legal pluralism. In the case of substantive deliberation emphasis is placed on the substantive values that are at issue rather than on the process of lawmaking.[79]

The Habermasian basis of the theoretical framework provides the groundwork for constructing a theory of coordination in which a number of 'pragmatic idealisations'[80] are built in that ensure that relevant participants have an autonomous voice in lawmaking processes. Deliberative democracy, and the legitimacy of lawmaking, are in Habermas' view based on discursive processes of opinion and will formation, relying on reason and the expression of private autonomy.[81] Lawmaking processes should be as non-hierarchical as possible and designed to maximize the

[79] Habermas, *Between Facts and Norms* (n 17) 287 ff.

[80] These pragmatic idealizations function as 'standards for a self-correcting learning process'; see J Bohman and W Rehg, 'Jürgen Habermas' in EN Zalta (ed), *The Stanford Encyclopedia of Philosophy* (Fall 2017 edition) <https://plato.stanford.edu/archives/fall2017/entries/habermas/>. See also J Habermas, *Wahrheit und Rechtfertigung. Beiträge zur Diskurstheorie des Rechts und des demokratischen Rechtsstaats* (Suhrkamp 1999) 35–39, 138–43, 674–77.

[81] ibid 103.

possibilities for deliberation.[82] Four suppositions are regarded as the most important:[83] '(i) no one capable of making a relevant contribution has been excluded, (ii) participants have equal voice, (iii) they are internally free to speak their honest opinion without deception or self-deception, and (iv) there are no sources of coercion built into the process and procedures of discourse'.

These suppositions are idealized, or counterfactual, since in reality discourses rarely fulfil all the conditions presupposed here.[84] Full inclusion, non-coercion, and equality are rarely all present at the same time in lawmaking discourses involving multiple polities and institutions, even more the case if the discourse is taking place beyond the borders of the nation-state. Stipulating what the rules of the game are—that is, these presuppositions—may, however, have an effect on the way in which discourses develop and inspire participants to approximate the ideal conditions for deliberation.[85]

Applied to the context of lawmaking in European private law, a number of potential opportunities for deliberation between lawmaking actors can be identified. First, at the level of legislatures, the EU Treaties have created legal mechanisms through which norm conflicts or discourses between the European Union and its Member States can be mediated. One such mechanism is the internal market provision laid down in Article 114 TFEU, through which the exact scope of competence of the European Union in market building can be demarcated. As has been exemplified by the European Union Court of Justice's (CJEU) take on the use of that provision, it creates a space within which constitutional issues can be battled out.[86] In order to fall within the market building competence of the EU legislator, legislative measures must be designed to prevent the emergence of obstacles to trade that are likely to arise.[87] However, subsequent case law suggests that the practical space for deliberation is limited, as the express and sometimes overly abundant reference to the internal market goals of the Union seem to be sufficient for legislation to pass the threshold of competence under Article 114.[88] Those opposed to EU legislative action will therefore have to make their voice heard in the legislative process itself,

[82] ACM Meuwese, *Impact Assessment in EU Lawmaking* (Kluwer Law International 2008) 42 <https://openaccess.leidenuniv.nl/bitstream/handle/1887/12589/Thesis.pdf>. See also J Black, 'Proceduralizing Regulation: Part I' (2000) 20 Oxford Journal of Legal Studies 597.

[83] See Bohman and Rehg, *The Stanford Encyclopedia of Philosophy* (n 80).

[84] T Risse, '"Let's Argue!": Communicative Action in World Politics' (2000) 54 International Organization 1, 17. See also J Habermas, 'Replik auf Einwände' in J Habermas, *Vorstudien und Ergänzungen zur Theorie des kommunikativen Handelns* (Suhrkamp 1995) 553.

[85] ibid.

[86] See Case C-376/98 *Germany v Parliament and Council* [2000] ECR I-8419, ECLI:EU:C:2000:544 (first *Tobacco Advertising* case).

[87] ibid para 86.

[88] See eg Case C-380/03 *Germany v Parliament and Council* [2006] ECR I-11573, ECLI:EU:C:2006:772 (second *Tobacco Advertising* case).

rather than subsequently.[89] In this process, it is likely that some of the preconditions for deliberative democracy are not (or not fully) met.[90]

A second space for deliberation is that connecting public and private regulators, for example in standardization processes in sectors of industry, and through the EU's Social Pillar project. The development of, for example, standards for terms of contract for services has steadily increased in Europe in the last decades. The EU's 'New Approach on Technical Standards and Regulation' was introduced as a model for creating technical and quality standards through co-regulation between private standard-setting bodies and the European Commission.[91] Although the European Commission in the 1980s intended to include services in this regime, it was not until the early 2000s that standards for services started to emerge. In recent years, however, standardization of services in the European Union has gradually appeared through bottom-up processes, that is through voluntary adoption of standards by the industry,[92] and has also found a legal basis in the EU Services Directive.[93] The use of standards in specific sectors has therefore gained importance, although at the same time little is known about the quality of such standards and their fit with other rules such as those of national contract and tort law.[94]

Third, the CJEU creates a space for deliberation through its position as a final adjudicator vis-à-vis the EU legislature and national courts and legislators. The CJEU, in its constitutional role at EU level, exercises checks and balances over the EU legislator. The *Tobacco Advertising* case mentioned earlier is but one example of the Court's power to delineate the position of the legislator.[95] The Court also moderates the space between EU law and national laws through infringement procedures against Member States and through the preliminary reference procedure, in which it rules on the interpretation of EU law in individual cases.

Finally, there is a fourth area for deliberation between lawmaking actors in European private law, albeit that it is harder to pin down exactly within which

[89] Drawing this conclusion for European contract law, see S Weatherill, *Contract Law of the Internal Market* (Intersentia 2016) 75 ff, 81.

[90] Compare Hesselink, 'Democratic Contract Law' (n 57) 123–24.

[91] H-W Micklitz, 'The Visible Hand of European Regulatory Private Law—The Transformation of European Private Law from Autonomy to Functionalism in Competition and Regulation' (2009) 28 Yearbook of European Law 3, 43, regards the New Approach as providing the leading regulatory concept underlying lawmaking in European private law.

[92] See P Delimatsis, 'Standardisation in Services—European Ambitions and Sectoral Realities' (2016) 41 European Law Review 513; C Busch, 'DIN-Normen für Dienstleistungen—Das Europäische Normungskomitee produziert Musterverträge' [2010] Neue Juristische Wochenschrift 3061.

[93] Directive 2006/123/EC on services in the internal market [2006] OJ L376/36.

[94] Only a few studies have been carried out that assess the quality of standards in specific fields. See eg BJ van Leeuwen, *European Standardisation of Services and Its Impact on Private Law. Paradoxes of Convergence* (Hart Publishing 2017); M Mataija, *Private Regulation and the Internal Market: Sports, Legal Services, and Standard Setting in EU Economic Law* (OUP 2016).

[95] See also Case C-236/09 *Association Belge des Consommateurs Test-Achats v Conseil des Ministres* [2011] ECR I-773, ECLI:EU:C:2011:100. Davies constructs the relationship between the Court and the legislature as a principal-agent relationship. See G Davies, 'The European Union Legislature as an Agent of the European Court of Justice' (2016) 54 Journal of Common Market Studies 846.

space—legally speaking—deliberation can take place. The field meant here is that of private lawmaking, or private regulation. Although research has revealed that private regulation is an increasingly used source of rules *and* that (national) courts are inclined to recognize rules developed through private regulation, the status of these type of rules remains debatable. To what extent they are binding, and to what extent they are legitimate, are questions that are not easily answered. The more important question from a substantive perspective, however, is whether the rules developed[96] through private regulation are in some way monitored for compliance with the objectives and values of EU law. It would seem that mechanisms to ensure this indeed exist. In the sphere of private regulation itself, quality monitoring mechanisms exist in the form of online reputation systems and online dispute resolution (ODR) solutions. These enable users to give feedback on the quality of goods and services and on the reliability of suppliers or other contractual counterparties. Further, rules developed by private actors are part of the broader lawmaking cycle within European private law, and can in various ways interact with public lawmaking in that area, for example through the incorporation of rules in contracts that are subsequently assessed by courts, or through the copying of rules into instruments of standardization or through other co-regulatory processes. Of course, it is likely that such processes are influenced by inequality between actors and potential coercion.[97]

In sum, there appear to be spaces for deliberative lawmaking in European private law, at least as an ideal model,[98] and therefore for a substantive deliberation between lawmaking actors. It is not the only model, as in practice other models for lawmaking may overlap or may be superimposed on the same constellation of lawmakers. One can think of intergovernmental lawmaking, parliamentary lawmaking, regulatory lawmaking, bureaucratic lawmaking, participatory lawmaking, and judicial lawmaking—all of which have been recognized in some way as 'models of EU lawmaking'.[99] Nevertheless, bearing in mind the rapid changes brought on by the rise of the platform economy and by servitization in the market for goods and services, the model of 'substantive deliberation' is important. It is the only one of these models that actively seeks to combine public and private regulation, as well as local, national, and EU lawmaking, in one framework for lawmaking.

[96] For examples, see the analysis of lawmaking in the platform economy in Chapters 6 and 7.

[97] See further Chapter 9.

[98] Each of the four spaces here identified only partly fulfils the ideal conditions set out in Habermas' theory. It may be a task of the EU legislature, as the most centrally placed actor in the legal pluralist framework within which laws are developed in European private law, to try to mitigate shortcomings in the deliberation process to the extent that is feasible. As the model of deliberative lawmaking is an ideal type, in real-life lawmaking only an approximation of that model can be attained.

[99] For a brief overview, see Meuwese, *Impact Assessment in EU Lawmaking* (n 82) 38 ff.

B. An Instrumental-Normative Approach

One part of the puzzle remains unsolved: is the idea of coordination not completely at odds with that of legal pluralism or, in other words, is 'coordinated legal pluralism' not a contradiction in terms? The framework for substantive deliberation proposed above indeed poses a particular theoretical challenge, in that even though the framework is conceptualized as being pluralist, it should ensure that core values and objectives of EU law—for example, those concerning the social market economy—are safeguarded. This gives rise to a paradox. Legal pluralism presumes that rules coexist without a formal hierarchy, whereas the coordination of rules to reach an outcome presumes steering of some sort. Even if such steering is not done through a command-and-control type system, it does restrict the otherwise free development of rules by different rule-making actors.

The solution for safeguarding the EU's values and objectives in European private law, it is submitted, could be to adopt an instrumental-normative approach. By this I mean an approach that does not interfere with lawmaking by different actors *unless* their rules fall below a certain level of consumer protection. The application of that benchmark, therefore, should be an *ultimum remedium*, to be invoked only in cases in which a deliberation of values between different rule sets does not by itself result in an outcome. One might indeed regard this as a 'coordinated' legal pluralism that enables a deliberation of values that allows an open dialogue between lawmaking actors, but with the safeguard that outcomes cannot go below the values embodied in EU market regulation. The approach is normative in the sense that it is based on the idea that legal pluralism, as the preferred perspective for lawmaking, should be preserved. Its normativity, however, does not extend so far as to hold that legal pluralism in itself should *always* be preserved. The combination with instrumentalism means that the framework should also safeguard the objectives and values of EU law, in particular those laid down in the EU Treaties.

Some further justifications for this approach are in order. I will first consider the position of a minimum set of common values in a strong legal pluralist theory, and then look into the relation between private law and instrumentalism.

1. Strong legal pluralism and common values

Critics might object that an agreement on a minimum set of common values is incompatible with a strong legal pluralist perspective. While that position may intuitively seem correct and certainly seem true for global legal pluralism, arguably, the same does not apply for pluralism in European private law. Three observations can be made, which highlight again that European private law is different from transnational private law. First, value pluralism can go hand in hand with consensus on a minimum set of values. It could be argued that in the European Union, other than at the global level, there is an overlapping consensus[100] on the categorical protection of weaker parties. This position would fit with most liberal-egalitarian understandings of European private law. Applying Rawlsian theory to European contract law, if contract law is considered part of the basic structure of society, justice would require that any distinction made between groups must be to the advantage of the least privileged.[101] In European private law, that principle is reflected in legislation aimed at the protection of weaker groups in society, such as consumers.[102] This means that, at least as a matter of principle, value pluralism in Europe exists in the shadow of a broader moral principle of protection of weaker parties.[103] In practice, the European Commission and other lawmaking actors do not always act in accordance with this principle, as debates in relation to the making of European private law have shown.[104] The long-term aim for all lawmaking actors involved in EU law should, however, in accordance with the Treaties be to pursue a social market economy (Article 3(3) TEU), part of which concerns the protection of weaker parties.[105]

Second, the values and objectives of EU law are not imposed on lawmaking actors but rather provide the underlying framework for the legal order that develops in its own space and time.[106] The balance between unity and diversity should be considered in relation to time. One can argue that the common values and objectives laid down in the EU Treaties provide the basis for a pragmatic legal order—rather than an established legal system—that can result in unity over time.[107] The boundaries of a pragmatic legal order are fluid, as norms are developed between different actors over time. Therefore, there is room for diversity and, while unity may develop over time, it is not a given that it will (hence 'putative'). From a normative perspective, which holds that legal pluralism is the better perspective and

[100] Muir Watt also points to Rawls' doctrine of overlapping consensus as a potential answer to the question whether there is a limit to the tolerance of alterity. See H Muir Watt, 'Conflicts of Law Unbounded: The Case for a Legal-Pluralist Revival' (2016) 7 Transnational Legal Theory 313, 347–48.

[101] MW Hesselink, 'Five Political Ideas of European Contract Law' (2011) 7 European Review of Contract Law 295, 302–03. Rawls probably did not consider contract law part of the basic structure of society, but others have applied his theory on the ground that contract law has important distributive effects. See eg AT Kronman, 'Contract Law and Distributive Justice' (1980) 89 Yale Law Journal 472.

[102] Hesselink, 'Five Political Ideas of European Contract Law' (n 101) 303. Hesselink emphasizes that the categorization of consumers as the weaker party may be unjust to small businesses who can also find themselves in a disadvantageous position against an economically stronger counter-party. See on this point Chapter 5, pp 110.

[103] Also MW Hesselink, 'Unjust Conduct in the Internal Market. On the Role of European Private Law in the Division of Moral Responsibility between the EU, its Member States and Their Citizens' (2016) 35 Yearbook of European Law 410, 419. cf J Rawls, 'The Domain of the Political and Overlapping Consensus' (1989) 64 New York University Law Review 233; J Rawls, *Justice as Fairness: A Restatement* (Harvard University Press 2001) 32–33.

[104] ibid, with reference to the internal market based agenda of the Commission, and the consumer focused position of European consumer organization BEUC.

[105] Compare Reich, *General Principles of EU Civil Law* (n 6) 38–39.

[106] See above, pp 52.

[107] Lindahl, *Authority and the Globalisation of Inclusion and Exclusion* (n 19).

should be preserved, one might even imagine that this putative order remains putative.

Third, in the governance of European contract law an element of voluntariness can be preserved for lawmaking actors, fitting with the main premise of strong legal pluralism: public autonomy.[108] As to common values, the instrumental-normative mechanism proposed in this book seeks to coordinate lawmaking towards the safeguarding of these values and objectives through mechanisms such as standardization, optional instruments, and the monitoring of online dispute resolution. These mechanisms are of a coordinating nature and they depend strongly on the voluntary participation of lawmaking actors, in particular those engaged in private regulation (businesses, standard-setting organizations). Moreover, they do not impose sanctions on actors who do not comply with the values and objectives of EU law but rather aim to use these values as a yardstick, to be used voluntarily by lawmaking actors in developing norms. The focus of the coordination process therefore is on the exchange of views on the substance of norms and not on the imposition of one legal order over another.[109] These governance mechanisms can also bring back a degree of legal certainty for norm addressees.

These three elements—overlapping consensus on common values, a putative legal order, and a coordinating mechanism based on voluntary participation—it is submitted, can to a large extent rebut the critique that common values are incompatible with strong legal pluralism in European contract law. They imply that the values and objectives of EU law can set a yardstick against which norms can be tested, yet that yardstick is not imposed on lawmaking actors but rather that it facilitates a substantive deliberation that includes and respects different viewpoints. It should be noted that this perspective recognizes the values and objectives laid down in the EU Treaties (in particular Articles 2 and 3 TEU) as a yardstick not just for private lawmaking actors but also for public lawmakers. They are broadly worded goals that leave room for different manifestations in EU law and in the national laws of the Member States, or in other words, for legal pluralism.

2. Private law and instrumentalism

Private law and instrumentalism can also seem unlikely bedfellows. In Western European legal systems private law is primarily seen as a system of rules that facilitates private law relationships. The content of those relationships is left to the parties involved, based on principles of autonomy and freedom of contract. Private law determines under what conditions agreements between parties are legally enforceable, based on a system of rights, principles, and practices that have been established in national legal systems. An instrumentalist approach, which sees law as an instrument that can be used in the pursuit of policy goals, seems at odds with the

[108] On which Chapter 2, p 39.
[109] For a further development of this argument see Chapter 9, pp 203.

facilitating function of private law. It would regard private law as a mechanism—amongst other fields of law—for the pursuit of policy goals. Instrumentalism is also a pragmatic mechanism that can be devoid of moral guidance, thereby making law the handmaiden of policy-makers or pursuers in society. Notably, 'in situations of sharp disagreement over the social good, if law is perceived as an instrument, individuals and groups within society will endeavor to seize the law, and fill in, interpret, and apply the law, to serve their own ends'.[110]

However, while it would seem true that instrumentalism sits uneasily with private law, most national legal systems have in some respects allowed policy goals into their private law systems. In the process of re-codifying German private law around the turn of the twentieth century, Von Gierke succeeded in bringing a few 'drops of socialist oil' into the civil code, the *Bürgerliches Gesetzbuch* (BGB).[111] Similar developments occurred in the private laws of other EU Member States that introduced rules of consumer protection into their civil codes or in separate consumer codes, often already in some form before EU legislation sought to harmonize consumer contract law.[112] Also in the case law of national courts, it is not uncommon to see discussions of policy arguments. There could be more space for such discussions in common law systems than in civil law systems,[113] considering that judges write their own opinions—rather than a unitary judgment—and therefore have more room for the discussion of arguments.[114] Above all, the openness of a private law system to instrumentalism would seem to depend on the willingness to look beyond established doctrinal structures, and on the acceptance of distributive functions of private law besides corrective justice.[115] The national private laws of the EU Member States reflect such openness to some extent. The role of instrumentalism in private law nevertheless remains contested in these systems and the position of social policy in private law is subject to fluctuating tendencies. Broadly speaking, a juridical rationality—in which private law issues are considered in light of the established system and doctrines of private law—prevails in most national systems.[116]

[110] B Tamanaha, *The Perils of Pervasive Legal Instrumentalism* (Wolf Legal Publishing 2008) 2.

[111] H-W Micklitz, *Brauchen Konsumenten und Unternehmen eine neue Architektur des Verbraucherrechts? Gutachten A zum 69. Deutschen Juristentag* (CH Beck 2012) 11–12, 26, with reference to O von Gierke, *Die soziale Aufgabe des Privatrechts* (Springer 1889).

[112] See eg on the development of unfair terms regulation P Nebbia, *Unfair Contract Terms in European Law. A Study in Comparative and EC Law* (Hart Publishing 2007) 23 ff. Separate consumer codes exist in France (the *Code de la consommation*) and Italy (the *Codice del consumo*).

[113] For a common law analysis, see A Robertson and HW Tang (eds), *The Goals of Private Law* (Hart Publishing 2009).

[114] cf M de SOl'E Lasser, *Judicial Deliberations: A Comparative Analysis of Transparency and Legitimacy* (OUP 2009).

[115] Compare W Lucy, 'What's Private about Private Law?' in A Robertson and HW Tang (eds), *The Goals of Private Law* (Hart Publishing 2009) 47, 49 ff.

[116] Chapter 5 examines the relationship between the juridical rationality of national private laws and the internal market rationality of EU law.

Even if the distinction between private law and instrumentalism could be upheld for national private laws, it is certainly not accurate to see European private law in this light. EU legislation in this field is based on specific policy goals that the European legislator seeks to pursue. Article 114 TFEU, concerned with the integration of the internal market, has provided the main basis for the harmonization of consumer contract law. Other important policy objectives of the Union, such as the pursuit of a social market economy, the protection of workers' rights, and environmental protection, have also resulted in legislation that impacts upon private law relationships.[117]

Instrumentalism, hence, is part and parcel of European private law. Hans Micklitz has even suggested that the better term to describe this area of the law is 'European Regulatory Private Law' (ERPL).[118] What matters for the proposed instrumental-normative perspective on lawmaking is how the pervasive instrumentalism reflected in the EU's internal market rationality relates to national private laws' juridical rationality. That question will be analysed in Chapter 5.

IV. Conclusions

Drawing together the lines set out in this chapter, the idea that Europe is special when it comes to lawmaking beyond the state can be upheld. Lawmakers, even if they are not subject to a formal hierarchy, operate in the shadow of the objectives and values laid down in the EU Treaties. The observance of these objectives and values, moreover, can be pursued in different ways, as different spaces exist for the deliberation of norms by lawmaking actors.

This chapter has elucidated three aspects of the theory. First, it has identified which criteria can be used for the demarcation of a Europeanist legal order based on common values, yet in some ways emergent or in flux. Second, it has extended the normative case for legal pluralism in transnational law to legal pluralism in European private law, focusing on the two principles that underlie normative legal pluralism (public autonomy and toleration). Although the same may not be true for all areas of EU law, the analysis has shown that a normative case can be made that supports the idea that European private law should be developed in a legal pluralist context rather than through top-down harmonization. Third, the chapter has argued that the objectives and values of EU law can be observed in lawmaking in European private law through an instrumental-normative approach that enables a substantive deliberation between lawmakers. That approach can be reconciled

[117] See Chapter 4. On environmental policy, see V Mak and E Terryn, 'Circular Economy and Consumer Protection. The Consumer as a Citizen and the Limits of Empowerment through Consumer Law' (2020) 43 Journal of Consumer Policy 227.

[118] Micklitz, 'The Visible Hand of European Regulatory Private Law' (n 91).

with strong legal pluralism on the grounds that it rests on an overlapping consensus between lawmakers with regard to those objectives and values, for example, the protection of weaker parties as part of the EU's objective to pursue a social market economy, and that the European legal order can be regarded as putative and hence open to further deliberation. Also, private actors have increasing an influence on the creation and monitoring of rules of contract and consumer law in Europe, which puts them on par—at least in relation to substance—with public regulators.

Strong legal pluralism, therefore, on the basis of the enquiry made in Chapters 2 and 3 emerges as the normatively preferred perspective on lawmaking in European private law. This approach challenges the view that every theory of pluralism in European private law in effect comes down to an 'ordered pluralism'.[119] Chapter 5 will assess that position in relation to existing theories of legal pluralism in European private law. Before that, Chapter 4 examines in more detail which values and objectives are common to the European project.

[119] Michaels, 'Why We Have No Theory of European Private Law Pluralism' (n 18) 158, with reference to M Delmas-Marty, *Ordering Pluralism. A Conceptual Framework for Understanding the Transnational Legal World* (N Norberg tr, Hart Publishing 2009).

4
Objectives and Values
Economic and Social Rights in European Private Law

Can the claim be upheld that legal pluralism in European private law is different from transnational private law at a more general, global level due to its allegiance to common values and objectives? This chapter puts forward an argument that it can, based on an analysis of the development of European consumer contract law through legislation and case law.* It aims to show that, while lawmaking in this field is embedded within the ordoliberal ideology on which the EU internal market was founded, it is shaped not only by economic rights but also by social rights. Those rights have a basis in Articles 2 and 3 of the Treaty on European Union (TEU),[1] which ground European cooperation in the common pursuit of a 'highly competitive social market economy', social justice, and equality, amongst other values and objectives. Although the idealism expressed in these provisions has not been translated into extensive legislative action at the EU or at the national level, the commitment to social rights can be observed in certain fields of EU law, including European consumer contract law.[2] While the balance between economic and social rights in this area is in flux, the EU Treaties in combination with secondary legislation, case law, and the EU Charter of Fundamental Rights[3] circumscribe a framework of shared values and objectives within which a substantive deliberation between lawmaking actors can take place. It can be argued, therefore, that the EU legal order has a normative basis that enables legal pluralist perspectives on lawmaking to go beyond procedural approaches.

The claims made in this introduction will be substantiated by an analysis of the development of European consumer contract law, with specific focus on the space given to social rights. Social rights, which extend to other aspects of consumers' lives such as employment, social inclusion, and environmental protection, are

* This chapter is based on and largely reproduces, but with significant revisions, the text of a previously published book chapter: V Mak, 'Social Considerations in EU Consumer Law: the Legislator, the Court and a Rhapsody in Blue' in D Ferri and F Cortese (eds), *The EU Social Market Economy and the Law. Theoretical Perspectives and Practical Challenges for the EU* (Routledge 2018) 213.

[1] Consolidated version of the Treaty on European Union [2012] OJ C326/01 (TEU).
[2] Other important areas are labour law and environmental law. See in more detail Chapter 10, pp 240–244.
[3] EU Charter of Fundamental Rights [2000] OJ C364/1.

Legal Pluralism in European Contract Law. Vanessa Mak, Oxford University Press (2020). © Vanessa Mak.
DOI: 10.1093/oso/9780198854487.001.0001.

often perceived to fall outside the realm of European consumer law,[4] although they have received more attention in the wake of the economic crisis.[5] Does that mean that they are of a secondary nature,[6] and exist solely in the shadow of the EU's internal market goals? While the answer to that question might still in essence be 'yes',[7] this chapter aims to show that the European Union has progressively come to express a greater commitment to the social rights of consumers, which is particular to the EU legal order in comparison to developments in transnational private law or in other, regional legal orders.[8] This development has not been linear, and the outcomes of it are not settled. A careful examination of the instances in which social considerations have persuaded the legislator or, more recently, the Court of Justice of the European Union (CJEU) to strengthen the position of consumers is the starting point for identifying where social rights reside in relation to economic rights within European consumer law. This analysis takes into account the political and economic thoughts that underlie legislative and court action in this area. The chapter therefore aims to unveil not only the position of social rights in the EU's internal market project but also to discuss how those rights are embedded in the political and economic context of the market. The analysis is underpinned by the traditional dichotomy between social rights and economic rights, noting that these terms here are only used for analytical purposes and, in EU consumer law, do not bear intrinsic normative weight.[9] Social rights are thus defined as all rights with a non-economic objective, exemplified by rights that pursue the protection of weaker parties in society, such as workers and consumers.[10]

The structure of the chapter is as follows. Section I describes the emergence of consumer law as part of the EU's pursuit of a social market economy. In order to establish what position was attributed to social rights in the early days of European consumer law, this section will seek to analyse the legislative action taken by the European institutions, taking into account the internal market itself, and the ideological bases on which it operated. Section II assesses how social rights are

[4] This was a main criticism of a group of scholars involved in the harmonization debate in European private law; Study Group on Social Justice in European Private Law, 'Social Justice in European Contract Law: A Manifesto' (2004) 10 European Law Journal 653.

[5] H-W Micklitz and I Domurath (eds), *Consumer Debt and Social Exclusion in the EU* (Ashgate 2015).

[6] I Benöhr, *EU Consumer Law and Human Rights* (OUP 2013) at 53.

[7] In particular, if one adopts Micklitz's perspective on 'access justice'; see H-W Micklitz, *The Politics of Justice in European Private Law. Social Justice, Access Justice, Societal Justice* (CUP 2018), discussed in Chapter 4. Weatherill appears to see more space in European contract law for policies going beyond internal market goals; see S Weatherill, *Contract Law of the Internal Market* (Intersentia 2016) 95 ff.

[8] For an elaboration of that comparison, see Chapter 7, p 160.

[9] Kaupa rightly points out that these terms, similar to other dichotomies, are otherwise not neutral. Deeming one set of rights economic and another not implies a certain worldview that can have normative implications. C Kaupa, *The Pluralist Character of the European Economic Constitution* (Hart Publishing 2016) 11–12.

[10] That definition is in line with Scharpf's, who speaks of rights and policies aimed at social protection and equality. FW Scharpf, 'The European Social Model: Coping with the Challenges of Diversity' (2002) 40 Journal of Common Market Studies 645.

currently being balanced with economic rights in EU consumer law: the Treaties, the EU Charter of Fundamental Rights, free movement(s) regulation, and harmonized consumer law. Private regulation has until now not been of great relevance to social rights in consumer law and, therefore, will not feature prominently in this chapter.[11] I will however come back to the relation between private regulation and social rights in the analysis of the platform economy in Chapters 6 and 7, as it is important to determine how the protection of all consumer rights—economic and non-economic—can be safeguarded when regulation moves towards the private sphere. Overall, while social rights appear to have gained recognition in legislative texts, it is submitted that the primary support for consumers' social position has instead come from the CJEU. Section III examines these 'glimmers of social justice' and evaluates what meaning they have in the broader fabric of European market regulation. Section IV concludes by evaluating the position of the Court within the wider framework of lawmaking in EU consumer law, and puts the primary responsibility for the promotion of social rights in this field back with the EU legislature. It also, in the run up to Chapters 6 and 7, seeks to identify some risks to the protection of social rights when lawmaking moves from public to private regulation.

I. Foundations of Consumer Law in the Internal Market

In order to understand what position economic and social rights hold in European consumer contract law, it is helpful first to consider the economic and political context within which consumer law developed. This section provides a brief overview of that development. Two preliminary points require clarification, namely: what is encompassed by the term 'European consumer law', and who are its addressees.

A. Tracing the Boundaries: European Consumer Law

Consumer law is not defined as such in the EU Treaties but the term is conventionally understood to include internal market regulation through the rules on free movement of goods and services aimed at removing legal barriers to trade (negative harmonization), and regulation through legislative harmonization in the form of directives and regulations that seek to lay down a uniform set of minimum rules for consumer protection (positive harmonization).[12] Positive harmonization

[11] Private regulation has had only a limited impact on social aspects of the consumer market, for example in projects concerning corporate social responsibility (CSR), where non-binding guidelines and codes of conduct have been developed. See A Heinemann, 'Social Considerations in EU Competition Law' in D Ferri and F Cortese (eds), *The EU Social Market Economy and the Law. Theoretical Perspectives and Practical Challenges for the EU* (Routledge 2018) 123, 135–36.

[12] S Weatherill, *EU Consumer Law and Policy* (2nd edn, Edward Elgar 2013) at 8.

of consumer law has been given effect through secondary legislation in the field of private law, in particular in consumer contract law and to a lesser extent in (product) liability law.

The addressees of consumer law are, primarily, consumers and businesses.[13] Consumers are generally defined as natural persons not acting in the course of a trade, business, or profession.[14] Businesses (or traders or suppliers), in an almost mirror image, are natural or legal persons acting in the course of a trade, business, or profession.[15] Consumer law, it should be noted, is concerned with final consumers. That is a significant difference with competition law, which often includes a much wider range of buyers affected by business behaviour, whether they are indirect or direct users, small or large, natural or legal persons (including businesses), intermediate buyers or final consumers.[16]

B. Four Ages of European Consumer Law

The substance of European consumer law often acknowledges the social rights of consumers; however, social rights tend to be considered secondary to economic rights. The underlying rationale for that distinction can be found within the economic and political foundations of consumer law in the internal market. Looking at the development of the EU internal market, four 'ages of consumer law' may be identified. While the first three—the founding of the internal market, its completion on the basis of the Single European Act of 1985, and its submergence into a broader, political order after the founding of the European Union—can be relatively well-defined, the fourth—post-crisis and post-*Aziz*[17]—is harder to assess. How meaningful are the examples of 'social justice' in European consumer law in the European market? The prevailing view,[18] substantiated in the following analysis, suggests that the primary ideology underlying the market is still a liberal one, even if the market has been driven by variations of liberalism over time.

[13] One might also consider consumer organizations as addressees, albeit that their role is secondary, as guardians of consumer interests from a collective perspective.

[14] The definition in Art 2(1) of Directive 2011/83/EU on consumer rights [2011] OJ L304/72 (Consumer Rights Directive), which is broadly reflective of other definitions used in European consumer legislation.

[15] The trader definition in Art 2(2) of the Consumer Rights Directive (n 14).

[16] A Albors-Llorens and A Jones, 'The Images of the "Consumer" in EU Competition Law' in D Leczykiewicz and S Weatherill (eds), *The Images of the Consumer in EU Law. Legislation, Free Movement and Competition Law* (Hart Publishing 2016) 43, 56.

[17] Case C-415/11 *Mohamed Aziz v Caixa d'Estalvis de Catalunya, Tarragona i Manresa (Catalunyacaixa)*, ECLI:EU:C:2013:164 (*Aziz*).

[18] Kaupa also acknowledges that the hegemonic narrative conceives of the European Union as a legal order based on liberal ideology; Kaupa, *The Pluralist Character of the European Economic Constitution* (n 9) 11.

First, the foundations of the internal market can be traced to the development of 'ordoliberalism' by legal and economic thinkers in Freiburg from the 1930s and in particular the late 1940s onwards. Ordoliberalism, also referred to as 'social liberalism', was conceived in post-war Germany as a model that can ensure that a free market reaches its theoretical potential in terms of production and growth by ensuring economic freedom for all market participants.[19] In this model, the role of the government is to ensure that there is free competition. The protection of individual liberty and equality therefore are values in themselves. That sets the model apart from neoclassical economics, in which the pursuit of economic efficiency is the primary goal.[20] From a viewpoint of political philosophy, the model must be distinguished from neoliberalism, since it does not in principle plead for a 'small' government. Instead it regards the government as an important guardian of economic freedom and holds that regulation of the market is needed to secure free competition between individuals. The government, for example through protection against cartels, must ensure that there are no legal obstacles to the functioning of the free market.[21]

Second, the idea of a free market that can sustain economic growth and—as the EC and EU Treaties expressly state as an aim—enhance the welfare of peoples across Europe appears to have worked well in the post-war era, when economic growth in the developed capitalist world experienced a 'Golden Age' in which wages and living standards more than doubled.[22] However, the boom of capitalist economies was due to a particular set of circumstances—including investment and an expansion of government spending to support post-war recovery and rebuilding—and came to an end when economic growth halted in the late 1970s. National governments across Europe turned towards neoliberal politics in response.[23] Privatization of public services and a move towards deregulation followed, both with an eye to managing the economy (and society) in the interest of private business. In this time when individual liberty pushed social policies to the side, the idea of a free market extending beyond national borders found fertile ground. The actions towards completion of the European internal market initiated by the Delors Commission in

[19] The term 'ordoliberalism' was first coined by Möller (H Möller, 'Liberalismus' (1950) 62 Jahrbücher für Nationalökonomie 24, 224), who added 'ordo' in reference to the *ORDO* journal—a leading economic journal at that time, founded by Franz Böhm and Walter Eucken of the Freiburg School in 1948 (D Gerber, 'Constitutionalising the Economy: German Neo-liberalism, Competition Law and the "New" Europe' (1994) 42 American Journal of Comparative Law 25, 31–32); Heinemann, 'Social Considerations in EU Competition Law' (n 8) 124 ff.

[20] Compare P Akman, 'Searching for the Long-Lost Soul of Article 82 EC' (2009) 29 Oxford Journal of Legal Studies 276, 276–277; G Monti, *EC Competition Law* (CUP 2007) 24.

[21] Ordoliberalists referred to this as *Ordnungspolitik* or 'indirect regulation', which means that the government does not direct the processes of the economy but merely establishes structural conditions within which those processes can function effectively. For a broader account, Gerber, 'Constitutionalising the Economy: German Neo-liberalism, Competition Law and the "New" Europe' (n 7) 47 and Monti, *EC Competition Law* (n 18) 23–24.

[22] J Stanford, *A Short Guide to the Economics of Capitalism* (2nd edn, Pluto Press 2015) 46.

[23] ibid 47–48.

the 1980s lent support to the establishment of economic freedom for all—but primarily for businesses—across the European Member States. The ordoliberal model of EC law at that time coincided with national neoliberal politics, albeit that the EC model aimed to reach its goals through a wave of regulation, rather than through deregulation.[24] Part of this regulation related to consumer law. The first Directive in this field was the Product Liability Directive of 1985.[25] It was followed by some twenty other directives and regulations concerning consumer rights in contract (mostly) and in tort, all adopted on the basis of the internal market competence of the European legislator. They include Directive 1993/13/EEC on unfair terms in consumer contracts, Directive 1999/44/EC on consumer sales, Directive 2005/29/EC on unfair commercial practices, and Directive 2011/83/EU on consumer rights.[26] This body of legislation is considered to have made a substantial impact on consumer protection in Europe. The recent 'Fitness Check' of European consumer and marketing law confirms that the key directives introduced in the 1990s and 2000s, when effectively applied, tackle the most important problems encountered by consumers in the European Union, also in online markets.[27] Those problems, in line with the focus on the internal market, are considered primarily of an economic nature.

In the meantime, however, the political constellation within which European consumer law developed went through another transformation. The central position of ordoliberal thought in Europe fit less well with the addition of European goals for cooperation that went beyond market integration. The Maastricht Treaty of 1992 by some is viewed as the end of the 'European economic constitution' that was solely focused on market integration through free competition. Maastricht 'demoted' the internal market to one part of a larger, political cooperation. In the same movement, ordoliberal thought became part of the opposition, rather than a supporting ideology for internal market policies.[28]

[24] According to Majone, privatization in national systems did not imply an end to all regulation but rather a changed role of the state: from producer of goods and services to an umpire whose function it is to ensure that economic actors play by the agreed rules of the game (G Majone, 'The Rise of the Regulatory State in Europe' (1994) 17 West European Politics 77, 80).

[25] Council Directive 85/374/EEC on the approximation of the laws, regulations and administrative provisions of the Member States concerning liability for defective products [1985] OJ L210/29 (Product Liability Directive).

[26] Council Directive 93/13/EEC on unfair terms in consumer contracts [1993] OJ L95/29 (Unfair Contract Terms Directive); Directive 1999/44/EC on certain aspects of the sale of goods and associated guarantees [1999] OJ L171/12 (Consumer Sales Directive); Directive 2005/29/EC concerning unfair business-to-consumer commercial practices in the internal market [2005] OJ L149/22 (Unfair Commercial Practices Directive); Consumer Rights Directive (n 14).

[27] The Consumer Rights Directive (n 14) was assessed separately. The results of the Fitness Check and of this assessment, as well as the supporting studies, can be accessed online at <ec.europa.eu/newsroom/just/item-detail.cfm?item_id=59332>. For a discussion of the position of social rights in these directives, see further pp. 87 below.

[28] C Joerges, 'What is Left of the European Economic Constitution?' (2005) 30 European Law Review 461, 474.

While that seems an accurate assessment for the post-1992 era,[29] it does not mean that the EU market has since then evolved towards a 'social model'.[30] The balance between liberal and social values in internal market regulation, as exemplified in private law, continues to be a matter of debate.[31] Until now, liberal motives appear to be stronger—for example, reflected in the strong emphasis in contract law on party autonomy—and indications of a more socially oriented approach limited to specific rules or (lines of) case law, sometimes in the field of European consumer law.[32] Notably, even in the field of EU consumer law the objective of ensuring a 'high level of consumer protection' throughout the EU appears primarily a corollary of internal market policy.[33] Nonetheless, alternative readings of the socio-economic underpinnings of EU law are also emerging. For example, Kaupa has posited that 'while neoliberalism continues to shape the Union's law and policies, the Treaty is yet not fully determined by it ... the Treaty allows for different readings in the light of competing socio-economic paradigms'.[34] The question is whether the tide may be turning in some areas of European consumer law. The CJEU's judgment in the *Aziz* case of 14 March 2013 can be seen as a radical support of social rights, in this case the right to housing, brought about through an active, socially inspired interpretation of consumer contract law by the Court.[35] Some authors have suggested that there may be a 'hidden constitutionalization' in the Court's judgment,[36] meaning that the Court is giving effect to constitutional rights (of consumers) through

[29] Some authors doubt the influence of ordoliberal thought on EU market integration altogether; JW Rutgers, 'The DCFR and the EC-Treaty' in MW Hesselink, C Mak, and JW Rutgers, 'Constitutional Aspects of European Private Law' (2009) 5 Centre for the Study of European Contract Law Working Paper Series 62 <http://ssrn.com/abstract=1413089> accessed 28 February 2020, as are all websites in this chapter.

[30] Although some social rhetoric is reflected in the Treaty (Art 2 EC Treaty as inserted by the Treaty of Amsterdam) and the promotion of social values continues to be pushed by those on the political left. See H Collins, *The European Civil Code. The Way Forward* (CUP 2008) 96 ff.

[31] MW Hesselink, 'Five Political Ideas of European Contract Law' (2011) 7 European Review of Contract Law 295; MW Hesselink, 'Democratic Contract Law' (2015) 11 European Review of Contract Law 81. Instructive comparisons have also been made by US legal theorists, A Bagchi, 'The Political Economy of Regulating Contract' (2014) 62 American Journal of Comparative Law 687.

[32] Whilst Hesselink, 'Five Political Ideas of European Contract Law' (n 29) proposes a pluralist view on the political foundations of European private law, that view seems normative rather than empirical in nature. It is commonly accepted that European private law, and the broader field of market integration, is governed by liberal thought, often at the expense of consumer protection and other social values; S Deakin, 'The Lisbon Treaty, the Viking and Laval Judgments and the Financial Crisis: in Search of New Foundations for Europe's "Social Market Economy"' in N Bruun, K Lörcher, and I Schömann (eds), *The Lisbon Treaty and Social Europe* (Hart Publishing 2012) 19. For a critical analysis, M Bartl, 'Internal Market Rationality, Private Law and the Direction of the Union: Resuscitating the Market as the Object of the Political' (2015) 21 European Law Journal 572, 580–81.

[33] H Unberath and A Johnston, 'The Double-Headed Approach of the ECJ Concerning Consumer Protection' (2007) 44 Common Market Law Review 1237, 1242.

[34] Kaupa, *The Pluralist Character of the European Economic Constitution* (n 9) 6.

[35] *Aziz* (n 17). For the facts of the case, see below pp 85.

[36] H-W Micklitz and N Reich, 'The Court and Sleeping Beauty: The Revival of the Unfair Contract Terms Directive (UCTD)' (2014) 71 Common Market Law Review 771, 800.

contract law. That would mean that social rights, in particular those laid down in the Charter, which fall within the definition of constitutional rights,[37] are of direct influence on the, otherwise economic, rights laid down in European consumer law. Whether the *Aziz* judgment is indeed such a turning point remains to be seen.

II. European Consumer Law: The State of Play

Having regards to the succinct overview conducted in section I, it does not seem surprising that social rights are secondary to economic rights in the EU's free movement regulation (negative harmonization) and mostly also in its harmonized consumer law (positive harmonization). Nevertheless, the CJEU's actively social interpretation of consumer contract law in *Aziz* suggests that there is a legal basis for the balancing of economic rights with social rights in European consumer law. In light of the secondary nature of social rights in free movement regulation and in harmonized contract law, however, a question arises: what legal basis is this, and where can it be found in EU law?

The answer to that question is not straightforward. The legal basis for a social rights based approach in EU consumer law is seldom clarified in the case law of the CJEU and has received limited attention in the literature.[38] Nonetheless, a closer look at the EU Treaties reveals that the legal basis for a social rights based approach in EU law can be identified which, it is submitted, comes from the values and objectives laid down in the EU Treaty—in particular the objectives of Article 3(3) TEU—and the Charter of Fundamental Rights. These will be discussed first, before reflecting on their relationship to free movement regulation and harmonized consumer law. The general line that will become apparent is that EU legislation gives expression to economic rights of consumers but, in line with its liberal underpinnings, does relatively little to pursue the social goals of Article 3(3) TEU. That role, as will be discussed in section III, is left to the Court of Justice.

[37] For a survey of social rights in European constitutions, C Fabre, 'Social Rights in European Constitutions' in G de Búrca, B De Witte, and L Ogertschnig (eds), *Social Rights in Europe* (OUP 2005) 15.

[38] For general explorations of social rights, values, and objectives, S Weatherill, *Law and Values in the European Union* (OUP 2016) in particular at 136–37; Benöhr, *EU Consumer Law and Human Rights* (n 6) 98 ff; F Dorssemont, 'Values and Objectives' in Bruun, Lörcher, and Schömann (eds), *The Lisbon Treaty and Social Europe* (n 30) 47, which focuses on labour law. Relevant to the argument set out here is also Kaupa's study of pluralism in the European economic constitution, which proposes that the Treaty leaves room for multiple, ie pluralist socio-economic interpretations. Kaupa, *The Pluralist Character of the European Economic Constitution* (n 9) 6–7 for the main premises of his argument.

A. Social Considerations in the Values and Objectives of the European Union

The basis for social rights in EU consumer law can be discerned in Article 3(3) TEU, although it does not refer to the field explicitly and does not even refer to the 'consumer' or 'consumer protection'. The provision refers to the establishment of the internal market as an aim of the Union. It goes on to set out a number of other objectives of EU law, some of which can encompass consumer protection goals. These include that the Union shall work for 'a highly competitive social market economy' and 'a high level of protection and improvement of the quality of the environment'. The Union shall also 'combat social exclusion and discrimination, and shall promote social justice and protection, equality between women and men, solidarity between generations and protection of the rights of the child'. While these objectives relate to broader societal goals, they provide the context within which the EU's consumer policy can further take shape. A more concrete specification of the Union's consumer policy objectives is laid down in the Treaty on the Functioning of the European Union (TFEU),[39] in particular in Articles 12, 114(3), and 169(1).[40] Those provisions can be read as an elaboration of the values expressed in Articles 2 and 3 TEU, in particular the 'social market economy' mentioned in Article 3(3) TEU.[41] Article 169(1) TFEU is the most elaborate of these three. It provides that '[i]n order to promote the interests of consumers and to ensure a high level of consumer protection, the Union shall contribute to protecting the health, safety and economic interests of consumers, as well as to promoting their right to information, education and to organise themselves in order to safeguard their interests'. Interestingly, the provision defines the interests of consumers as much broader than purely economic, referring to health and safety, as well as to a 'right to information' and to education. All of these could be regarded as non-economic and therefore social rights.[42] Other, specific basis for the protection of social rights are laid down in Articles 151 and 168(1) TFEU, which respectively concern employment and social protection and health protection.

The practical usefulness of these Treaty provisions for consumers, however, is limited. Rather than providing a direct cause of action, as constitutional rights in certain national systems or fundamental rights in the European Convention on Human Rights (ECHR) do,[43] these provisions can in general not be invoked by individual citizens in litigation against other parties. Citizens only have standing before the CJEU

[39] Consolidated version of the Treaty on the Functioning of the European Union [2012] OJ C326/47 (TFEU).

[40] Formerly both contained in Art 153 of the Treaty establishing the European Community (Consolidated version 2002) [2002] OJ C325/33 (EC Treaty).

[41] Weatherill, *Law and Values in the European Union* (n 38) 136–37.

[42] The reference to a right to organize themselves, on the other hand, would be a fundamental right, which is found also in many national constitutions.

[43] Art 43 of the European Convention for the Protection of Human Rights and Fundamental Freedoms (opened for signature 4 November 1950, entered into force 1953) (ECHR).

in cases where they have been directly affected by an EU regulatory act that did not require implementing measures,[44] or in cases where a question is referred to the Court for a preliminary ruling on the basis of Article 267 TFEU.

These Treaty provisions could however, at least in theory, give ground to other legal actions. They might form the basis for an allegation that an EU legislative measure is invalid, in case of consumer protection if the measure is thought to fail to meet the requirements stipulated in Article 169(1) TFEU with regard to a high level of protection.[45] The likelihood that the Court will find such a violation is, however, low. It would mean that the Court has to establish that there has been a manifest legislative neglect on the part of the EU legislature to take into consideration the protective quality of the harmonized rule or a manifest error of appraisal regarding the applicable conditions.[46] The Court will not soon be inclined to reach that conclusion. It would furthermore seem that the EU legislature can easily prevent (the impression of) that kind of neglect from arising by simply citing Article 169(1) TFEU in the impact assessment and in the Preamble to the adopted legislation.[47] As practical examples often illustrate, the EU legislature is prone to including generous references to the 'pursuit of a high level of consumer protection' in its proposals in the field of consumer law, and in the subsequent legislation. Impact assessments also, seeking to gather the political momentum needed for legislation to be adopted, tend to emphasize the proposed legislations importance for the pursuit of consumer protection.[48]

The relevance of Article 3(3) TEU, therefore, lies primarily in its expression of social rights as part of the EU's objectives. It can be read as ancillary to Article 2 TEU, which establishes the values on which the Union is built. These values are common to the Member States in a society in which pluralism, non-discrimination, tolerance, justice, solidarity, and equality between women and men prevail. Together, Articles 2 and 3 TEU make clear that the Union, although it started out as a market-building project, has in its primary legislation firmly adopted values and objectives that go beyond an economic cooperation. The question is then whether these provisions are more than a kind of mission statement for the Union. As subsequent sections will demonstrate, other EU legislative measures give rise to stronger legal effects.

[44] Art 263 TFEU, which also states that a natural or legal person may institute proceedings against an act addressed to that person or which is of direct and individual concern to them. The term 'act' here is intended to refer not to regulatory acts but to individual acts of EU institutions.

[45] Weatherill, *Law and Values in the European Union* (n 38) 137.

[46] ibid.

[47] ibid.

[48] For a critique of the way in which impact assessments have been used in European private law, EAG van Schagen, 'The Hidden Potential of Regulatory Impact Assessments (RIAs) in the Private Law *Acquis*' (2014) 22 European Review of Private Law 69, who concludes that RIAs have much potential to improve the quality of private law but only if shortcomings, such as unsubstantiated assumptions and a lack of neutrality, are addressed.

B. The EU Charter of Fundamental Rights

Although likely to be seen as tangential to consumer rights laid down in EU Directives and Regulations, the EU Charter of Fundamental Rights has proven to become increasingly influential in consumer cases. The *Aziz* case has already been mentioned as a potential harbinger for the 'constitutionalization' of European contract law,[49] even if that case did not actually cite the Charter directly. The case concerned the potential unfairness of terms included in the mortgage agreement between Mohamed Aziz, a Moroccan national who lived and worked in Spain, and Spanish bank Catalunyacaixa. After the financial crisis hit Spain, Aziz, like many other borrowers, was unable to repay the instalments of his mortgage loan. The bank ordered repayment of the debt and, after Aziz failed to pay, obtained a court order for a judicial auction and eviction of Aziz and his family from the residence. Shortly before the eviction, however, Aziz had instigated proceedings at the court of first instance in Barcelona with the aim of obtaining a declaration that certain terms in the mortgage contract were unfair. Importantly, the aim of these proceedings was also to establish that while the case on the potential unfairness of terms in the mortgage agreement was pending, the parallel proceedings for auction and eviction should be stalled. As Spanish legislation did not attach suspensory effect to such declaratory proceedings, the judge at first instance referred the case to the CJEU with the question whether that legislation constituted a limitation of consumer protection, since it involves a clear impediment to the consumer's exercise of rights of action or judicial remedies of such a kind as to guarantee the effective protection of his rights.[50] The CJEU gave an affirmative answer to this question, thereby making it possible to protect consumers from eviction procedures during the time that proceedings on unfair terms in mortgage contracts are pending. In response, the Spanish legislator has amended the relevant legislation.[51] Follow-up case law has cited the Charter,[52] as have other cases in the field of consumer law, as will be discussed later in this chapter.

The most obvious consumer law provision is Article 38 which states that 'Union policies shall ensure a high level of consumer protection'. The added value of this provision alongside Articles 114 and 169 TFEU, however, seems limited. It seems somewhat anachronistic to conceive of 'consumer protection' as a fundamental right in the classical sense, and therefore the general consensus appears to be that

[49] Above, pp 80.

[50] *Aziz* (n 17) [31]. The judge at first instance, José Maria Fernández Seijo, has become a national celebrity in Spain due to this case.

[51] Although the initial legislation, as it turned out, did still not comply with the effectiveness principle of EU law; Case C-169/14 *Juan Carlos Sánchez Morcillo and María del Carmen Abril García v Banco Bilbao Vizcaya Argentaria SA*, ECLI:EU:C:2014:2099 (*Sánchez Morcillo I*).

[52] ibid [35]. In a Slovakian case with similar facts to the Spanish cases, the Court ruled that the national legislation at issue in the proceedings did comply with the requirements of Art 47 of the Charter; Case C-34/14 *Monika Kušionová v SMART Capital as*, ECLI:EU:C:2014:2189 (*Kušionová*).

the provision does nothing more than consolidate the EU's commitment to consumer protection within the Treaties and as observed in internal market and free movement regulation.[53] Of greater relevance is Article 47 of the Charter.[54] This provision stipulates that '[e]veryone whose rights and freedoms guaranteed by the law of the Union are violated has the right to an effective remedy before a tribunal'. The CJEU has discovered this provision as a mechanism through which to give effect to consumer rights laid down in EU legislation, emphasizing the obligation that it places on the Member States to ensure that citizens have effective remedies that allow them to enforce rights derived from EU law in national courts. Article 47 can therefore be seen as the embodiment of the principle of effectiveness of EU law, which through its elevation to a 'fundamental right' has given the Court an impetus to appeal to it in consumer cases, in particular in those that are closely related to other, perhaps more classical fundamental rights.[55] The protection achieved through Article 47 in the Spanish mortgage cases, heralded by *Aziz*,[56] for example, has enhanced the protection of citizens against the loss of their family home, which is laid down in Article 7 of the Charter as: '[e]veryone has the right to respect for his or her ... home'. In sum, the Charter, like the EU Treaties, contains rights that reflect that consumer protection encompasses more than solely the economic interests of consumers. It can provide a legal basis also for cases in which social rights, such as the right to housing, are at stake.

C. Free Movement Regulation and Harmonized Consumer Law

Despite the firm footing that social rights appear to have in the Treaties and in the EU Charter of Fundamental Rights, they are less visible in more specific applications of EU consumer law. The two legs of EU law that concern the regulation of the consumer market, free movement regulation and harmonized consumer law, seem to focus primarily on economic rights. That is not surprising, as both are tied to the internal market goals of the Union. Their aim is, either through negative or

[53] S Weatherill, 'Article 38—Consumer Protection' in S Peers and others (eds), *The EU Charter of Fundamental Rights: A Commentary* (Hart Publishing 2014) para 38.04, who states that 'Article 38 draws on existing material in EU law, and is not a leap into the unknown or the little known'.

[54] For early explorations on the potential of Art 47, N Reich, 'The Principle of Effectiveness and EU Contract Law' (2013) II Osservatorio del diritto civile e commerciale 337; C Mak, 'Rights and Remedies: Article 47 EUCFR and Effective Judicial Protection in European Private Law Matters' in H-W Micklitz (ed), *Constitutionalization of European Private Law* (OUP 2014) 236.

[55] Art 47 is however also used in cases involving traders. The CJEU's decision in *Biuro podróży 'Partner'* confirmed that traders, when rights derived from the Unfair Contract Terms Directive are enforced against them, also are entitled to judicial safeguards, based on *their* right—rather than the consumer's—to an effective remedy grounded in Art 47 of the Charter; Case C-119/15 *Biuro podróży 'Partner' v Prezes Urzędu Ochrony Konkurencji I Konsumentów*, ECLI:EU:C:2016:987.

[56] See above pp 80, and in more detail below, p 89 ff.

through positive harmonization, to bring the laws of the EU Member States closer and thereby to eliminate barriers to trade. For consumers this means that the underlying aim of the regulatory approach of EU consumer law is to ensure that they can pass the threshold for taking part in, and benefiting from, the internal market. In the words of Micklitz, EU consumer law pursues 'access justice' (*Zugangsgerechtigkeit*).[57] Nonetheless, social rights or policies are recognized as factors that may potentially restrict market integration objectives. The balance for now, however, appears to lean towards economic rights and market integration.

In free movement regulation the internal market objective is clearly paramount. On the basis of free movement rules—laid down in Article 26 TFEU, with further provisions for goods laid down in Articles 28–37 TFEU and for services in Articles 56–62 TFEU[58]—regulations at Member State level that form a real or potential barrier to trade in the internal market can be set aside. There is some room for limiting the free movement, as can be seen in particular in relation to goods, but that space is narrowly demarcated. An exception exists for non-discriminatory prohibitions or restrictions on the free movement of goods that are equivalent to quantitative restrictions, if they can be justified 'on grounds of public morality, public policy or public security; the protection of health and life of humans, animals or plants; the protection of national treasures possessing artistic, historic or archaeological value; or the protection of industrial and commercial property'.[59] Justifications for such restrictions also stem from the case law of the CJEU, where an exception has been recognized for provisions that are 'necessary in order to satisfy the mandatory requirements relating in particular to the effectiveness of fiscal supervision, the protection of public health, the fairness of commercial transactions and the defence of the consumer'.[60] In practice, however, cases in which national measures are set aside appear to be more numerous than cases in which prohibitions or restrictions to the free movement of goods are deemed justified. An explanation for that trend may be that the CJEU by setting aside national legislation that restricts trade gives a boost to the integration of the internal market. Economic concerns therefore often trump social considerations.

In harmonized consumer law, the balance between economic and social rights is largely similar, but not completely the same. The legal basis for harmonization in EU consumer law, the aim of which is to approximate the laws of the Member States in specific areas of consumer (private) law, has in practice always been Article

[57] H-W Micklitz, 'The Visible Hand of European Regulatory Private Law—The Transformation of European Private Law from Autonomy to Functionalism in Competition and Regulation' (2009) 28 Yearbook of European Law 3, 13.

[58] Arts 49–55 TFEU (freedom of establishment), Arts 63–66 TFEU (free movement of capital), and Art 21 and Titles IV and V TFEU (free movement of persons) are less relevant for consumer law and are therefore not discussed here.

[59] Art 36 TFEU.

[60] Case 120/78 *Rewe-Zentral AG v Bundesmonopolverwaltung für Branntwein*, ECLI:EU:C:1979:42 (*Cassis de Dijon*), at [8].

114(3) TFEU. That means that the harmonization of consumer law is tied to the goal of integration of the internal market. The content of harmonizing legislation largely reflects this underlying market ideology. Directives in the field of consumer contract law are often aimed at empowerment of consumers through information rights. Examples are Directive 2011/83/EU on consumer rights, Directive 90/314/EEC on package travel, Directive 2008/48/EC on consumer credit, Directive 2014/17/EU on consumer mortgage credit,[61] as well as Directive 93/13/EEC on unfair terms and Directive 2005/29/EC on unfair commercial practices that seek to ensure that consumers receive information that is clear, intelligible, fair, and not misleading.[62] The idea that information on the characteristics of products and services can empower consumers by helping them make sound purchase decisions is connected to neo-classical economic theory, in which consumers are perceived as rational actors. That paradigm is leading in EU consumer legislation.[63] Still, sometimes stronger consumer protection rights are included, for example, in the form of warnings, prohibitions, or other measures that aim to support social policies. The most prominent example is the restriction placed on the availability of credit with an eye to protecting consumers against over-indebtedness.[64] A little more remote is the potential effect of the remedies laid down in Directive 1999/44/EC on consumer sales:[65] by making repair a primary remedy for non-conformity, the Directive contributes to sustainability goals.[66] Express provision is therefore made for consumer protection rights in specific instances. Nevertheless, the overall picture that emerges in relation to harmonized consumer law is that, at least on paper, it is concerned with economic rights more than with social rights. The survey of the EU Treaties, the Charter of Fundamental Rights, and secondary legislation in EU consumer law made in this section thus confirms two things. First, it has revealed that there is a legal basis for social policies in EU consumer law. That legal basis follows from Article 3(3) of the EU Treaty, in combination with the consumer law provisions laid down in Articles 12, 114(3), and 169(1) TFEU. However,

[61] Consumer Rights Directive 2011/83/EU on consumer rights (n 14); Council Directive 90/314/EEC on package travel, package holidays and package tours [1993] OJ L158/59 (Package Travel Directive); Directive 2008/48/EC on credit agreements for consumers [2008] OJ L133/66 (Consumer Credit Directive); Directive 2014/17/EU on credit agreements for consumers relating to residential immovable property [2014] OJ L60/34 (Consumer Mortgage Credit Directive).

[62] Unfair Contract Terms Directive (n 26); Unfair Commercial Practices Directive (n 26).

[63] For an excellent account of the influence of neo-classical and behavioural economics on EU consumer law: A Alemanno and A-L Sibony (eds), *Nudge and the Law: A European Perspective* (Hart Publishing 2015).

[64] See the obligation laid down in Art 18 of the Consumer Mortgage Credit Directive (n 61), which holds that credit providers must refuse mortgage loans if the consumer does not pass the creditworthiness assessment. This requirement is new in comparison to the Consumer Credit Directive (n 61).

[65] Consumer Sales Directive (n 26). The Directive will be replaced by Directive (EU) 2019/771 on certain aspects concerning contracts for the sale of goods [2019] OJ L136/28, applying to contracts from 1 January 2022.

[66] Sustainability is covered on a more general level by the reference to 'improving the quality of the environment' in Art 3(3) TEU.

because they can only in limited circumstances be directly invoked by consumers, the Treaties are not the main source for social rights in EU consumer law. More direct causes of action can be based on the Charter, in particular on Article 47, and on social rights laid down in consumer law Directives. The second conclusion, nonetheless, is that social rights take up a secondary position in relation to economic rights in the legislation. To see how these rights have in recent years gained importance, we need to turn to the case law of the CJEU.

III. The CJEU and Social Justice

The *Aziz* case of 2013 could represent a turning point for the protection of social rights through EU consumer law.[67] Whether the case is indeed the first step in that direction is of course something that we cannot predict at this time. The case law of the Court in consumer law does, however, carry the seeds of an approach that promises more in terms of the pursuit of social rights and policies in the future. Two elements are important, one substantive, the other relating to the position of the Court in the institutional framework of the Union. First, on the substantive point, the Court appears sometimes to promote social justice over economic goals in consumer contract law cases. Second, the position of the Court in relation to national courts and legislators enables 'strategic litigation' by consumers or others who seek to pursue social goals. It should be noted that the term 'social justice' in relation to the CJEU's case law is used in a specific context, and is narrower than that of 'social rights' more generally discussed in this chapter.[68] It has, in EU consumer law, primarily emerged in relation to consumer contract law, which deals with the rules applicable to business-to-consumer transactions. Generally speaking, social justice is concerned with redistributive effects that may be achieved through private law, or more specifically contract law. Social justice objectives can frame the autonomy of contracting parties beyond economic interest.[69] Autonomy might for example be restricted on grounds of equality or non-discrimination, or in the rare circumstance of 'social *force majeure*'.[70]

The CJEU's judgment in the *Aziz* case and related follow-up judgments can be regarded as instances in which the Court has let social justice concerns

[67] For the facts of the case, see above, pp 85.

[68] That general distinction is between social and economic rights, in which social rights are defined as all non-economic rights. Compare above, pp 75.

[69] T Wilhelmsson, 'Varieties of Welfarism in European Contract Law' (2004) 10 European Law Journal 712; Study Group on Social Justice in European Private Law, 'Social Justice in European Contract Law: A Manifesto' (n 4).

[70] An example is the universal service obligation laid down in Directive 2009/72/EC concerning the supply of electricity, which prohibits disconnection of electricity to vulnerable consumers in critical times [2009] OJ L211/55; N Reich, *General Principles of EU Civil Law* (Intersentia 2014) at 82–83.

intervene with the autonomy of the contracting parties.[71] In *Aziz* the Court held that a Spanish procedural rule allowing eviction on the grounds of non-payment of mortgage instalments should be set aside in cases where a consumer had instigated proceedings against the mortgage lender to challenge unfair terms in the mortgage agreement.[72] *Sánchez Morcillo* confirmed that ruling, with explicit reference to Article 47 of the Charter, and established that the Spanish legislator needed to do yet more work to ensure that its procedural law offered effective judicial remedies for consumers to enforce their rights derived from Directive 1993/13/EEC on unfair terms.[73] In a roundabout way, therefore, the Court lent support to the right to housing which, although not referred to in the judgment, is laid down in Article 7 of the EU Charter of Fundamental Rights. Article 7 enshrines the right to respect of private and family life, including respect of one's home.[74] The case therefore goes beyond what might have been expected on the basis of Directive 93/13/EEC on unfair terms.

One explanation for the prominent position of the CJEU in the social justice debate may be that the institutional framework in which the Court operates enables 'strategic litigation'. The Court's role has been attributed to the possibilities that EU law provides to consumers who have run out of options for protection in their own legal systems, either because of a lack of protective rights or—in practice more important—the inability to enforce them. Micklitz posits that the absorption of consumer law into mainstream private law has led to an expulsion of protection from consumer law, a process reinforced by EU law's choice for an average consumer who is rational, autonomous, and self-confident.[75] However, there is room within the system of EU law to find other ways of achieving just outcomes, namely by using the reference procedure of the CJEU. That route could lead to outcomes that are unavailable in national law but, if the Court is willing to take a proactive stance, can be introduced through a conceptualization of social justice values in

[71] *Aziz* (n 17); *Kušionová* (n 52). Compare also Joined Cases C-154/15 and C-307/15 *Francisco Gutiérrez Naranjo v Cajasur Banco SAU*, ECLI:EU:C:2016:980.

[72] *Aziz* (n 17).

[73] *Sánchez Morcillo* (n 51). On the particularities of the new Spanish legislation, see also Joined Cases C-482/13, C-484/13, C-485/13, and C-487/13 *Unicaja Banco SA v José Hidalgo Rueda and others*, ECLI:EU:C:2015:21; Case C-8/14 *BBVA SA v Pedro Peñalva López*, ECLI:EU:C:2015:731; Case C-421/14 *Banco Primus v Jesús Gutiérrez García*, ECLI:EU:C:2017:60.

[74] Another legal basis might potentially be found in Art 34(3) of the Charter, which concerns the right to social housing and housing assistance. In both cases, however, it is important to realise that the provisions do not provide a legal basis for individual actions by consumers, as Art 47 can. The provisions rather seem to have the character of principles, or of fundamental rights to be guaranteed and protected by public authorities. Compare Micklitz and Reich, 'The Court and Sleeping Beauty: the Revival of the Unfair Contract Terms Directive (UCTD)' (n 34) 800 and the Opinion of Advocate-General Cruz Villalón, Case C-176/12 *Association de médiation sociale v Union locale des syndicats CGT and others*, ECLI:EU:C:2013:491, at [45], referring to the distinction between 'rights' and 'principles' included in Art 52(5) of an earlier version of the Charter.

[75] H-W Micklitz, 'The Expulsion of the Concept of Protection from the Consumer Law and the Return of Social Elements in the Civil Law: A Bittersweet Polemic' (2012) 35 Journal of Consumer Policy 283, 289.

European contract law. In the words of Micklitz: '[f]rom a theoretical point of view, the European-inspired "consumer law without protection" provides an open goal-mouth for the conceptual design of a modern European contract law, of which the civil law scholars in Germany and throughout Europe are taking advantage'.[76]

The premises for an active, or perhaps even activist role, of the CJEU in relation to social rights in EU consumer law therefore are present. Of course, this rather bold idea of the role of the CJEU raises the question *how* the Court should approach cases in which market values and social justice values influence the outcome of the case. The lack of methodological transparency in the Court's reasoning in private law cases has been amply documented, for example in relation to general principles, but also more specifically in relation to the 'constitutionalization' of European contract law.[77] The general gist of analyses of the CJEU's case law in the field suggests that there are examples of cases in which the Court explicitly pursues social justice goals through private law, but that it is hard to discern a consistent line or even a theoretical framework underlying the Court's approach. Rather than attributing an active role to the Court for bringing in social values into EU market regulation,[78] the status quo seems to point to a more hesitant take on that role. It might well be that the Court, through limitations to the rights existing in EU law that it gets to rule on, is simply not in a position to set out a consistent social justice response in European market regulation.[79] Instead, the cases can probably only be considered 'glimmers' of social justice in a market otherwise informed by liberal values.[80]

[76] ibid 290. In a recent article, Van Duin emphasizes that Art 47 of the Charter promotes individual rights protection for both parties, therefore also for traders. A van Duin, 'Metamorphosis? The Role of Article 47 of the EU Charter of Fundamental Rights in Cases Concerning National Remedies and Procedures under Directive 1993/13/EEC' (2017) 6 Journal of European Consumer and Market Law 190, 197.

[77] C Mak, 'The One and the Many: Translating Insights from Constitutional Pluralism to European Contract Law Theory' (2013) 21 European Review of Private Law 1189; C Sieburgh, 'A Method to Substantively Guide the Involvement of EU Law in Private Law Matters' (2013) 21 European Review of Private Law 1156.

[78] For an 'optimistic' view, H-W Micklitz, 'The ECJ between the Individual Citizen and the Member States—A Plea for a Judge Made European Law on Remedies' in H-W Micklitz and B De Witte (eds), *The European Court of Justice and the Autonomy of the Member States* (Intersentia 2012) 349, 392.

[79] On effective remedies in EU law, D Leczykiewicz, '"Where Angels Fear to Tread": The EU Law of Remedies and Codification of European Private Law' (2012) 8 European Review of Contract Law 47, 58.

[80] Other authors have been bolder in suggesting that a coherent approach might be developed. H Collins, 'The Revolutionary Trajectory of EU Contract Law towards Post-national Law' (paper presented at the Final Workshop: European Regulatory Private Law. 'A European Advantage in Transnational Lawyering?', EUI, Florence, 26–27 May 2016), who suggests that fundamental rights of EU law can provide a new 'rule of recognition' (in the vein of Hart's concept of law) for European private law.

IV. Conclusion

The discussion conducted in this chapter leads to the conclusion that EU consumer contract law is still mainly concerned with the economic rights of EU citizens, although it contains openings for the pursuit of social rights and policies. The foregoing has shown that there is a legal basis, or that there are perhaps several, for balancing economic and social rights in EU consumer law. Articles 2 and 3(3) TEU include social rights firmly within the values and objectives of EU law. More specific consumer protection rules laid down in Articles 12, 114(3), and 169(1) TFEU confirm that social rights, in the sense of non-economic rights, are part and parcel of the EU's internal market project. At least symbolically, therefore, the Treaties lend support to social rights in consumer law. Nonetheless, for now the legislator has remained fairly inactive in promulgating social rights in this field. That might be explained by the difficulty of moderating legislative competences between the European Union and its Member States, in particular in areas that go beyond market-building.[81] As is well-known,[82] social policy is still primarily determined at Member State level. EU consumer legislation, such as harmonized rules of contract or tort law, therefore primarily deal with issues related to facilitating business-to-consumer transactions in the internal market. Information rights for consumers, aiming to 'empower' consumers as rational market actors, are more prominent in this legislation than other, more protective rules that support social goals, such as the protection of consumers against over-indebtedness through consumer credit law.

The CJEU, at the same time has stepped into the void left by the legislator and in recent case law has achieved the protection of social rights of consumers through contract law. That development, fuelled by a growing reliance on the EU Charter of Fundamental Rights, could provide a useful route for the integration of social considerations in EU consumer law. The Court, moreover, is of great practical significance for the protection of consumers' social rights as it provides a judicial route for the protection of individual rights even in cases where consumers (or traders) cannot obtain that protection within their national legal system. The *Aziz* case is rightfully seen as an example of 'strategic litigation', where the possibility to submit a preliminary reference to the CJEU was used by the national court to obtain an

[81] K Lörcher, 'Social Competences' in Bruun, Lörcher, and Schömann (eds), *The Lisbon Treaty and Social Europe* (n 30) 165, 166, who emphasizes 'the desire of Member States to limit the extension of the Union's [social] competences as much as possible'.

[82] See D Ferri and F Cortese, 'Introduction' in Ferri and Cortese, *The EU Social Market Economy and the Law* (n 11) 8, who nonetheless emphasize that the limited competence of the EU in social matters might be compensated by the broader social patterns engrained in its constitutional structure, including its social market economy objectives. In a similar vein, Micklitz observes that '[t]he "justice deficit" of the EU when measured against national welfare state standards should not overshadow the social and societal dimension of the EU and the EU private law order'. See H-W Micklitz, *The Politics of Justice in European Private Law* (n 7) 12.

outcome that national, Spanish legislation did not allow. The decision effectively led to the protection of consumers against eviction from their home during the time that proceedings on the potential unfairness of terms in their mortgage agreement was pending. The broader reach of this judgment lies in the question whether it signals a move towards the greater protection of social, or constitutional rights through private law. The CJEU may have paved the way for such a development in EU consumer law. At the same time, the Court is constrained in what it can achieve, since it only rules on a case-by-case basis and is dependent on the cases that come before it. While the CJEU can be an important recourse for individual rights protection, therefore, the baton will have to be returned to the EU legislator to promote the further development of social rights in European consumer law. The recent Fitness Check of the major consumer law Directives appears to be a missed opportunity in this regard, but perhaps future initiatives from the legislature will put social rights in a more prominent place. That would do justice to the values and objectives laid down in the EU Treaties.

Within the framework of economic and social values and objectives of EU law, as described in this chapter, lawmaking actors can develop new rules for consumer and contract law. The theoretical position developed in Chapter 3 puts forward that an instrumental-normative approach should be adopted that enables lawmaking actors to self-legislate, but with the safeguard that the values and objectives of EU law are observed. The next chapter considers how that perspective fits with existing theories of legal pluralism in European private law. Can strong legal pluralism be maintained?

5

Pluralism in European Private Law

It has been said that European private law reflects a preference for 'ordered pluralism'.[*,1] That term, read against the background of broader debates on legal pluralism in EU law, characterizes the field as pluralist rather than monist, yet not radically or strongly legal pluralist. It recognizes that the primary position of monist, state-based legal systems as promulgators of rules has gradually been supplanted in EU law discourse by a pluralist perspective in which multiple legal systems and legal sources coexist within and beyond the state.[2] In the field of private law, increasingly relevant sources of rules are the case law of the Court of Justice of the European Union (CJEU) and private regulation through rulemaking and standardization in specific sectors of industry.[3] At the same time, ordered legal pluralism implies that the relation between these legal systems and legal sources is not completely free, other than 'radical' or 'strong' legal pluralist theories which hold that rules can coexist without a formal hierarchy. Strong legal pluralist theories tend to be characterized by a distinction between state law and other sources of norms. The suggestion of legal pluralism is that norms created outside the framework of state lawmaking can also be regarded as 'law', or in any event as rules that have a law-like effect on societies or individuals.[4] In cases of conflicts between rules originating from different legal systems—for example national and EU constitutional laws, national and EU private laws, or national private law and private regulation—various mechanisms may result in an outcome that is imposed through a hierarchy. That, however, does not have to be a formal, legal hierarchy;

[*] This chapter is based on and largely reproduces, but with significant revisions, the text of a previously published article: V Mak, 'Pluralism in European Private Law' (2018) 20 Cambridge Yearbook of European Legal Studies 202.

[1] R Michaels, 'Why We Have No Theory of European Private Law Pluralism' in L Niglia (ed), *Pluralism and European Private Law* (Hart Publishing 2013) 139, 158.

[2] That broad idea gives rise to a diverse range of further questions on which legal systems can be recognized and whether it is normatively desirable to maintain legal pluralism. For a recent overview of the field, see G Davies and M Avbelj (eds), *Research Handbook on Legal Pluralism and EU Law* (Edward Elgar 2018).

[3] A trend noted by H-W Micklitz, 'The Visible Hand of European Regulatory Private Law—The Transformation of European Private Law from Autonomy to Functionalism in Competition and Regulation' (2009) 28 Yearbook of European Law 3, who sees this as part of a process of 'politicization' of European private law in which new forms of governance are emerging. See also JM Smits, 'Plurality of Sources in European Private Law, or: How to Live with Legal Diversity?' in R Brownsword and others (eds), *The Foundations of European Private Law* (Hart Publishing 2011) 323; JM Smits, 'Het privaatrecht van de toekomst' (2015) 52 Tijdschrift voor Privaatrecht 517.

[4] See W Twining, *General Jurisprudence* (CUP 2009) 88–121, 362–75.

Legal Pluralism in European Contract Law. Vanessa Mak, Oxford University Press (2020). © Vanessa Mak.
DOI: 10.1093/oso/9780198854487.001.0001.

ordering can also emerge from the normative, institutional, political, or cultural context in which a conflict plays out.[5]

Normatively, strong legal pluralism is appealing, as it promotes a framework for lawmaking in which multiple viewpoints and values can be taken into account. Other than a monist system, it therefore gives space to the realization of public autonomy—the ability to self-legislate through democratic mechanisms—of different groups or communities. This includes lawmaking by formal, public legislators and regulatory actors, but it can also apply to informal lawmaking by private actors when rules extend beyond individual relationships and, for example, are meant to regulate an entire sector of industry.[6] Ordered legal pluralism goes some way towards establishing a framework within which that space for autonomy also exists and could therefore also normatively be preferred over monism. However, in comparison to strong legal pluralism, it cannot make the same case for realizing public autonomy as it imposes boundaries on that autonomy through ordering mechanisms that are based on a hierarchy between lawmakers or legal orders. Simply said, and acknowledging that a full argument for strong legal pluralism requires a more comprehensive analysis,[7] strong legal pluralism normatively can be considered more appealing than ordered legal pluralism for all those addressed by laws, and all involved in lawmaking.

Debates on lawmaking in European private law have not fully come to grips with these perspectives on legal pluralism. The dominant focus of discussion in this field, in particular in its early days, has been on formal lawmaking, that is, lawmaking concerning the harmonization of national private laws through EU regulations and directives. Whilst more recent studies recognize the influence of the case law of the CJEU and of the growing body of private regulation, different views exist on their relation vis-à-vis state law and EU law. In light of, in particular, the rise of private regulation[8] as a source of lawmaking beyond the state, it seems timely to take stock of legal pluralist positions in European private law. In which ways have existing theories brought forward our understanding of processes of lawmaking in

[5] Nico Krisch's theory of systemic legal pluralism, for example, uses 'interface norms' that determine when one systems should tolerate a rule emanating from another legal system as a mechanism to mediate legal pluralism. A loophole in this framework is that more powerful actors can impose their most favoured rules on others. See P Capps and D Machin, 'The Problem of Global Law' (2011) 74(5) Modern Law Review 794, 808. On ordered legal pluralism, see also M Delmas-Marty, *Ordering Pluralism. A Conceptual Framework for Understanding the Transnational Legal World* (N Norberg tr, Hart Publishing 2009) 14, who prefers ordered pluralism over the perceived unruliness of strong legal pluralism.

[6] Private autonomy, by contrast, is the ability to freely give shape to individual relationships between private parties. Individual autonomy can also be regulated so as to contribute to the pursuit of societal goals See H Dagan, 'Between Regulatory and Autonomy-Based Private Law' (2016) 22 European Law Journal 644, 647 ff. Moreover, it can morph into public autonomy when rules adopted in individual private law relationships become a template for regulation. See pp 114 below.

[7] For an elaboration of the normative argument, see Chapter 2, p 35 ff.

[8] I use a broad definition of private regulation that includes regulation by private actors through contracting, self-regulation, and co-regulation.

European private law? And is it possible to develop a theory of strong legal pluralism in this field that takes account of formal as well as private lawmaking, or are we bound to fall back on a European preference for ordering?

This chapter assesses some of the leading theories of legal pluralism in European private law. It analyses how 'ordered' existing theories of pluralism in European private law are by considering what space they give to deliberation between lawmakers at different levels of regulation. The chapter also considers at which points the theories may need refinement in order to include all relevant lawmakers, formal and other, in a legal pluralist constellation. The task will be broken down by focusing on a number of specific points of contestation within broader private law theory discussions.[9]

I. Theoretical Framework and Outline

The lens through which theories of legal pluralism will be examined is that of the diverging rationalities of European private law,[10] on the one hand, and national private laws on the other.[11] Rationalities concern frameworks of discussion and questions asked within those frameworks, not the answers given or the ideologies that inspire such answers.[12] For the sake of highlighting the main tensions between European private law and national private laws, and also because it is hard to capture them in all of their complexities, the rationalities used here should be seen as ideal types.

The rationality of European private law, focused as it is on the integration of the internal market, can be regarded as primarily instrumentalist. Private law in this context is used as an instrument towards achieving the policy objectives of EU law. These objectives are primarily related to the integration of the internal market,[13] and the framework within which European private law is perceived is therefore

[9] Another example of this approach can be seen in Michaels, 'Why We Have No Theory of European Private Law Pluralism' (n 1).

[10] Here in the meaning of private law developed at the EU level. The term can also be used in reference to the entire body of rules on European private law, including national laws.

[11] The term 'rationalities' is used by R Michaels, 'Of Islands and the Ocean: The Two Rationalities of European Private Law' in R Brownsword and others (eds), *The Foundations of European Private Law* (Hart Publishing 2011) 139, who distinguishes, as ideal types, the instrumentalism underlying European private law from the 'juridical' rationality underlying national private laws. See also H-W Micklitz, 'Perspektiven des europäischen Privatrechts—Ius commune praeter legem?' (1998) 6 Zeitschrift für europäisches Privatrecht 253; CU Schmid, 'The Instrumentalist Conception of the Acquis Communautaire in Consumer Law and its Implications on a European Contract Law Code' (2005) 1 European Review of Contract Law 211; M Bartl, 'Internal Market Rationality, Private Law and the Direction of the Union: Resuscitating the Market as the Object of the Political' (2015) 21 European Law Journal 572.

[12] Michaels, 'Of Islands and the Ocean: The Two Rationalities of European Private Law' (n 11) 142.

[13] ibid, who rightly notes that the goals of EU law since its inception have been extended to goals that go beyond the internal market project. See also V Mak, *The Character of European Private Law* (inaugural lecture, Tilburg University 2015) 9–10.

one of pragmatic, purposive rule making. As said, this is an ideal type. There is a competing narrative of protection of the individual through legal rights, which encompasses broader (social) values and objectives, albeit as a corollary to the internal market project.

The rationality of national private laws, by contrast, can be characterized differently, perhaps as juridical. The legal system itself, rather than the economic and political context within which rules are created and operate, sets the framework for discussion. In this framework, legal questions are answered on the basis of legal texts and legal precedents rather than extra-legal goals.[14] Private law in that perspective is also a reflection of market ordering, but the system is not *aimed* at market integration. Rather, private law systems seek to balance the interests of private parties in relation to transactions, liability, and property on the basis of rights, principles, and practices that have been established over centuries. The underlying principles of private law systems that guide the balancing of interests are autonomy and fairness. In this rationality, which as an ideal type has a broader span than the instrumentalist rationality of EU law, there is room for questions of market regulation but also of corrective or redistributive justice.[15] The expression of this framework in national laws takes the form of doctrinal lawmaking based on consistency and purity of the legal system.

These two rationalities rub against each other when rules developed at the EU level are introduced into national laws. Sometimes they fit, but other times the pragmatic, internal market focused nature of the rules upsets the juridical rationality of national private laws. There is space within the legal framework of the European Union, however, to balance the two rationalities. To begin with, the interaction between EU law and national laws is fluid in places, for example because their relation is mediated through the principles of subsidiarity and proportionality. Lawmaking will therefore always occur through an interplay between the European Union and the Member States. Further, since many rules of private law are introduced through EU directives, the Member States often have some leeway in the implementation process to adapt rules to their national systems. Finally, cutting across EU law and national private laws, private lawmakers create their own rules through contracting, self-regulation, and co-regulation, thereby potentially influencing the substance of new rules of private law. The idea of legal pluralism in European private law therefore can be maintained. The question is however, bearing in mind the competing rationalities of European private law and national private laws, how much *space* there is for deliberation between lawmaking actors at each level. In that respect, we come back to the perspective of sociological accounts

[14] Michaels, 'Of Islands and the Ocean: The Two Rationalities of European Private Law' (n 11) 142.

[15] Compare Study Group on Social Justice in European Private Law, 'Social Justice in European Contract Law: A Manifesto' (2004) 10 European Law Journal 653. cf also Micklitz, who regards private law as part of economic law. See K Purnhagen and P Rott (eds), *Varieties of European Economic Law and Regulation. Liber Amicorum for Hans Micklitz* (Springer 2014).

of legal pluralism in which the focus is on the evolution of social norms and 'spaces' of governance and regulation, rather than on the state as the authoritative locus for lawmaking.[16] The answer to the question of space can give some leads as to whether we are looking at a strong legal pluralist constellation, or an ordered one.

To answer the question about space for deliberation, I will assess existing theories of legal pluralism in European private law in a discussion of three specific points of contestation. These points roughly correspond to three ways in which legal orders can be unpacked so as to get a better perspective on legal pluralism: who makes rules, what substance do these rules have, and how does lawmaking take place? In other words, which actors, norms, and processes are at play?[17] Some overlap between these categories is inevitable in an analysis of the theories. I will tackle them in the following order: substance (or 'norms'); approaches to lawmaking ('processes', with some overlap with 'norms'); and the role of private parties in lawmaking vis-à-vis the role of the state and the European Union ('actors').

Starting with norms, I will analyse the types of justice underlying private law rules at the national and EU level. Considerations of justice, be it corrective, redistributive, or otherwise, are fundamental to all private law systems in the world. An analysis of the notions of justice underlying EU and national private laws can clarify the relation between them, and the extent to which systems can be coordinated towards safeguarding similar values and objectives without losing the space for deliberation and contestation of norms that is essential for maintaining legal pluralism.

Second, I will consider the tension between doctrinal approaches to private law and pragmatism. Can existing private laws be responsive to new developments in society, or are other regulatory responses required even if they cut across established doctrines? This question may come across as one that lawyers would ask if their frame of reference is the (national) legal system that they are familiar with and, so to speak, 'grew up in'.[18] However, the doctrinal question is relevant beyond that framework. In a legal pluralist perspective, the responsiveness of doctrinal approaches (or of legal systems) is a measure of the available space for deliberation and contestation of norms. If legal systems can accommodate new norms within existing doctrines, norm conflicts between legal orders are avoided and pluralism is essentially nipped in the bud. If not, then the boundaries of autonomy

[16] See eg S Sassen, *A Sociology of Globalization* (WW Norton 2007). See also Chapter 3, pp 52.

[17] This three-pronged framework is developed by Zumbansen as a methodology for studying the transnational legal sphere and makes it possible to consider norms from a perspective that is neutral on whether norms are part of an official legal system, and also independent from the territorial grounding of law in a particular jurisdiction. See P Zumbansen, 'Defining the Space of Transnational Law: Legal Theory, Global Governance and Legal Pluralism', Comparative Research in Law & Political Economy, Research Paper No 21/2011, 7 <http://digitalcommons.osgoode.yorku.ca/clpe/59> accessed 28 February 2020, as are all websites in this chapter.

[18] Compare P Legrand, 'Against a European Civil Code' (1997) 60 Modern Law Review 44.

and toleration within a legal pluralist constellation are touched upon,[19] and some mechanism of managing pluralism will have to kick in. In European private law, an example of responsiveness can be seen in the way that EU law and national laws have dealt with the integration of consumer protection rules into private laws. I group this discussion of responsiveness under 'processes' but note that examples given will of course relate to substance and therefore also provide further content for the 'norms' aspect of legal pluralist theories.

Third, and finally, I will discuss the role of private parties in lawmaking in relation to the role of states and of the European Union. In particular within the framework of contract law, which in Europe is based on autonomy and freedom of contract, businesses and consumers have much leeway to determine the terms on which they wish to enter into transactions. That means that through individual choice, they can determine which rules they wish to be applicable to their contracts. In theory, the contractual choices of many businesses and consumers in Europe could reveal preferences for specific rules, which legislators and regulators may then copy into rules of private law. Yet, in European private law as in national laws, limitations to that freedom exist in the form of mandatory rules that cannot be contracted out of. Examples are rules of consumer or employee protection. A relevant question is therefore to what extent the individual choice of private actors can influence lawmaking in European private law or, in other words, to what extent private actors can be considered lawmaking actors.

These three points of contestation can be connected to three major streams of thought in the legal theory of pluralism in European private law. In this chapter, I group them around the work of three scholars: Hans Micklitz, Martijn Hesselink, and Jan Smits.[20] While they are not the only authors who have written in this field, they have put forward positions that are distinct and that highlight relevant tensions between the EU internal market rationality and national laws' juridical

[19] This conception of legal pluralism draws on studies of cosmopolitan and postnational pluralism, which hold that the legal framework should create or maintain a space for deliberation between different communities. It should do that first, by giving voice to *public autonomy*. Second, the interaction between different communities should be based on *toleration* of other values or viewpoints. See N Krisch, *Beyond Constitutionalism: The Pluralist Structure of Postnational Law* (OUP 2010), 99, 100–01, 103. For a 'restatement' based on the theory put forward in his book on *Global Legal Pluralism*, see P Schiff Berman 'Non-State Lawmaking through the Lens of Global Legal Pluralism' in MA Helfand (ed), *Negotiating State and Non-State Law. The Challenge of Global and Local Legal Pluralism* (CUP 2015) 15, 27.

[20] Michaels in an earlier study selected the theories of Wilhelmsson, Smits, and Legrand as 'three of [legal pluralism's] most prominent proponents'. See Michaels, 'Why We Have No Theory of European Private Law Pluralism' (n 1) 140. I have chosen Micklitz's work as the primary representative of a theory engaging with justice in European private law. It is of course not the only theory and the discussion will also take into account the work of Wilhelmsson and others on social justice. From Hesselink's work, which also deals with justice issues, I take up the discussion on pragmatism in European private law as a separate issue. Further, while Legrand's position is interesting because of his strong outcry *against* harmonization of European private law, his view seems to have lost some momentum, in part because growing political divides between the EU Member States in recent years have resulted in a more nationalist approach to lawmaking in European private law.

rationality. Their work can therefore form a useful starting position for determining the state of play in the field of European private law, and a fulcrum for examining contrasting positions taken by other authors. Notably, all three authors have their intellectual roots in the legal traditions of continental European civil law systems. Theoretical work on legal pluralism in European private law seems to have attracted fewer authors from the common law.[21] The importance of the authors' background should however not be overplayed, as the theoretical, and political economy-oriented nature of their selected works transcends the common law/civil law distinction.

I will deal with each area of contestation by providing a brief description, followed by a critical analysis. Some of the lines emerging from the analysis will be drawn together in a separate section on strong legal pluralism. The chapter concludes with a short recapitulation and reflection on the relevance of strong legal pluralism for future research in European private law.

II. Justice and the Rationalities of Private Law

One of the leading visions on legal pluralism in European private law was proposed by Hans Micklitz, who earlier than others reached the conclusion that the obstacles to harmonization in the field—such as insurmountable differences in legal culture and legal norms, but also a lack of political will—would prevent the adoption of a full-fledged European Civil Code or even of a (smaller) Common European Sales Law.[22] He developed an alternative perspective on lawmaking in the field, in which the emphasis comes to lie on the interaction between legal orders, in particular the EU and the national laws of the Member States, and the question regarding which degrees of integration can be observed between them.[23] In this framework, the rules and principles of European private law developed by the EU legislator and

[21] Indicative can be the list of authors, exclusively with a civil law background although some have worked in common law systems, included in L Niglia (ed), *Pluralism and European Private Law* (Hart Publishing 2013).

[22] See H-W Micklitz, 'Failure or Ideological Preconceptions? Thoughts on Two Grand Projects: the European Constitution and the European Civil Code' in K Tuori and S Sankari (eds), *The Many Constitutions of Europe* (Ashgate 2010) 109, and sources there cited.

[23] Micklitz's project works with four models: (i) conflict and resistance; (ii) intrusion and substitution; (iii) hybridization; and (iv) convergence. Conflict and resistance explores the possible ways in which national systems may try to resist the influence of European private law and seeks to clarify boundaries as to where EU law begins and national private law ends. Intrusion and substitution focuses on the introduction by the EU legislator of regulatory rules in private law, in a 'self-sufficient' manner, ie where the creation and enforcement of rules are all encompassed in the EU legal order. Hybridization is concerned with the enforcement of rights arising from EU law through national remedies, and therefore aims for a merging of the two levels. Convergence, finally, looks at ways in which the two levels can be brought closer together without actually merging them. It focuses not just on mandatory or default rules, but also includes new modes of governance, co-regulation, and self-regulation.

the European Court of Justice (CJEU) are conceived of as the potential seeds from which a 'self-sufficient legal order' of European private law may grow.[24]

Regardless of the analytical and normative merits of this perspective, one important contribution of this theory is that it exposes the underlying rationales of private law rules developed in EU law in comparison to national private laws. The former are thought to be narrower and primarily related to creating access to the internal market for businesses and consumers, whereas national private laws combine market regulation with considerations of redistributive justice. The term 'access justice' or *Zugangsgerechtigkeit*, coined by Micklitz, sits somewhere in between the allocative (libertarian) justice that characterizes market law and the expressions of social distributive justice seen in national laws.[25] It embodies the idea that the rules of European private law developed by the European legislator and the Court are meant to empower actors to pass the threshold to taking part in the internal market. However, although this in theory means that all workers and consumers should be included in the market and by extension in society, as is Micklitz's normative claim,[26] one may wonder to what extent European private law delivers on that promise. European private law in consumer markets has mostly been developed through harmonizing legislation. The justifications for such harmonizing legislation put forward by the European Commission over the past decades almost without failure cite that businesses should not be deterred from entering foreign markets by difference in national legislation, whereas consumers should have the confidence that they enjoy similar buyer protection in other Member States as they do in their own country[27] so that they can 'reap the benefits of the internal market'. Micklitz has posited that this aspect of European private law should be named European Regulatory Private Law (ERPL), as it is the reflection of EU internal market policy applied to private law relationships. ERPL, other than national private laws, is infused with regulatory aims tied to the internal market and pays no—or in any case less explicit—heed to questions of social distributive justice. It may even restrict the space for national policy-making rooted in social or uniquely local policy concerns.[28]

[24] H-W Micklitz and Y Svetiev (eds), 'A Self-Sufficient European Private Law—A Viable Concept?', EUI Working Papers LAW 2012/31, 6.

[25] H-W Micklitz, *The Politics of Justice in European Private Law. Social Justice, Access Justice, Societal Justice* (CUP 2018) 18 ff. See earlier H-W Micklitz, 'Social Justice and Access Justice in Private Law', EUI Working Papers LAW 2011/02, 22 ff.

[26] H-W Micklitz, *The Politics of Justice in European Private Law* (n 25) 20.

[27] These justifications of course also follow from Art 114 of the Consolidated version of the Treaty on the Functioning of the European Union [2012] OJ C326/47 (TFEU), which is the main legal basis for harmonization of private law in the EU. Nevertheless, the EU Treaties contain objectives and values that go beyond the internal market rhetoric.

[28] H-W Micklitz, 'Introduction—Social Justice and Access Justice in Private Law' in H-W Micklitz (ed), *The Many Concepts of Social Justice in European Private Law* (Edward Elgar 2011) 3; H-W Micklitz 'Monistic Ideology versus Pluralistic Reality—Towards a Normative Design for European Private Law' in L Niglia (ed), *Pluralism and European Private Law* (Hart Publishing 2013) 29, 38; H-W Micklitz 'The Forgotten Dimension of European Private Law' in L Azoulai, *The Question of Competence in the European Union* (OUP 2014) 125. See also Y Svetiev, 'The EU's Private Law in the Regulated

The problem could also be framed more broadly, not only as one of different rationales underlying legislation but as one of different rationalities, in which the rationality of European private law is instrumentalist whilst that of national private laws can be characterized as juridical.[29] The contrast between the rationalities of European private law and of national private laws is particularly stark when it is studied, as Micklitz and his research team did, in the context of so-called regulatory silos. These silos, or sectors, refer to the specific sectors of industry in which the European Union has intervened in private law relationships as part of a broader regulatory strategy to liberalize markets and open them up to competition. Examples are the telecommunications and energy sectors,[30] the financial services sector,[31] insurance, tourism, and healthcare.[32] The descriptive account of the ERPL project holds that these different market sectors functioning as relatively closed entities, each with its own rationality[33]—although all are embedded in the EU's internal market project and also share that overarching rationality—which influences the making of rules, the substantive standards, and the enforcement mechanisms in that particular sector.[34] Moreover, the presence of sector-specific lawmaking actors—in particular representatives of the industry who take part in standardization processes—is presented as a factor of such prominence that it prevents, or hinders, the introduction of rules developed by external lawmakers. The substance of rules may therefore come out in favour of the established interests of the more powerful market players.[35] While EU law may intervene to at least safeguard access to justice in such markets, as other actors will be bound by rules emanating from the EU legislator, the relatively closed lawmaking process makes it unlikely that distributive policies are pursued by lawmakers in each of these sectors.

Although the ERPL project has provided a stimulating and necessary alternative perspective to the harmonization debate, it is vulnerable to criticism,[36] as other legal pluralist accounts may be more complete, from an analytical or descriptive

Sectors: Competitive Market Handmaiden or Institutional Platform?' (2016) 22 European Law Journal 659, 660, who states that negative integration is so deeply entrenched in the CJEU's case law that it makes EU law unable to accommodate national regulatory autonomy.

[29] See p 96 above.

[30] Discussed by Svetiev, 'The EU's Private Law in the Regulated Sectors' (n 28). See also M Cantero Gamito, 'The Transformation in the Making of Private Law via Telecommunications Regulation' in Micklitz and Svetiev, 'A Self-Sufficient European Private Law—A Viable Concept?' (n 24) 89.

[31] See eg I Domurath, *Consumer Vulnerability and Welfare in Mortgage Contracts* (Hart Publishing 2017); G Comparato, *The Financialization of the Citizen. Social and Financial Inclusion through European Private Law* (Hart Publishing 2018).

[32] BJ van Leeuwen, *European Standardisation of Services and Its Impact on Private Law. Paradoxes of Convergence* (Hart Publishing 2017).

[33] cf MW Hesselink, 'Private Law, Regulation, and Justice' (2016) 22 European Law Journal 681, 683.

[34] Micklitz and Svetiev, 'A Self-Sufficient European Private Law—A Viable Concept?' (n 24) 78.

[35] This finding resonates the concerns put forward by Bartl, 'Internal Market Rationality, Private Law and the Direction of the Union' (n 11).

[36] For reflections on the project by Hesselink, Bartl, Dagan, and Mulder, see the special issue of the European Law Journal (2016) 22(5).

standpoint as well as in relation to the scope that they see for normative considerations of justice. I will discuss two points of contention in relation to the project's theoretical basis. The points of contention relating to the ERPL project stem from: (i) its analysis of the process of lawmaking in regulated sectors, or silos; and (ii) the perception that European regulatory private law is subservient to the goal of achieving access to the internal market for all businesses and consumers but has a limited role in social policy.

The first aspect, the analysis of silos as part of the ERPL project, appears to underestimate the relevance of cross-sector lawmaking in European private law. The existent rules of private law, in particular consumer law, contain a number of instruments that apply to all contracts between businesses and consumers in the European Union, without distinction between sectors of industry. Examples are the Consumer Rights Directive,[37] the Unfair Contract Terms Directive,[38] and the Consumer Sales Directive.[39] Considering that these directives lay down minimum rules for consumer protection in business-to-consumer (B2C) contractual relations, the rationality of lawmaking in different sectors at least in some part overlaps. While it may be true that the specific rationality of a given sector—for example, telecoms or energy—can influence which other rules are developed in relation to B2C contracts, all lawmaking actors in the sector are obliged to abide by the rules laid down by EU law.[40] Therefore, it may be that some of these rules have relatively more importance in one sector than another, depending on their relation to standards, national legislation, or other rules applicable in the sector, but they can never be left out or diverged from to the detriment of the consumer. That cross-sectoral effect of EU law on private law relationships in the different market sectors needs to be taken into account in any theory that wishes to give a full account of lawmaking in European private law.

The previous point leads to a second consideration. Substantively, the directives that apply across sectors lay down a number of consumer rights that are quintessentially European, and yet go beyond what would be needed to achieve access justice for consumers. The right of withdrawal, the control of unfair terms, and the harmonized remedies for non-conformity are the main examples of such rights.[41] Withdrawal, which means the possibility for consumers to rescind a contract within fourteen days after either the conclusion of a contract or the delivery

[37] Directive 2011/83/EU on consumer rights [2011] OJ L304/64 (Consumer Rights Directive).

[38] Council Directive 1993/13/EEC on unfair terms in consumer contracts [1993] OJ L95/25 (Unfair Contract Terms Directive).

[39] Directive 1999/44/EC on certain aspects of the sale of consumer goods and associated guarantees [1999] OJ L171/12 (Consumer Sales Directive). This Directive was repealed in 2019 and will be replaced by a new consumer sales directive. See below, p 118.

[40] Of course, unless EU law itself makes exceptions for specific sectors.

[41] Some even regard them as pillars of a pragmatic system that could develop into a loosely coherent European private law. See Hesselink, 'Private Law, Regulation, and Justice' (n 33) 685–87 for a further development of this argument.

of goods,[42] has become a well-known and often exercised right in European consumer contracts. It enables consumers to buy goods through online or other distance media—for example, clothes—and try them at home before deciding whether to keep them.[43] The second example, the control of unfair terms, aims to eliminate terms laid down in general terms and conditions used by traders that in some way infringe upon consumer rights or that upset the balance of fairness between the contracting parties.[44] The third category, remedies for non-conformity, has ensured that consumers in Europe can count on having a set of remedies available if goods that a trader delivers to them do not live up to the contract. These include repair, replacement, price reduction, and termination.[45] Although some national variation exists,[46] the Directive has succeeded in its aim to guarantee these remedies for consumer sales contracts in the European Union.[47] Similar remedies will be introduced for digital content contracts.[48]

It is striking that these rights, in particular through their interpretation by the CJEU, have gone beyond what is required from an access justice perspective. In particular, the Unfair Terms Directive has given a major impulse to consumer protection, not just in relation to the economic position of consumers but also in relation to social inclusion and redistribution. National courts have discovered the Directive as a route through which to attack unfair mortgage credit contracts, and thereby indirectly to prevent the eviction of debtors and their families from their homes.[49] The remedies for non-conformity and the right of withdrawal intervene perhaps to a lesser extent in consumers lives—having

[42] The Consumer Rights Directive (n 37), Art 9 harmonizes the right of withdrawal for all consumer contracts concluded through distance communication.

[43] Statistics on consumer sales in the European Union reveal a steady increase of the percentage of online sales as part of all consumer sales in Europe, which is linked to a growing trust of consumers in online shopping and a better knowledge of their rights. See European Commission, 'EU Consumer Conditions Scoreboard 2017' <http://ec.europa.eu/newsroom/just/item-detail.cfm?item_id=117250>, 10.

[44] Unfair Contract Terms Directive (n 38) Arts 3, 6.

[45] Consumer Sales Directive (n 39) Art 3.

[46] Notably in the United Kingdom, albeit that Brexit will perhaps diminish the relevance of that deviation. For an explanation on the continued prominence of damages as a remedy over specific performance, see P Giliker, 'The Consumer Rights Act 2015—A Bastion of European Consumer Rights?' (2016) 37 Legal Studies 78. See also V Mak, 'Specific Performance in English Consumer Sales Law' in JM Smits, D Haas, and G Hesen (eds), *Specific Performance in Contract Law: National and Other Perspectives* (Intersentia 2008) 121.

[47] The recent 'Fitness Check' of European consumer and marketing law confirms that the key directives introduced in the 1990s and 2000s, when effectively applied, tackle the most important problems encountered by consumers in the EU, also in online markets. The results of the Fitness Check and of this assessment, as well as the supporting studies, can be accessed online at <ec.europa.eu/newsroom/just/item-detail.cfm?item_id=59332>.

[48] Directive (EU) 2019/770 on certain aspects concerning contracts for the supply of digital content and digital services [2019] OJ L136/1 (Digital Content Directive). Member States should implement the Directive by 1 July 2021 and its rules will apply to the delivery of digital content, also for contracts concluded before that date, from 1 January 2022. See Digital Content Directive, Art 24.

[49] This example refers to Case C-415/11 *Mohamed Aziz v Caixa d'Estalvis de Catalunya, Tarragona i Manresa (Catalunyacaixa)*, ECLI:EU:C:2013:164.

their direct impact in economic rather than social terms—but also lean towards consumers' interests rather than those of traders. Consumers are given not just any remedy for non-conformity, but the ones that are thought to empower them most; and the right of withdrawal is a highly consumer-friendly way in which goods can be ordered and assessed, and returned if the consumer wishes, all at the trader's expense.[50]

The fact that these rights go beyond what is needed to help actors pass the threshold for participation in the internal market signifies that ERPL is not fully informed by access justice as a benchmark for its substance.[51] European regulatory private law appears to engage with social justice or interpersonal justice too,[52] albeit that it is unclear to what extent, and under what conditions, the European legislator and the Court are driven to recognize rules that go beyond the basic standards required for consumers' participation in the internal market and, by corollary, their inclusion in society. Interestingly, Micklitz's theory of ERPL may actually, even if it is not presented as such, give an opening to the further development of a framework within which social interests are taken into account in the making of European private law. His work on the constitutionalization of European private law acknowledges the influence of non-economic rights, in particular fundamental rights, on private law relationships through EU law. Nevertheless, the pursuit of market access is regarded as a precondition for the engagement of the EU Court and legislator with such rights.[53] The addition suggested by other perspectives on justice is that, while it may be descriptively valid to see the connection to market access as a prerequisite for judicial review or legislative action, there also is a normative side to the inclusion of non-economic rights in European regulatory private law. Besides access justice (focused on providing market access to all, including weaker actors, in the EU market), the extension of ERPL to non-economic interests requires that justifications are found for choices made with regard to interpersonal justice in private law relationships.[54] For example, while it may be conceded that minimum rules on unfair contract terms in consumer contracts

[50] With one exception, namely that the consumer will have to pay the costs for returning the goods, through the medium that he desires; see Case C-511/08 *Handelsgesellschaft Heinrich Heine GmbH v Verbraucherzentrale Nordrhein-Westfalen eV*, ECLI:EU:C:2010:189 and now Consumer Rights Directive (n 37), Art 13. The consumer will however obtain a refund of the price of the goods as well as the delivery costs that he paid when ordering them. Moreover, in practice many traders provide consumers with the means to return goods at no additional cost.

[51] cf Hesselink, 'Private Law, Regulation, and Justice' (n 33).

[52] On interpersonal justice, ibid 691–92. Interpersonal justice concerns the effects of private law on individuals and includes, but is not limited to, the correction of wrongs.

[53] See eg H-W Micklitz and C Sieburgh, 'Primary EU Law and Private Law Concepts' in H-W Micklitz and C Sieburgh (eds), *Primary EU Law and Private Law Concepts* (Intersentia 2017) 1, 42–43; H-W Micklitz and N Reich, 'The Court and Sleeping Beauty: The Revival of the Unfair Contract Terms Directive (UCTD)' (2014) 51 Common Market Law Review 771.

[54] Hesselink, 'Private Law, Regulation, and Justice' (n 33) 691.

can encourage more actors to take part in the internal market, there is still the question whether the consequences attached to unfairness in private law relationships are balanced, taking into account both the interests of the consumer as well as those of the trader. Therefore, Micklitz's access justice framework can be construed so as also to include normative choices relating to social justice, interpersonal justice, and redistribution.

By giving space to access justice and social redistributive justice, the theory can moreover transcend the perceived dichotomy between the instrumental rationality of EU internal market law and the juridical rationality of national private laws. Redistributive justice, as has been said,[55] is still often perceived as falling within the realm of national private law systems. That notion begs reconsideration in light of the finding that European regulatory private law includes considerations of social justice. More generally, this finding in relation to Micklitz's theory of access justice seems to be corroborated by examples from the case law of the CJEU[56] and by a broader reconceptualization of social justice in EU law that may result in greater attention for the vulnerable in Europe.[57] In some areas of European (regulatory) private law, such as in consumer law, a call for greater attention for the redistributive effects of EU law has already been made. It has been said that 'risk-distribution is already a feature of EU consumer law' and that EU law should be more explicit in recognizing that it has a social welfare function in this respect.[58]

Taking stock, a strong legal pluralist perspective can open up a space for normative deliberation of concepts of justice in European private law. The ERPL framework provides a basis on which such a theory could be developed. The above analysis lays bare some ways in which the theory might already be able to accommodate a space for deliberation between the differing rationalities of European and national private laws. There are some additional responses conceivable from a strong legal pluralist perspective, which I will return to in section V, after the discussion of 'processes' and 'actors'.

[55] See p 101 above.

[56] In particular the Court's references to the EU Charter of Fundamental Rights in private law cases appear to boost social justice in European private law. See eg H Collins, 'Building European Contract Law on Charter Rights' in H Collins (ed), *European Contract Law and the Charter of Fundamental Rights* (Intersentia 2017) 1. See in detail Chapter 4.

[57] For a recent analysis, in which a comparison is made with the national context in the United Kingdom, see C O'Brien, *Unity in Adversity: EU Citizenship, Social Justice and the Cautionary Tale of the UK* (Hart Publishing 2017).

[58] G Howells, C Twigg-Flesner, and T Wilhelmsson, *Rethinking EU Consumer Law* (Routledge 2018) 332. See also the earlier analyses of a social welfare model in European (consumer) contract law in T Wilhelmsson, *Social Contract Law and European Integration* (Dartmouth 1995) and—as part of a more general overview of different approaches—T Wilhelmsson, 'Varieties of Welfarism in European Contract Law' (2004) 10 European Law Journal 712, and N Reich, *General Principles of EU Civil Law* (Intersentia 2014) 82–83.

III. Doctrinal and Pragmatic Approaches

Moving from norms to processes, another aspect of legal pluralism in European private law concerns the approaches to lawmaking that are chosen. On the one hand, there are doctrinal approaches to private law, which build on the idea of private law as an evolved system of rules, principles, and practices;[59] on the other side stand pragmatic approaches that aim to resolve societal problems in an efficient and user-friendly manner as they arise in practice. These approaches are reflected in the dichotomy between the juridical rationality associated with national private laws, of which doctrinal approaches are part, and the instrumental rationality of EU law, in which pragmatic solutions can be found beyond the internal, juridical framework.[60] They are nonetheless more specifically focused, in that they are concerned with the *ways in which* law can tackle societal problems (in other words, processes), rather than on a more abstract level with the broader framework of discussion within which questions are asked. As Hesselink observes:

> the main difference between the classical national systems of private law in the member states and European private law is not its regulatory nature but its more pragmatic style. European private law is far less doctrinal and, consequentially, much more user-friendly (for unsophisticated users) and more future-proof than the [German Civil Code] BGB and other national civil codes, even after their recent reforms.[61]

The dichotomy between doctrinal and pragmatic approaches in European private law is most acutely observed in the relation between general private law and specific rules of consumer law. The introduction of consumer law rules can, as a deviation from general contract law, be seen as a pragmatic response driven by the European legislator's legal harmonization agenda for the integration of the internal market. As such, it is a relevant case study for determining the space for deliberation, and hence for legal pluralism, between the European and national legal orders. The greater the resistance to pragmatic solutions, and conversely the greater the desire to integrate new rules into existing doctrinal systems, the less space there seems to be for the coexistence of norms in a strong legal pluralist constellation.[62]

The distinction between doctrinal and pragmatic aspects of European private law is highlighted by Hesselink, who argues that the pragmatic nature of European private law can give it an advantage over classical, doctrinal private law for parties that require efficient and user-friendly solutions in conflicts of low complexity and

[59] See MW Hesselink 'How Many Systems of Private Law are there in Europe?' in L Niglia (ed), *Pluralism and European Private Law* (Hart Publishing 2013) 199.
[60] See pp 96 above.
[61] Hesselink, 'Private Law, Regulation, and Justice' (n 33) 688.
[62] See also above, pp 97.

value.[63] Indeed, European private law stands out from national laws as virtually all instruments in this field have been directed towards the regulation of B2C relationships.[64] Notably, one explanation for that focus is that the EU's legislative competences are restrained by the principles of subsidiarity and proportionality. While a case can be made for the harmonization of consumer contract laws with the aim of pursuing the integration of the internal market and, through mandatory rules, ensuring a high level of consumer protection, that case is harder to make for business-to-business (B2B) transactions. Most of those transactions are, due to the freedom of contract, governed by rules determined by the parties themselves, rather than mandatory rules. The parties can also choose which (national) law governs the contract, within the boundaries set by private international law. Besides that, the European Union, however, does not seem to have competence to harmonize facilitative or 'default' rules of contract law.[65] Nevertheless, as a consequence of this B2C focus of European private law the substance of rules may diverge from general private law. Characteristics associated with B2C transactions are that they mostly reflect low-value transactions, that most disputes between parties do not reach the courts because of this low value as well as other barriers,[66] and that consumers benefit from more user-friendly mechanisms for dispute resolution such as mediation or arbitration.[67] These characteristics are pragmatic in nature and to some extent make consumer contract law drift away from classical, doctrinal private law, as found at the national level in the EU Member States.[68]

[63] Hesselink, 'Private Law, Regulation, and Justice' (n 33) 686–87.

[64] Two projects that proposed regulation of B2B relationships failed. The Common European Sales Law (CESL) intended to include not only B2C contracts within its scope, but also B2B contracts in which one of the parties was a small or medium-sized enterprise. See European Commission, 'Proposal for a Regulation of the European Parliament and of the Council for a Common European Sales Law' COM(2011) 635 final, Art 7. An enquiry into the need for regulation of unfair commercial practices in B2B relations only after a long time led to legislative proposals. On this topic, see A Renda and others, 'Study on the Legal Framework Covering Business-to-Business Unfair Trading Practices in the Retail Supply Chain. Final Report' (European Union 2014) <http://ec.europa.eu/internal_market/retail/docs/140711-study-utp-legal-framework_en.pdf>. A proposal for a Directive on unfair trading practices in business-to-business relationships in the food supply chain (COM(2018) 173 final) was adopted in December 2018. In 2019, also, a new EU regulation was adopted concerning transparency of online platforms. See Regulation (EU) 2019/1150 on promoting fairness and transparency for business users of online intermediation services [2019] OJ L186/57.

[65] N Reich, 'A European Contract Law, or an EU Contract Law Regulation for Consumers?' (2005) 28 Journal of Consumer Policy 383, 391 ff. According to Reich, an exception may be made for B2B contracts involving a small or medium-sized enterprise. See pp 110 ff below.

[66] Studies show that many consumers avoid court proceedings because of their high costs, long duration, and uncertain outcomes. See eg I Ramsay, 'Consumer Redress and Access to Justice' in CEF Rickett and TGW Telfer (eds), *International Perspectives on Consumers' Access to Justice* (CUP 2003) 17, who highlights that for many low-income consumers complaint mechanisms will not be as effective as they are for middle-income consumers.

[67] Hesselink, 'Private Law, Regulation, and Justice' (n 33) 686. See also Calliess' analysis of online dispute resolution (ODR) mechanisms. G-P Calliess, 'Online Dispute Resolution: Consumer Redress in a Global Market Place' (2006) 7 German Law Journal 647.

[68] Hesselink, 'Private Law, Regulation, and Justice' (n 33) 687–88.

Going beyond this description of the status quo, a broader analysis of the interplay between doctrinal and pragmatic approaches in European private law can give insight into the space for deliberation between the two approaches. In other words, it can indicate whether there is room for legal pluralism, for example by allowing pragmatic approaches to coexist besides doctrinal national laws, or whether legislators seek to knead pragmatic solutions into the mould of doctrinal systems. Also vice versa, the question can be asked whether doctrinal laws should transform in response to pragmatic solutions introduced in one area of private law. In both cases, practice shows doctrinal laws to be resistant to the integration of pragmatic solutions, thereby (perhaps inadvertently) supporting legal pluralism. The first situation, the adaptation of pragmatic solutions to fit existing doctrinal legal frameworks, is an evergreen of harmonization projects in European private law. In most cases where the European legislator proposed harmonizing rules, these were laid down in EU directives, thus leaving space for the national legislator to implement rules in a manner befitting their existing legal system. Some Member States made an effort to adapt their existing legislation in specific places to integrate B2C rules into general private law, whilst others preferred the verbatim copying of EU legislation into self-standing statutory instruments without addressing their relation to general private law.[69] The variety of approaches chosen, and the resulting continued divergence of rules despite attempts at harmonization, have led some authors to conclude that the harmonization of European private law 'seems to have reached a dead-end'.[70] As a consequence, pragmatic rules of European consumer law coexist with doctrinal rules of general contract law. This situation may be characterized as legal pluralist, albeit of an ordered variety, since rules emanating from EU law will trump those of national laws in cases where conflicts arise and may then cut across the doctrinal system of those national laws. One area in which this has happened is unfair terms regulation in consumer contracts.[71]

The second situation, the transformation of doctrinal laws in response to pragmatic solutions, also emphasizes the resistance of doctrinal laws to change. One test case confirming this is the question whether the rules on withdrawal, unfair terms and remedies for non-conformity that have been developed for B2C contracts can be extended to general contract law, in particular to B2B contracts, which resonates with some of the questions that were raised in relation to ERPL's

[69] The latter is the approach chosen in UK law, whilst eg Germany and the Netherlands have integrated most European private law directives into their civil codes.

[70] H Schulte-Nölke, 'The Brave New World of EU Consumer Law—Without Consumers, or Even Without Law?' (2015) 4 Journal of European Consumer and Market Law 135.

[71] The case law of the CJEU in relation to the *ex officio* assessment of unfair terms by national courts has cut across national rules of procedural law and has also, primarily in the *Aziz* judgment, influenced the assessment of unfairness in the light of the open norm of 'good faith' in contract law. See eg C Mak, 'The One and the Many: Translating Insights from Constitutional Pluralism to European Contract Law Theory' (2013) 21 European Review of Private Law 1189, 1207–08; OO Cherednychenko, 'The Impact of Fundamental Rights' in C Twigg-Flesner (ed), *Research Handbook on EU Contract Law and Consumer Law* (Edward Elgar 2016) 109, 131–33.

silos approach.[72] The rationality underlying these rules, as explained above, reflects a pragmatic approach to the needs of consumers, in particular in cases where disputes arise. That moment—that is, the occurrence of a dispute—is indeed pivotal to the relevance of private law rules in practice, as it puts to the test which rights can actually be given effect by parties.[73] The clearer those rights are, the lower the costs of dispute resolution, and the more likely that the consumer will get a satisfactory outcome.[74] This argument therefore supports a pragmatic approach to private law, in which rights are introduced that are unambiguous and easily enforced, such as the right of withdrawal or the right to avoid unfair contract terms.

Until now, however, national private laws have remained fairly resistant to the expansion of pragmatic solutions beyond B2C relations to also include B2B relationships.[75] One explanation is that the term 'B2B relationships' is broad and undifferentiated. It places all business-to-business transactions into one category, whereas in practice significant differences may exist between large and small, or even micro-sized businesses run by one person. Some smaller companies will be equally vulnerable as consumers when it comes to assessing their legal position at the time of entering into a contract or being able to put pressure on the other party or to obtain a remedy if the performance of the contract is unsatisfactory. For those types of cases, it could be argued that consumer protection rules should be extended to other categories of weaker parties.[76] Some support may be garnered therefore for the idea that B2B contracts in which one of the parties is a small or medium-sized enterprise (SME) should be treated in a similar way to consumer contracts, as there is a similar economic or power imbalance between the two contracting parties.[77] Examples already exist of cases in which consumer protection is extended to transactions between businesses in which one is an SME. In Germany and the Netherlands, for example, SMEs may in certain circumstances benefit from an extension of consumer protection against unfair terms in contract law. The mechanism by which this is done is called *Reflexwirkung* or *reflexwerking*, meaning

[72] See above, p 103.

[73] On the importance of remedies in contract law, see earlier V Mak, *Performance-Oriented Remedies in European Sale of Goods Law* (Hart Publishing 2009) 1–2.

[74] cf Hesselink, 'Private Law, Regulation, and Justice' (n 33) 686.

[75] European private law has also remained focused on B2C transactions, although B2B transactions have on occasion been considered, but eventually not been subjected to legislative action. See eg Renda and others, 'Study on the Legal Framework Covering Business-to-Business Unfair Trading Practices in the Retail Supply Chain' (n 64).

[76] The debate could be extended also to other types of weaker parties, such as employees or those who are at risk of harm caused by environmental factors and climate change ('green victims').

[77] This idea inspired the choice for the proposed CESL to be applicable to B2C contracts and to B2B contracts in which one of the parties is an SME. See note 64 above. A small enterprise is defined in EU law as a company with fewer than fifty staff and a turnover or balance sheet total of less than €10 million. A medium-sized enterprise is defined as a company with fewer than 250 staff and a turnover of less than €50 million or a balance sheet total of less than €43 million. See Commission Recommendation 2003/361/EC of 6 May 2003 concerning the definition of micro, small, and medium-sized enterprises [2003] OJ L124/36.

that courts can mirror the application of these rules onto B2B contracts in which one of the parties is a small business.[78]

Nonetheless, the extension of consumer laws to B2B transactions is not common practice. One important reason for being hesitant in this respect is that the treatment of SMEs (in some instances) as consumers makes the legal framework doctrinally more complex. Whilst it can lead to just outcomes in individual cases, overall the effect would be a blurring of categories. Besides the distinction between consumers and businesses—which is already obscure in some aspects[79]—it would introduce a third category of 'small businesses who are treated as consumers'. As a result, the sometimes difficult questions of demarcation between consumers and businesses would not disappear; they would simply arise at a different point, namely in identifying which businesses qualify as 'small' enough to benefit from consumer protection. The difficulties of differentiating between different types of actors within categories, moreover, can already be observed on the other side of the equation, in relation to the consumer definition. EU consumer law has introduced its own definitions of the 'average consumer' and the 'vulnerable consumer', which differ sufficiently from the definitions in national laws to cause doctrinal upheaval.[80] One reason to keep working with traditional, doctrinal categories of consumers and businesses is therefore in itself also pragmatic, albeit from the perspective of the legal system rather than the parties affected by it: complexity is minimized.[81] It is not surprising therefore that laws are, doctrinally, resistant to the instrumental nature of European private law.[82]

Overall, a number of factors can work against the integration of pragmatic solutions into a broader framework of doctrinal private law. The coexistence of pragmatic solutions besides doctrinal laws is however also a confirmation that a space exists for legal pluralism in European private law, in terms of process (pragmatic vs doctrinal solutions) as well as norms (the substance of B2C rules vs general contract law, on which see section I, above). In terms of process, moreover, the observation that the pragmatic approach of European consumer law has until now not been integrated into general contract law does not mean that it cannot still have

[78] See eg MBM Loos and I Samoy 'Introduction' in MBM Loos and I Samoy (eds), *The Position of Small and Medium-Sized Enterprises in European Contract Law* (Intersentia 2014) 1, 3; EH Hondius, 'The Notion of Consumer: European Union versus Member States' (2006) 28 Sydney Law Review 89, 96.

[79] See in Dutch, M Schaub, 'Wie is consument?' (2017) Tijdschrift voor Consumentenrecht 30.

[80] For an analysis of English, Dutch, and German cases on financial services for consumers, see V Mak, 'The "Average Consumer" of EU Law in Domestic and European Litigation' in D Leczykiewicz and S Weatherill (eds), *The Involvement of EU Law in Private Law Relationships* (Hart Publishing 2013) 33.

[81] Hesselink's view that the pragmatic pillars of European contract law can be influential because they have a wide territorial scope, with harmonized rules applying in all EU Member States, whereas national doctrinal laws diverge—see Hesselink, 'Private Law, Regulation, and Justice' (n 33) 687—therefore only seems superficially true. It is important also to consider how the rules of European contract law integrate with those national doctrinal laws.

[82] On resistance in European private law, see also G Comparato, *Nationalism and Private Law in Europe* (Hart Publishing 2014) ch 3.

transformative effects in the future. I will consider that question in relation to the rise of the platform economy and the emergence of an intermediate category of 'prosumers' in the section on strong legal pluralism.

IV. Private Actors as Lawmakers

The third point, which goes to the heart of legal pluralism, is what role private actors have in lawmaking in European private law. In a juridical rationality their place would be seen as subordinate to democratically chosen, state legislatures. In a legal pluralist constellation, however, that role changes. Strong pluralist theories downplay the role of the state by taking the sociological perspective in which multiple legal orders coexist, at local and global levels but also within the territory of the state. In that perspective, private actors are included as norm-creating actors besides or within the state. In other words, formal and informal lawmaking[83] can be regarded as equally important for private law practice. That perspective coincides (at least in part) with the instrumentalist rationality of European private law, since private actors can be regarded as active contributors to the integration of the internal market through law.

One particular proponent of this approach is Jan Smits, who has advocated a choice-of-law based theory of radical legal pluralism in European contract law. What makes his theory a 'radical' form of pluralism is that, besides adopting a sociological perspective of coexisting legal orders, it takes a second step: focusing on individual choice, the theory suggests that private actors are not necessarily governed by the law of one state or the norms of one societal group, but instead are allowed to 'opt out' of the law of their state and to 'opt in' to another norm set. That enables private actors to choose the rules that they find most favourable to their purposes or situation.[84]

Smits' conception of radical legal pluralism in European private law at first glance adheres to the premises of strong legal pluralism. It relies on the (both public and private) autonomy of private actors to choose the rules that apply to them and that enable them to reach their objectives. Also, other actors are presumed to recognize the choices made by private actors; that is, they regard the rules chosen by private actors as valid even if they themselves do not agree with those rules. The framework therefore presumes toleration by other actors. An additional feature of the theory holds that the freedom of private actors to choose the rules applicable to their transactions creates a 'law market',[85] and that in this market a competition of

[83] Here used as synonyms for public regulation promulgated by the state or other government actors or by the European Union, and private regulation in the form of rules made by private actors through contracting practice, self-regulation, or co-regulation.

[84] JM Smits 'A Radical View of Legal Pluralism' in L Niglia, *Pluralism and European Private Law* (Hart Publishing 2013) 161, 162.

[85] EA O'Hara and LE Ribstein, *The Law Market* (OUP 2009).

rules will result in the emergence of the 'best' rule for contracting in the market.[86] The notion of regulatory competition, as this process is called, is based on the economic theory of jurisdictional competition, which goes back to Charlies Tiebout.[87] Fitting the economic model of a market, it assumes that law can be viewed as a product created by states—the supply side—and chosen by private actors—the demand side. The theory of regulatory competition, therefore predicts that under the right conditions a 'law market' can operate in which lawmakers compete for their law to be chosen by private actors.

This perspective on legal pluralism has however also attracted criticism, in particular because it relies on the capacity of private parties (including weaker ones) to make suitable choices.[88] In many cases private parties will not be able to assess the best suitable law for the purposes of their transaction properly. For example, consumers or small businesses will not carry out a full regulatory enquiry before entering into a cross-border transaction, whereas larger businesses may well hire (in-house) counsel to advise on legal aspects before marketing their products in various foreign markets. Furthermore, even if private parties do have a preference for a particular choice-of-law, they may not be in a position to enforce it. If the other party to the contract has a stronger bargaining position, in all likelihood the preferences of that party will prevail.[89] Here is not the place to go into a full discussion of the limitations of the theory.[90] Nonetheless, these particular criticisms do point to a broader question relating to the political economy of individual-choice-based theories of radical legal pluralism.

The idea of individual choice nevertheless seems attractive as a means to do justice to the autonomy of contracting parties. Autonomy, however, is not the only value that deserves to be supported through the governance framework of European private law. Equally, if not more important, are the protection of weaker parties or issues of social justice, as was seen in section II. Questions that arise are whether a law market based on individual choice can guarantee that the welfare of all members of society, including weaker parties who are less able to exercise a choice to their own benefit, is being pursued. Can sufficient safeguards for the

[86] JM Smits, *The Making of European Private Law* (Intersentia 2002) 64, who however expresses a preference for a permanent free movement of rules rather than fixation of the most favourable rule through codification; N Reich, 'Competition Between Legal Orders: A New Paradigm of EC Law?' (1992) 29 Common Market Law *Review* 861.

[87] C Tiebout, 'A Pure Theory of Local Expenditure' (1956) 64 Journal of Political Economy 416; and see G Rühl, 'Regulatory Competition in Contract Law: Empirical Evidence and Normative Implications' (2013) 9 European Review of Contract Law 61, 64, and sources there cited.

[88] B Lurger, 'A Radical View of Pluralism? Comments on Jan Smits' in L Niglia, *Pluralism and European Private Law* (Hart Publishing 2013) 173, 174.

[89] S Vogenauer, 'Regulatory Competition through Choice of Law and Choice of Forum in Europe: Theory and Evidence' (2013) 21 European Review of Private Law 13, 19 states that a party will only be able to impose contractual terms if it has superior bargaining power.

[90] ibid for an in-depth analysis. See also Lurger, 'A Radical View of Pluralism? Comments on Jan Smits' (n 88).

protection of fundamental values and objectives, such as legal certainty, consumer protection, and environmental protection,[91] be provided if private actors are considered as actors with (at least a shared) responsibility for lawmaking?

The answer to these questions is complex, because the theory on individual choice in European contract law at some points is underdeveloped. Yet, it is exactly in relation to these broader goals—concerning the protection of fundamental values and objectives of the EU private law order—that the theory of radical legal pluralism in European private law may be improved. I will elaborate this idea by first analysing three aspects of criticism of Smits' theory of radical legal pluralism. In the next section, on strong legal pluralism, I will come back to these and elaborate some responses as to how these aspects could still provide the groundwork for a strong legal pluralist theory for European private law.

First, despite its name, Smits' theory in the end is anything but 'radical'.[92] The theory only engages with facilitative rules, not with mandatory rules. Its assertion that private actors should be allowed to choose the contract law that best fits their interests, in that light, does not add much to our general understanding of private law. The facilitative character of contract law seen in Western legal systems already places the emphasis on the autonomy of private parties. Where the real limitations of that autonomy arise, is in relation to mandatory rules. Businesses cannot contract out of mandatory consumer protection, as is reflected in conflict-of-laws rules.[93] Free choice of rules would only seem to be available for business-to-business contracts, and even in those cases it may be that limitations arise if one of the parties involved is a small or medium-sized enterprise.[94] The theory, therefore, can only provide an incomplete governance strategy for European contract law.

Second, in its final stage, the theory does not actually choose a 'strong' legal pluralist perspective. In its application to questions of lawmaking, it reverts back to formal lawmaking by the state. The 'best' or 'most favoured' rules that are assumed to come up through choice-of-law in contracts between private parties are supposed to provide material for law reform. Such reform assumes the adoption of new legislation by the state.[95] Not only from a theoretical perspective, but also empirically, that is a problematic point. It cannot be established that legislators in

[91] These objectives correspond to those laid down in Art 3(3) of the Consolidated version of the Treaty on European Union [2012] OJ C326/01 (TEU) for the European social market.

[92] Michaels, 'Why We Have No Theory of European Private Law Pluralism' (n 1) 151.

[93] For Europe, see Art 6(2) of Regulation (EC) 593/2008 on the law applicable to contractual obligations [2008] OJ L177/6 (Rome I), which stipulates that businesses cannot by contract derogate from the minimum protection that consumers have under the law of their country of residence.

[94] The proposal for CESL was tailored specifically to contracts in which one of the parties is perceived as weaker, either as a consumer or as an SME. Compare 'Proposal for a Regulation of the European Parliament and of the Council on a Common European Sales Law' COM(2011) 635 final, Art 7.

[95] Vogenauer, 'Regulatory Competition through Choice of Law and Choice of Forum in Europe' (n 89) see also F Chirico and P Larouche, 'Conceptual Divergence, Functionalism and the Economics of Convergence' in S Prechal and B van Roermund (eds), *The Coherence of EU Law: The Search for Unity in Divergent Concepts* (OUP 2008) 463, 487 ff.

the European Union have adapted their contract laws in response to competition between contract laws in practice. It is true that many contract laws in Europe have seen reform in the last twenty years. Examples are Germany, the Netherlands, and a number of the EU's newer Member States (Estonia, Hungary, Lithuania, Poland, and Romania).[96] Whether these adaptations were in response to choices of law in practice, or whether they incorporated rules or approaches that had been favoured in practice, however, cannot be deduced from the available data.[97]

Third, a substantive problem related to the 'law market' idea is that it often overlooks power relations. The suggestion seems to be that of a market for law in which ideas can be freely traded, without intervention from special interests ('*herrschaftsfrei*').[98] In reality, the likelihood is that businesses with stronger market power will be able to impose their preferred rules on weaker parties, or that the solution preferred by the more numerous will prevail.[99] A moderating solution is found in conflict-of-laws rules, which place policy constraints on the market, for example in the form of consumer protection rules.[100] That, however, brings us back to the other two criticisms, namely that the theory thus reverts back to one of 'weak' or 'juridical' legal pluralism rather than strong legal pluralism, and that it does not explain how mandatory rules fit with the idea of individual choice by private actors.[101]

By itself, therefore, individual choice theory appears insufficiently equipped to support a strong legal pluralist perspective on European private law. Nonetheless, the arguments put forward by Smits could form the basis of defining private actors as lawmakers in a strong legal pluralist theory; they only require refinement. The same is true for the other points of contestation, concepts of justice ('norms') and approaches to lawmaking ('processes'). I will now on the basis of the analysis set out in the previous sections come to some conclusions as to how a theory of strong legal pluralism in European private law may be further developed.

[96] Rühl, 'Regulatory Competition in Contract Law' (n 87) 77.

[97] While the reform of the German law of obligations according to parliamentary documents was inspired by a desire to be at the forefront of lawmaking in Europe, the substance of the reforms does not reflect the adoption of rules copied from practice in Europe. See in more detail V Mak, 'Private Actors as Norm-Setters through Choice-of-Law': The Limits of Regulatory Competition' in C Cauffman and JM Smits (eds), *The Citizen in European Private Law: Norm-Setting, Enforcement and Choice* (Intersentia 2016) 99, 106; Deutscher Bundestag 11 October 2001, Plenarprotokoll 14/192, 18758; H Däubler-Gmelin, 'Die Entscheidung für die so genannte Große Lösung bei der Schuldrechtsreform—Zum Entwurf Eines Gesetzes zur Modernisierung des Schuldrechts' (2001) Neue Juristische Wochenschrift 2281.

[98] Michaels, 'Why We Have No Theory of European Private Law Pluralism' (n 1) 152.

[99] ibid.

[100] Compare H Eidenmüller, 'Recht als Produkt' (2009) 64 JuristenZeitung 641.

[101] Michaels, 'Why We Have No Theory of European Private Law Pluralism' (n 1) 152–53.

V. The Strong Legal Pluralist Response

This chapter started with the question whether legal pluralism in European private law can be construed as a strong, rather than an ordered, legal pluralism. The idea underlying that inquiry is that strong legal pluralism is normatively appealing because it does justice to the public autonomy of all lawmaking actors, formal and private. It recognizes the power to self-legislate for these actors and it allows norms to coexist outside a formal, legal hierarchy.

To determine the viability of a strong legal pluralist theory in European private law, the chapter has examined three aspects that can serve as a methodological lens through which to regard pluralism: norms, processes, and actors. Existing theoretical positions engaging with these aspects, notably the ones of Micklitz, Hesselink, and Smits, have been found to go some way towards laying the groundwork for a strong legal pluralist framework in European private law. Yet, none is able to completely shrug off the ordering imposed by state-based perspectives on lawmaking. While one might conclude from this that the state is, and will remain, the primary locus for lawmaking, that conclusion would in some respects be too rash. The state is likely to continue to be the central actor in lawmaking processes—as legal pluralists will also agree—but that does not rule out the possibility that a space for legal pluralism can exist for issues that are of a transnational nature, as is the case for European private law. This section sets out a brief response as to how points of contestation arising from the examined theories could be refined from a strong legal pluralist perspective.

A. Justice and the Rationalities of Private Law

Returning to 'norms' first, the analysis of ERPL presented above confirms that the theory as it stands, and as it is further developed in scholarship, is extremely relevant for our understanding of the rationalities of European private law. At the same time, the theory seems open to further development in some respects. The question whether European private law serves goals of access justice or also social distributive justice reveals a contested area in the theory that is of fundamental importance for how we perceive the coordination of lawmaking between different actors. That question reverberates in the corollary question how the interplay between regulated sectors and the broader, cross-sectoral approach to European private law functions. A theory of strong legal pluralism may be refined by mirroring it against these dilemmas, with which it is also concerned. The responses could then be as follows.

The first point, concerning the role of European private law in regulated markets, raises a deeper question on the effects that rules have once they are put in practice, or the distinction between 'law in the books' and 'law in action'. While it can be established that there are rules that apply across sectors—namely the rights of withdrawal, unfair terms control, and remedies for non-conformity in consumer contracts—that does not yet tell us whether these rules apply in the same way in each context. If it is true, as the ERPL project posits, that regulation in each sector operates along the lines of a sector-specific rationality, it may well be that some of that rationality rubs off on these general rules of European private law. Looking at remedies for non-conformity, it could for example be the case that repair is the most used remedy in one market, perhaps because it is considered to contribute to environmental sustainability,[102] while replacement prevails in another market. One may wonder whether the consequence for an individual consumer in the first market would be that his or her right of replacement—after all, the consumer may choose between repair or replacement[103]—is effectively diminished. Such questions would require further, empirical research in order to determine how remedies operate in practice in different sectors, whether their practical application diminishes consumer protection, and whether action is required to re-establish a general approach to remedies for non-conformity across sectors.

Second, the finding that access justice is not the only benchmark for the substance of European private law but that it is in some ways complemented by social justice is of relevance for the elaboration of the normative substance of rules. What is interesting for this particular field is that European private law, in comparison to global, transnational private law, is created in an institutional setting that already contains mechanisms for managing pluralism that go some way towards the recognition of common social values and goals. Coordination of lawmaking may for example be more readily achieved within the EU's institutional context, in which legislators and policy makers at national and EU level coordinate their lawmaking and in which also often note is taken of comparative legal solutions adopted by other Member States, than in legal orders with a lesser degree of regional cooperation between states or other lawmakers.[104] In this regard it is relevant also that the EU legal order is based on a number of common values and objectives, notably the ones laid down in Article 3(3) TEU. The rich debate on the rationalities of European private law, which revolves around the perceived dichotomy between internal market objectives and social policies, signifies that the precise content of the values and objectives set out in the EU Treaties continues to be in flux. Nonetheless, the presence of shared values and objectives in the Treaties provides a basis for mutual trust between the Member States, and therefore for toleration of norms created

[102] The European legislator has made the connection between repair and sustainability, eg in its new directive for consumer sales. See Directive (EU) 2019/771 on certain aspects concerning contracts for the sale of goods, and repealing Directive 1999/44 [2019] OJ L136/28 (new Consumer Sales Directive), recital 32.

[103] Currently following from Consumer Sales Directive (n 39) Art 3(3); in the new Consumer Sales Directive (n 102) Arts 9(1), 11.

[104] For an elaboration of this argument, see Chapter 2, pp 22.

by others,[105] as well as an explicit basis for taking account of social justice goals. That realization may be a stepping stone towards identifying a space for deliberation between lawmakers in which norms can coexist.

B. Doctrinal and Pragmatic Approaches

The second point of contestation, 'processes', raises other challenges. It has been seen that the introduction of new rules in European private law often leads to a clash between, on the on hand, pragmatic solutions proposed as part of EU harmonization—for example in consumer law—and, on the other hand, the established doctrinal systems of national private laws. On a more fundamental level this can be considered a clash between the instrumentalist rationality of European private law and the juridical rationality of national private laws. The resistance of doctrinal laws often results in a lack of integration of the two approaches, and thereby effectively in the continuance of a legal pluralist constellation. Where doctrinal laws remain unresponsive to fundamental change, but accept the existence of pragmatic solutions, the two rationalities can coexist side by side. That may however only be a temporarily sustainable position, as societal changes can require that changes are made that will affect the doctrinal structures of private laws in a more fundamental way. One aspect of 'processes' of lawmaking in a legal pluralist constellation, therefore, is to conceive of ways in which a space for deliberation between doctrinal and pragmatic lawmaking can be given shape. This problem is hard to discuss on an abstract level and I will therefore use an example for analysis. Staying with the business and consumer categories from section II, the next challenge to doctrinal classifications comes from the emergence of new types of actors, 'prosumers', in the platform economy.

This is a more complex problem than the question whether B2C protection should be extended to general contract law, as it overturns the idea that consumers are purchasers and therefore on the demand side of the market. The platform economy enables individuals to take part in the market by offering goods and services to consumers worldwide even if they are not professional traders. It has blurred the lines between the concepts of 'consumer' and 'business'. In the legal definition used in most jurisdictions, a natural person not acting in the course of a business, trade, or profession would be regarded as a consumer, vis-à-vis a business as a natural or legal person who is operating in one of those ways. In the new economy, a natural person with the same characteristics, but now on the other side of a transaction, namely as a seller or service provider rather than a buyer, all of a sudden is transformed into a 'prosumer', in other words a consumer who produces

[105] Toleration, it should be recalled, is one element required in a legal pluralist theory of lawmaking in European private law. See p 41 above.

goods and services.[106] The question is whether the law should respond by treating this 'prosumer' as a new category, or whether existing doctrinal approaches can be applied in ways that meet the needs of consumers, businesses, and others who are active in the platform economy.

Saliently, this problem has elements that lift it beyond the juridical rationality of (national) private laws. Prosumers have emerged in particular as participants in the so-called 'platform economy', that is, the market for goods and services that has been created by online platforms, which allows individuals to offer products to consumers around the world. Technology, in the form of online platforms, has enabled such peer-to-peer or consumer-to-consumer transactions, and has thereby provoked a significant shift of power balances in the market for consumer goods and services.[107] Individual sellers or suppliers who would normally have very limited resources for the sale and marketing of their goods or services can make use of online platforms to provide them with a space where they can place their products on the market.[108] That is true not only within their own national markets but also much more broadly as online platforms operate across state borders. Prosumers who make use of online platforms, therefore, are excellently placed to offer their goods and services outside their own country and, in the European Union, to contribute to the integration of the EU internal market. From that perspective, facilitating peer-to-peer transactions becomes relevant for the EU legislature. Therefore, the discussion on whether the 'prosumer' should be recognized as a separate legal category takes on significance also within the instrumentalist rationality of EU law.

What is required in terms of facilitating transactions between prosumers and other actors, such as consumers? Some lessons may be taken from the development of consumer law until now.[109] While many existing laws would treat prosumers as professional traders under certain circumstances—for example, whether their aim is to make a profit, what the organizational structure of their operation is, and with what frequency they sell goods or services—only a few systems limit the legal responsibilities of prosumers in comparison to other, more experienced professional traders.[110] At the same time, regulatory scholarship has recognized for

[106] The term 'prosumer' was first coined by A Toffler, *The Third Wave* (Bantam Books 1980). An alternative term, the 'hybrid consumer' is used by C Riefa, 'The Reform of Electronic Consumer Contracts in Europe: Towards an Effective Legal Framework?' (2009) 14 Lex Electron 17.

[107] Not only prosumers have benefited from this shift; the gains from the platform economy also go in a large part to the major platforms themselves, such as Airbnb, Google, Facebook, and Amazon.

[108] For an exploration of the rise of the platform economy, see A Sundararajan, *The Sharing Economy* (MIT Press 2016) 69 ff.

[109] For an assessment of the consumer notion in e-commerce law over time, see EM Weitzenboeck, 'Looking Back to See Ahead: The Changing Face of Users in European E-Commerce Law' (2015) 23 Artificial Intelligence Law 201, who makes a case for maintaining consumer protection and letting general contract law deal with the emergence of new users, such as prosumers.

[110] See MBM Loos and others, 'Digital Content Contracts for Consumers. Analysis of the Applicable Legal Frameworks and Suggestions for the Contours of a Model System of Consumer Protection in Relation to Digital Content Contracts, Final Report: Comparative Analysis, Law & Economics

some time now that the emergence of prosumers in various sectors might require new approaches to regulation. Findings to this effect have been made in relation to the Internet, for example with regard to privacy, copyright, censorship, social networks, and net neutrality;[111] the energy and telecommunications markets;[112] and, most recently, digital content.[113] This 'regulatory disconnection' between rules and practice is perceived as problematic, since regulation sometimes overshoots its goal and sometimes falls short in protection. Prosumers that are placed within the category of consumers enjoy a protection that they may not need (over-inclusion), whilst they are under-included in the category of professionals and therefore not subject to legal duties that would otherwise apply to traders.[114] On the other hand, where prosumers are treated as professional traders, their responsibilities towards consumers may be unduly strict considering the small(er) size of their enterprise. In order for the legal framework to support the active participation of consumers-as-producers in the market, and thereby to contribute to innovation and higher quality of goods and services,[115] it is thought therefore that regulation should be tailored more specifically to prosumers. This means that regulation at all levels—national and EU, but also self-regulation, for example through standardization—should address the question whether rules take account of prosumers, and if not, what changes are needed to achieve that.[116]

Even with that realization, the doctrinal challenge will not be easily overcome. The objections to the introduction of a 'third category' that were raised above,[117] equally apply to the introduction of a prosumer category for the platform economy.

Analysis, Assessment and Development of Recommendations for Possible Future Rules on Digital Content Contracts. With an Executive Summary of the Main Points' (study performed for the European Commission 2011) 42–44 <ec.europa.eu/justice/consumer-marketing/files/legal_report_final_30_august_2011.pdf>. The trio 'profit–organization–frequency' in practice allows courts some useful tools to distinguish between professional and non-professional traders. Germany and the Netherlands attach particular importance to the appearance of the prosumer, ie whether they present themselves as a consumer or a trader.

111 I Brown and CT Marsden, *Regulating Code: Good Governance and Better Regulation in the Information Age* (MIT Press 2013).

112 A Butenko and K Cseres, 'The Regulatory Consumer: Prosumer-Driven Local Energy Production Initiatives', Amsterdam Law School Research Paper No 2015-31, Amsterdam Centre for European Law and Governance Research Paper No 2015-03 <https://ssrn.com/abstract=2631990>.

113 Loos and others, 'Digital Content Contracts for Consumers' (n 110).

114 Butenko and Cseres, 'The Regulatory Consumer: Prosumer-Driven Local Energy Production Initiatives' (n 112) 30.

115 In the energy market, for example, the emergence of prosumers is likely to have far-reaching consequences. They impact upon sustainability (prosumers use solar panels to generate electricity), competition in the energy market, contractual relations between the prosumer and the operator of a grid, and potentially also international relations between countries concerning energy trade. For an overview and a research agenda, see R Leal-Arcas, F Lesniewska, and F Proedrou, 'Prosumers: New Actors in EU Energy Security', Queen Mary School of Law Legal Studies Research Paper No 257/2017, 33–34 <https://ssrn.com/abstract=3010714>.

116 Brown and Marsden also correctly point out the need to include prosumers in policy-making processes, eg through civil society representation. See Brown and Marsden, *Regulating Code* (n 111) 202.

117 See p 111 above.

One solution for resolving such problems might be to revert to monism and see the EU legislator as the lawmaker who has ultimate authority.[118] Perhaps, however, a space for the gradual development of rules that provide a better fit with societal developments can be provided in a pluralist framework, for example through pragmatic solutions developed in soft law and through the influence of civil society. It has been observed that private regulation tends to respond more rapidly to new societal and technological developments,[119] which is of course not surprising seeing that the introduction of formal regulation requires many more steps to be taken through democratic legislative processes. The role of private actors in law-making should therefore in any event receive greater attention in discourses on European private law. Still, existing theories of legal pluralism in European private law have not reached an understanding as to how private actors are, or should be, involved in that process. One concern is whether the involvement of private actors can vouchsafe that fundamental objectives and values of EU law, such as consumer protection, are guaranteed. That brings us to the third point of contestation: the role of private actors as lawmakers.

C. Private Actors as Lawmakers

The discussion of Smits' theory of radical legal pluralism revealed a number of weak points in the reliance on individual choice theory as a basis for a strong legal pluralist perspective, in which private actors are regarded as lawmakers. Even if there is substance in these criticisms, they should not lead to the conclusion that a conclusive theory of strong legal pluralism in European private law cannot be conceived. Taking each point in turn, the responses to the criticisms raised may be as follows.

First, the problem of facilitative and mandatory rules. Although it is true that mandatory rules place restrictions on private actors' individual choice, in practice such restrictions mean very little if parties do not enforce them. Consumers may have legal protection against unfair terms in contract law as laid down in Directive 93/13/EEC, but how many of them actually benefit from that protection? Whilst cases do make it to court, often at the application of traders who seek to obtain payment from a consumer,[120] research suggests that many terms that would qualify as 'unfair' are present in traders' terms and conditions but remain unchallenged.[121]

[118] A plea for monism is made by Hesselink, 'How Many Systems of Private Law are there in Europe?' (n 59) 244–47.

[119] See eg Brown and Marsden, *Regulating Code* (n 111) 202.

[120] In which case judges are obliged under EU law to *ex officio* assess the unfairness of terms in the contract. See Cases C–240/98 to 244/98 *Océano Grupo Editorial SA v Roció Murciano Quintero* [2000] ECLI:EU:C:2000:346.

[121] C Riefa, *Consumer Protection and Online Auction Platforms. Towards a Safer Legal Framework* (Ashgate 2015) 125 ff.

The focus that Smits' theory of radical legal pluralism places on facilitative rules, therefore, is not actually unfounded. It appears to reflect the reality of contracting in the European market, as well as in other market incidentally, in which the autonomy of contracting parties prevails. Even if, say, 20 per cent of consumers factually enjoy the protection laid down in legislation, 80 per cent do not because legal protection does not assert itself, or because a transaction is concluded to the satisfaction of both parties despite the presence of potentially unfair terms in the contract. Obviously the first situation—the lack of enforcement of rules—should not be encouraged; it is important that adequate mechanisms are maintained for those situations where consumers do encounter problems and wish to obtain remedies from traders.

In this respect, it is important to find ways to ensure that consumer protection is guaranteed. As said earlier, rather than portraying the relationship between mandatory and facilitative rules as a stark conflict, legal pluralist theories may look for ways to mediate between those types of rules. Again, starting from a practical perspective: choice-of-law by private actors can be steered through instruments that are not mandatory in nature but that do—like mandatory rules—channel parties' choices towards consumer protection. Examples are standardization in contract law, or the use of optional instruments. The effect of such instruments can potentially be significant even if only a minority of contracting parties makes use of them. Economic theories have held that change can be realized in markets if a small, but sophisticated group of users actively compares alternatives and, on that basis, adopts a preferred solution.[122] In this case, the adoption of standards or optional instruments in contracting by a small group of users might provide an impetus for establishing consumer protection rules of European private law as the main substantive benchmark in the EU consumer market.[123]

The response that the first point of criticism could be more theoretical than real, however, does not hold up in relation to the second aspect. Radical legal pluralism's fall-back on the state as the ultimate lawmaking actor cannot be seen as anything other than a concession to weak legal pluralism. To portray the theory as strong legal pluralism is in that light not sustainable. It is important to note, nonetheless, that a legal pluralist theory that seeks to conceptualize the process of lawmaking in private law in all its facets—from inception to usage to acceptance as 'law' to

[122] It has been suggested in other contexts that competition—with an eye to innovation—can sufficiently take place if a small number of top players in the market engage in choice. This is the 'informed minority' argument attributed to Alan Schwartz and Louis L Wilde. See A Schwartz and LL Wilde, 'Imperfect Information in Markets for Contract Terms: The Examples of Warranties and Securities Interests' (1983) 69 Virginia Law Review 1387; A Schwartz and LL Wilde, 'Product Quality and Imperfect Information' (1985) 52 The Review of Economic Studies 251.

[123] Giesela Rühl has relied on this mechanism as part of an argument in favour of regulatory competition between national legal systems. See Rühl, 'Regulatory Competition in Contract Law' (n 87) 68. In that context, however, the effect of the use of rules by a sophisticated minority is also dependent on the subsequent adoption of such rules by legislators.

(perhaps) formal legislation to enforcement—cannot adopt a state-centred focus. As an explanatory and as a normative theory, it must include norms created by non-state actors in its conception of all stages of lawmaking. Even if norms created by private actors do not go through a process of acceptance by formal legal institutions, they may still be regarded as, and used by norm-addressees, as if they were binding law.[124] In particular, in instances where rules created by non-state actors are not tested against regulation or legislation emanating from the state or another democratically chosen legislator, it is important to have other means through which the substance of these rules can be monitored, such as through court proceedings, alternative dispute resolution mechanisms, or monitoring by (government or independent) supervisory bodies. Private actors can then be held accountable for upholding certain minimum standards, such as in relation to consumer or employee protection, health and safety, and environmental protection.

Third, the substantive problem that power relations influence the outcome of norm-creating processes is indeed of great importance. A theory of legal pluralism in European private law should engage with this question. Private actors engaged in standard-setting in a regulated sector, for example, are thought to reinforce extant interests of producers.[125] This is a difficult point to tackle, in part because many aspects remain unclear. On the one hand, there seems sufficient evidence that the participants in lawmaking through standardization are indeed often, and mostly businesses, whereas consumer interests are represented by a minority of representatives.[126] The risk of collusion, deception, and strategic behaviour of producers in standardization processes has been recognized.[127] Yet, it has not been proven that the outcome of standardization processes is to the detriment of consumers. Moreover, no clear picture exists of the influence of European or national rules of consumer law, or contract or tort law, in the different sectors. Those issues require further consideration, especially now that standardization as a lawmaking tool is

[124] Of course, questions of legitimacy arise in relation to private regulation. An in-depth discussion is beyond the scope of this chapter. For an overview of the debate in this field, see G-P Calliess and P Zumbansen, *Rough Consensus and Running Code* (Hart Publishing 2010) 130 ff, referring in particular to the concept of 'affectedness' developed by David Held which ties any assessment of democracy to the quality by which a group has been affected by a decision. See Held, 'Democratic Accountability and Political Effectiveness from a Cosmopolitan Perspective' (2004) 39 Government and Opposition 364. See also Chapter 2, pp 33.

[125] See eg N Gandal and P Régibeau, 'Standard-Setting Organisations. Current Policy Issues and Empirical Evidence' in P Delimatsis (ed), *The Law, Economics and Politics of International Standardisation* (CUP 2015) 394, 402, who state: 'Not surprisingly, the more expertise a given member [of a standard-setting organization; *VM*] has and the more human capital that member is willing to invest into the process, the greater the influence on the design of the standard. Accordingly, large intellectual property holders and large potential users will generally have significantly more weight within the SSO than smaller firms or than final consumers.'

[126] In Europe, the European Association for the Co-ordination of Consumer Representation in Standardisation AISBL (ANEC) represents consumer interests in standardization processes.

[127] See eg OECD Competition Committee, 'Standard Setting', Policy Roundtables 2010 <https://www.oecd.org/daf/competition/47381304.pdf>.

steadily gaining importance.[128] The European Commission's annual standardization work package for 2017 proposed the development of horizontal standards for services, whilst the annual package for 2016 already contained a number of standardization projects that could affect consumer services, such as parcel delivery, smart metering, healthcare services, accessibility of services for persons with disabilities, eLearning courses, and online dispute resolution for e-commerce.[129]

In sum, a theory of strong legal pluralism can serve to sharpen the vision set out in Smits' radical legal pluralist theory of European private law. It shares the notion that norms created at all levels of regulation—formal and informal—should be included. Its improvements exist in elucidating that the limitation of individual choice by mandatory rules is empirically not as prevalent as it might seem; that, when lawmaking shifts towards private regulation, alternative mechanisms might be found to ensure that the (consumer) protection laid down in mandatory rules is nonetheless ensured; and that further empirical work is required to assess the impact of power relations on the substance of rules.

VI. Conclusions

Various aspects considered, Michael's observation that many theories of legal pluralism in European private law are not theories of strong legal pluralism, but of ordered legal pluralism,[130] seems to hold up. Although nuances can be discerned, the existing theories largely confirm that EU law's internal market rationality stands apart from and can override the juridical rationality of national private law systems. In relation to justice—the first dichotomy—the pursuit of access justice through EU law can result in rules that are aimed at empowering consumers and businesses to pass the threshold for taking part in the internal market, without having specific regard to questions of social distributive justice. As a corollary, however, social justice can be a factor in determining the substance of rules, for example of fairness in consumer transactions. The analysis of the second dichotomy, between doctrinal and pragmatic approaches, shows that pragmatic rules aimed for example at consumer protection can cut across the doctrinal approaches of national private law systems. Nonetheless, doctrinal systems can be resistant to changes that would increase the complexity of the law. For the third dichotomy, between formal and private regulation, existing theories have not come up with a conclusive answer

128 Van Leeuwen's conclusion that the tool is underdeveloped, despite the European Commission's rhetoric, therefore appears to be rapidly overtaken by the emergence of projects concerning the standardization of services and service contracts in national systems as well as at EU level. See further Chapter 8, pp 190.

129 COM(2016) 357 final, 3–4, and COM(2014) 500 final, 3. See also Schulte-Nölke, The Brave New World of EU Consumer Law' (n 70) 137; C Busch, 'DIN-Normen für Dienstleistungen—Das Europäische Normungskomitee produziert Musterverträge' (2010) Neue Juristische Wochenschrift 3061.

130 Michaels, 'Why We Have No Theory of European Private Law Pluralism' (n 1) 158.

on how to construe the role of private actors as lawmakers in a true legal pluralist manner. The rules created by private actors ultimately require the assumption of rules into formal law.

At the same time, the analysis has revealed several instances in which inroads are made on the 'ordered' conception of legal pluralism. It may be that these provide the premises for the development of a strong legal pluralist theory for European private law after all. The primary observation that I make is that each of the existing theories in some way confirms that the conception of 'who makes law' is in flux. The rise of private actors as lawmakers has been noted and has, for example for Smits, been a ground for developing a bottom-up perspective on lawmaking. Further, the emergence of 'prosumers' as a potential new category of legal subjects, but also as lawmakers, raises new doctrinal questions. The ERPL project, finally, has paid particular attention to the emergence of standardization and co-regulation in lawmaking processes.

Second, while national legal systems may doctrinally resist change, there can be other ways through which laws can be responsive to societal developments. In lawmaking processes, greater heed could be paid to the role of soft law or civil society, through which transformations often take place much sooner than through formal laws. In relation to the justice objectives of European private law, it is interesting to observe that the integration of social justice into lawmaking processes at EU level seems to be gaining ground on the pursuit of 'access justice'. The framework of EU law provides a space for deliberation of values and objectives in European private law, for example through the values and objectives laid down in Article 3(3) TEU and through the EU Charter of Fundamental Rights, yet that space has not been used often in legislation and case law. If the trend to include social justice considerations continues, for example in the case law of the CJEU, EU law may become instrumental in pursuing social goals through private law, and thereby enter into the domain that is often perceived to fall within the Member States' responsibility. In a pluralist perspective, this means that rules developed at EU level may diverge from Member States' laws, and that therefore norm conflicts may arise that will require mediation. Which mechanisms can be invoked to 'manage' pluralism—such as standardization, model rules, or co-regulatory lawmaking processes—acquires new importance in this context?

Taking stock, therefore, the analysis of actors, norms, and processes involved in lawmaking in European private law reveals a field that has matured, but that is now at the threshold of a re-evaluation and perhaps a new transformation in lawmaking. The increasing importance of private regulation combined with a sensitivity to social justice issues almost inevitably leads to the question: which mechanisms can be maintained or created for ensuring that the values and objectives of EU law and of national private laws are safeguarded? That question goes beyond the frameworks provided by existing theories of ordered legal pluralism. It demands a new attempt at the development of a strong legal pluralist theory for European private law. The previous chapters have aimed to sketch the contours of such an approach. In the following chapters, the proposed theoretical approach will be tested against two case studies on lawmaking in European contract law. Does the instrumental-normative approach proposed in the earlier chapters resonate with practical experiences with lawmaking in European contract and consumer law?

6
The Platform Economy
Regulatory Instruments

The sharing economy has grown exponentially in recent years. The term denotes the market within which goods and services are exchanged between individuals, or 'peers', which is distinct from the market in which consumers obtain goods and services from businesses, that is, professional entities.[1] A defining element is also that the performances rendered by individuals make use of otherwise neglected resources. In other words, the sharing economy stimulates the use of resources that would otherwise be wasted. The use of these resources also often implies that goods or services are supplied by private persons rather than businesses. The line between consumers and producers therefore becomes blurred, resulting in the emergence of 'prosumers'.[2]

In this market, online platforms play an important role in connecting individuals who wish to take part in the exchange of goods and services. The term 'platform economy' can therefore also aptly be used to describe these emerging models for exchange. Examples of platforms abound: Airbnb for apartment and house rentals; Uber for taxi services; Lyft for ride-sharing services; TaskRabbit for cleaning services, and Feastly for cooking and meal sharing.[3] They roughly operate along similar lines. The platform enables users to offer goods or services, which others can book or purchase, and it provides means of communication by which users can connect to set up their deal. Most platforms charge fees to their users, but otherwise (claim to) have no part in the exchanges that are established through their platform. Airbnb, for example, enables guests and hosts to connect for the purpose of renting an apartment or a house. The rental contract is created and applies between host and guest only and does not involve the platform. Airbnb's terms and conditions, moreover, specify a list of limitations of liability towards both parties.[4]

In some ways, it might be thought that existing private laws should be able to cope with legal problems that arise in relation to platform services. Contracts

[1] An accessible yet comprehensive introduction, including an analysis of regulatory responses to the rise of platforms, is provided by A Sundararajan, *The Sharing Economy* (MIT Press 2016).

[2] See eg PP Swire, 'When Should "Consumers-as-Producers" Have to Comply with Consumer Protection Laws?' (2008) 31 Journal of Consumer Policy 473.

[3] For more examples see Sundararajan (n 1) 3.

[4] Although these may not hold up in jurisdictions with strong consumer protection laws, such as EU Member States. See V Mak, 'Private Law Perspectives on Platform Services. Airbnb: Home Rentals between AYOR and NIMBY' (2016) 5 Journal of European Consumer and Market Law 19.

Legal Pluralism in European Contract Law. Vanessa Mak, Oxford University Press (2020). © Vanessa Mak.
DOI: 10.1093/oso/9780198854487.001.0001.

between users will be governed by the law designated by the rules of private international law, and the same is true for the contracts between the platform and its users, albeit that the platform will often seek to impose a choice of law. Liability in tort will likewise be dealt with under national laws, as designated by the rules of private international law. Still, one may wonder whether that approach—which falls back on national private laws—can suffice, in particular in a market where many transactions involve parties from different jurisdictions. It is well-known that most consumers—or here, users—do not always make use of the rights that they have under consumer or private laws. Barriers such as costs, a lack of knowledge of relevant legislation, and the often small amounts of money involved in consumer transactions prevent consumers from taking legal action.[5] These problems are even greater in a cross-border context than they are in the national context.[6] Therefore, the solution of legal issues through litigation seems an unattractive and unlikely route for many platform users. On top of these practical problems, many legal issues have not been clarified for the platform economy. While online platforms in the European Union can escape liability in relation to products advertised on their platforms due to the host exemption for information service providers,[7] they often provide other services such as secure payment systems, communication systems, or online dispute resolution. It is however often not clear to what extent platform operators can be held liable for unsatisfactory performance in relation to these services as it can be hard to establish whether the platform qualifies as an intermediary or franchise under national laws and may be held liable in that capacity.[8]

An important observation—and this is where the development of the platform economy makes the case for a new approach to lawmaking that fits with the legal pluralist perspective advocated in this book—is that platforms themselves are actively working to provide mechanisms that can, at least partly, overcome the problems of enforcing consumer rights. They have an interest in securing trust between users who, even more than consumers in the offline world, are at a disadvantage in establishing the quality of goods and services and the reliability of their counterparty.[9] Platforms therefore use mechanisms that can fill in the 'regulatory void'.[10] Examples of such mechanisms are codes of conduct or guidelines that prescribe

[5] These are well-known obstacles to access to justice. See eg C Hodges, I Benöhr, and N Creuztfeldt-Banda, 'Consumer-to-Business Dispute Resolution: the Power of CADR' (2012) 13 ERA Forum 199, 201, who note that 'above all, courts are not user-friendly for today's citizens'.

[6] N Reich, 'Transnational Consumer Law—Reality or Fiction?' (2009) 27 Penn State International Law Review 859, 861.

[7] Directive 2000/31/EC on certain legal aspects of information society services, in particular electronic commerce, in the Internal Market [2000] OJ L178/1 (E-Commerce Directive), Arts 14 and 15.

[8] See C Wendehorst, 'Platform Intermediary Services and Duties under the E-Commerce Directive and the Consumer Rights Directive' (2016) 5 Journal of European Consumer and Market Law 30.

[9] O Lobel, 'The Law of the Platform' (2016) 101 Minnesota Law Review 87, 146 ff. See further Chapter 7.

[10] That term is used by V Hatzopoulos, *The Collaborative Economy and EU Law* (Hart Publishing 2018) 190.

the quality, safety, non-discrimination, or other policies that users should comply with; online review systems that provide a reputational feedback mechanism in which users can leave feedback on services rendered or the qualities of other users (eg as a guest on Airbnb); and online dispute resolution centres that enable users to solve disputes through an online mediator provided by the platform.[11] The reality of lawmaking in the platform economy therefore implies a shift from a framework in which mandatory consumer laws are developed for the benefit but outside the reach of businesses and consumers, to a bottom-up approach in which each are active participants. Consumers become active participants in the regulatory process that defines the applicable rights, for example through writing and relying on online reviews. Moreover, since disputes between businesses and consumers often—because of the low values at stake—are not litigated in court, the rules determined by businesses in private regulation may give the final say on the outcomes in individual disputes.

While these are innovative, useful, and practical initiatives, they raise questions in relation to private lawmaking, for example in terms of legitimacy and accountability.[12] This chapter and the next one will touch upon these questions to some extent. Their focus is however more specific: in the light of the central theme of this book, a study of lawmaking in the platform economy can provide practical insights in the space for deliberation that various formal and informal lawmakers have. Furthermore, the substance of emerging norms can be tested against the objectives and values of existing rules of European and national private laws to establish whether these are adhered to, or not. Taken together these two routes of enquiry—focusing on processes of lawmaking as well as on the substance of norms—can lead to a better understanding of the role of private actors in lawmaking.

The structure of this and the following chapter is as follows. This chapter focuses on the instruments for regulation that lawmaking actors in the platform economy in Europe have used until now. They include a mix of public regulation, co-regulation, codes of conduct, soft law projects to develop model rules, and reputational feedback systems. Also, online dispute resolution can in practice be a source of norms, albeit that the development of norms in that context is less structured. Chapter 7 assesses whether the norms laid down by these various instruments meet the objectives and values of European private law. To that end, as an illustration, the rules on transparency developed in relation to platforms will be compared with the broader framework of EU law and national private laws. Transparency is chosen as a case study since it is one of the first topics

[11] See Lobel, 'The Law of the Platform' (n 9) 142 ff, with examples of self-regulation by eBay, Uber, and Lyft.

[12] Many of these are familiar. For an analysis of private lawmaking in the transnational sphere, see F Cafaggi, 'The Many Features of Transnational Private Rule-Making: Unexplored Relationships Between Custom, Jura Mercatorum and Global Private Regulation' (2015) 36 University of Pennsylvania Journal of International Law 101.

that lawmakers at different levels of regulation have started to get involved in, as will be seen below, and therefore sufficient material is available for comparison. That this is an early topic for lawmakers to engage with is perhaps not surprising. Transparency requirements are some of the least invasive instruments of regulation. They do not necessarily touch upon the substantive conditions under which goods and services are offered to consumers but simply require traders to be honest and clear about their products and business practices so that consumers can make informed decisions about purchases. Regulating transparency therefore is a mechanism to empower consumers through information and it is still far away from other, more paternalistic measures of consumer protection.[13] The question is then whether transparency requirements for online platforms towards their users, and for traders on those platforms towards consumers, offer levels of consumer protection that are similar to the requirements prescribed by EU law. In that context, a distinction will have to be made between business-to-consumer (B2C) transactions, to which EU consumer law by definition applies,[14] and B2B or consumer-to-consumer (C2C) transactions that fall outside the scope of EU consumer law and are regulated by default by national, general private laws.[15] In the first instance, for transparency aspects regulated by EU consumer law the question will be one of compliance: do online platforms and their users comply with, and enforce, the requirements laid down by EU law? For aspects falling outside the scope of EU consumer law, as well as for B2B and C2C transactions, the assessment will be of a more speculative nature. The question there will be whether the rules applicable to those situations, as they have been or are being developed at various levels of regulation, fit within the normative framework developed in EU law. The investigation of instruments in this chapter, combined with the normative assessment in Chapter 7, will give some clues as to the conditions that need to be fulfilled for an instrumental-normative approach to lawmaking to work in practice.

I. Instruments for Regulation in the Platform Economy

The emergence of the platform economy has occurred in stages, with online platforms gradually entering different markets for goods and services. Due to the spontaneous nature of the emergence of new businesses in the platform economy, and their variety in terms of activities and of issues that may require regulation, the

[13] See S Weatherill, *EU Consumer Law and Policy* (2nd edn, Edward Elgar 2013) 92–94, who notes that 'in the EU there is a suspicion that harmonisation at the level of information provision, rather than direct control of contract content, represents the line of least political resistance'.

[14] Provided that platform activities are directed at consumers in Europe, compare Regulation (EC) 593/2008 of 17 June 2008 on the law applicable to contractual obligations [2008] OJ L177/6 (Rome I), Art 15. For reasons of scope, this chapter will not discuss issues of private international law in detail.

[15] The assessment will extend to B2B transactions, since consumer protection can have some reflective or radiating effects in cases involving small or medium-sized enterprises.

regulatory actions that have been taken in the platform economy are of a patchwork nature. Some platforms have developed codes of conduct, sometimes in relation to specific issues, for example a non-discrimination policy for users.[16] Some have developed rules through a process of negotiation with legislative actors, reaching a memorandum of understanding on a particular problem, such as preventing the sale of counterfeit goods through online platforms.[17] Further, platform users have been able to make their own contribution to lawmaking through the use of online review systems which can have a significant impact on the maintenance of quality standards of platforms. Finally, regulators at various levels of regulation—local, national, and European—have gradually started to develop regulation in order to curb some of the problematic aspects of the platform economy.

To get a grasp on how lawmaking actors operate, and how they navigate the space for deliberation with other actors, the following sections will examine these instruments for lawmaking in more detail. The order of discussion follows the spectrum for private regulation (codes of conduct) to in-between forms (co-regulation) to legislation and regulation, and potential regulation (soft law). Two flanking mechanisms that can also be norm-producing or norm-enforcing will complete the analysis: online reputation systems and online dispute resolution.

II. Codes of Conduct

On 1 November 2016, short-term accommodation rental platform Airbnb launched a non-discrimination policy which it made mandatory for all its users.[18] The policy was adopted in response to a Harvard University study which found that applications from guests with distinctively African-American names were 16 per cent less likely to be accepted than those of guests with distinctively Caucasian names.[19] Airbnb now requires all of its users explicitly to commit to their non-discrimination policy or, alternatively, not to be able to make bookings through the system. Other platforms also have introduced codes of conduct. Examples are Facebook's 'community standards'[20] and Uber's 'community guidelines'.[21]

[16] Airbnb introduced a code of conduct on non-discrimination in 2016. See further section II below and Chapter 7, pp 171 ff.

[17] See the Memorandum of Understanding on the Sale of Counterfeit Goods over the Internet developed by the European Commission together with stakeholders from civil society. Further below, section III.

[18] See https://www.airbnb.com/help/article/1523/general-questions-about-the-airbnb-community-commitment accessed 28 February 2020, as are all websites in this chapter.

[19] B Edelman, M Luca, and D Svirsky, 'Racial Discrimination in the Sharing Economy: Evidence from a Field Experiment' (2017) 9 American Economic Journal: Applied Economics 1; see also <https://www.nytimes.com/2016/09/09/technology/airbnb-anti-discrimination-rules.html>.

[20] See <https://www.facebook.com/communitystandards/>.

[21] Which amongst other things stipulate 'you shouldn't touch or flirt with other people in the car'. See <https://www.uber.com/legal/community-guidelines/us-en/>.

Codes of conduct can be low-key instruments for agreement on certain standards of behaviour within organizations or, as the examples discussed here show, for anyone engaging with others within or through an organization. Many companies have adopted codes of conduct, for example in relation to quality standards concerning sustainable production, or a safe work environment for their employees.[22] Legally, however, the status of codes of conduct is only moderately strong. While courts in certain circumstances follow the rules laid down in a code of conduct even if it diverges from the default rules of the applicable law, the general view is still that such codes are instruments of soft law that have validity only if the applicable, formal law recognizes them through its own mechanisms.[23] Such mechanisms may be open norms concerning usage, or good faith, or the incorporation of codes of conduct into a contract.[24] A study of the status of codes of conduct in the Netherlands reveals that courts are even fairly open to the recognition of codes of conduct as binding.[25] In transnational law, codes of conduct and other voluntary standards are also used widely, and legally they can be considered binding for example as reflections of trade usage.[26] Interestingly, in European private law the basis for attaching stronger legal consequences to codes of conduct has been laid through references in several EU directives.[27] The Unfair Commercial Practices Directive sanctions traders who falsely claim to be a signatory to a code of conduct, or who do not comply with a code of conduct to which they are bound.[28] Moreover, codes of conduct may be referred to in substantiating the open norm of 'professional diligence' that is central to assessing whether a commercial practice is unfair.[29] Further, the Timeshare Directive encourages traders to inform consumers

[22] See OECD, 'Codes of Corporate Conduct: Expanded Review of their Contents', OECD Working Papers on International Investment 2001/06 <https://www.oecd.org/daf/inv/investment-policy/WP-2001_6.pdf>.

[23] This can be regarded as a form of toleration in the mediation of legal pluralism; compare N Krisch, *Beyond Constitutionalism: The Pluralist Structure of Postnational Law* (OUP 2010) 100–01.

[24] M-C Menting, *Industry Codes of Conduct in a Multi-Layered Dutch Private Law* (dissertation Tilburg 2016, unpublished) 261–62 <https://pure.uvt.nl/ws/portalfiles/portal/23090135/Menting_Industry_07_12_2016_emb.pdf>.

[25] Menting, *Industry Codes of Conduct in a Multi-Layered Dutch Private Law* (n 24) 261–62, who finds that lower courts are inclined to recognize codes of conduct as binding if there is agreement between the parties to the court proceedings that one of the parties was bound to the code. This includes situations where such agreement, procedurally, is established because the counterparty does not contest it in court. The Supreme Court, however, stays within the boundaries of what is considered formal law under Art 79 of the Dutch Code on Judicial Organisation (*Wet op de Rechterlijke Organisatie*, Staatsblad 1827, 20).

[26] For a comparative perspective on trade usage, see V Mak, 'According to Custom ...? The Role of "Trade Usage" in the Proposed Common European Sales Law (CESL)' (2014) 10 European Review of Contract Law 64.

[27] Menting, *Industry Codes of Conduct in a Multi-Layered Dutch Private Law* (n 24) 86 ff.

[28] Directive 2005/29/EC concerning unfair business-to-consumer commercial practices in the internal market [2005] OJ L149/22 (Unfair Commercial Practices Directive), Annex I, Arts 5(5) and 6(2)(b). Non-compliance with commitments contained in codes of conduct by which the trader has undertaken to be bound is sanctioned only where (i) the commitment is not aspirational but firm and is capable of being verified, and (ii) the trader indicated in a commercial practice that he is bound by the code.

[29] Unfair Commercial Practices Directive (n 28), Arts 5(2) and 2 sub h.

of their codes of conduct, whereas the Consumer Rights Directive obliges traders to provide such information in relation to distance and off-premises contracts.[30] Codes of conduct can also be referred to when assessing whether a product was safe under the Product Safety Directive.[31] Until now, however, examples of the use of such codes of conduct in European private law are sparse and it is therefore not possible to draw firm conclusions with regard to their practical relevance at this time.

Nonetheless, the use and usability of codes of conduct has from time to time led to a reappraisal of their status. It has been argued that they can have stronger validity provided that certain conditions are met. Generally speaking, the choice is between two models: a model in which private regulation is considered valid if it complies with substantive rules of any kind, as long as they do not infringe good moral or public order; or a model in which private regulation is considered valid if it complies with a set of minimum procedural criteria, such as transparency, a minimum degree of participation of norm addressees, and a pre-established allocation of duties.[32] The first would be an attractive model as it enables substantive processes of lawmaking or, in other words, substantive deliberation. It has garnered some support in the literature,[33] but its relative open-endedness makes it hard to monitor, which may explain why this model has so far not prevailed in practice.

The procedural model, on the other hand, has been adopted by lawmakers at the EU level as well as in national systems. At the EU level, the 2013 Interinstitutional Agreement (IIA) on better lawmaking introduced a general framework for the use of self-regulation.[34] The conditions required for valid lawmaking through self-regulation include consistency with EU law, transparency, representation of the parties involved, and representativeness of the general interest; also, the rules should not be related to fundamental rights or situations where political options are at stake, nor should they affect the principles of competition or the unity of the internal market.[35] The 2013 IIA has since been superseded by a revised better regulation agenda of the European Commission, accompanied by guidelines for better regulation.[36] While the express conditions under which private regulation

[30] Directive 2008/122/EC on the protection of consumers in respect of certain aspects of timeshare, long-term holiday product, resale, and exchange contracts [2009] OJ L33/10 (Timeshare Directive), Art 14(1) and recital 22; Directive 2011/83/EU on consumer rights [2011] OJ L304/64 (Consumer Rights Directive), Art 6(1)(n) and 6(5).

[31] Directive 2001/95/EC on general product safety [2002] OJ L11/4 (Product Safety Directive), Art 3(3).

[32] I Giesen, *Alternatieve Regelgeving en Privaatrecht* (Kluwer 2007) 53.

[33] Giesen, *Alternatieve Regelgeving en Privaatrecht* (n 32) 141. His observation in 2007 was that even the procedural conditions for the validity of self-regulation required further development.

[34] European Parliament, Council and European Commission, 'Interinstitutional Agreement on Better Law-making' [2003] OJ C321/1, para 17.

[35] ibid.

[36] European Commission, Communication from the Commission to the European Parliament, the Council, the European Economic and Social Committee and the Committee of the Regions, 'Better Regulation for Better Results—An EU Agenda', COM(2015) final; European Commission, Commission Staff Working Document, 'Better Regulation Guidelines' SWD(2017) 350.

is considered valid are dropped, the guidelines do offer a general framework based upon the general principles of effectiveness, efficiency, coherence, proportionality, and subsidiarity.[37] In combination with these general policy documents, the European legislator in various private law directives has expressly encouraged industry and consumer organizations to develop rules through codes of conduct or other voluntary instruments at EU level.[38] At least on paper, therefore, the procedural framework for developing legally binding codes of conduct appears strong.

At the same time, however, the European framework for private regulation has been criticized for lacking practical effect. While some codes of conduct have been developed at EU level, primarily in the areas of free movement and competition law,[39] empirical studies indicate that the Better Regulation agenda has not led to a greater use of codes of conduct or other forms of private regulation.[40] Only in some instances, it has been found, has a successful mix of public and private regulation emerged at the instigation of an EU regulator. Such an example is the field of advertising,[41] in which actors at the national level have been particularly active developers of codes of conduct and private enforcement mechanisms. More recently, the Court of Justice of the European Union (CJEU) downplayed the importance of codes of conduct in the context of unfair commercial practices. Whilst Directive 2005/29/EC recognizes circumstances in which traders can be held liable for not complying with codes of conduct to which they proclaim to be bound,[42] the Court held that the Directive does not preclude national legislation which does not confer a legally binding nature on a code of conduct.[43]

[37] European Commission, 'Better Regulation Guidelines' (n 36) 3–4.

[38] See eg Timeshare Directive (n 30), Art 14(1) and recital 22; Product Safety Directive (n 31), Art 8(2); Directive 2006/114/EC concerning misleading and comparative advertising [2006] OJ L376/21 (Directive on Misleading and Comparative Advertising), Art 6 and recital 18; E-Commerce Directive (n 7), Art 16; Directive 2007/65/EC on the coordination of certain provisions laid down by law, regulation or administrative action in Member States concerning the pursuit of television broadcasting activities [2007] OJ L332/27 (Audiovisual Media Services Directive, or: AMSD), Art 4(7), Art 9(2), and recital 44. The AMSD is under review but will in its revised form contain similar provisions; see European Parliament Briefing, 'Regulating Online TV and Radio Broadcasting' (April 2018) <http://www.europarl.europa.eu/RegData/etudes/BRIE/2018/620217/EPRS_BRI(2018)620217_EN.pdf>.

[39] Menting, *Industry Codes of Conduct in a Multi-Layered Dutch Private Law* (n 24) 260–61.

[40] See PWJ Verbruggen, 'Private Regulation in EU Better Regulation. Past Performance and Future Promises' (2017) 19 European Journal of Law Reform 121, 128. Also, C Cecot and others, 'An Evaluation of the Quality of Impact Assessment in the European Union with Lessons for the US and the EU', AEI-Brookings Joint Center for Regulatory Studies Working Paper 2007 No 07-09 <https://ssrn.com/abstract=984473>, who note that private regulation is increasingly considered in EU impact assessments as an alternative to legislation but also that, if an alternative is chosen, it is often the alternative of 'not regulating'.

[41] Verbruggen, 'Private Regulation in EU Better Regulation' (n 40) 130.

[42] Unfair Commercial Practices Directive (n 28) Art 6(2).

[43] Case C-109/17 *Bankia SA v Juan Carlos Marí Merino and others*, ECLI:EU:C:2018:735. The case concerned Art 10, which prescribes that '[t]his Directive does not exclude the control, which Member States may encourage, of unfair commercial practices by code owners and recourse to such bodies by the persons or organisations referred to in Article 11 if proceedings before such bodies are in addition to the court or administrative proceedings referred to in that Article'.

The overall conclusion on the use of codes of conduct, however, does not have to be so bleak. First, the empirical studies carried out in relation to the EU's Better Regulation agenda have only taken account of the use of private regulation as an instrument for EU policy-making. Therefore, they do not take account of issues falling outside the competence of the European Union which might be regulated through private regulation, perhaps in combination with, or at the level of, national law. The rise of private regulation in relation to the platform economy would seem to fall outside the reach of EU law in some respects, for example in relation to prosumers or the protection of those buying in peer-to-peer transactions rather than as a consumer. In that context, private regulation is increasing, and its quality may well improve if a mix of public and private law, EU law, and national law is pursued.[44] Second, other studies, like Menting's, indicate that the use of private regulation and the recognition of codes of conduct as legally binding has increased in certain national systems. For platforms this means that the use of codes of conduct can be an effective means of regulating the behaviour of users which, under certain conditions, is considered legally valid.

My argument in this regard goes beyond procedural conditions for the legal validity of codes of conduct. Following the line set out in the earlier chapters of this book, lawmaking through private regulation should also be part of the substantive deliberation between lawmakers. Although practice has relied on procedural mechanisms for establishing the legal validity of codes of conduct, the platform economy is largely devoid of such mechanisms as many issues between platforms and users are resolved outside the courts. In the absence of judicial assessment of codes, it is submitted, the substantive model might take on new significance as it provides an alternative way of establishing legal validity that has found recognition in scholarship. It is important then, that the substance of such codes can be monitored to safeguard the observance of core objectives and values of EU law and national laws. Furthermore, the practical framework for deliberation between lawmakers will have to facilitate the exchange, comparison, discussion, and potential adaptation of substantive rules.

III. Co-Regulation: A Memorandum of Understanding

Another instrument for regulating online platforms can be co-regulation, that is, the cooperation between platform operators and legislators or regulators to establish rules for a specific problem. The platform economy has until now in Europe remained fairly un-regulated due to the wish of the EU legislator to enable innovation by new market entrants.[45] While legislation is slow to emerge, cooperation

[44] The European Union is currently hesitant to regulate; see section IV below.

[45] European Commission, Communication from the Commission to the European Parliament, the Council, the European Economic and Social Committee and the Committee of the Regions, 'Online

between the European Commission and online platforms has led to a few instruments that seek to regulate specific problems in the platform economy. They are an EU Internet Forum that seeks to curb terrorist content on the Internet, a Code of Conduct on Illegal Online Hate Speech, a Memorandum of Understanding on the Sale of Counterfeit Goods over the Internet,[46] and, more recently, a Product Safety Pledge.[47] In particular the third initiative, on counterfeit goods, is relevant for the development of rules on transparent and fair behaviour, and potential liability, of online platforms. It is also an illustrative example of coordination of lawmaking between public and private lawmaking actors.

The first version of the Memorandum of Understanding (henceforth the MoU) on the sale of counterfeit goods precedes the EU's broader involvement in the Digital Single Market. It dates from 2011 and was intended as a specific response to the problematic enforcement of intellectual property rights concerning products advertised and sold on the internet. Rather than burdening rights holders and other stakeholders with enforcement through litigation, the European Commission sought to establish a mechanism for the proactive tracking and terminating of rights infringements. It opted for dialogues with stakeholders, in particular online platform operators and rights holders, with the aim of developing voluntary agreements on workable and practical solutions for enforcement of intellectual property rights on the Internet.[48] This dialogue resulted in the MoU on the sale of counterfeit goods over the Internet in 2011, which was signed by thirty-three companies and trade associations, including Amazon, eBay, Nike, Adidas, Lego, Mattel, Microsoft, Lacoste, Burberry, Procter & Gamble, and Unilever.[49]

An evaluation of the MoU in 2013 revealed a number of best practices but also found that the assessment of the effectiveness of the instrument was difficult to measure without more precise benchmarks. A new memorandum was drafted which included specific 'key performance indicators' (KPIs) for assessing the

Platforms and the Digital Single Market. Opportunities and Challenges for Europe', COM(2016) 288 final, which expresses a preference for self-regulation by platforms and an intention to investigate limited regulatory action to safeguard transparency; 5, 12–15.

[46] European Commission, 'Digital Single Market: Commission calls for swift adoption of key proposals and maps out challenges ahead' (Press release, Brussels 10 May 2017) <http://europa.eu/rapid/press-release_IP-17-1232_en.htm>.

[47] European Commission, 'European Commission and four online marketplaces sign a Product Safety Pledge to remove dangerous products' (Press release, 25 June 2018) <http://europa.eu/rapid/press-release_IP-18-4247_en.htm>. The signatories are Alibaba, Amazon, eBay, and the French platform Rakuten. For the full text of the pledge, see European Commission, 'Product Safety Pledge. Voluntary commitment of online marketplaces with respect to the safety of non-food consumer products sold online by third party sellers' <https://ec.europa.eu/info/sites/info/files/voluntary_commitment_document_4signatures3-web.pdf>.

[48] European Commission, Report from the Commission to the European Parliament and the Council on the Functioning of the Memorandum of Understanding on the Sale of Counterfeit Goods via the Internet, COM(2013) 209 final, 5.

[49] Memorandum of Understanding on the Sale of Counterfeit Goods over the Internet (Brussels, 4 May 2011); signed version at <http://ec.europa.eu/DocsRoom/documents/10468/>.

effectiveness of the MoU in an objective, reliable, and transparent manner.[50] These were, for example, the number of search results that link to an offer of counterfeit goods, or the number of listings that were removed as a result of an alleged infringement of the right owners' intellectual property rights.[51] The revised MoU of 2016 was signed by nineteen parties: five Internet platforms, eight rights holders, and six associations. They include, amongst others, Alibaba, Amazon, eBay, Adidas, Chanel, Lacoste, Nike, and Procter & Gamble.[52]

The MoU on counterfeit goods resulting from the dialogue that the European Commission engaged in with stakeholders is an inspiring example of the way in which cooperation between public and private lawmakers can be encouraged and facilitated. It seems to have reached promising results until now. Both the 2011 and the 2016 MoUs have effectively contributed to decreasing the number of counterfeit goods on online marketplaces.[53] Moreover, the dialogue with private actors was set up in such a way that they had ample space for developing their own methods for the enforcement of intellectual property rights, within the boundaries of what could reasonably achieved in terms of monitoring, costs, and so on.[54] Therefore, these actors appear to have been able to give voice to their public autonomy, that is their ability to self-legislate. In terms of process, this dialogue between public and private actors is at first glance an example of how lawmaking in a strong legal pluralist context can work in practice.

The proof of the pudding is in the eating, however, and it remains to be seen whether the normative aspect of lawmaking in European private law, as advocated in this book, has also been met. The question is whether the resulting norms, rules, and practices safeguard the objectives and values of EU and national laws. I will consider that question in the next chapter. It is clear, however, also from a more general perspective, that the signatories of the MoU have a commitment to the objectives of EU law. Paragraphs 31–33 of the MoU, in both the 2011 and the 2016 versions, stipulate minimum rules in relation to consumer confidence, information,

[50] European Commission, Commission Staff Working Document 'Overview of the Functioning of the Memorandum of Understanding on the Sale of Counterfeit Goods via the Internet. Accompanying document to the Communication from the Commission to the European Parliament, the Council and the European Economic and Social Committee: A Balanced IP Enforcement System Responding to Today's Societal Challenges, COM(2017) 707 final', SWD(2017) 430 final, 1.

[51] SWD(2017) 430 final (n 50) 3–4.

[52] For a full list see SWD(2017) 430 final (n 50), Appendix I. See also Memorandum of Understanding on the Sale of Counterfeit Goods over the Internet (Brussels, 21 June 2016); signed version at <http://ec.europa.eu/DocsRoom/documents/18023/attachments/1/translations/>.

[53] See <https://ec.europa.eu/growth/industry/intellectual-property/enforcement/memorandum-understanding-sale-counterfeit-goods-internet_en>, with reference to SWD(2017) 430 final (n 50) and COM(2013) 209 final (n 48). Efforts to control online offers for counterfeit goods have also been made through consumer education; see European Consumer Centres' Network (ECC-Net), 'The Impact of Counterfeiting on Online Consumer Rights in Europe' (March 2017).

[54] Notably, proactive and preventive measures that rights holders and Internet platforms have committed to under the MoU are only required for as far as they are 'commercially reasonable' and 'technically feasible'. See SWD(2017) 430 final (n 50) 8, and paras 6, 9, 15, 16, and 27 of the 2016 MoU.

and protection. These rules intend to protect consumers against losses suffered when they fall for a scam and buy counterfeit products from websites. Internet platforms in those cases allow customers to keep the counterfeit goods, and many offer a refund or a guarantee of some sort. Platforms that act as sellers themselves, moreover, are obliged under Directive 99/44/EC on consumer sales to offer consumers a refund or replacement of the counterfeit goods.[55] At least on paper, therefore, core objectives are acknowledged by the signatories of the MoU.

IV. Legislation and Regulation

It has already been said that public regulation of the platform economy is slow to emerge. Still, the European legislator as well as national legislators and regulators are not principally against regulating online platforms, and they have expressed a willingness to introduce regulation where it is required. The first examples of regulation have started to appear.[56]

In its 2016 Communication concerning online platforms, the European Commission identified several problems with regard to transparency towards businesses and consumers, for example in relation to payments for listings of search engine results, the identification of the actual supplier of services or products, possible misleading practices including fake reviews, and lack of transparency on use of data and search results which could harm suppliers' business activities.[57] It carried out a fact-finding exercise in relation to B2B practices in the online environment, which resulted in a proposal for an EU regulation on fairness and transparency in platform-to-business (P2B) relationships.[58] The Regulation was adopted in 2019. It intends to fill a gap in the EU framework for consumer and competition law concerning misleading or unfair information. Whilst consumers in B2C relationships

[55] Directive 99/44/EC on certain aspects of the sale of consumer goods and associated guarantees [1999] OJ L171/12 (Consumer Sales Directive). The Directive will be replaced by Directive (EU) 2019/771 on certain aspects concerning contracts for the sale of goods, and repealing Directive 1999/44 [2019] OJ L136/28. The new Directive should be implemented by the EU Member States by 1 July 2021, and apply to consumer sales contracts concluded from 1 January 2022.

[56] I use the term 'regulation' here as a general reference to legislation and other forms of public regulation originating from EU and national legislatures, as well as regulators at other levels of government. This corresponds with the finding of Koop and Lodge that, even if the term 'regulation' is often not explicitly defined in scholarship, it is generally agreed that 'prototype regulation' 'is characterized by interventions that are intentional and direct—involving binding standard-setting, monitoring, and sanctioning—and exercised by public-sector actors on the economic activities of private-sector actors.' C Koop and M Lodge, 'What is Regulation? An Interdisciplinary Concept Analysis' (2017) 11 Regulation and Governance 95, 105.

[57] Communication on Online Platforms 2016 (n 45) 10, 12.

[58] European Commission, 'Proposal for a Regulation of the European Parliament and of the Council on promoting fairness and transparency for business users of online intermediary services', COM(2018) 238 final. The Regulation was adopted on 20 June 2019. See Regulation (EU) 2019/1150 on promoting fairness and transparency for business users of online intermediation services [2019] OJ L186/57 (P2B Regulation).

are protected against unfair business practices and unfair contract terms through harmonized rules laid down in EU directives,[59] businesses enjoy only the protection against misleading and comparative advertising of Directive 2006/114/EC.[60] That Directive protects against misleading advertising but it does not cover some problematic business practices that occur between online platforms and their business users. Examples are: unexplained changes in terms and conditions without prior notice; the delisting of goods or services and the suspension of accounts without a clear statement of reasons; lack of transparency related to the ranking of goods and services and of the undertaking offering them; unclear conditions for access to and use of data collected by providers; and a lack of transparency regarding the favouring of providers' own competing services.[61] Further, even in the absence of a contractual relationship, business users can be affected by the ranking practices of online search engines.[62] The Regulation can be seen as a significant step towards the protection of businesses against unfair trading practices in the platform economy. Saliently, the Regulation covers some of the same problems that were identified earlier in studies on B2B unfair commercial practices carried out under the aegis of the European Commission,[63] but which had not led to legislative action.

Further, the EU legislature in April 2018 presented a New Deal for Consumers, which aims to amend a number of existing EU consumer law directives.[64] A Directive based on the part of the New Deal dealing with the modernization of consumer law was adopted in 2019 and should be implemented into national laws by 28 November 2021, and applied from 28 May 2022.[65] The Directive contains

[59] In particular the Unfair Commercial Practices Directive, or UCPD, (n 28), and Directive 1993/13/EEC on unfair terms in consumer contracts [1993] OJ L95/29 (Unfair Contract Terms Directive). The UCPD also allows actions by competitors against traders guilty of unfair practices, but only provided that consumer interests have been harmed. See Art 11 of the Directive, and Joint Cases C-261/07 *VTB-VAB NV v Total Belgium NV* and C-299/07 *Galatea BVBA v Sanoma Magazines Belgium NV* [2009] ECR I-2949, ECLI:EU:C:2009:244; Case C-304/08 *Zentrale zur Bekämpfung unlauteren Wettbewerbs eV v Plus Warenhandelsgesellschaft mbH* [2010] ECR I-00217, ECLI:EU:C:2010:12; Case C-540/08 *Mediaprint Zeitungs- und Zeitschriftenverlag GmbH & Co KG v Österreich-Zeitungsverlag GmbH* [2010] ECR I-10909, ECLI:EU:C:2010:660. See also V Mak, 'Full Harmonization in European Private Law: A Two-Tracked Concept' (2012) 20 European Review of Private Law 213; B Keirsbilck, *The New European Law of Unfair Commercial Practices and Competition Law* (Hart Publishing 2011) 246 ff.

[60] Directive on Misleading and Comparative Advertising (n 38).

[61] See P2B Regulation (n 58).

[62] ibid.

[63] See A Renda and others, 'Study on the Legal Framework Covering Business-to-Business Unfair Trading Practices in the Retail Supply Chain. Final Report' (European Union 2014) <http://ec.europa.eu/internal_market/retail/docs/140711-study-utp-legal-framework_en.pdf>; European Commission, 'Green Paper on Unfair Trading Practices in the Business-to-Business Food and Non-Food Supply Chain in Europe', COM(2013) 37 final.

[64] European Commission, 'Proposal for a Directive of the European Parliament and of the Council amending Council Directive 93/13/EEC of 5 April 1993, Directive 98/6/EC of the European Parliament and of the Council, Directive 2005/29/EC of the European Parliament and of the Council and Directive 2011/83/EU of the European Parliament and of the Council as regards better enforcement and modernisation of EU consumer protection rules' COM(2018) 185.

[65] Directive (EU) 2019/2161 as regards the better enforcement and modernisation of Union consumer protection rules [2019] OJ L328/7 (Modernisation Directive).

some provisions concerning online platforms. The most conspicuous provision is perhaps the amendment of the Consumer Rights Directive, adding a new Article 6a(1)(b), which imposes an obligation on online marketplaces to indicate whether a supplier is acting in a professional capacity or as a private party. The online marketplace should establish that classification on the basis of a declaration from the supplier. This provision, already included in the initial proposal for a Modernisation Directive, has attracted criticism for being difficult to use in practice. Without objective criteria indicating in which circumstances a supplier is considered to act in a professional manner, it will be very hard for suppliers to determine when they cross the threshold from 'hobbyist' to professional trader.[66] That point is underlined by recent case law from the CJEU which held that a person who placed eight separate advertisements on an online platform should not automatically be considered a 'trader' in the sense of Directive 2005/29/EC on unfair commercial practices or Directive 2011/83/EU on consumer rights. It is up to national courts, on a case-by-case basis, to assess whether a person is 'acting for purposes related to his trade, business, craft or profession' and hence a trader.[67] Interestingly, the European Law Institute (ELI) Draft Model Rules on Online Platforms seek to solve the problem by imposing a more extensive duty on platform operators 'to take adequate measures to prevent traders from appearing on the platform as non-traders', which entails that they may rely on information provided by the supplier as to its status 'unless the platform operator knew or ought to have known that this information is incorrect'.[68] The potential relevance of the ELI Draft Model Rules is discussed in more detail below and in Chapter 9.[69]

Furthermore, it is unclear what consequences a failure to comply with this requirement will have for the online marketplace or for the supplier. It may be that the (also new) sanctions of the CRD apply, or that such a failure omits to a misleading omission under Article 6(1)(g) of Directive 2005/29/EC on unfair commercial practices, but whether those are the intended consequences is unclear.[70] The Modernisation Directive also imposes a duty on online marketplaces to inform consumers whether consumer rights stemming from EU consumer legislation apply or not to the contract concluded (Article 6a(1)(c)). While that would

[66] C Twigg-Flesner, 'Bad Hand? The "New Deal" for EU Consumers' (2018) 15 Zeitschrift für das Privatrecht der Europäischen Union 166, 172.

[67] Case C-105/17 *Komisia za zashtita na potrebitelite v Evelina Kamenova*, ECLI:EU:C:2018:808, at [37]. The Court, following Advocate General Spuznar's Opinion, did identify a number of circumstances that might indicate that a person is acting as a trader, such as whether the sale on the platform was carried out in an organized manner, whether it was intended to generate a profit, and whether the seller had technical information and expertise relating to the products which she offered for sale which the consumer did not necessarily have. See para 38 of the Court's judgment.

[68] Draft Instrument of the European Law Institute (ELI), *Model Rules on Online Platforms*, version voted on by ELI members on 28 February 2020, Art 14(3).

[69] See below, p 144 ff; Chapter 9, p 214.

[70] Twigg-Flesner, 'Bad Hand? The "New Deal" for EU Consumers' (n 66). Compare also, on offline sales, Case C-149/15 *Sabrina Wathelet v Garage Bietheres & Fils SPRL*, ECLI:EU:C:2016:840.

practically be a useful gesture, the provision is in essence superfluous, as the consumer dealing with a professional trader is by definition entering into a B2C transaction and therefore enjoys the protection of EU consumer law. The significance of these provisions however remains to be seen once the Directive is transposed into national laws and its rules take effect in practice. In the European Union, only Denmark currently has legislation on this point, stipulating that '[i]f two private parties enter into a contract with the assistance of an active third party (an intermediary), the contract between the seller and the buyer is considered a B2C contract if the customer is a consumer'. The seller in that case has to comply with consumer law and, notably, some information requirements stemming from consumer regulation are extended to the platform.[71] The model rules developed by a working group of the ELI, discussed in the next section, also introduce provisions concerning the liability of platforms. These provisions could potentially have far-reaching effects on platform liability, albeit that the rules are non-binding and require voluntary adoption by the parties involved.[72]

Also at the national level, initiatives have been taken to regulate online platforms. In Europe, the frontrunners in this domain are France and Italy. France adopted a legislative act, the *Loi Lemaire* or *Loi pour la République numérique*, on 7 October 2016 to deal with a number of issues concerning the digital society. The Act deals with privacy and data protection, the right to be forgotten, digital inheritance, data portability, and data storage. For the platform economy, the *Loi pour la République numérique* includes important provisions on transparency and fairness towards consumers.[73] It contains specific provisions, amending the French consumer code, that oblige platform operators to provide their non-professional users with transparent information on their terms of use and some context-specific issues. That includes information on the ways in which the placement of listings on a website is determined, on sponsorship or other financial links between platforms and suppliers, and on the status of the other contracting party (ie whether they are a professional or a non-professional trader).[74] The means by which platforms should ensure transparency were further clarified by two legislative decrees in October 2017, entering into force on 1 January 2018.[75] The required information

[71] M Jull Sørensen, 'Private Law Perspectives on Platform Services: Uber. A Business Model in Search of a New Contractual Legal Frame?' (2016) 5 Journal of European Consumer and Market Law 15, 17.

[72] Draft Instrument of the European Law Institute, *Model Rules on Online Platforms*, version available on 28 February 2020, Arts 19 and 20. For a discussion on the function of model rules, see section V below, and Chapter 9, p 214.

[73] Loi No 2016-1321 du 7 octobre 2016 pour une République numérique. The full text of the law (in French) is available at <https://www.legifrance.gouv.fr/affichTexte.do;jsessionid=CCB0E73C69E80F3D28A0914D8E2FD0F6.tplgfr23s_3?cidTexte=JORFTEXT000033202746&categorieLien=id>.

[74] Art L 111-7 of the *Code de la consommation*.

[75] Décret No 2017-1434 du 29 septembre 2017 relatif aux obligations d'information des opérateurs de plateformes numériques; and Décret No 2017-1435 du 29 septembre 2017 relatif à la fixation d'un seuil de connexions à partir duquel les opérateurs de plateformes en ligne élaborent et diffusent des bonnes pratiques pour renforcer la loyauté, la claret et la transparence des informations transmises aux consommateurs. The text of the decrees (in French) is available at <https://www.legifrance.gouv.fr/

should be made available on an easily accessible part of the platform's website, and it should be reachable from every page of that website.[76] Non-compliance with the rules can be sanctioned by the *Commission nationale informatique et libertés (Cnil)*, the French data protection authority, with a fine of €3 million, which is a multiplication by twenty of the previous maximum fine.[77]

While the *Loi pour la République numérique* and its accompanying decrees appear to place significant transparency obligations on platform operators, one caveat is in order: the law only applies to platforms whose website is accessed by 5 million individual visitors per month.[78] That means that consumers can only rely on these specific information rights in relation to large platforms, such as Amazon or Airbnb. In relation to smaller platforms, they will nonetheless still have the general protection that consumers enjoy against misleading practices or unfair terms.[79] An explanation for that difference is that the legislator wishes to maintain space for innovation, which often occurs in its initial stages through the activities of small(er) start-ups. Burdening such small or medium-sized traders with additional information duties might stifle innovation.[80]

In Italy, legislation has also been proposed in relation to the sharing economy. The Sharing Economy Bill of 2016 aims to lay down rules on fairness, taxation, compensation, and consumer protection. It proposes that all platforms should sign up to a sharing economy register and provide documents for the approval of the Italian competition authority AGCM.[81] These documents should contain, inter alia, the terms and conditions that the platform applies to its contracts with consumers. Furthermore, for security reasons the Bill prescribes that if payments are made to the platform they should always be made electronically, and user profiles need to be verifiable through several mechanisms in order to prevent the use of fake profiles.[82] The bill seeks to impose tax obligations on platform operators, which the Italian revenue is thought to miss out on when platforms operate outside the framework of existing regulation, for example in the markets for taxi services

affichTexte.do;jsessionid=CCB0E73C69E80F3D28A0914D8E2FD0F6.tplgfr23s_3?cidTexte=JORFTEXT000035720908&dateTexte=>; and at: <https://www.legifrance.gouv.fr/affichTexte.do;jsessionid=CCB0E73C69E80F3D28A0914D8E2FD0F6.tplgfr23s_3?cidTexte=JORFTEXT000035720925&dateTexte=>.

[76] Décret No 2017-1434 (n 75).

[77] See <https://www.economie.gouv.fr/republique-numerique>. The Cnil may also, if an infringer does not mend its practices after a warning, opt for a publication of the offence, or an injunction.

[78] Décret No 2017-1435 (n 75).

[79] In France, the Unfair Commercial Practices Directive (n 28) is implemented in the *Code de la consommation* (Art L 121-1 ff), and so is the Unfair Contract Terms Directive (n 59) (Art L 212-1).

[80] B Bozdoganoglu, 'Tax Issues Arise from a New Economic Model: Sharing Economy' (2017) 8 International Journal of Business and Social Science 119, 132. See also Camera dei Deputati, Atto Camera: 3564, Proposed Sharing Economy Bill, Art 3.

[81] ibid. See also P Grifoni and others, 'Sharing Economy: Business Models and Regulatory Landscape in the Mediterranean Areas' (2018) 11 International Business Research 62, 74.

[82] Camera dei Deputati, Atto Camera: 3564, Proposed Sharing Economy Bill, Art 4.

or vacation rentals.[83] Fines for non-compliance with the rules can be significant: a platform operator may become liable for 25 per cent of its income generated during the time that the platform operated without a registration.[84]

Notably, not all (former) European jurisdictions are in favour of regulating the platform economy. The UK House of Lords, in a 2016 report, recommended for now not to intervene with platforms through regulation.[85] The report considered the competition, consumer law, and data protection aspects of online platforms. Experts heard by the House of Lords committee in its inquiry confirmed that the platform economy by its nature disrupts existing law. They are quoted as submitting that '[o]ur view is that legal disruption is not an accident of the platform economy, it is a core feature. Digital platforms obviously challenge the law, and this is a key feature and consequence of their operations. They like to show how the law is out-of-date with the new economy'.[86] Other witnesses emphasized the risk of stifling innovation when choosing to regulate the platform economy, pointing in particular at the burden and cost that regulation might impose on small and medium-sized enterprises and European start-ups.[87] Most witnesses, however, also underlined the importance of protecting fundamental rights of citizens, and the need for regulation to safeguard those rights.[88] Whilst the House of Lords committee rejects general regulation of the platform economy due to the risk of stifling innovation, it accepts that specific regulation is needed to secure consumer protection, data protection, and competition law so that they are sufficiently robust to protect the public interest and to deter abusive behaviour.[89]

The House of Lords report paints a balanced, realistic picture of the stakes that are at play in the debate on whether or not to regulate the platform economy. The arguments weighed here can explain why many European jurisdictions for now have not adopted horizontal regulation for the platform economy. Notably, these arguments are very similar to the ones considered by the European Commission in its 2016 Communication on online platforms. They fit within the liberal political ideology that underlies the EU's objectives and values.[90] However, the reticent attitude of the legislature creates a greater space for lawmaking by other actors, some of which may require monitoring to ensure that core objectives and values of EU law are safeguarded. In the European legal order, both the EU and national legislatures are bound to have a role in that process.

[83] Bozdoganoglu, 'Tax Issues Arise from a New Economic Model: Sharing Economy' (n 80) 132.

[84] ibid.

[85] House of Lords, Select Committee on European Union, 10th Report of Session 2015–16, 'Online Platforms and the Digital Single Market' (April 2016).

[86] ibid 90, quoting A Strowel and W Vergote.

[87] ibid 91, quoting A Ezrachi and M Stucke, as well as cloud storage provider Skyscape Cloud Services Ltd.

[88] ibid 91, citing European consumer organization BEUC, amongst others.

[89] ibid 91–92.

[90] On which, see Chapter 4.

V. Soft Law

In the absence of, or potentially as preliminary to the regulation of certain aspects of the platform economy at least one soft law initiative has been instigated: the ELI project on Model Rules on Online Intermediary Platforms.[91] The project has its origins in Osnabrück, where researchers affiliated with the European Legal Studies Institute (ELSI) of the university took the first steps towards identifying which regulation may be needed in the platform economy. In the triangular relationship between a platform and the parties who contract with each other through the intermediary platform, the contractual relationship and potential liability of parties towards each other is already fairly well covered by EU law and national laws. If the relationship is one between a business and a consumer, harmonized rules of European consumer law provide a range of rights and remedies for sales and services. For B2B contracts and C2C contracts, the general rules of national private laws provide solutions. Where rules are lacking, however, is in relation to the other two sides of the triangle: the position of the platform towards the two contracting parties who use the platform as an intermediary. The Osnabrück group concentrated on this area in its initial Discussion Draft of a Directive on Online Intermediary Platforms.[92] The project was later adopted by the ELI and continued under the chairmanship of Hans Schulte-Nölke, together with project reporters Christoph Busch, Gerhard Dannemann, Aneta Wiewiórowska-Domagalska, and Fryderyk Zoll.

Several aspects of this project are of interest from a lawmaking perspective. First, like earlier soft law instruments, the drafting of new rules is instigated by a group of legal academics and then continued under the aegis of a European institution. That process was also the route by which the Principles of European Law (PEL) were developed as projects of the Study Group on a European Civil Code.[93] The Principles were later used as a basis for the European Commission's academic project for a Draft Common Frame of Reference (DCFR),[94] together with rules developed by the Acquis Group[95] and the Principles of European Contract Law

[91] See <https://www.europeanlawinstitute.eu/projects-publications/current-projects-feasibility-studies-and-other-activities/current-projects/online-platforms/>.

[92] C Busch and others, 'Discussion Draft of a Directive on Online Intermediary Platforms' (2016) 5 Journal of European Consumer and Market Law 164.

[93] For an overview, see H Beale, 'European Contract Law: The Common Frame of Reference and Beyond' in C Twigg-Flessner (ed), *Cambridge Companion to European Union Private Law* (CUP 2010) 116.

[94] Study Group on a European Civil Code and European Research Group on Existing EC Private Law (Acquis Group), *Principles, Definitions and Model Rules of European Private Law. Draft Common Frame of Reference (DCFR)* (full edition, Sellier 2009).

[95] European Research Group on the Existing EC Private Law (Acquis Group), *Contract I: Pre-contractual Obligations, Conclusion of Contract, Unfair Terms* (Sellier 2007) and *Contract II: General Provisions, Delivery of Goods, Package Travel and Payment Services* (Sellier 2009).

(PECL).[96] Incidentally, many of the members of the original academic groups continued their work once the draft rules became part of the Commission's project to develop a DCFR. The same is the case with the Osnabrück/ELI project on online intermediary platforms.[97] This indicates an interplay between private and public lawmakers, with advantages from both sides. The private origin of rules makes that they can be developed fairly openly, initially outside the framework of formal legislation and the rules prescribed there, and with the direct input of private stakeholders. The adoption by a public lawmaker at a later stage can channel the rules into a framework for formal lawmaking, thereby giving them the legitimacy of a democratic lawmaking procedure. While the ELI is not a formal lawmaking institution, it was designed as a counterpart to the American Law Institute (ALI), which has an enormous standing as an independent scholarly lawmaking organization in the United States.[98] Rules promulgated through the ELI can therefore perhaps also be regarded as publicly legitimized. It may then be hoped that the Model Rules for online intermediary platforms fare better than the DCFR, which has remained an academic text with little practical uptake.[99]

Further, the initial Discussion Draft for online intermediary platforms aimed at the development of an EU Directive, while the project has under the ELI been reframed as the development of model rules. The difference is significant: one implies the introduction of formal legislation, that is, likely to include mandatory rules, whilst the other aims to provide parties with a set of rules that they can incorporate into their contract if they so wish. This difference in nature is likely to have an impact on the substance of rules. The drafters of model rules have more freedom to include rules that, for example, allocate liability towards an online platform, since it is possible in contract to divert from the default rules laid down in existing legislation.[100] The drafters of new legislation will have to consider whether they wish to amend existing rules, and whether they believe it is politically feasible to have new legislation to that effect adopted. In the case of online platforms, what

[96] Commission on European Contract Law, *Principles of European Contract Law. Parts I and II* (partly revised edn, Kluwer 1999) and *Part III* (Kluwer 2002) <https://www.jus.uio.no/lm/eu.contract.principles.parts.1.to.3.2002/>.

[97] For a list of participants, see the ELI website referred to in n 91.

[98] The ALI derived that standing from the regular citation of its Restatements by the courts; see L Liebman, 'The American Law Institute: A Model for the New Europe?' in F Cafaggi and H Muir-Watt, *Making European Private Law. Governance Design* (Edward Elgar 2008) 209, 214.

[99] Its greatest recognition may be that the DCFR has in a significant number of national court cases been referred to as a source of European principles of civil law. G Kalouta, 'The Draft Common Frame of Reference in the Courts' in M Andenas and D Fairgrieve (eds), *Courts and Comparative Law* (OUP 2015) 696 discusses approximately thirty cases. Citations by the European Court of Justice, however, are limited to seven citations by the Advocates General of the CJEU, five of which are from Advocate General Trstenjak. See Kalouta at 711–15.

[100] For example, the host exemption laid down in Arts 14 and 15 of the E-Commerce Directive (n 38).

is problematic is that it is not even clear in many jurisdictions if and how existing legislation applies to the relationship between platforms and their users.[101]

In sum, soft law has a few advantages over public regulation, in particular that it is developed (often) in closer contact with the stakeholders who will be affected by the rules. Also, since the rules are not binding unless parties incorporate them into their contract, the drafters of soft law principles and model rules have more leeway to decide upon the substance of rules. This mechanism for lawmaking therefore provides a tool primarily for private actors to give shape to their legal relationships, of course always within the limits of mandatory rules of national or EU law if they apply.[102]

VI. Reputation Systems

In the platform economy a regulatory function can also be fulfilled by a group of private actors that typically does not actively engage in norm creation: consumers. The enforcement of consumer law is often seen as a function of regulators, who can remove and prevent illegal or fraudulent traders from operating in the market, and ensure the compliance of traders with the law and associated codes.[103] In the platform economy, however, consumers can quite easily contribute to the monitoring and correction of trader behaviour through so-called reputation systems.[104] Reputation systems are mechanisms that enable users to share information about the transactional behaviour of other users, and of the quality of products or services offered through a platform.[105] They can take the form of online reviews that can be posted on a platform's website, or of star ratings to indicate how satisfied users were with products or with the services rendered by the platform or by other users. Not only do these mechanisms serve a trust function in the platform economy, providing information about quality and reliability to users who otherwise do not know each other,[106] they also generate information that platform operators can use

[101] For an overview of issues concerning the platform economy, including problems of classification and liability, see the special issue (2016) 5(1) of the Journal of European Consumer and Market Law (EuCML).

[102] See for a further discussion of the role of model rules in a legal pluralist constellation of lawmakers Chapter 9, p 214.

[103] C Hodges, 'The Consumer as Regulator' in D Leczykiewicz and S Weatherill (eds), *The Images of the Consumer in EU Law. Legislation, Free Movement and Competition Law* (Hart Publishing 2016) 245, 245.

[104] ibid 250, noting that many businesses maintain consumer care departments that seek to obtain information from consumers on the quality and safety of products, which can be fed back into the production process. See also C Busch, 'Crowdsourcing Consumer Confidence. How to Regulate Online Rating and Review Systems in the Collaborative Economy' in A De Franceschi (ed), *European Contract Law and the Digital Single Market. The Implications of the Digital Revolution* (Intersentia 2016) 223.

[105] ibid 226.

[106] See Lobel, 'The Law of the Platform' (n 9) 146–48. Also, Sundararajan, *The Sharing Economy* (n 1) 60 ff.

to assess and, where required, adapt their products or services. Since the information is posted online and available for all the world within seconds, reputation systems can be a powerful tool for bringing attention to bad practices of online traders and 'naming and shaming' them into compliance with regulation. It has been said that with the rise of the Internet: 'Reputations will count as never before. So possibilities for power shift to the citizen-consumer.'[107] Consumers therefore, through online reputation systems, can become active participants in the monitoring of trader behaviour.

Notably, consumers are not the only ones who can use reputation systems as a means to support trust in the platform economy. Users of online platforms can also include professional traders. They may, for example, post reviews on the reliability of consumers who purchase their products, such as with regard to the quality and speed of communication and overall attitude towards facilitating the delivery and receipt of goods.[108] However, the regulatory function of traders is likely to be of less relevance in the platform economy than that of consumers, if only for the reason that traders are often on the offer side of the market and therefore the party whose performance needs to be monitored. Still, like consumers they may use online review systems to rate and influence the behaviour of online platforms.

Besides this regulatory function, reputation systems can also have an influence on lawmaking. The information posted by users can, from a socio-legal perspective, provide lawmakers with data on consumer expectations with regard to the quality of goods, services, communication, and other aspects of platforms' and consumers' behaviour. With regard to the latter, consumer behavioural studies have in recent decades gained importance as tools for lawmaking, in particular as a means to test whether the information paradigm of consumer law works, or whether it needs refinement or even replacement with another model that takes better account of cognitive limitations in human decision-making.[109] The increasing use of data analysis methods in legal practice and legal scholarship, moreover, might open up new pathways for the processing of data from online reviews in order to obtain useful insights on consumer expectations that can be fed back into lawmaking processes.[110]

There is also, however, the question whether reputation systems themselves need to be regulated. Practice has revealed that in order for reputation systems to operate satisfactorily certain conditions need to be fulfilled.[111] First, the system itself must be transparent. This means that it must be made clear to users, for example through

[107] M Scammell, 'The Internet and Civic Engagement: The Age of the Citizen-Consumer' (2000) 17 Political Communication 351.

[108] An example is eBay.

[109] For an analysis of the impact of behavioural studies on lawmaking in Europe, see A Alemanno and A-L Sibony, *Nudge and the Law. A European Perspective* (Hart Publishing 2015).

[110] V Mak, TFE Tjong Tjin Tai, and A Berlee (eds), *Research Handbook on Data Science and Law* (Edward Elgar 2018).

[111] See Busch, 'Crowdsourcing Consumer Confidence' (n 104) 234 ff.

online accessible policies, how reviews are processed, and whether they are subjected to any kind of review before publication. The French *Loi pour la République numérique* has introduced obligations of this kind in Article 24(2). Further, the system design can influence the quality and reliability of reviews themselves, and certain aspects will therefore have to be taken into account in designing an online reputation system. For the submission of reviews, a choice can be made between an open or closed system, meaning a system through which anyone can post reviews or a system that only allows users to post after a confirmed transaction.[112] That choice influences the reliability of reviews. After all, if anyone can post, there is no guarantee that reviewers have actually visited the apartment, used the taxi service, ordered the book, eaten at the restaurant, and so on, before writing a review about their experience. Other aspects to consider in the design of a reputation system are whether anonymous reviews should be allowed, whether reciprocal reviewing can be minimized so that users are not influenced by what their counterparty says about them,[113] and whether paid reviews should be admitted.[114]

The question whether or not regulate reputation systems is on the agenda of public and private regulators at national and EU level. The Danish Ombudsman has introduced Guidelines on the Publication of User Reviews,[115] and several national consumer associations have adopted their own recommendations.[116] The ELI working group for Model Rules on Online Intermediary Platforms has also drafted a proposed rule on this matter. A first version was published in Article 8 of its Discussion Draft and stipulated a duty on the platform operator to 'provide information about the modalities of collection, processing and publication of ratings and reviews' and to 'comply with standards of professional diligence'.[117] That rule was inspired by the co-regulatory approach that has for many years been used in the area of product safety, according to which a general clause in legislation is fleshed in more legal and technical detail by the European standardization bodies.[118] The

[112] ibid 235.

[113] Studies have revealed that the quality of reviews is influenced by the design of a reputation system, and can be improved eg by shielding reviews from users until both parties to a transaction have had an opportunity to review each other; see G Bolton, B Greiner, and A Ockenfels, 'Engineering Trust: Reciprocity in the Production of Reputation Information' (2013) 59 Management Science 265. On the shortcomings of many online reputation systems, see also SH Ranchordás, 'Online Reputation and the Regulation of Information Asymmetries in the Platform Economy' (2018) 5 Critical Analysis of Law 127, 134 ff.

[114] Busch, 'Crowdsourcing Consumer Confidence' (n 104) 236–37.

[115] Danish Consumer Ombudsman, *Guidelines on Publication of User Reviews* (1 May 2015) <https://www.consumerombudsman.dk/media/49717/guidelines.pdf>. See Busch, 'Crowdsourcing Consumer Confidence' (n 104) 229.

[116] In Germany: *Empfehlungen an Betreiber von Bewertungsplattformen* issued by the consumer association *Verbraucherzentrale Bundesverband eV* in December 2012 <https://www.vzbv.de/sites/default/files/downloads/Bewertungsportale-Empfehlungen-vzbv-2012.pdf>.

[117] C Busch and others, 'Discussion Draft of a Directive on Online Intermediary Platforms' (n 92), Discussion Draft Art 8. See also C Busch, 'Commentary on Article 8' in C Busch and others (eds), *Model Rules on Online Intermediary Platforms* (Jagiellonian University Press 2019) 77.

[118] C Busch and others, 'Discussion Draft of a Directive on Online Intermediary Platforms' (n 92) 165.

final version of the Model Rules on Online Platforms stipulates that reputational feedback systems that comply with voluntary standards, such as (still to be developed) national or European standards, or international standards, are presumed to be in conformity with the requirements of professional diligence.[119] One such standard already exists, namely the recently adopted ISO standard 20488:2018 on online consumer reviews.[120] As an alternative, the Model Rules also provide their own requirements of professional diligence for reputation systems.[121]

VII. Online Dispute Resolution

A final source of norm creation that is relevant for the platform economy is online dispute resolution, or ODR.[122] If a dispute arises between parties contracting through a platform, or between a user and the platform, parties may well resort to this form of dispute resolution if they fail to find a solution through negotiation with their counter-party. The alternative, litigation through the courts, is often not chosen, as it is too costly in comparison to the loss suffered, in particular in consumer cases; the length of procedures is generally long; and the transnational context within which platforms operate means that parties will often have to litigate in jurisdictions other than their own.[123] In the platform economy, many platforms offer online dispute resolution services as a means to overcome such problems. Airbnb, for example, operates a resolution centre that enables users to claim a refund in certain circumstances or to resolve other issues,[124] as does eBay.[125]

It has been argued that online dispute resolution mechanisms could have a regulatory function if certain conditions are fulfilled.[126] Those conditions are primarily twofold: that data on the market activities of traders can be captured through dispute resolution systems, and that the data can be recycled in such a way that the

[119] For a more detailed discussion, see C Busch, 'Verbraucherschutz in der Platformökonomie', WISO Diskurs 15/2018 (Friedrich Ebert Stiftung 2018) 11 <http://library.fes.de/pdf-files/wiso/14618.pdf>.

[120] See on this Chapter 9, pp 210.

[121] Draft Instrument of the European Law Institute, *Model Rules on Online Platforms*, version available on 28 February 2020, Art 6.

[122] See in more detail for Europe, P Cortés, *The Law of Consumer Redress in an Evolving Digital Market* (CUP 2018); and P Cortés, *Online Dispute Resolution for Consumers in the European Union* (Routledge 2011).

[123] These problems have been long-standing, in particular in transnational consumer law, and efforts have been made at the national and transnational level to develop alternatives to court litigation. See eg G-P Calliess, 'Transnational Consumer Law: Co-Regulation of B2C-E-Commerce' in O Dilling, M Herberg, and G Winter (eds), *Responsible Business. Self-Governance and Law in Transnational Economic Transactions* (Hart Publishing 2008) 225.

[124] For a user guide developed through the Airbnb online community, see <https://community.withairbnb.com/t5/Tips-Tutorials/Request-Money-Using-The-Resolution-Center-A-Community-Help-Guide/m-p/414759>.

[125] <https://resolutioncenter.ebay.com/>. For a discussion of eBay's resolution system, see Calliess, 'Transnational Consumer Law: Co-Regulation of B2C-E-Commerce' (n 123) 21–22.

[126] Hodges, 'The Consumer as Regulator' (n 103) 246–47 for an outline of this argument.

feedback from these systems pushes traders towards compliance with applicable laws and regulations. Existing regimes for alternative dispute resolution already do this to a certain extent—in a more developed form, in comparison to other countries, in the United Kingdom[127]—and the advancement of further use of data has great potential for improving standards and identifying poor practices.[128] In addition, the regulatory function would increase if the dispute resolution operated, and gathered and exchanged data, in a pan-European structure so that trends can be charted in the application of relevant EU regulation across the Union.[129]

Like reputation systems, ODR could moreover have effects that go beyond its regulatory function. The data gathered from ODR procedures could also have an influence on lawmaking as they provide information on trader and consumer behaviour, just like reputation systems do.[130] For example, eBay's preferred dispute resolution service provider SquareTrade uses the patterns that it observes in disputes as data to improve their menu-driven software for direct negotiations between parties.[131]

There is a caveat to the reference to ODR in lawmaking, however, which is that the current systems operate far from satisfactorily. Concerns about online dispute resolution in consumer cases include, importantly, whether consumers can count on receiving the level of mandatory consumer protection that they would enjoy under the national law of their country of residence. It has been suggested that the only way to guarantee this, even if it would form a barrier to cross-border e-commerce, is always to make alternative dispute mechanisms and ODR in consumer cases ultimately subject to state courts.[132] Noting that the promotion of cross-border consumer transactions might be in need of transnational solutions, others have argued in favour of greater transparency of the level of consumer protection offered by different national and transnational regimes, without subjecting cases necessarily to the ultimate authority of state courts.[133] Here, as more generally, the case may also be made that it seems more straightforward to achieve a level of collaboration between lawmakers in the European Union than between those at

[127] Examples are the UK Financial Ombudsman Service, Communications Ombudsman, Energy Ombudsman, Legal Ombudsman, ABTA complaint system, and Motor Codes complaint system. See C Hodges, I Benöhr, and N Creutzfeldt-Banda (eds), *Consumer ADR in Europe* (Hart Publishing 2012).

[128] Hodges, 'The Consumer as Regulator' (n 103) 255.

[129] ibid 255. Besides substantive rules that have been subject to EU harmonization, the main procedural instrument for which monitoring would be relevant is Regulation (EU) No 524/2013 on online dispute resolution for consumer disputes [2013] OJ L165/1.

[130] See above, p 147.

[131] S Abernethy, 'Building Large-Scale Online Dispute Resolution and Trustmark Systems' (paper presented at the UNECE Forum on ODR 2003 by the President/CEO of SquareTrade) <https://www.mediate.com/Integrating/docs/Abernethy.pdf>. See also Calliess, 'Transnational Consumer Law: Co-Regulation of B2C-E-Commerce' (n 123) 22.

[132] See Reich, 'Transnational Consumer Law—Reality or Fiction?' (n 6) 867–68.

[133] Calliess, 'Transnational Consumer Law: Co-Regulation of B2C-E-Commerce' (n 123) 35, 42.

the transnational level, where the multitude of fora in which common standards are discussed and promoted still seems to be a serious problem.[134]

VIII. Conclusions

As things stand, the instruments of lawmaking that in the European Union have been applied to the platform economy show a mixed picture. They include rules developed at the transnational level and those that apply solely at the national level; rules that are part of 'formal' law and therefore binding versus rules of self-regulation or of soft law that are not automatically binding but that may nonetheless be considered binding by a court in certain circumstances; and beyond rules also other norm-creating instruments, such as reputational feedback systems or ODR, through which the processing of individual or aggregated data on disputes can provide information to lawmakers on trader and consumer behaviour.

Interestingly, the rules brought in through private regulation, at least in amount, eclipse the rules laid down in legislation and regulation. An explanation for this phenomenon was already hinted at in the introduction to this chapter—the development of private regulation has been driven by the wish of platforms to build trust amongst users—and will be further explored in Chapter 7. For users, in particular consumers without in-depth legal knowledge, that shift from public to private regulation will not be particularly noticeable. To some extent instruments developed in the private sphere function in a similar way as nation-state legal systems rely on rules, remedies, and enforcement mechanisms. For example, while an online reputation systems may provide information that helps assess the quality and reliability of a user or service, if it turns out that the actual performance falls short, the user will still want to have a remedy.[135] In that case, recourse to an ODR system can provide a mechanism for obtaining compensation or another solution.

From a lawmaking perspective, however, the shift towards private regulation is significant. Seen against the background of EU law, it fits with a move away from legislative harmonization and towards co-regulation and standardization, or, in other words, a move away from 'economization' to 'politicization' of European private law, to use the words of Micklitz.[136] In that perspective, the focus shifts from the black-letter law approach of EU market integration through legal harmonization to a governance approach. Governance 'opens the perspective and puts

[134] G-P Calliess and P Zumbansen, *Rough Consensus and Running Code. A Theory of Transnational Private Law* (Hart Publishing 2010) 180.

[135] Calliess, 'Transnational Consumer Law: Co-Regulation of B2C-E-Commerce' (n 123) 18.

[136] H-W Micklitz, 'The Visible Hand of European Regulatory Private Law—The Transformation of European Private Law from Autonomy to Functionalism in Competition and Regulation' (2009) 28 Yearbook of European Law 3, 7–8.

emphasis on the law-making process, on the development and use of new regulatory instruments, and on feasible enforcement mechanisms'.[137]

These observations concern the form of the instruments. In the following chapter, the substance of the various instruments will be examined in more detail to determine which aspects of the platform economy they actually cover and whether their rules safeguard the objectives and values of EU law.

[137] ibid 8.

7
The Normative Side
Transparency in the Platform Economy

The approach advocated in this book is an instrumental-normative one. It requires that a result is achieved through law (hence instrumental), and that this result amounts to the safeguarding of the objectives and values of EU law, such as consumer protection (and in that way is normative). The topic of this chapter, the platform economy, provides fruitful ground for testing if and how that approach can be implemented. I will focus on one prominent issue—transparency in contracting—to examine what opportunities lawmaking actors have so far taken in terms of regulating the market, or engaging in deliberations concerning regulation, and whether this has resulted in rules that safeguard the objectives and values of EU law. Whereas the focus therefore is on 'norms', the chapter also provides insights on the actors and processes that are at play in the platform economy.

That enquiry is structured as follows. First, a brief analysis is presented of the transparency rules laid down in EU consumer law, their interpretation by the European Court of Justice (CJEU), and their relation to national private laws. This analysis serves to sketch the normative framework for transparency in EU law, which notably in some respects extends beyond consumer transactions and also seeks to protect (small) businesses. Importantly, while this enquiry reveals a framework that itself contains inconsistencies and contested aspects in the development of rules at the European Union and the national level (section 7.II), ultimately the EU framework does appear to be sufficiently robust to provide normative guidance for ensuring a minimum level of consumer protection (section 7.III).

In the second part of the chapter, the rules on transparency that have emerged in the platform economy will be recalled from Chapter 6 and assessed in the light of this normative framework of EU consumer law. This comparative assessment will first chart the relevant legal relationships in the platform economy, focusing on the tripartite relationship between the platform and users contracting through it (section 7.VI). The rules applying to these relationships will then be examined in detail through case studies of two major online platforms: Airbnb and Amazon (section 7.V). Those studies reveal that transparency requirements in the platform economy are often not applied by platforms, nor enforced through public legislation or regulation, but that private regulation has emerged as an instrument that can nonetheless provide users with similar kinds of protection as found in EU

Legal Pluralism in European Contract Law. Vanessa Mak, Oxford University Press (2020). © Vanessa Mak.
DOI: 10.1093/oso/9780198854487.001.0001.

consumer law. In some instances, the transparency requirements in private regulation even go beyond that level of protection. Nevertheless, close monitoring is still required as platforms are not driven by the same motives or responsibilities as legislators or regulators, for example with regard to protecting the individual or collective interests of consumers. The chapter wraps up with a conclusion that takes stock of the framework for transparency in EU law, the empirical evidence found in relation to transparency rules in the platform economy, and the roles of different lawmaking actors.

Methodologically, the chapter takes the approach of a functional comparison between the rules developed at different levels of regulation. Functionalism here means that the effects of rules rather than the rules themselves will be the focus of the enquiry. That entails that '[i]nstitutions, both legal and non-legal, even doctrinally different ones, are comparable if they are functionally equivalent, if they fulfil similar functions in different legal systems'.[1] As will be seen, the European Commission's line, which expressed a preference for private regulation by platforms instead of regulating them, has largely been followed in practice.[2] That is relevant not only in view of which lawmakers are involved but also in terms of the normative choices that have until now been made. It means that platform operators have a strong influence on the rules that govern transactions through platforms and, with most of the platforms active in the European Union being operated by US companies, that private regulation is coloured by values prevailing in the United States rather than in Europe.[3] The balance between the transparency framework laid down in EU consumer law and those new rules emanating from private regulation has yet to be struck.

I. Transparency in EU Consumer Law

Transparency, in the form of market transparency,[4] is a cornerstone of EU consumer law and policy. It is based on the idea that consumers with sufficient

[1] While there is no definitive definition of functionalist comparative law, these are elements that all theories agree on. See R Michaels, 'The Functional Method of Comparative Law' in M Reimann and R Zimmermann (eds), *The Oxford Handbook of Comparative Law* (OUP 2019) 345.

[2] Europe is nonetheless regarded as a major player who could through regulation deal with concerns regarding competition, the control of data, distribution of profits, and the protection of democratic processes against misinformation; see eg 'Europe takes on the tech giants' *The Economist* (London, 23 March 2019).

[3] Highlighting the difference between Europe and Asia in this respect, N Ferguson, *The Tower and the Square* (Penguin Books 2017) 413. Whereas Europe has chosen to 'capitulate and regulate', Asia has opted to 'exclude and compete', meaning that US companies are kept out of markets where possible and that the creation of regional competitors is stimulated through government schemes.

[4] Transparency is also an important general principle of EU administrative law and governance. See Art 15 of the Consolidated version of the Treaty on the Functioning of the European Union [2012] OJ C326/47 (TFEU), Art 1 of the Consolidated version of the Treaty on European Union [2012] OJ C326/01 (TEU), and Arts 41 and 42 of the EU Charter of Fundamental Rights [2000] OJ C364/1. For an analysis of the development and implications of that principles, see A Buijze, *The Principle of Transparency*

information about goods and services available in the market will be able to make rational decisions about purchases. From a contractual perspective that idea is appealing because it should ensure that consumer expectations in relation to goods and services are met. Taking a broader market perspective, if consumers care about quality, the effect of this approach should be that the quality of goods and services offered increases.[5] As a regulatory technique, finally, the focus on transparency is attractive because it abides by the principle of party autonomy that prevails in general contract laws: it provides consumers with tools to come to a purchasing decision, but it does not touch the content of the contract.[6]

The legislative basis of the value[7] of transparency in EU consumer law is somewhat hidden at the more general level of the Treaties, where it could perhaps be considered part of the internal market provision of Article 114 TFEU. However, it becomes significantly more specific in secondary legislation. The majority of EU directives in the field of consumer law introduce information requirements for traders towards consumers in relation to the characteristics of goods and services and other aspects that are relevant in the pre-contractual stage.[8] The transparency requirements in relation to information are generally twofold: the consumer needs to have received or be able to access the relevant information, for example in the form of general terms and conditions of the trader, and the information must be understandable to the 'average consumer' at whom it is directed.[9] The first requirement is often referred to as formal transparency, whilst the second aspect is deemed substantive transparency.[10]

in EU Law (dissertation Utrecht 2013) <https://dspace.library.uu.nl/handle/1874/269787> accessed 28 February 2020, as are all websites in this chapter; A Buijze, 'The Six Faces of Transparency' (2013) 9 Utrecht Law Review 3; S Prechal and M de Leeuw, 'Dimensions of Transparency: The Building Blocks for a New Legal Principle?' (2007) 0 Review of European Administrative Law 51.

[5] For a broader discussion of the economic rationale underlying the EU consumer market, see I Ramsay, *Consumer Law and Policy* (3rd edn, Hart Publishing 2012) chapter 2.

[6] See S Weatherill, *EU Consumer Law and Policy* (2nd edn, Edward Elgar 2013) 92–94.

[7] Some authors speak of the 'transparency principle'; see eg MBM Loos, 'Transparency of Standard Terms under the Unfair Contract Terms Directive and the Proposal for a Common European Sales Law' (2015) 23 European Review of Private Law 179. While the definition of principles, values, and the like is not set in stone, the term principle in the context of EU law seems to imply something with a legal nature. Seeing that transparency is related foremost to market policy, I prefer to speak of it as a value.

[8] Information requirements also relate to practical information about the trader (eg address and other contact details), price, interest rates, and information about the right of withdrawal. For a discussion see Weatherill, *EU Consumer Law and Policy* (n 6) 95 ff.

[9] Loos, 'Transparency of Standard Terms' (n 7) 180. The connection of the transparency test to the average consumer of EU unfair commercial practices law was made by the European Court of Justice in the *Kásler* case. See Case C-26/13 *Árpád Kásler and Hajnalke Káslerné Rábai v OTP Jelzálogbank Zrt*, ECLI:EU:C:2014:282 (*Kásler*), at [74].

[10] Loos, 'Transparency of Standard Terms' (n 7) 180. The distinction appears to have been coined by F d'Usseaux, 'Formal and Substantive Aspects of the Transparency Principle in European Private Law' [1998] Consumer Law Journal 320; see JA Luzak and M Junuzović, 'Blurred Lines: Between Formal and Substantive Transparency in Consumer Credit Contracts' (2019) 8 Journal of European Consumer and Market Law 97.

Transparency is therefore well embedded within EU consumer law. Nonetheless, critics have pointed out that, to put consumers on par with traders in the market for goods and services, it is not enough to provide them with information. The behavioural studies referred to earlier in this book have revealed that consumers are hindered by cognitive limitations and can therefore not always come to a well-informed and well-reasoned decision. To counter the criticism that transparency by itself is not sufficient to ensure consumer protection, EU law also gives consumers a post-contractual right of withdrawal, and it maintains a fairness assessment—within boundaries—through the Unfair Contract Terms Directive (UCTD).[11] The fairness test has been given further substance through the case law of the CJEU.[12]

While the framework for transparency seems rather straightforward, it contains some aspects that have not been fully fleshed out, as well as some inconsistencies between different Directives. This differentiation can be attributed to the European legislature's initially somewhat unstructured, and later, hampered efforts at harmonization. In the first instance, directives were introduced for specific areas of consumer law over a twenty-year period with little or no attention for how new rules, for example concerning information, related to those laid down by other directives. When, from the early 2000s on, the European Commission started investing in the review and modernization of consumer law, some gains were made in achieving greater consistency.[13] However, the gains are very modest if one compares them to the ambitious initiatives that were launched during that time. The review of the consumer *acquis* started out with approximately twenty directives but ended with two, and some aspects of two others, in the 2011 Consumer Rights Directive. The Commission's proposal for a Common European Sales Law (CESL) did not make it,[14] and neither did the Draft Common Frame of Reference (DCFR) give rise to new legislative proposals. The Commission's pursuit of full, rather than minimum harmonization, moreover, was also largely unsuccessful. This means that many directives only harmonize rules in part, and leave many issues at the discretion of the EU Member States.

[11] Directive 1993/13/EEC on unfair terms in consumer contracts [1993] OJ L95/29 (Unfair Contract Terms Directive).

[12] Case C-415/11 *Mohamed Aziz v Caixa d'Estalvis de Catalunya, Tarragona i Manresa (Catalunyacaixa)*, ECLI:EU:C:2013:164; Case C-488/11 *Asbeek Brusse*, ECLI:EU:C:2013:341; Case C-342/13 *Katalin Sebestyén v Zsolt Csaba Kővári, OTP Bank, OTP Faktoring Követeléskezelő Zrt, Raiffesien Bank Zrt*, ECLI:EU:C:2014:857.

[13] The most prominent example is the harmonization of the cooling-off period for the consumer's right of withdrawal, which was set at fourteen calendar days for the majority of consumer contracts. See Directive 2011/83/EU on consumer rights [2013] OJ L304/64 (Consumer Rights Directive), Art 9. The Consumer Rights Directive also harmonizes information requirements for most consumer contracts. For an overview, see JA Luzak and V Mak, 'The Consumer Rights Directive' in AS Hartkamp and others (eds), *De invloed van het Europese recht op het Nederlandse privaatrecht* (Kluwer 2014) 67.

[14] The proposal for a Common European Sales Law (CESL) was withdrawn at the end of 2014. For an overview of its legislative history, see M Király, 'The Rise and Fall of Common European Sales Law' (2015) (2) ELTE Law Journal 31.

The framework for transparency in EU consumer law, therefore, contains many rules that differ between directives. I will highlight some, by way of illustration, to show what these differences mean in practice. The overall argument put forward here—that the EU framework can enable an instrumental-normative approach to lawmaking—however can still be maintained. The variation between detailed rules, it is submitted, does not dilute the general value of transparency to the extent that normative guidance is lost.

II. Transparency in Detail

One example of divergence between the legal systems of the EU Member States concerns the consequences of breaching the transparency rule laid down in Article 5 of the UCTD. Most importantly, whilst it is in some legal systems presumed that a breach of the transparency rule laid down in Article 5 UCTD implies unfairness and therefore gives ground to set aside the infringing term, that view is rejected in other Member States, in particular in the United Kingdom.[15] Such differentiation is possible since the Directive does not specify which sanctions should be attached to a breach of the transparency rule. The view prevailing in Dutch and German law is that a breach of the transparency requirement makes a contract term unfair, and hence that the term can be rescinded. This view is in accordance with the CJEU judgment in the *Amazon* case, concerning a choice of law clause in a seller's general terms and conditions, where it was held that:[16]

> a term in the general terms and conditions of a seller or supplier which has not been individually negotiated, under which the contract concluded with a consumer in the course of electronic commerce is to be governed by the law of the Member State in which the seller or supplier is established, is unfair in so far as it leads the consumer into error by giving him the impression that only the law of that Member State applies to the contract, without informing him that under Article 6(2) of the Rome I Regulation he also enjoys the protection of the mandatory provisions of the law that would be applicable in the absence of that term, this being for the national court to ascertain in the light of all the relevant circumstances.

[15] In general, it remains to be seen whether existing, implemented EU law continues to follow the line set out by the EU legislature and the CJEU.

[16] Case C-191/15 *Verein für Konsumenteninformation v Amazon EU Sàrl*, ECLI:EU:C:2016:612 (*Amazon*), at [71]. German law already held the view that a breach of the transparency requirement implies unfairness, a position codified in § 307(1) of the *Bürgerliches Gesetzbuch* (German Civil Code). For the Netherlands, see MBM Loos, *Algemene voorwaarden* (Boom juridische uitgevers 2018), para 242.

In the United Kingdom, however, the Law Commission and the Scottish Law Commission have in the past chosen a different position. Although they initially proposed legislation that would sanction a term that breached the transparency requirement as an unfair term, the Commissions came back on that proposal and suggested that transparency should only be seen as one factor in the assessment of (un)fairness, together with all the other circumstances of the case.[17] That position could still be maintained, despite the Court's judgment in *Amazon*, it has been argued. The judgment after all does not say that the infringement of the transparency rule *automatically* implies unfairness of the contract term.[18] Nevertheless, the better view seems to be that a lack of transparency does make the term unfair. It hampers the consumer's ability to assess the economic consequences of the term, as required by the Court's judgment in *Kásler*,[19] and thereby is at odds with the consumer's interest in informed consent and reasonable expectations.[20]

As another example, focusing on the relation between the UCTD and other EU consumer law directives, the application of transparency in EU consumer law is not always consistent. It has been noted that the two-pronged transparency test of the UCTD, which includes a formal and a substantive aspect, differs from the Consumer Credit Directive (CCD),[21] which opts for a formal assessment only.[22] The formal requirement is that the consumer has had an opportunity to read the terms of the contract, whereas the substantive test also requires that the average consumer could have understood the economic consequences of the term. It is not entirely clear how the transparency requirements of the UCTD and the CCD relate to one another, but it appears that credit providers can suffice with fulfilling just the formal stage. In its case law on consumer credit contracts, the CJEU has lent support to that approach, in particular in the *Home Credit Slovakia* case.[23] At the same time, in other case law concerning consumer credit agreements, the Court been asked to rule on the application of the transparency test from the UCTD. In *Kásler* the Court held that, where the UCTD is turned to for assessing transparency, the

[17] The Law Commission and the Scottish Law Commission, 'Unfair Terms in Consumer Contracts: Advice to the Department for Business, Innovation and Skills' (March 2013) <https://www.lawcom.gov.uk/project/unfair-terms-in-consumer-contracts/>, 82–84, in particular para 6.60.

[18] This position was taken by the Appeal Committee of the Dutch institute for financial complaints, Kifid, which found that a term lacking transparency may not only be interpreted in a negative manner, but also in a positive sense by the consumer. See *Commissie van Beroep Klachteninstituut Financiële Dienstverlening* 6 November 2017, 2017–37.

[19] *Kásler* (n 9).

[20] Compare JW Rutgers, 'Case Note: Court of Justice of the European Union 28 July 2016, Case C-191/15 *Verein für Konsumenteninformation v Amazon EU Sàrl*, ECLI:EU:C:2016:612' (2017) 64 Netherlands International Law Review 163, 173; Loos, *Algemene voorwaarden* (n 16) 242.

[21] Directive 2008/48/EC on credit agreements for consumers [2008] OJ L133/66 (Consumer Credit Directive).

[22] Luzak and Junuzović, 'Blurred Lines: Between Formal and Substantive Transparency in Consumer Credit Contracts' (n 10), who plead for a policy change by the European Commission in this respect, applying the substantive test also to consumer credit contracts.

[23] Case C-42/15 *Home Credit Slovakia a.s. v Klára Bíróová*, ECLI:EU:C:2016:842.

fulfilment of the formal requirements is not enough but must be complemented by a substantive test to see whether the average consumer would have understood the economic consequences of the term before entering into the contract.[24] While that broader interpretation is potentially favourable to consumers,[25] and has garnered some support in the literature,[26] the Court does not say whether it should also be applied to cases where the formal requirements of the CCD have been followed and complied with. It may therefore, until further clarification is given by the EU legislature or the Court, in individual cases be held that compliance with the CCD information requirements in a formal sense is sufficient for consumer credit contracts. In such circumstances, national courts may actually still comply also with the UCTD if they find that the challenged term was 'clear and comprehensible' to the consumer, which depends on a factual assessment by the national court.[27]

III. Transparency as a General Value

That means that as a normative benchmark, the framework of EU law does not provide a specific, incontestable answer to every problem that can arise with regard to information in consumer contracts. The rules laid down in directives such as the UCTD and the CCD are in some respects still open to interpretation and it will depend on national courts to decide how to apply the rules in individual cases. While this could be regarded as a failure of the harmonization of European private law,[28] from a different perspective it could be that the different interpretations given to the two Directives simply reflects an intermediate step in the development of a doctrine of transparency in European consumer law. The field is dynamic rather than static.

[24] *Kásler* (n 9) [74]-[75]. See also Case C-186/16 *Paula Andriciuc and others v Banca Românească SA*, ECLI:EU:C:2017:703, and Case C-621/17 *Gyula Kiss v CIB Bank Zrt*, ECLI:EU:C:2019:820. See also MBM Loos, 'Transparency Under the UCTD: Could You Please Explain what these Terms are Supposed to Mean?' (2020) 9 Journal of European Consumer and Market Law 25, who points out that the CJEU's judgment in *Kiss* gives an opening for assessing transparency in relation to the individual—rather than the average—consumer in para 82 of the case.

[25] Hungarian legislation has, after the judgment in *Kásler*, rendered all terms invalid that, in consumer credit contracts, use the buying rate of foreign currency for calculating the loan payment, but the selling rate for calculating the instalments for repayment. Also, Art 23 of Directive on credit agreements for consumers relating to residential immovable property [2014] OJ L60/34 (Consumer Mortgage Credit Directive) can be seen as a response to the detriment caused by loans indexed in foreign currency. See A Fejős, 'Mortgage Credit in Hungary' (2017) 6 Journal of European Consumer and Market Law 139.

[26] Luzak and Junuzović, 'Blurred Lines: Between Formal and Substantive Transparency in Consumer Credit Contracts' (n 10) 7.

[27] That line was adopted by the Croatian Supreme Court in the *Franak* case; see E Mišćenić, 'Croatian Case "Franak": Effective or "Defective" Protection of Consumer Rights?' (2016) 5 Harmonius Journal of Legal and Social Studies in South East Europe 184, 203–05.

[28] For a critical analysis, see M Junuzović, 'Transparency of (Pre-)Contractual Information in Consumer Credit Agreements: Is Consistency the Missing Key?' [2018] 14 Croatian Yearbook of European Law & Policy 69.

At the same time, that does not mean that the EU framework—when put to the test—cannot fulfil the requirements of an instrumental-normative approach to lawmaking. On the contrary: the information rights of consumers are all derived from the general value of transparency, which is firmly embedded in a framework of regulation on pre-contractual information requirements for consumers, and protection against unfair commercial practices and unfair terms.[29] That is different from, for example, the United States, where consumer protection in contract law has developed to a more limited extent. That distinction can be explained by differences in the ideologies that inform legal regulation. While the United States and the European Union both combine the goal of pursuing interstate or cross-border trade with the pursuit of a high level of consumer protection, US consumer contract law is overall more strongly informed by market policies and efficiency concerns than European contract law. This difference, arguably, goes back to the rise of law and economics scholarship in the Chicago School from the 1970s and 1980s onwards, which legitimated deregulation and promoted competition.[30] By comparison, consumer law in the European Union is primarily based on the EU's internal market competences but its content goes beyond market concerns.[31] In competition or antitrust law, furthermore, it can be seen that non-economic goals are more significantly embedded in European case law.[32] Also in substance, EU consumer contract law contains rules that go beyond market interests, such as the protection against over-indebtedness laid down in the Mortgage Credit Directive of 2014.[33]

For Europe, the commitment to consumer protection is reflected in the EU Treaties which beside the internal market provision of Article 114 TFEU also include a broader basis for harmonization of consumer law in Article 169 TFEU. That provision, together with the general principles of subsidiarity, proportionality, and sincere cooperation set forth in Articles 5(3), 5(4), and 4(3) of the Treaty on European Union (TEU), can be a basis for a shared responsibility of the EU and the Member States in the development of consumer law beyond the (economic) objectives of the EU internal market.[34] Even if that legal basis has until now hardly been used, it evinces a greater commitment of the European Union to objectives

[29] Consumer Rights Directive (n 13); Directive 2005/29/EC concerning unfair business-to-consumer commercial practices in the internal market [2005] OJ L149/22 (Unfair Commercial Practices Directive); Unfair Contract Terms Directive (n 11).

[30] For a comparison of the European Union and the United States on this point, see H-W Micklitz, *The Politics of Justice in European Private Law. Social Justice, Access Justice, Societal Justice* (CUP 2018) 148–51.

[31] S Weatherill, *Contract Law of the Internal Market* (Intersentia 2016) 95 ff. See also Chapter 4, pp 80.

[32] See DD Sokol, 'Troubled Waters Between US and European Antitrust' (2017) 115 Michigan Law Review 955, 958.

[33] Consumer Mortgage Credit Directive (n 25).

[34] For an elaboration of this argument see K Gutman, *The Constitutional Foundations of European Contract Law: A Comparative Analysis* (OUP 2014).

and values that are not purely of an economic nature, but that are part of the EU social market economy.[35] Evidence of that commitment is also seen in the introduction of specific rules for the protection of 'vulnerable' consumers, for example in the energy sector and, more generally, in unfair commercial practices regulation.[36]

The institutional framework and common legal bases of the European Union also make it a stronger normative setting in comparison to transnational cooperation in the field of private law. For a broader discussion of this point, I refer to the discussion in Chapters 2 and 3.

Practically, nonetheless, the relative openness of the value of transparency in EU law means that doctrinal challenges are likely to come up in cases where specific outcomes are sought. If lawmaking through the various instruments discussed in the previous chapter leads to different degrees of transparency—for example in the types and extent of information duties resting on suppliers with regarded to the products or services offered—one can fall back on the framework for transparency of EU law to determine which degree fits best within that broader framework. The boundaries of transparency are then defined: formal transparency is the minimum requirement and, for most consumer contracts, substantive transparency adds another layer. In other words, the recipient must at least have been given an opportunity to take notice of the relevant terms and conditions, and as a second step, the economic consequences of those terms must have been understandable to the average consumer. In some cases, as for consumer credit contracts, formal transparency suffices.

Although the framework of EU consumer law gives guidance in this respect—and relatively speaking quite a lot—there is a caveat, which is that the transparency rules developed by the EU legislator and the CJEU take on slightly different hues when they are implemented and applied in the Member States' legal systems. There, notions of good faith and fairness in general contract law influence to what extent consumers are protected against unfair terms, misleading advertising, or other infringements of transparency. Furthermore, the consequences of setting aside contract terms due to unfairness or misleading advertising differ from one Member State to another. In some, but not all, legal systems an individual action is available to consumers to rescind or terminate a contract if an unfair commercial

[35] See Weatherill, *Contract Law of the Internal Market* (n 31) 95 ff; K Gutman, 'The Development of Consumer Law in the US: Comparisons with the EU Experience' (2012) 4 Journal of European Consumer and Market Law 212, 221. Also Chapter 4. The commitment to consumer protection is also visible in the procedural mechanisms that are available for the enforcement of rights. In the United States, access to justice is restrictive in comparison to the European Union. Even if EU consumers are less likely to seek redress through the courts, due to the deterrent effect of a 'loser pays' rule in litigation, they benefit from the availability of well-developed regimes for alternative dispute resolution. See J Fischer, 'Consumer Protection in the United States and European Union: Are Protections Most Effective Before or After a Sale?' (2014) 32 Wisconsin International Law Journal 308, 323–24.

[36] M Bartl, 'Socio-Economic Imaginaries and European Private Law' in PF Kjær (ed), *The Law of Political Economy: Transformations in the Function of Law* (CUP, 2020), SSRN https://ssrn.com/abstract=3317374.

practice has been established.[37] National courts, for example, are struggling with the question whether substitution of terms is allowed in cases where an unfair term is rescinded. Are they allowed, in the light of the CJEU's interpretation of Directive 93/13/EEC on unfair terms, to fall back on default rules of national contract law to supplement contracts? The CJEU's judgment in *Kásler* appears to confirm that approach, but the reach of that judgment is contested. Some judges read it as a blanket permission to substitute terms, for example to replace an unfair interest clause with the legal interest rate. However, a better reading of the judgment is that the CJEU considers the deterrent effect that the striking out of unfair terms should have to prevail over other considerations, such as the principles of equivalence. That means that courts should not in all cases be allowed to substitute terms, and thereby help out the trader, but that they can only do so in the circumstance that the contract cannot exist without the offending term.[38]

The question is whether these uncertainties in relation to individual cases are problematic in the broader scheme of things. The doctrinal challenge lies in reconciling prevailing approaches in national private laws with the transparency framework developed in EU law, and actively confirmed by the CJEU in a consumer-friendly way. Recalling the discussion in Chapter 5, this can be seen as a clash between the juridical rationality of national private laws and the instrumental rationality of EU law. It also reflects the 'double-headed approach' of EU law, signalled by Unberath and Johnston.[39] The integration of the internal market is pursued on the one hand by setting aside national legislation that raises barriers to trade, which means that consumer protection that goes further than market integration requires is deemed invalid, whilst on the other hand the CJEU seeks to

[37] See eg Belgium, on which R Steennot, 'Belgium: Private Law Remedies for Breach of the Prohibition of Unfair Commercial Practices' (2015) 4 Journal of European Consumer and Market Law 188; the Netherlands, on which V Mak, 'Unfair Commercial Practices and Dutch Private Law' (2015) 4 Journal of European Consumer and Market Law 246; and the United Kingdom, on which J Devenney, 'Private Redress Mechanisms in England and Wales for Unfair Commercial Practices' (2016) 5 Journal of European Consumer and Market Law 100. The New Deal for Consumers of 2018 proposed an amendment of Art 11a of the Unfair Commercial Practices Directive to the effect that contractual and non-contractual remedies should be available to consumers, including as a minimum the possibility for the consumer to unilaterally terminate the contract; see European Commission, 'Proposal for a Directive of the European Parliament and of the Council amending Council Directive 93/13/EEC of 5 April 1993, Directive 98/6/EC of the European Parliament and of the Council, Directive 2005/29/EC of the European Parliament and of the Council and Directive 2011/83/EU of the European Parliament and of the Council as regards better enforcement and modernization of EU consumer protection rules' COM(2018) 185 final, proposed amendment of Art 11a of Directive 2005/29/EC. The final version of the Modernisation Directive contains a more generally phrased provision on individual remedies in contract and tort; see Directive (EU) 2019/2161 as regards the better enforcement and modernization of Union consumer protection rules [2019] OJ L328/7, new Art 11a of Directive 2005/29/EC (note that the provision is labelled 'Art 11 bis' in other language versions).

[38] Also of this opinion, AS Hartkamp, C Sieburgh, and W Devroe (eds), *Cases, Materials and Text on European Law and Private Law* (Hart Publishing 2017) 70. See also C Leskinen and F de Elizalde, 'The Control of Terms that Define the Essential Obligations of the Parties under the Unfair Contract Terms Directive: *Gutiérrez Naranjo*' (2018) 55 Common Market Law Review 1595, 1610.

[39] H Unberath and A Johnston, 'The Double-Headed Approach of the ECJ Concerning Consumer Protection' (2007) 44 Common Market Law Review 1237.

emphasize and confirm the reach of EU law by interpreting and applying measures of EU consumer law in a very consumer-friendly way. The question is how problematic this is. One may consider the interplay between EU law and national private law doctrines as a dialectic process that serves to further develop and sharpen notions of transparency and fairness in contract and consumer law. Even if it contains open areas, the framework of EU law at least formulates objectives and values defining the context within which that process takes place. That some issues have not been resolved, such as the question of whether deleted terms may be substituted with others, should not be seen as a disqualification of the EU framework to provide normative guidance. In national doctrinal systems, after all, it often also takes time for issues to be resolved and doctrines to be fleshed out.

Therefore, it is submitted that the general framework of transparency can still provide sufficient guidance to lawmaking actors to use it as a benchmark in an instrumental-normative approach to lawmaking in European private law. It rests on two notions of transparency—formal and substantive—that are applied horizontally to most areas of EU consumer contract law. The divergent approach taken with regard to consumer credit is notable, but it is not unlikely that further development of regulation in that field will also eventually move towards a substantive transparency test.[40] Even if it does not, as consumer credit law is largely developed and applied in a specific sector, the common approach set out for EU consumer contract law in general can be taken as a reflection of the main framework for the objectives and values of EU law.

Having examined the normative framework for transparency, the following two sections turn to the question whether the instrumental goal, to safeguard a minimum level of consumer protection, can in practice be met. In the case study presented here, that question translates into whether transparency between contracting parties in the platform economy meets at least the benchmark set by EU law.

IV. Transparency, for Whom?

To answer that question, a differentiation between categories of transactions has to be made based on the personal scope of those transactions. Different regimes are applicable to business-to-consumer (B2C), business-to-business (B2B), and consumer-to-consumer (C2C) transactions. B2C transactions are governed by EU consumer law and are subject to specific transparency requirements; those which fall outside its scope but may be covered by transparency requirements from other sources. In the context of online platforms, the occurrence of these different

40 For a plea to this effect, compare Luzak and Junuzović, 'Blurred Lines: Between Formal and Substantive Transparency in Consumer Credit Contracts' (n 10).

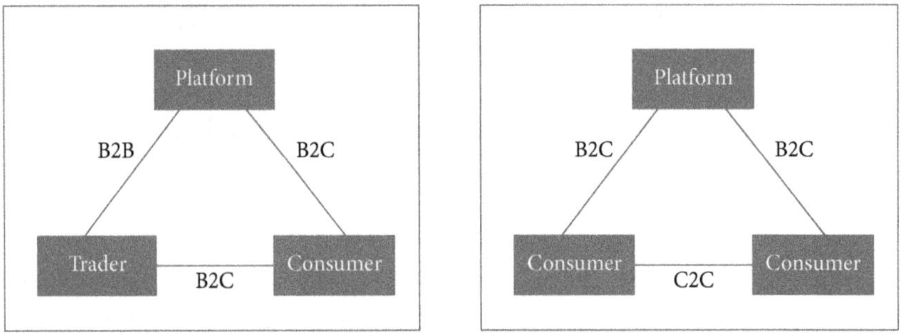

Figure 7.1 Tripartite relationships in the platform economy

categories varies. It is dependent in particular on whether the seller or service provider classifies as a professional trader or as a non-professional supplier, which for the sake of brevity I will also call a consumer.[41] By way of illustration, the pictures in Figure 7.1 are representative of the two main variations.

The first category for which to assess whether transparency requirements are being met in the platform economy are B2C transactions. They can occur between a platform and its consumer users, and between traders and consumers who contract through a platform. This category may seem straightforward because it is subject to the EU's specific rules for consumer law, such as laid down in the CRD, the UCTD, the CCD, and other directives. Whether transparency requirements are met, therefore, in the first instance is a question of compliance. In the European Union, national authorities are primarily responsible for the collective enforcement of consumer law,[42] whilst courts provide redress to consumers in individual cases in which their rights have been infringed.[43] The European Commission itself also has powers of enforcement together with the enforcement authorities of the Member States.[44] The Commission together with the pan-European network of national authorities invoked their powers of enforcement against Airbnb in 2018

[41] The term is not strictly correct if one considers consumers always to be on the demand side of the market, as most legal systems do. Alternatives are 'peer' or perhaps 'prosumer'.

[42] Examples are the Authority for Consumers and Markets (ACM) in the Netherlands; the *Direction générale de la concurrence, de la consummation et de la repression des frauds (DGCCRF)* in France; and (until Brexit) the Competition and Markets Authority (CMA) in the United Kingdom. For a full list of consumer protection authorities in the EU Member States, see <https://www.eba.europa.eu/consumer-corner/national-competent-authorities-for-consumer-protection>.

[43] Collective redress through courts has until now not been established across the European Union. However, a proposal for a collective redress procedure has been published as part of the New Deal for Consumers. See European Commission, 'Proposal for a Directive of the European Parliament and of the Council on representative actions for the protection of the collective interests of consumers, and repealing Directive 2009/22/EC' COM(2018) 184 final.

[44] There are two pan-European networks for the enforcement of consumer law: the Consumer Protection Cooperation Network (CPC Network) for national enforcement authorities and the European Consumer Centres Network (ECC-Net) for consumer organizations. See P Cortés, *The Law of Consumer Redress in an Evolving Digital Market* (CUP 2018) 21 ff.

on the ground that the company was in breach of transparency requirements towards consumers.[45] As a result of that action, Airbnb agreed to comply with rules of EU consumer law.[46] Besides the enforcement of existing rules of consumer law, a normative question is whether B2C transactions should be more strictly regulated in order to ensure that the EU's consumer protection goals are met. For the purposes of the case study presented in this chapter it is relevant to determine in that light whether the general transparency framework of EU law would require stronger protection than existing rules of EU consumer law currently offer. That is, it should be noted, a regulatory question in which the interests of innovation and regulation will have to be weighed and in which the EU legislature has significant scope to decide whether or not to introduce new legislation. It is not obvious, therefore, that the normative benchmark for transparency in EU law requires that regulatory action is taken. The primary focus of the assessment will therefore be on the question whether actors in the platform economy live up to existing rules on transparency in EU law.

The second category concerns C2C contracts. The platform economy changes the supply side of the market so that suppliers are often (but not always) private individuals rather than professional traders. Consumers, that is those on the receiving end of transactions, therefore in many cases buy from non-professional parties. Those transactions are not governed by EU consumer law since they do not concern B2C transactions but by the general contract laws of the Member States.[47] In some cases it could nonetheless be justifiable that buyers should have the same protection that they would enjoy if their counterparty was a professional trader. One example, directly related to transparency, is where it is unclear to the buyer that she is dealing with a non-professional trader. In that case, responsibility can under the EU's New Deal for Consumers potentially be directed to the platform operator, who could be held liable in respect of some (information) duties that would normally rest on the trader in a B2C relationship.[48]

More generally, it is a question of whether parties on the demand side of peer-to-peer transactions made through platforms should be given some protection to compensate for what they would otherwise have in a B2C relationship. One would surmise that some aspects of peer-to-peer transactions should be of the same

[45] European Commission, 'EU Consumer Rules: The European Commission and EU Consumer Authorities Push Airbnb to Comply' (Press release, 16 July 2018), <europa.eu/rapid/press-release_IP-18-4453_en.htm>.

[46] See more below, pp 170.

[47] Private international law, in the absence of a choice of law by the parties, directs the applicable law towards the country of residence of the seller or service provider. See Regulation (EC) No 593/2008 of the European Parliament and of the Council on the law applicable to contractual obligations (Rome I) [2008] OJ L177/6, Art 4(1)(a) and (b). For contracts relating to a right *in rem* in immovable property or to a tenancy of immovable property the applicable law is the law of the country where the property is situated; see Art 4(1)(c). For short-term lets, the law of the landlord's habitual country of residence applies; see Art 4(1)(d).

[48] See Chapter 6, pp 139.

standard, for example when it comes to safety or the availability of amenities. An Airbnb rental will only be able to compete with a regular hotel room if guests can be sure that the accommodation complies with electrical and fire safety standards, so that they can sleep safely. Also, the accommodation should have a (private) bathroom, towels, and linens, if it is to be considered comparable to a hotel room. While many of these aspects can be agreed upon through contract, and regulated by the default rules of general contract laws, there can still be an inequality in the relationship between the parties. A host knows more about the state and quality of their apartment and, conversely, a guest knows more about their reliability and cleanliness.[49] Current debates centre on the question how to balance, on the one hand, the interests of consumers on the receiving end of peer-to-peer transactions with, on the other hand, the interests of non-professional suppliers through platforms.[50] Private regulation, or self-regulation, by platforms is hailed as an instrument that could potentially secure a certain level of protection for consumers who are on the receiving end of the platform's as well as the supplier's services.[51] In the case studies below, I will assess whether that approach has until now been successful.

The third category of transactions in the platform economy are B2B contracts. This category mainly encompasses contracts between platforms and their business users, such as professional traders who offer goods or services through a platform. Other contracts falling within this category could be those between traders selling to other businesses through a platform. While consumer law is not applicable to these types of transactions it is nevertheless useful to consider the transparency requirements also in relation to B2B contracts, for two reasons. First, in cases where one of the parties is a small business, similar asymmetries between the parties may exist as in B2C relationships. For that reason, some legal systems allow the application of consumer protection rules to business contracts in cases where a small business is deemed to deserve protection (*Reflexwirkung*).[52] Second, the European Union has identified transparency in B2B relationships as a first area in which to introduce specific transparency requirements for the platform economy. In 2018, it proposed a Regulation on fairness and transparency for business users of online intermediary services. The Regulation was adopted in June 2019.[53] Business

[49] Discussing this information asymmetry, see M Cohen and A Sundararajan, 'Self-Regulation and Innovation in the Peer-to-Peer Sharing Economy' (2015) 82 The University of Chicago Law Review Dialogue 116, 120.

[50] See V Hatzopoulos, *The Collaborative Economy and EU Law* (Hart Publishing 2018) 52 ff for a summary of the debate.

[51] ibid 54.

[52] Arguing that the rationales for protection are the same in B2C and B2B relationships, MW Hesselink, 'Unfair Terms in Contracts Between Businesses' in J Stuyck and R Schulze (eds), *Towards a European Contract Law* (Sellier 2011) 131.

[53] Proposal for a Regulation of the European Parliament and of the Council on promoting fairness and transparency for business users of online intermediary services, COM(2018) 238 final; Regulation (EU) 2019/1150 on promoting fairness and transparency for business users of online intermediation services [2019] OJ L186/57 (P2B Regulation).

users, for example, would benefit from transparency in relation to the placement of listings on online platforms, in particular if a more prominent placement is dependent on sponsorship or payment.

Finally, a new type of actor, the 'prosumer', has been said to emerge in the platform economy. This is the term used for the blurred category of private individuals who engage in the semi-professional sale of goods or offer of services. Existing laws struggle with the classification of prosumers. Counting them as consumers runs the risk of over-inclusion, since they may not need the protection that the law extends to consumers. On the other hand, if they are treated as traders, the rules applicable to businesses may place unduly strict requirements on prosumers, who are usually small or micro-enterprises. It has been suggested, therefore, that this type of consumer-trader should be governed by a new category, the prosumer. Still, until now the discussion on how to regulate transactions involving prosumers has remained mostly of a theoretical nature.[54]

The concurrence of transactions of a different nature—B2C, B2B, C2C, and transactions involving prosumers—is one factor that makes it hard to come up with fitting regulation for online platforms.[55] An exacerbating factor is that the business models of platforms differ significantly and that this can also influence the balance of interests between parties.[56] Uber, for example, has defined many of the terms under which its drivers (ie suppliers) can operate through the platform, including how the price of their service is calculated and which quality ratings drivers must obtain in order to continue driving for Uber. That is different for other platforms, such as Airbnb, which mostly only have facilitative function that allows parties to contract—on the terms they decide—through the platform. Because of these differences, it is not easy to find a one-size-fits-all solution for the regulation of platforms.[57] That can in part explain why regulation is slow to emerge and why, if it does, it is through a mixture of various instruments.

The private law relationships between platforms and their users, therefore, are governed by norms laid down in EU law, national laws, and primarily also in private regulation with variations in whether a relationship qualifies as B2C, C2C, or B2B. It is now time to consider the substance of the norms applied to these relationships.

[54] See I Brown and CT Marsden, *Regulating Code: Good Governance and Better Regulation in the Information Age* (MIT Press, 2013) 183 ff, and Chapter 5, pp 118.

[55] That problem has also been signalled by Hatzopoulos. For a schematic overview see Hatzopoulos, *The Collaborative Economy and EU Law* (n 50) 55.

[56] Compare C Wendehorst, 'Platform Intermediary Services and Duties under the E-Commerce Directive and the Consumer Rights Directive' (2016) 5 Journal of European Consumer and Market Law 30.

[57] The case law of the European Court of Justice reflects these differences, as Uber is not considered to be an 'information society service' in the sense of the E-Commerce Directive, whereas Airbnb is. See Case C-390/18 *Airbnb Ireland*, ECLI:EU:C2019:1112; Case C-320/16 *Uber France SAS v Nabil Bensalem*, ECLI:EU:C:2018:221; and Case C-434/15 *Asociación Profesional Élite Taxi v Uber Systems Spain SL*, ECLI:EU:C:2017:981.

V. Lawmaking in Action

What outcomes have been achieved in the platform economy and how do they measure up to the framework for transparency in EU law? The patchwork process through which new rules are being developed makes it difficult to give a straightforward answer to that question. New online platforms are created almost every day and each develops its own rules and practices. My approach, therefore, is to examine two of the major online platforms that are active in Europe—Airbnb and Amazon—as case studies for lawmaking in European private law. From those case studies, some more general conclusions may be drawn.

The method used for the case studies is a functional one.[58] I will compare rules developed by various lawmaking actors in the light of the two aspects of transparency that are present in EU consumer law, the formal and the substantive. They entail that the consumer needs to have received or be able to access the relevant information, eg in the form of general terms and conditions of the trader; and that the information must be understandable to the 'average consumer' at whom it is directed.[59] I will take account of both aspects, so as to make the most comprehensive comparison. That seems fitting for the chosen case studies, moreover, since neither platform is specifically concerned with consumer credit, to which the more limited test of formal transparency applies.

Practically, the case studies zoom in on rules that are central to the business model of the platform. For Airbnb the focus is on rules concerning the description of the accommodation offered and associated aspects. For Amazon the focus is on the modalities of sale.

A. Case Study I: Airbnb

Airbnb is a US firm, founded in California in 2008, that through its website enables users to enter into (mostly) short-term rental agreements for holiday accommodation. The idea behind the platform is sympathetic: it allows people to stay at the houses of complete strangers and to thereby experience the way 'locals' live, rather than staying at a hotel. The company started out small but, even as it is now valued at US$38 billion,[60] continues to present the platform as a 'community'.[61] That should not obfuscate, however, that the operations of the platform have in the

58 Michaels, 'The Functional Method of Comparative Law' (n 1).
59 See Loos, 'Transparency of Standard Terms' (n 7).
60 See <https://www.forbes.com/sites/greatspeculations/2018/05/11/as-a-rare-profitable-unicorn-airbnb-appears-to-be-worth-at-least-38-billion/#3fc0a3912741>.
61 See <https://www.airbnb.com/diversity>, which runs the headline 'Our diverse global community makes Airbnb possible'.

meantime been professionalized in many respects. For the purposes of this case study, the following developments in terms of applicable laws, or rules, are relevant.

1. Applicable rules

To begin with, for its operations in Europe Airbnb has to comply with mandatory rules of EU law.[62] That includes EU consumer law in particular, which is applicable to the legal relationships between Airbnb and its users: hosts as well as guests.[63]

Furthermore, issues not covered by EU legislation are subject to the rules of the relevant national law that applies to the relationship between Airbnb and the user, which in the company's general terms and conditions is stipulated to be Irish law.[64] It should be noted that, in accordance with Article 6(2) of the Rome I Regulation, the terms also stipulate that consumers do not lose the protection given by the law of their country of residence. Relevant rules of national law could be the rules concerning the liability and other responsibilities of intermediaries.[65] It is beyond the scope of this chapter to make a full comparative investigation for Airbnb in all EU Member States. Generally speaking, however, it appears that rules concerning intermediaries are only applicable to platforms in limited circumstances. In the Netherlands, for example, it has been held that a platform can only be treated as an intermediary if it is 'more than a noticeboard' enabling users to connect. An indication of that can be that the platform is the only means by which users can get in contact with each other, as the platform shields the contact data of the other party from them.[66] I will leave this issue aside for reasons of scope and complexity.

Turning to the legal relationships between users of the platform, these are often of a peer-to-peer or C2C nature, and only sometimes B2C. They are therefore mostly subject to the general or specific rules of contract law of an EU Member State. Potentially, the rules regulating tenancy contracts may apply, albeit that exceptions can apply to short-term lease contracts. The applicable law will have to be determined according to private international law, and in case of tenancy is likely to be the law of the country where the landlord has his habitual place of residence.[67] The balance between the contracting parties in these C2C situations is different from a B2C relationship. In general contract law, the balance is considered to be equal, and

[62] The company has a subsidiary based in Ireland, which is the contractual counterparty for all users resident in Europe. See <https://www.airbnb.com/terms>. Outside the United States, specific subsidiaries for China and Japan are also based in Ireland, which is attractive for companies because of its tax regime.

[63] The two standing parts of the triangle in Figure 7.1.

[64] <https://www.airbnb.com/terms>.

[65] See also Chapter 6, p 140.

[66] See Dutch Supreme Court, 15 October 2015, *Duinzigt v X*, ECLI:NL:HR:2015:3099.

[67] Rome I Regulation (n 47), Art 4(1)(d), which contains a specific rule for tenancy agreements for temporary private use for a period of not more than six consecutive months. For other contracts relating to immovable property, the law of the country where the accommodation is located applies; see Art 4(1)(c).

buyers do not enjoy consumer protection. They are, however, not entirely without protection, as they can invoke rights relating to mistake, misrepresentation, fraud, duress, abuse of circumstances, and such if they were misled or pressured into concluding a contract. Furthermore, guests of Airbnb properties could potentially invoke rules concerning the liability or other responsibilities of intermediaries. On that ground, they may be protected against conflicts of interests, or situations where information regarding the status of their counterparty is not disclosed to them, making them believe that they contract with a trader rather than a consumer. Unfortunately, the position and potential liability of platforms as intermediaries is still widely divergent between jurisdictions. Although the rules proposed in the EU's New Deal for Consumers aim to regulate some responsibilities, the resulting Directive on the modernization of consumer protection rules introduces only limited aspects of the relationship between platform and users.[68] The European Law Institute (ELI) Model Rules on Online Platforms go further, introducing liability for platforms that have failed to comply with transparency requirements towards users or that have a dominant influence on the contract between the parties.[69] Seeing that the rules are non-binding, they will not be discussed in more detail in this chapter.

2. Transparency

In terms of compliance with transparency requirements, Airbnb fell short of the standards set by EU consumer law in its relations with users. In July 2018, the European Commission, together with the pan-European network of consumer authorities, started enforcement discussions with Airbnb on the ground that the company failed to comply with mandatory transparency requirements towards consumers.[70] In particular, terms relating to the price (including extra fees such as service and cleaning charges) were said to be insufficiently clear to consumers before the conclusion of a contract. In response to this action, Airbnb agreed to commit to compliance with rules of EU consumer law.[71]

While enforcement of EU consumer law is one route through which to ensure transparency, other options exist, for example through national legislation or through instruments of private regulation. On the legislative side, action has been limited. The only example of specific legislation for transparency of online platforms, until now, is French law.[72] Airbnb has however also invested in private

[68] For a discussion, see Chapter 6, pp 140.

[69] Draft Instrument of the European Law Institute, *Model Rules on Online Platforms*, version available on 28 February 2020, Arts 19 and 20.

[70] European Commission, 'EU Consumer Rules: The European Commission and EU Consumer Authorities Push Airbnb to Comply', press release (n 45).

[71] European Commission, 'EU Consumer Rules: Airbnb Commits to Complying with European Commission and EU Consumer Authorities' Demands' (Press release, 20 September 2018) <http://europa.eu/rapid/press-release_IP-18-5809_en.htm>.

[72] The French *Loi pour la République numérique*, Loi No 2016-1321 du 7 octobre 2016 pour une République numérique. The full text of the law (in French) is available at <https://www.legifrance.

regulation.[73] Codes of conduct, online reviews, and online dispute resolution (ODR) mechanisms have helped to enhance transparency about the description and quality of the service that users can expect from the platform, as well as from the host or guest with whom they conclude a contract for the rental of accommodation.

Notably, most of these instruments are relevant to enhancing transparency in the relationship between users of the platform, the hosts and guests in a peer-to-peer relationship. EU and national consumer laws do not apply directly to these C2C relationships, which are governed primarily by the general contract rules of national laws, but the rules of consumer law may nonetheless have an indirect effect through the instruments of private regulation developed by the platform. Codes of conduct and community guidelines are soft mechanisms through which Airbnb can persuade hosts and guests to abide by certain conditions in their transactions with each other. I will leave aside the question whether these codes and guidelines constitute terms of the contract between Airbnb and its users, or whether they should be seen as implied terms in the contract between the users, which raises complex formal questions.[74] In the following I will focus on the substance of the rules laid down in private regulation and compare them to the transparency regime of EU consumer law. Through that exercise an evaluation can be made as to whether private regulation, directly or indirectly, achieves similar degrees of formal and substantive transparency as prescribed by EU law. I will also make a few brief observations on how the rules compare to the general contract laws of EU Member States representing the major legal traditions in the European Union—Germany, France, and (until Brexit occurs) England—to highlight how private regulation by the platform in any event improves the position of guests in comparison to default rules of general contract law.

Airbnb has introduced codes of conduct in response to problems encountered in practice. This has led, for example, to a set of 'community standards' on safety and security which were (so it appears) developed in response to cases where guests got injured or otherwise harmed at their rented accommodation,[75] and to

gouv.fr/affichTexte.do;jsessionid=CCB0E73C69E80F3D28A0914D8E2FD0F6.tplgfr23s_3?cidTexte=JORFTEXT000033202746&categorieLien=id>. For a discussion of the main aspects of the *Loi*, see Chapter 6, pp 141.

[73] The importance of private regulation as a means for trust-building in the largely unregulated platform economy was highlighted already by O Lobel, 'The Law of the Platform' (2016) 101 Minnesota Law Review 87, 146 ff.

[74] See Chapter 6, pp 132 ff.

[75] One striking example concerns the case of a German woman who discovered hidden cameras at her Airbnb rental in California. A brief summary of the case (in German) can be found in *Suddeutsche Zeitung* 14 January 2016, 'Deutsche Touristin entdeckt versteckte Kamera in Airbnb-Wohnung'. For the complaint filed with the court, see <http://ia801508.us.archive.org/24/items/gov.uscourts.cand.293740/gov.uscourts.cand.293740.1.0.pdf>. Other, rare cases concern instances where guests have died at properties rented through Airbnb; see 'Death in Airbnb rental raises liability questions' *New York Times* (New York, 13 November 2015); and <https://medium.com/matter/living-and-dying-on-airbnb-6bff8d600c04#.lcj7jb9yw>.

a non-discrimination policy in response to research revealing a high percentage of rejected bookings in the United States for African-American users of the platform.[76] Interestingly, the rules laid down in these codes of conduct at least reflect the transparency requirements of EU consumer law, and in some respects go further than is required by EU law. Airbnb's community standards, to begin with, focus on five aspects: safety, security, fairness, authenticity, and reliability.[77] Some of the rules postulated here correspond with rights that, in most legal systems, are enforceable through contract, tort, or criminal law. In relation to transparency, the following stipulations are of interest:[78]

- Authenticity

Your Airbnb experiences should be full of delightful moments and surprising adventures. Since our community is built on trust, authenticity is essential—it requires a balance of shared expectations, honest interactions, and accurate details.

- Misrepresenting yourself

You should not provide a false name or date of birth, use listings for commercial purposes without your host's permission, have events or parties without your host's approval, maintain duplicate accounts, or create an account if you're under 18.

- Misrepresenting your spaces

You should not provide inaccurate location information, have incorrect availability, mislead people about the type, nature, or details of your listing, substitute one listing for another, set up fake or fraudulent listings, leave fraudulent reviews, engage in deceptive pricing, or fail to disclose hazards and habitability issues.

- Experiences that are merely transactions

Airbnb began as a way to allow people to share their homes. Though Airbnb has grown since the early days, and home sharing has expanded around the world, we still expect that every listing is not just a transaction, but a place for others to belong.

A misrepresentation with regard to the advertised accommodation may amount to a misleading practice under EU Directive 2005/29/EC on unfair commercial practices. Required is that the average consumer would have made a different economic decision if he or she had been aware of the correct information

[76] B Edelman, M Luca, and D Svirsky, 'Racial Discrimination in the Sharing Economy: Evidence from a Field Experiment' (2017) 9 American Economic Journal: Applied Economics 1.
[77] See <https://www.airbnb.com/trust/standards>.
[78] ibid.

(Article 5 of the UCPD). Formally, however, this applies only if the transaction is of a B2C nature, meaning that the host can be classified as a professional trader.[79] Airbnb itself as platform operator escapes liability if misleading information is published on its website by a third party. Even if the information would qualify as illegal, the platform would in most cases still be exempt from liability on the ground of the so-called host exemption of the E-Commerce Directive.[80] The rules on 'misrepresenting yourself' and 'misrepresenting your spaces' otherwise correspond with rules on mistake and misrepresentation in English law, *Irrtum* in German law, and *erreur* in French law.[81]

Nevertheless, some rules laid down in Airbnb's community standards go further than these legal rights prescribe. The final stipulation on 'experiences that are merely transactions' is a case in point. It states the expectation that 'every listing is not just a transaction, but a place for others to belong'. That requirement goes beyond legal default rules on tenancy and, even if it could be contractually agreed upon between parties, it is something that most tenancy agreements do not specify. Should tenancy law not apply, for example because of an exception for short-term rentals, the default rules of general contract law will also not entitle guests to hold the expectation of a 'place to belong'. How to interpret this community guideline in terms of transparency, however, is another question. As an expression of formal transparency, it communicates to users that they are entitled to something more than the provision of a room in exchange for money. But what does this addition mean? Substantive transparency, that is, ensuring that the information is understandable to the average consumer, appears not to be met to the same degree. However, taking account of other Airbnb codes of conduct, one might be able to come up with a more precise interpretation of what it means 'to belong'. Airbnb for example introduced a non-discrimination code of conduct in 2016.[82]

A second mechanism that contributes to transparency are online review systems. For Airbnb, its online review system even functioned as a catalyst for the successful implementation of its non-discrimination policy. This shows that transparency can help achieve substantive goals. A field experiment on discrimination of guests seeking to book accommodation through Airbnb reveals that discrimination on the basis of race can be decreased by providing more information.[83] The study started from the finding that guests with African-American-sounding names were on average 19.2 per cent less likely to book an accommodation than those with

[79] Unfair Commercial Practices Directive (n 29).
[80] Directive 2000/31/EC on certain legal aspects of information society services, in particular electronic commerce, in the Internal Market [2000] OJ L178/1 (E-Commerce Directive), Arts 14 and 15.
[81] See H Beale and others, *Cases, Materials and Text on Contract Law* (2nd edn, Hart Publishing 2010) 441 ff.
[82] See Chapter 6, p 131.
[83] R Cui, J Li, and DJ Zhang, 'Reducing Discrimination with Reviews in the Sharing Economy: Evidence from Field Experiments on Airbnb', SSRN <https://ssrn.com/abstract=2882982>.

Caucasian sounding names. Adding peer reviews, even if only one positive review was added, evened out the differences between these two categories. The acceptance rate for guests with white sounding names in the experiment came out at 56.2 per cent, and the one for guests with African-American-sounding names at 58.1 per cent.[84] Interestingly, the acceptance rate also evened out if a negative review was added. The authors of the experiment put forward several potential explanations for that effect.[85] It may be that the host's prior beliefs about the behaviour of African-American guests were even lower than the review indicates. It could also be that the host's opinion improves because a review signifies that the guest has completed transactions on Airbnb before, indicating that the guest is likely to be more familiar with the process, that his or her identity is truthful, and that the guest has been accepted by other hosts in the community which establishes a social norm that the guest should be accepted. Altogether, therefore, a well-designed online review system can have a positive effect on the compliance of users with social norms and, as a corollary in case of non-discrimination, with legal rights.

More generally, empirical studies have shown that consumers regard online reviews as an important source of information at the pre-contractual stage. A 2013 study by the European Consumer Centres' Network (ECC-Net) found that 82 per cent of respondents read online consumer reviews before making a purchase.[86] For online reviews to fulfil an information function at the pre-contractual stage, it is however vital that the information posted by users is reliable.[87] As discussed in the previous chapter,[88] several mechanisms can be used to promote the reliability of information. In the case of Airbnb several choices have been made in the design of its online review system to ensure greater reliability of reviews. The system, for example, is a closed system that only allows registered users to post reviews of accommodations after they have actually stayed there.[89] Furthermore, the system is designed in a reciprocal manner, meaning that hosts and guests do not see the other party's review of them until they have written and posted their own review. This design is thought to enhance the reliability of information given, since it prevents users from adapting their own review in the light of positive or negative information given about them by the other party.[90]

[84] ibid 3.

[85] ibid 23–24.

[86] ECC-Net, 'Trust Marks Report 2013. Can I Trust the Trust Mark?' (October 2013) 51. Other online sources reveal varying, but always high numbers. It seems likely that at least 80–90 per cent of consumers reads consumer reviews before making online purchases.

[87] Also European Parliament, 'Online Consumer Reviews. The Case of Misleading or Fake Reviews' (Briefing, October 2015) <http://www.europarl.europa.eu/thinktank/en/document.html?reference=EPRS_BRI(2015)571301>.

[88] See Chapter 6, pp 147.

[89] This differs from platforms such as Tripadvisor, which allow anyone to post reviews, therefore lacking a verification of whether reviewers have even visited the places that they write about.

[90] G Bolton, B Greiner, and A Ockenfels, 'Engineering Trust: Reciprocity in the Production of Reputation Information' (2013) 59 Management Science 265, who studied how the quality of online reviews can be influenced, using eBay as a case study. Anecdotal evidence confirms that the system

The third instrument of private regulation on Airbnb that aims to maintain certain standards between the users of the platform is its Dispute Resolution Center. In theory, such an online dispute resolution facility could generate outcomes that the platform could use to help improve its services. For that to happen, two conditions need to be fulfilled:[91] the system needs to gather data on trader behaviour, and there should be a feedback system that loops these data back to the trader and forces them to comply with applicable laws and regulation. Those requirements of course apply to situations where the dispute resolution deals with disputes between customers and the trader. In the case of Airbnb we are looking at another side of the transactional triangle, namely the relation between the users: the host and the guest. The use of an ODR system can force these parties to comply with regulation, for example to pay out damages to the other party in case of harm caused to persons or things. In an indirect way, the system can nonetheless also influence the platform operator. For example, by gathering data on disputes between hosts and guests, Airbnb can learn on which points its service may be improved, and it has done so already. For example, in response to complaints about (the lack of) facilities at the rented accommodation, the platform can push hosts to post more and better information about the space. If an accommodation is accessible only by stairs, it is not suitable for wheelchair users, and the host should post information to that effect on the online listing. The code of conduct for hosts now reflects this by stipulating as tips under 'Accurate listing details' that hosts should

> [l]et guests know if there are parts of the listing that are off-limits, like a garage or the attic' and that they should '[b]e honest about unexpected factors that will impact your guest's stay. Your guests deserve to know if your neighbours just started a noisy construction project or if they'll have to climb 8 flights of stairs to get to your place.[92]

Nevertheless, reports on the functioning of Airbnb's dispute resolution centre suggest that the system does not function to everyone's satisfaction. Users complain that the system does little to weed out false claims, that hosts and guests who seek to prevent extortion by the other party should be careful to record information on the state of the accommodation upon check in and check out, for example

has this effect, but also that reviews are still always subjective. See eg 'Surviving a bad Airbnb review' *New York Times* (New York, 19 January 2018), where the author describes that she left out information on missing cleaning products from her review because she enjoyed her overall stay at the accommodation. Had she known that the host would write a negative review about her sloppy cleaning (sic), she would have included that information.

[91] See C Hodges, 'The Consumer as Regulator' in D Leczykiewicz and S Weatherill (eds), *The Images of the Consumer in EU Law. Legislation, Free Movement and Competition Law* (Hart Publishing 2016) 245, 246–47. Further Chapter 6, pp 149.

[92] <https://www.airbnb.com/hospitality>.

by taking photographs of broken furniture or unsafe situations, and that one has to invest a significant amount of time and energy in order to be successful.[93] Whether these reports are representative of the level of service provided by Airbnb's dispute resolution centre is hard to assess. The complaints posted on websites have not been subjected to a fact check, and even if they are true, they may reflect only a small percentage of the overall number of Airbnb rentals in a given period. Furthermore, logical explanations may exist for the aspects of the ODR system that users complain about and that perhaps they would accept as normal in other, offline situations. The dispute resolution centre, for instance, works with a limited number of employees who have a significant case load to get through each day. They have to prioritize claims—for example, intervene sooner in cases where a guest feels physically threatened or harassed by a host than in cases of damaged furniture—and they are dependent on the supporting documentation that hosts and guests submit to them to come to a fair solution.[94] Like most ODR systems, the gains of a dispute resolution centre lie in obtaining a quick solution to problems that arise between parties who have only weak connections, as they are basically strangers. Whether the outcomes are satisfactory and whether they are comparable to the solution that parties would have reached through litigation on a national court is very difficult to say without empirical evidence. For Airbnb, this is as true as it is for other online platforms.

Recapitulating, it appears that for approximately the first ten years of its existence Airbnb fell short of complying with the transparency requirements of EU consumer law, which apply to the relationship between the platform and its consumer users as a B2C relationship. Although the European Commission, together with national consumer authorities, instigated actions against this practice which led to a promise from Airbnb to commit to complying with the rules of EU consumer law, it is unlikely that this will solve the problem completely. As platforms innovate, situations are bound to come up again in which European rules of consumer law are not, or are insufficiently, taken into account. That is partly due to the fact that Europe does not compete with the United States in the development of online platform services, but instead has 'capitulated' and merely seeks to keep them in check through regulation.[95] Regulation, however, is usually one step behind innovation.[96] Private regulation, to some extent however can fill the void, since it

[93] For guidance from experienced Airbnb users, see <https://thebudgetsavvytravelers.com/2018/07/23/airbnb-dispute-resolution-center-process-qa-how-to-win/>.

[94] See the report from an alleged former case manager at Airbnb at <https://howtoairbnb.com/a-former-employee-just-spilled-the-beans-about-airbnbs-deepest-darkest-secrets/>. Note that it is hard to verify the source from which this information came and that no conclusions can be attached to it in terms of reliability, even though the comments come across as reasonable.

[95] Ferguson, *The Tower and the Square* (n 3). See also Introduction, pp 10.

[96] The term 'regulatory disconnect' reflects this in both a horizontal dimension (time) and a vertical dimension (level of generality); see A Butenko and P Larouche, 'Regulation for Innovativeness or Regulation of Innovation?' (2015) 7 Law, Innovation and Technology 52.

allows for a much faster development of new rules that can instantaneously be put in practice. The case study of Airbnb reveals that the platform has indeed invested in private regulation in several ways—codes of conduct, an online review system, an ODR centre—and in some cases has thereby introduced rules that protect consumers to the same, or a greater, extent as EU consumer law promises.

B. Case Study II: Amazon

The second case study focuses on Amazon. Although also an online platform, the company has other characteristics and a different business model than Airbnb, and some of the findings with regard to transparency in contracting therefore have a different nuance. Amazon was established in 1994 as an online bookstore.[97] It has since diversified its range of products, selling music, videos, toys, clothes, and other consumer goods, and has become one of the largest online retailers in the world. Its main competitor in the Asian market and increasingly also globally is Alibaba, which in China maintains a larger market share than Amazon.[98] Further, in specialized markets such as in film and television, the company competes with specialized providers such as Netflix, HBO, and national broadcasting companies. In the following, I will focus on the sale of goods, which still makes up the main part of Amazon's activities.

1. Applicable rules

Amazon's business model differs from Airbnb—and also from Alibaba—in that the company is itself a retailer, whereas Airbnb functions as an online platform that connects third-party users. That implies that some problems that were identified in the previous section with regard to transparency obligations do not apply. Since the relationship between Amazon, as an online retailer, and a customer is a direct one, rules of consumer law will apply in cases where the customer is a non-professional party. However, Amazon also functions as a marketplace where external suppliers are able to offer their goods. It is estimated that, with a steady increase in recent years, now just over 50 per cent of all products sold on Amazon's marketplace are sold by third-party traders.[99] That percentage is likely further to increase, as the

[97] See <https://edition.cnn.com/interactive/2018/10/business/amazon-history-timeline/index.html>.

[98] Alibaba holds a 60 per cent market share in the Chinese e-commerce market. See D Newman, 'Alibaba vs Amazon: The Battle of Disruptive Innovation beyond Traditional E-Commerce' Forbes (24 October 2018) <https://www.forbes.com/sites/danielnewman/2018/10/24/alibaba-vs-amazon-the-battle-of-disruptive-innovation-beyond-traditional-e-commerce/#2ef67f0b1759>.

[99] Measured for 2018; see <https://www.statista.com/statistics/259782/third-party-seller-share-of-amazon-platform/>. In 2015 the number was approximately 40 per cent; see JK Winn, 'The Secession of the Successful: The Rise of Amazon as Private Global Consumer Protection Regulator' (2016) 58 Arizona Law Review 193, 201, with reference to 'Technologies Transforming Transportation: Is the Government Keeping Up?', Hearing Before the Subcommittee On Surface Transportation and

company encourages the growth of third-party transactions, which are more profitable due to lower overhead costs and the possibility to charge fees for storage and shipping of goods.[100] This part of Amazon's marketplace is similar to Airbnb from the platform operator's perspective: they offer a platform that facilitates the conclusion of contracts and are a third party to the transaction between users. The transactions between users, that is between traders and customers, are B2C contracts in cases where third-party traders are professional sellers. Transactions may also be classified as peer-to-peer, which will be the case if a trader is not a professional party.[101] In the first case, rules of consumer law are applicable, in the second case the application of transparency duties will have to be determined on the basis of other rules, for example the general rules of contract law of the (national) law applicable to the contract.

Amazon therefore operates both as a direct retailer and as an intermediary platform enabling sales by third-party traders, with varying obligations with regard to transparency towards purchasers of goods. To most consumers, however, the overall service offered through the platform will appear as uniform. The reason for that is that the company prescribes very strict rules to third-party traders, making their service levels comply with the overall Amazon brand. These rules are laid down in the seller agreement that Amazon concludes with third-party sellers and associated policies.[102]

2. Transparency

In terms of substance, the level of consumer protection for purchases through Amazon is high. For the purposes of this case study, three sets of standard terms and conditions have been considered: (i) the terms applicable to purchases by consumers buying from Amazon;[103] (ii) the terms applicable to purchases by

Merchant Marine Infrastructure, Safety, and Security, 114th Congress 1 (2015) (statement of Paul Misener, Vice President for Global Public Policy, Amazon).

[100] Alibaba, by comparison, only accommodates sales by third-party traders. It does so without charging listing fees, thereby promoting entrepreneurship and giving small traders an opportunity to lift themselves out of poverty. See P Mourdoukoutas, 'Why Alibaba is More Profitable than Amazon' Forbes (6 May 2018) <https://www.forbes.com/sites/panosmourdoukoutas/2018/05/06/why-alibaba-is-more-profitable-than-amazon/#764829916788>.

[101] See above, p 164.

[102] See the 'Policies and agreements' page on Amazon Seller Central Europe <https://sellercentral.amazon.co.uk/gp/help/external/help-page.html?itemID=521&language=en_GB&ref=efph_521_bred_G1801>. For the purpose of this case study I use Amazon UK as a representative example for terms applicable in Europe, since these terms have been drafted in English. Other European Amazon sites are Amazon.de, Amazon.fr, and Amazon.es. Their terms and conditions are available in translation and are similar to the UK version, although on occasion specific national rules or policies apply. I will not discuss these specificities in detail but will mention one or two examples.

[103] Accessible through a link at the bottom of the main page of Amazon.co.uk <https://www.amazon.co.uk/gp/help/customer/display.html/ref=footer_cou?ie=UTF8&nodeId=201909000>. This page displays the Conditions of Use & Sale and also gives access to a range of other policies, eg concerning privacy, supply chain standards, and intellectual property rights.

consumers buying from a professional third-party trader through Amazon; and;[104] (iii) the terms applicable between Amazon and third-party traders.[105] As said, the first two are similar, so that consumers' purchasing experience through the Amazon website is standardized to ensure high quality levels. Focusing first on these, Amazon appears to provide a high level of transparency to consumers at various stages of concluding a purchasing contract. That is seen first in the relatively straightforward accessibility of terms and conditions for consumers. A link to the applicable terms is visible at the bottom of Amazon's main page and it connects consumers within a few clicks to relevant conditions and policies.[106] The substantive transparency of terms also appears to be in order. The terms and conditions are phrased in comprehensible language,[107] albeit that they make use of legal terminology that will not be familiar to many consumers. Nevertheless, sentences are relatively short, phrased in a direct manner,[108] and they appear to convey the information required by EU consumer directives in relation to, inter alia, e-commerce transactions, privacy, intellectual property rights, applicable law, jurisdiction, and the consumer's right of withdrawal. To give an example, Amazon's clause concerning the applicable law to a contract of sale between the platform and a consumer reads:[109]

> These conditions are governed by and construed in accordance with the laws of the Grand Duchy of Luxembourg, and the application of the United Nations Convention of Contracts for the International Sale of Goods is expressly excluded. If you are a consumer and have your habitual residence in the EU, you

[104] For information on conditions relating to such sales, Amazon refers consumers to the Participation agreement between itself and third-party traders (see n 105) through its Conditions of Use & Sale (n 103) Art 12. Alongside the contract between the consumer and the third-party trader, Amazon provides consumers with the Amazon A-to-Z guarantee; also see Art 12.

[105] The Participation agreement, or Amazon Services Europe Business Solutions Agreement <https://sellercentral.amazon.co.uk/gp/help/external/201190440?language=en-GB&ref=mpbc_3216781_cont_201190440>. Associated policies <https://sellercentral.amazon.co.uk/gp/help/external/help-page.html?itemID=521&language=en_GB&ref=efph_521_bred_G1801> and at related pages referred to in footnotes below.

[106] Winn, 'The Secession of the Successful: The Rise of Amazon as Private Global Consumer Protection Regulator' (n 99) at 206 already noted the prominent display and accessibility of terms. She tested the terms against the twelve principles for fair e-commerce developed by Americans for Fair Electronic Commerce Transactions (AFFECT), a coalition of consumer, business and library customers of mass-market digital products. The principles were developed under the leadership of Jean Braucher; see J Braucher, 'New Basics: Twelve Principles for Fair Commerce in Mass-Market Software and Other Digital Products' in JK Winn (ed), *Consumer Protection in the Age of the 'Information Economy'* (Ashgate 2006) 177.

[107] Confirming Winn's finding, see Winn, 'The Secession of the Successful: The Rise of Amazon as Private Global Consumer Protection Regulator' (n 99) 206.

[108] Both aspects, according to empirical studies of consumer behaviour, appear to enhance consumer comprehension. See M Elshout and others, 'Study on Consumers' Attitudes towards Terms and Conditions (T&Cs). Final Report' (European Commission 2016) <https://ec.europa.eu/info/sites/info/files/terms_and_conditions_final_report_en.pdf>.

[109] Conditions of Use & Sale (n 103) Art 14.

additionally enjoy the protection afforded to you by mandatory provisions of the law of your country of residence.

This provision is in accordance with Articles 3 and 6(2) of the Rome I Regulation,[110] which entitles parties to make a choice of law for the law of a state, whilst respecting mandatory rights of consumer protection that consumers enjoy in their country of residence. The exclusion of the UN Convention on Contracts for the International Sale of Goods (CISG) is valid in accordance with Article 6 CISG, albeit that its relevance for Amazon sales is likely to be minimal. The Convention applies to international business contracts, not to B2C contracts.[111]

Another example can be Article 14 of the Conditions of Use & Sale, which informs the consumer of his right of withdrawal from the contract.[112] The consumer has the right to rescind the contract without giving any reason, and without incurring any costs other than those for returning the goods, until fourteen calendar days from the delivery of the goods or, in case of services or digital content not supplied in a tangible medium, the conclusion of the contract.[113] Further, the consumer must be informed of his right of withdrawal. Failure to provide this information is sanctioned by extending the withdrawal period until twelve months after the delivery of the goods.[114] Including the information on the right of withdrawal in the terms and conditions is a low-cost manner of escaping that sanction. Amazon has complied with these requirements in Article 14 of its Conditions of Use & Sale. On a minor aspect, one may nonetheless wonder whether the stipulation that Amazon will 'reimburse delivery charges for the least expensive type of delivery offered by us' is valid. The CJEU has held that consumers who exercise the right of withdrawal are entitled to reimbursement of delivery costs, so as not to discourage consumers from exercising their right of withdrawal.[115] The judgment seems to imply that the actual delivery costs need to be reimbursed, which with regard to Amazon would imply that consumers would be entitled to a full reimbursement even if they had chosen a more expensive delivery option than standard shipping.

[110] Rome I Regulation (n 47). It also remedies the complaint that the consumer should be made aware of the additional protection that the national law of their country of residence may provide. Compare *Amazon* (n 16).

[111] UN Convention on Contracts for the International Sale of Goods (opened for signature 11 April 1980, entered into force 1 January 1988) 1489 UNTS 3 (CISG), Arts 1(1) and 2(a).

[112] This provision applies to third-party traders under certain conditions; see the Amazon Services Europe Business Solutions Agreement (n 105), Art S-2.2.

[113] Consumer Rights Directive (n 13), Art 9(1) and (2).

[114] Consumer Rights Directive (n 13), Art 10(1). The trader can shorten that period by providing the required information to the consumer, at which time a period of fourteen calendar days commences; see Art 10(2).

[115] Case C-511/08 *Handelsgesellschaf Heinrich Heine GmbH v Verbraucherzentrale Nordrhein-Westfalen eV* [2010] ECR I-3047, ECLI:EU:C:2010:189, at [52]–[54]. The case concerned the interpretation of Art 6 of Directive 97/7/EC on the protection of consumers in respect of distance contracts [1997] OJ L144/19, which has since been repealed and superseded by the Consumer Rights Directive (n 13).

As an aside, these findings are mostly confirmed when running the Conditions of Use & Sale through the analysis tool for unfair terms 'Claudette', developed by Hans Micklitz and Giovanni Sartor at the European University Institute.[116] In this respect, Amazon's standard terms and conditions perform very well in comparison to other online platforms. It should be borne in mind, however, that Claudette is currently a relatively crude tool for making this assessment and that it cannot reach the same degree of accuracy as a human trained in EU consumer law. As its algorithms are further developed it might become more accurate in its assessment of terms.

Besides complying with rules of EU consumer law, Amazon provides consumers with a significant amount of relevant information through its website, in many cases going beyond the requirements of EU law or national contract laws. The website gives information on the quality of products through star rankings and online reviews provided by purchasers, and it provides consumers with recommendations of products that they 'may also like' if they have looked at, or purchased a specific product.

The high level of consumer protection secured through Amazon's terms and policies, however, is not mirrored on the side of other users of the platform: third-party traders. The rules applicable to third-party traders are perhaps transparent—although they are not easily accessible for external parties who have not registered as sellers with Amazon—[117] but they impose a very strict governance regime on traders. In this respect, it is worthwhile to extend the analysis beyond transparency of terms. It can be seen that Amazon not only requires third-party traders to comply with their agreement with Amazon and all associated policies but also that strict performance targets are imposed. Traders 'should be working toward achieving and maintaining a level of customer service that meets the following seller performance targets for every product they sell': an order defect rate of less than 1 per cent; a cancellation rate of less than 2.5 per cent; and a late dispatch rate of less than 4 per cent.[118] Other metrics that are taken into account to measure the trader's performance are percentages of orders that have received negative feedback from consumers; an A-to-Z guarantee claim; or a service credit card chargeback.[119] Traders can monitor their performance through an online tool provided by Amazon. Those who do not meet their targets are generally given a warning and

[116] See <http://www.claudette.eui.eu>. Some results are incorrect—eg Claudette picks up on the applicable law and jurisdiction clauses as potentially unfair—which may be explained by the programme's independent reading of sentences rather than in combination. This means that additions in a follow up sentence which add nuance and make terms comply with EU law are not picked up on. The programme is of course still in its developing stages and it is likely that legal text analysis tools such as Claudette will improve in the future.

[117] For this case study, I located the relevant terms and policies—listed in n 105—through a Google search, which led me to the Amazon Seller Central Europe website. While parties signing up as sellers appear to be directed to this page, there are no visible links on Amazon.co.uk (or other Amazon websites) that enable other users to find the information on the Seller Central website.

[118] See <https://sellercentral.amazon.co.uk/gp/help/external/200370550?language=en_GB&ref=efph_200370550_cont_521>.

[119] ibid.

will then have sixty days to improve their performance measurably, or risk having their accounts suspended.[120]

These terms are strict and they can in practice be very hard for third-party traders to comply with. Although in Europe the plight of these traders has been recognized and acted upon by the EU legislator, the Regulation on transparency and fairness in platform-to-business relations[121] is unlikely to create a more equal balance between platforms and traders. The Regulation requires that the delisting of goods or the suspension of accounts is accompanied by a statement of reasons. Whereas that requirement can enhance transparency, it does not prevent platforms from holding third-party traders to very strict terms and conditions, and from suspending their accounts in case they do not meet the company's targets.

The requirements imposed on third-party traders with regard to performance appear to be harsh also because of Amazon's enforcement practice. Disputes between traders and customers are resolved through Amazon's dispute resolution centre. Complaints made by traders indicate that Amazon will often rule in favour of the retail customer, even contrary to its own regulations, for example if the trader has complied with all requirements for an A-to-Z guaranteed sale and goods fail to arrive.[122] The balance between the rights of consumers and businesses, or more generally buyers and sellers, that characterizes national contract laws seems to be missing here.

Amazon's business model therefore differs from Airbnb by imposing a much stricter governance framework for transactions between users. The company's extensive regulation of the services rendered by third-party traders means that transparency as well as quality of service can be maintained at a consistent and high level for customers purchasing goods through the website. Practically, therefore, Amazon's practices comply with many of the requirements found in EU consumer law. The company has even served 'as a transmission vector for bringing European consumer rights into the American market'.[123] The driver for this strong focus on consumer rights and enforcement is Amazon's policy to always put customer satisfaction first, which has been a cornerstone of the company's popularity and growth.[124]

For the purpose of establishing the functioning of private regulation, Amazon's case provides again a falsification of the idea that private regulation leads to lower

[120] ibid.

[121] See Chapter 6, pp 138.

[122] In that case, the Selling Policies—formerly the Amazon Marketplace Community Guidelines—prescribe that Amazon will not hold traders responsible for a claim. See Winn, 'The Secession of the Successful: The Rise of Amazon as Private Global Consumer Protection Regulator' (n 99) 202. See also <https://sellercentral.amazon.co.uk/gp/help/external/G27951?language=en_GB>.

[123] Winn, 'The Secession of the Successful: The Rise of Amazon as Private Global Consumer Protection Regulator' (n 99) 208; JK Winn and M Webber, 'The Impact of EU Unfair Contract Terms Law on US Business-to-Consumer Internet Merchants (2006) 62 Business Law 209.

[124] Winn, 'The Secession of the Successful: The Rise of Amazon as Private Global Consumer Protection Regulator' (n 99) 210–11.

levels of consumer protection. In practice, consumers are often given stronger entitlements than they would have under default rules of contract law. However, benefits for consumers do not come for free but have ramifications for other stakeholder groups in society. The trade-off of Amazon's strong customer satisfaction policy is that third-party traders often have to accept solutions that are to their detriment and in many cases not even fair if the applicable rules—imposed by Amazon itself—are taken into consideration. Further, the service level that Amazon provides to customers can be maintained because the company recruits employees for their warehouses at often ungenerous terms. Reports continue to reveal issues with regard to unsafe work environments, low wages, long working hours, and constant surveillance.[125]

C. Conclusions from the Case Studies

Returning to the question of consumer protection that is central to this chapter, the two case studies provide a useful overview of the regulatory landscape of the platform economy. They reveal a mix of public and private regulation at work. EU consumer law is sometimes directly applicable, namely where it concerns the relationships between the platform and its consumer users. In that case, the maintenance of the EU's 'high level of consumer protection' is a matter of enforcement rather than of lawmaking. The case of Airbnb illustrates that enforcement does not necessarily require sanctions but can also be achieved through mutual actions by the authorities and the platform. Still, enforcement can be problematic as consumer authorities have to work with limited resources and generally are not in a position to follow up on compliance with EU consumer law of all general terms and conditions used by businesses.

Further, platforms and users can fall back on general rules of private law of the EU Member States. Those laws provide some further protection in cases where transparency towards users is in issue, in particular for C2C and B2B relationships, in the form of legal actions based on mistake, misrepresentation, fraud, duress, abuse of circumstances, or pre-contractual liability based on tort law. It will not always be clear to consumers which actions are available to them, in particular if they are contracting with parties in other countries and possibly under rules of national law.

[125] See eg S Ghosh, 'Peeing in trash cans, constant surveillance, and asthma attacks on the job: Amazon workers tell us their warehouse horror stories' *Business Insider* (London, 3 May 2018) <https://www.businessinsider.nl/amazon-warehouse-workers-share-their-horror-stories-2018-4/?international=true&r=US>; C Lieber, 'Amazon warehouse workers in Europe spent Black Friday protesting' Vox (27 November 2018) <https://www.vox.com/the goods/2018/11/27/18114735/amazon-warehouse-workers-europe-protests-black-friday>.

The case study on Airbnb reveals, however, that the platform itself has developed transparency rules that in some cases go further than the requirements of EU law or national contract laws. Examples are codes of conduct, online review systems, and—although perceived to have achieved only limited success—ODR mechanisms. Also contract terms themselves, as seen in the case study on Amazon, can ensure high levels of transparency towards consumers, as well as an overall policy to secure high levels of customer satisfaction. In these respects, platforms are taking responsibility to ensure high levels of transparency for users.

Importantly, however, the drivers of consumer protection on online platforms are primarily based on business and marketing practices. Online platforms only thrive if they can attract users who trust that the services rendered by or through the platform are safe and of a high quality. Hence, platforms have an interest in ensuring customer or user satisfaction. As was seen in the case study on Amazon, that can be at the cost of protecting other parties that find themselves in a weaker bargaining position vis-à-vis the platform, such as third-party traders.

VI. Analysis

Bringing together the several strands that run through this chapter, the following observations can be made in relation to lawmaking in the platform economy. Primarily, that the instrumental-normative approach to lawmaking in European private law advocated in this book appears to have empirical grounding: the norms that have emerged roughly meet the minimum level of consumer protection of EU law. Noteworthy is, however, that there is variation. In some respects, consumer protection issues remain unregulated, or rules laid down in legislation and public regulation are difficult to enforce. On the other hand, private regulation has stepped in to fill that gap, and occasionally introduces rules that go beyond transparency requirements laid down in EU law.

For the bigger picture of lawmaking in European private law, the study of transparency in the platform economy made in this chapter highlights several points that have come to the fore in previous chapters. In relation to norms, the emergence of the platform economy can be seen as a paradigmatic example of legal pluralism in action. The decline of public regulation, and the consequent shift towards private regulation, has created opportunity for the development of norms by a range of actors, including platforms and platform users. That diversification of lawmaking, at least initially, has led logically to a variety of norms developed and applied to private law relationships in the platform economy. That is laudable to the extent that norms are a reflection of public autonomy, but it is not beneficial to transparency (of the rules themselves, this time) and enforcement.

In time, rules may grow closer together if 'best practices' are exchanged between actors.[126]

In the dialectic relation between EU law's market integration rationality and national laws' juridical rationality, the shift towards private regulation raises deeper concerns that require continuous monitoring. Whereas legislators in Europe have a duty to safeguard the interests of consumers—or more broadly, citizens—private actors operate according to other drivers. The two case studies reveal varying dynamics. In Amazon's case, where the online platform is a retailer of goods that aims to standardize its levels of service and quality attached to its brand, there is a strong driver for ensuring consumer satisfaction. This results in well-developed rules of private regulation that offer high levels of consumer protection, as tested here in relation to transparency in contracting. That high level of consumer protection, however, comes at a cost. Third-party traders operating through the platform are held to very strict rules that are far removed from the balancing of fairness in European or national private laws.[127]

The case study on Airbnb, on the other hand, reveals that rules developed for a peer-to-peer platform for services operate are influenced by other drivers that are not inherently focused on consumer satisfaction or consumer protection. The development of codes of conduct, online review systems, and ODR mechanisms is only in part driven by the wish to enhance consumer or user protection. The motivation for platforms to invest in such mechanisms is that they are a means to sustain the platform's operations. The platform economy requires mechanisms that instil trust between users who do not know each other and who are often far apart in geographical distance. For platforms to attract users they need to secure 'systems of stranger trust'.[128] While that can in practice lead to norms that comply with or go beyond the level of consumer protection of EU law, that is not a given. Platform operators are in a position to monitor which measures are needed to maintain trust and to attract users, and they could, subject to the characteristics of the market, choose to downgrade protection.

This problem is particularly salient in the platform economy, which is strongly focused on services. Platforms have emerged as competitors to companies in regulated markets and have, due to innovative solutions, rapidly attracted large amounts of users. In these circumstances, when the demand side of a market increases significantly and many consumers wish to purchase goods or services from a certain platform, the platform has a powerful position to determine its user terms and conditions. Consumers are likely to still use the platform, for example because it has the largest range of suppliers and therefore the

[126] The next chapter will delve deeper into mechanisms for lawmaking that can be adopted to 'manage' legal pluralism in European private law.

[127] The recently adopted P2B Regulation aims to introduce some protection for small businesses in relation to fairness and transparency; see P2B Regulation (n 53).

[128] A term used by Lobel, 'The Law of the Platform' (n 73) 146.

largest offer of a particular type of good or service in the market. In the platform economy, situations where one operator becomes the biggest or only player in the market are common. Airbnb, Uber, and Facebook are examples of platforms that hold the largest market share in their respective markets. Once a tipping point has been passed where one player becomes the biggest in the market, the safeguarding of consumer protection comes under pressure. Although competition law is the first mechanism that could provide a response,[129] consumer law can act as a safety net if competition law fails to secure sufficient quality of goods or services, or information about those goods and services.[130] Whether consumer law can give an adequate response, however, is uncertain in the light of the examination made in this chapter. Dominant platforms have lesser incentive to work on customer satisfaction as they have already secured their position in the market.

Doctrinally, lawmaking in the platform economy also creates new challenges. As was seen, the rules developed through private regulation sometimes go beyond party expectations that would be actionable through doctrines of national private law systems. Questions may arise as to whether such promises can or should be enforced through contract law, or in other words, which consumer expectations should be deemed reasonable if one considers national laws and practices. Further, the question whether consumers in C2C relations concluded through a platform should benefit from consumer protection touches upon categorizations that are deeply embedded in private law systems. The rationale for protection, nonetheless, may well be present. Consumers in C2C relations through platforms are likely to have chosen goods or services that to them are comparable to those offered by traders, hence in a B2C relationship. Airbnb again can serve as an example. Guests booking through the platform are likely to choose an Airbnb rental as an alternative to hotel accommodation, yet they wish to enjoy similar amenities and safety levels.[131] They should on that ground perhaps enjoy similar consumer protection through contract law as they would have in B2C relationships. Some discussion is taking place on this matter, but mostly in relation to the responsibilities that could be placed on platforms in cases where it is unclear to consumers that they are not dealing with a professional trader. The normative question deserves further debate.

Overall, the legal pluralist challenges that arise in relation to the platform economy are connected to the same thing: the role of private actors as

[129] See R Podszun and S Kreifels, 'Digital Platforms and Competition Law' (2016) 5 Journal of European Consumer and Market Law 33. For an economic perspective on 'tipping points' in data-driven markets, of which the platform economy is a typical example, see JO Prüfer and C Schottmüller, 'Competing with Big Data', Tilburg Law School Legal Studies Research Paper Series No 06/2017, SSRN <https://ssrn.com/abstract=2918726>.

[130] J Drexl, *Die wirtschaftliche Selbstbestimmung des Verbrauchers* (Mohr Siebeck 1998).

[131] See above, pp 165.

lawmakers. This chapter has provided empirical support for the hypothesis that private actors in European private law act as lawmakers, autonomously and largely outside the reach of public legislation or regulation. While the norms emanating from the private sphere can, and often are, of a level that corresponds with EU law's consumer protection framework, there is a risk that norms fall below that level. The development of norms by private actors is market-driven, rather than based on regulatory goals. To secure the objectives and values of EU law, therefore, other mechanisms will have to monitor, and where necessary correct, the outcomes reached in private regulation. Some options were mentioned in an earlier chapter:[132] the use of standardization in contract law, the use of optional instruments or model laws, and monitoring through online dispute resolution. The next chapter will examine these in detail.

[132] Chapter 5, p 125.

8
More Normativity
Standardization

Are the case studies on online platforms representative for consumer markets governed for a large part through contracting and private regulation? A third case study can provide material for comparison and for testing the robustness of the findings. That case study will focus on standardization, which presents itself as the most significant example of private governance in European consumer markets. Standardization can be defined as a process of private regulation whereby private actors engage in the development of standardized norms for particular sectors of industry or for particular types of contract.

Notably, standardization does not take place completely in the private sphere, as is the case for online platforms where contractual terms, codes of conduct, and private governance mostly remain untested in court or in (co-)regulatory processes.[1] Standardization can take the form of self-regulation, but in Europe it is more often an expression of co-regulation between the European legislator and private actors who are stakeholders in a specific sector or industry, for example businesses or consumers in the energy market. Harmonized standards, which are developed by European standard-setting organizations (ESOs) at the instigation of the European legislator, are the prime example of such processes. In the European Union they make up a significant part of the work of standard-setting bodies.[2] That finding is relevant to the enquiry into legal pluralism as it means that norms developed through standardization are to some extent kept in check by public institutions, and that standardization is therefore perhaps not a true example of strong legal pluralism. My contention is, however, that it would be too simple to dismiss standards from the pluralist framework. The claim put forward in this chapter is that standardization in European contract and consumer law, even though it is embedded in public governance, gives expression primarily to norms developed by private actors. It therefore can be regarded as a source of private regulation that

[1] Lindahl has argued that online platforms like eBay, which are governed through contracts and online dispute resolution (ODR), can be regarded as global legal orders; see H Lindahl, *Authority and the Globalisation of Inclusion and Exclusion* (CUP 2018) 149–56.

[2] About 30 per cent of the European Standards published by the European Committee for Standardization (CEN), one of the main ESOs, are harmonized standards. See https://www.cen.eu/you/EuropeanStandardization/Pages/default.aspx accessed 28 February 2020, as are all websites in this chapter.

Legal Pluralism in European Contract Law. Vanessa Mak, Oxford University Press (2020). © Vanessa Mak.
DOI: 10.1093/oso/9780198854487.001.0001.

contributes to the development of norms through a substantive deliberation with other sources, in particular EU law and national contract and tort laws. The balancing between EU law's market rationality and national private laws' juridical rationality that characterizes European private law can also be observed in this process of deliberation.[3]

This chapter will first substantiate the claim that standardization is an expression of private regulation in a legal pluralist constellation by describing in more detail what place standardization has in the EU's governance framework, with particular focus on harmonized standards (section I). The private character of these standards is emphasized by their application through voluntary use by the standards' addressees (section II). Concluding that an important space for deliberation on the substance of such standards exists in the interplay between EU law and norms laid down in national contract and tort laws, section III will examine the substantive quality of harmonized standards. This part of the case study can determine whether the instrumental-normative approach to lawmaking put forward in this book resonates in practice. It will do so, following the Court of Justice of the European Union's (CJEU's) judgment in *Schmitt v TÜV Rheinland* (henceforth *Schmitt*),[4] by comparing the quality of standards for medical devices against the national contract and tort laws of a small number of representative EU Member States. Quality, in this context, will be assessed on the basis of the protection that rules can ensure for consumers or patients, in accordance with the goals and values of the relevant EU legislation. More specifically, protection will be assessed in relation to two aspects that are fundamental to private law—in particular tort law—namely the potential to prevent against harm, and the ability to compensate those who have suffered harm.[5] Section IV will conclude, focusing on how the case study in this chapter can inform the instrumental-normative approach to lawmaking put forward in this book. Even if actual outcomes sometimes fall short of preventing harm or compensating for it, lawmaking actors in Europe appear to be working towards the same objectives.

I. Standardization in Europe

This chapter focuses on harmonized standards as a case study for lawmaking in European private law from a legal pluralist perspective. Besides the use of harmonized standards, other types of standardization are also present in the European market, for instance national standards and standards developed by international

[3] On the rationalities underlying European private law, see in detail Chapter 5, pp 96–97.
[4] Case C-219/15, *Elisabeth Schmitt v TÜV Rheinland LGA Products GmbH*, ECLI:EU:C:2017:128.
[5] Deterrence and compensation are generally regarded as goals of tort law; see eg D Nolan, 'Causation and the Goals of Tort Law' in A Robertson and HW Tang (eds), *The Goals of Private Law* (Hart Publishing 2009) 165. See further below, p 196.

standard-setting bodies. Whereas an examination of other standards could also give insight in the substantive norms developed by private standard-setting bodies, the choice to focus on harmonized standards is inspired by their central position in the developing case law of the CJEU on standards. That case law touches upon the central themes of this book—in particular the space for a substantive deliberation of norms and values between lawmaking actors, which the Court reframes but also preserves in its case law on harmonized standards. Before discussing that case law in detail, this section and the next provide some background on the place of harmonized standards in the broader framework of standardization in Europe.

Starting with a definition, standards can either take the form of technical standards, prescribing the essential requirements that products should comply with, or services standards, which prescribe standard norms for services contracts. While in relation to services contracts standardization is a relatively recent phenomenon in European lawmaking, the creation and use of technical standards has a longer history in Europe as well as internationally.

Internationally, the best-known standard-setting organization is the International Organization for Standardization (ISO).[6] In the European Union, besides national organizations, the major ESOs are the European Committee for Standardization (CEN), the European Committee for Electrotechnical Standardization (CENELEC), and the European Telecommunications Standards Institute (ETSI).[7] These standard-setting bodies can independently determine new standardized rules but they are also involved in co-regulation through the New Approach to Technical Harmonization and Standards.

The New Approach, which is no longer so new anymore,[8] was introduced by the European legislature in 1985 as a model for creating technical and quality standards through co-regulation between private standard-setting bodies and the European Commission.[9] Even though it was originally intended as an instrument for the control of product safety standards, that aim failed, and a separate directive was required to deal with that issue.[10] The New Approach has nonetheless stimulated the creation of standards in a range of other areas, such as construction, cosmetics,

[6] For information and access to ISO standards, see <https://www.iso.org/home.html>.

[7] Regulation (EU) No 1025/2012 on European standardisation [2012] OJ L316/12, recital 4. See also <https://www.cencenelec.eu/Pages/default.aspx>.

[8] Revisions have been introduced, however, most recently in 2015. See Directive (EU) 2015/1535 laying down a procedure for the provision of information in the field of technical regulations and of rules on Information Society services [2015] OJ L241/1.

[9] Micklitz regards the New Approach as providing the leading regulatory concept underlying lawmaking in European private law; see H-W Micklitz, 'The Visible Hand of European Regulatory Private Law—The Transformation of European Private Law from Autonomy to Functionalism in Competition and Regulation' (2009) 28 Yearbook of European Law 3, 43.

[10] Directive 92/59/EC on general product safety [1992] OJ L228/24, which has since been replaced by Directive 2001/95/EC on general product safety [2002] OJ L11/4. Compare Micklitz, 'The Visible Hand of European Regulatory Private Law' (n 9) 40.

energy efficiency, electronics, healthcare engineering, and sustainability.[11] The European Commission in the 1980s intended to include services in this regime, yet it was not until the early 2000s that standards for services started to emerge. In recent years, however, standardization of services in the European Union has gradually appeared through bottom-up processes, that is, voluntary adoption of standards by the industry, and has also found a legal basis in the EU Services Directive.[12] Furthermore, in 2013 the European Commission mandated the three ESOs to identify topics for horizontal service standards. This led to the selection of three specific areas for the development of standards, starting in 2016: performance measurement, service contracts, and service procurement.[13]

II. Voluntary Character

Standards are instruments of private regulation, which are in some markets or industries preferred over public regulation due to their greater flexibility and the idea that they are an actual and direct reflection of the rules favoured by parties in those markets.[14] The voluntary character of standards—in their creation, adoption, and use—is essential to maintaining these aspects. In the European Union, however, the creeping influence of public regulation on standards is raising questions as to how much space is left for voluntary action by private actors.

The embeddedness of standards in public governance structures can be seen in three congruent developments concerning harmonized standards at the EU level of regulation. First, harmonized standards have become subject to *ex-ante* approval by the European Commission, confirmed by publication in the official journal.[15] Second, the CJEU has held that EU free movement rules apply to private certification bodies, meaning that standards developed by these bodies can be set aside if they infringe the free movement provisions.[16] Third, the Court has held that harmonized standards are part of EU law and therefore subject to interpretation by the Court.[17]

[11] For an overview, see <https://ec.europa.eu/growth/single-market/european-standards/harmonised-standards_en>.

[12] Directive (EC) 2006/123 on services in the internal market [2006] OJ L376/36. See P Delimatsis, 'Standardisation in Services—European Ambitions and Sectoral Realities' (2016) 41 European Law Review 513; C Busch, 'DIN-Normen für Dienstleistungen—Das Europäische Normungskomitee produziert Musterverträge' (2010) Neue Juristische Wochenschrift 3061.

[13] See <http://ec.europa.eu/growth/single-market/services/service-standards_en>. Delimatsis, 'Standardisation in Services' (n 12) 530 ff.

[14] H Schepel, *The Constitution of Private Governance: Product Standards in the Regulation of Integrating Markets* (Hart Publishing 2005) 31, also pointing out that public regulation is often regarded as scoring better on accountability and legitimacy.

[15] In more detail Chapter 9, pp 209.

[16] Case C-171/11 *Fra.bo SpA v Deutsche Vereinigung des Gas- und Wasserfaches eV (DVGW)—Technisch-Wissenschaftlicher Verein*, ECLI:EU:C:2012:453. Notably, this ruling applies to all standards developed by private certification bodies, not only harmonized standards developed by ESOs.

[17] Case C-613/14 *James Elliott Construction Ltd v Irish Asphalt Ltd*, ECLI:EU:C:2016:821.

Notwithstanding the creeping influence of public institutions on standardization, one aspect that preserves the private nature of standards is that their use still depends on voluntary adoption by a standard's addressees. Even if harmonized standards have been developed, manufacturers, other economic operators, and conformity assessment bodies remain free to choose another technical solution to demonstrate that they have complied with essential requirements laid down in EU directives or regulations.[18]

The private nature of norms developed by standard setting-organizations is preserved also by the hesitance of EU institutions to impose regulatory consequences on the non-compliance with standards. The CJEU has been unwilling to develop the goals laid down in EU law directives into more concrete liability rules, for which it would have had the opportunity in *Schmitt*. Hence, harmonized standards in combination with national laws determine on which grounds and in which circumstances liability can arise. I turn to that case law now.

III. Standards, Courts, and National Laws

The Court of Justice has recently clarified how it regards the relation between harmonized standards and the national contract and tort laws of the EU Member States. The decision in *Schmitt* is emblematic in this respect.[19]

TÜV Rheinland is a German, private certification body for medical devices. It was one of several national certification bodies that became involved in litigation in the wake of the PIP scandal. The PIP litigation concerned physical harm suffered by women whose silicone breast implants, manufactured by Poly Implant Prothèse (PIP), ruptured and started leaking. As it turned out, the manufacturer had a practice of using industrial silicone gel rather than silicone gel intended for medical use, and used this seemingly randomly in the production of the breast implants. This practice had largely escaped the attention of supervisory authorities.[20] The scandal affected thousands of women in a number of EU Member States.[21] Damages claims were filed in several jurisdictions, including the United Kingdom, Germany, France, and the Netherlands. They were directed not only at the manufacturer's insurer but also at doctors and clinics who had provided breast implant procedures,

[18] Schepel, *The Constitution of Private Governance* (n 14) 231–32. See also <https://ec.europa.eu/growth/single-market/european-standards/harmonised-standards_nl>.

[19] *Schmitt* (n 4).

[20] Although the US supervisory agency Food and Drug Administration (FDA) discovered that PIP breast implants contained sub-standard industrial silicone gel in 2000, after which the implants were temporarily taken off the US and French markets.

[21] For a study of the risks associated with PIP breast implants, see the independent report published by an expert group of the UK National Health Service (NHS) in 2015; B Keogh, 'Poly Implant Prothèse (PIP) Breast Implants: Final Report of the Expert Group' (NHS 2015) <https://www.gov.uk/government/publications/poly-implant-prothese-pip-breast-implants-final-report-of-the-expert-group>.

at national public health agencies, and finally at the EU certification body, TÜV Rheinland, that was meant to supervise PIP's activities and through inspections ensure that EU quality and safety standards were being complied with in the production of silicone breast implants.[22] TÜV Rheinland, in this context, was a so-called notified body, an organization registered with the European Commission and approved as an actor that carries out conformity assessment procedures for specific EU directives.[23] The CJEU ruled that a notified body is not under a general obligation to carry out unannounced inspections, to examine devices, or to examine the manufacturer's business records, but that this is different where there is evidence indicating that a medical device may not comply with the requirements laid down in Directive 93/42.[24] In that case, the notified body has to comply with Article 16(6) of the Directive, which requires it, taking account of the principle of proportionality, to 'suspend or withdraw the certificate issued or place any restrictions on it unless compliance with such requirements is ensured by the implementation of appropriate corrective measures by the manufacturer'. Further, failure of the notified body to fulfil its obligations under the Directive may result in liability, to be determined however according to rules of national law.[25]

The Court's judgment, therefore, opens up the possibility for notified bodies to be held liable by individual citizens who have been harmed by products over which the notified body has exercised insufficient supervision. At the same time, however, the Court is not willing to rule that notified bodies *should* be held liable, and under what exact conditions, leaving that question for national courts to decide on the basis of national tort law. Also, the case leaves open the possibility for separate actions against hospitals or doctors who had used the defective medical devices on the basis of national tort or contract law. The way in which liability is assessed in the interplay between standards and national laws is directly relevant to the central question of this chapter, concerning the quality of norms (section III.B). However, it is also relevant to see that legal pluralism is preserved due to the CJEU's unwillingness to develop liability rules under EU law. This can be perceived as a conflict between the EU's internal market rationality and national laws' juridical rationality (section III.A).

22 See BJ van Leeuwen, 'PIP Breast Implants, the EU's New Approach for Goods and Market Surveillance by Notified Bodies' (2014) 5 European Journal of Risk Regulation 338.

23 Decision No 768/2008/EC on a common framework for the marketing of products [2008] OJ L218/82. See for further information <https://ec.europa.eu/growth/single-market/goods/building-blocks/notified-bodies_en>.

24 *Schmitt* (n 4) [47].

25 ibid paras 51–60.

A. (Non-)liability under EU Law

In relation to the question of liability of supervisory authorities, the Court might in *Schmitt* have gone further than it did. The Court followed its earlier decision in *Paul*, a case concerning the potential liability of public supervisory authorities in financial markets, where it held that the relevant EU directives in that field could 'not be regarded as conferring on individuals, in the event that their deposits are unavailable as a result of defective supervision on the part of the competent national authorities, rights capable of giving rise to liability on the part of the State on the basis of Community law'.[26] However, that decision did not as such restrict the Court to come to a similar conclusion in *Schmitt*. The aim of the applicable EU legislation was different, and therefore *Paul* would not need to be followed in relation to medical devices; a point forcefully made by Norbert Reich.[27] In its recitals, the Medical Devices Directive explicitly states as one of its aims that 'medical devices should provide patients, users and third parties with a high level of protection'.[28] This could have been a ground for the Court to find liability of notified bodies under EU law in cases where supervision had fallen short, fitting with the principle of effectiveness.[29] The circumstances were different in *Paul*, where it would have gone against the aim of the applicable EU legislation to hold public supervisory agencies liable. In that case, Directives 94/19, 77/80, 89/299, and 89/646 aimed to create a single license system for credit institutions.[30] The legislation was not, or at least not directly, concerned with the protection of end-users.

It has been suggested that the CJEU perhaps shied away from a firm standpoint on liability of notified bodies because it predicted that liability would follow under the applicable German rules of tort law. The finding that supervisory action would have required TÜV Rheinland to suspend PIP's manufacturing license when evidence surfaced concerning the possible defectiveness of their products could be a basis for liability. The German statutory rules (*Schutzgesetz*) have a broad

[26] Case C-222/02 *Peter Paul, Cornelia Sonnen-Lütte and Christel Mörkens v Bundesrepublik Deutschland* [2004] ECR I-9425, at [51].

[27] N Reich, 'Product Liability and Beyond: An Exercise in Gap-Filling' (2016) 24 European Review of Private Law 619, 638.

[28] Directive 93/42/EEC concerning medical devices [1993] OJ L169/1 (Medical Devices Directive). This directive will be replaced in the Spring of 2020. See Regulation (EU) 2017/745 on medical devices [2017] OJ L117/1 (Medical Devices Directive) and <https://ec.europa.eu/growth/sectors/medical-devices/regulatory-framework_nl>.

[29] Compare PWJ Verbruggen and BJ van Leeuwen, 'The Liability of Notified Bodies under the EU's New Approach: The Implications of the PIP Breast Implants Case' (2018) 43 European Law Review 394, 400.

[30] Directive 94/19/EC on deposit-guarantee schemes [1994] OJ L135/5; First Council Directive 77/780/EEC on the coordination of laws, regulations and administrative provisions relating to the taking up and pursuit of the business of credit institutions [1977] OJ L322/30; Council Directive 89/299/EEC on the own funds of credit institutions [1989] OJ L124/16; Second Council Directive 89/646/EEC on the coordination of laws, regulations and administrative provisions relating to the taking up and pursuit of the business of credit institutions and amending Directive 77/780 [1989] OJ L386/1.

protective scope.[31] While it cannot be surmised from the judgment what motivated the Court to rule as it did, it cannot per se be assumed that considerations about the outcome in the case pending before the national court was decisive. The CJEU does not engage with outcomes in pending cases, and it is not obliged to, having an interpretative function only in preliminary reference procedures. Although the Court occasionally answers preliminary questions in such a way that the outcome is prescribed, research on judicial dialogues confirms that the Court sometimes avoids answering questions so as to leave space for the national court to reach a suitable outcome within the context of the applicable rules of national law and the circumstances of the case.[32] The procedural autonomy of the Member States can also explain the Court's hesitance to find liability under EU law. Holding notified bodies liable and stipulating the conditions under which liability can be found would interfere with the national procedures for individual actions in tort law. The Court is balancing in these types of cases between the two rationalities described in Chapter 5: the EU's internal market rationality, which would support the pursuit of goals laid down in EU legislation and can be seen as instrumental in nature; and the juridical rationality of the Member States, which seeks to preserve the balance between rules, principles, and practices developed in national legal systems.[33]

B. Standards and National Private Law

The substance of the case is left to national law. Here, the balance has to be struck between the interests of end-users, producers, and the notified bodies who are responsible for certification and inspection. At this level, some findings can be made about the quality of standards in comparison to rules of national contract and tort law. Quality, in this regard, will be assessed on the basis of the rules' ability to realize the objectives and values of EU law, which in this case are summarized in the Medical Devices Directive's aim of providing 'patients, users and third parties with a high level of protection'.[34] More specifically, quality will be assessed on the basis of the rules' ability to prevent harm, and to compensate for harm if it does occur, reflecting the goals commonly reflected in tort and contract laws.

As will be seen, the *ex-ante* level of consumer or patient protection laid down by standardization can be high—meaning that it can prevent harm—yet it can fall

[31] Verbruggen and van Leeuwen, 'The Liability of Notified Bodies under the EU's New Approach' (n 29) 401.

[32] See eg T Tridimas, 'The ECJ and the National Courts: Dialogue, Cooperation, and Instability' in A Arnull and D Chalmers (eds), *The Oxford Handbook of European Union Law* (OUP 2015) 403, 409–10 (distinguishing judgments grounded on outcome, guidance, or deference to national courts); J Krommendijk and MA Loth, *Europese rechters in gesprek. Verhalende annotaties* (Boom Juridisch 2018) 65–66.

[33] Chapter 5, pp 96–97.

[34] Medical Devices Directive (n 28), recitals.

short due to insufficient monitoring and enforcement mechanisms. I will discuss the PIP case in more detail by way of illustration. Factually, PIP is an interesting case because it could not be said with certainty whether breast implants made with industrial silicone gel, even if they leaked, led to a greater risk of cancer or other health issues.[35] The applicable standard for medical devices may therefore have been over-regulating by prohibiting the use of this type of gel, although there are of course many reasons to have concerns regarding the use of industrial gel in products meant for medical use and, more particular, implantation in the human body. At the same time, the standard could only have been effective if it had been monitored properly. In the absence of effective monitoring, national private laws can compensate those who have suffered harm. Private law's *ex-post* responses are more nuanced, but they may also lead to a less encompassing protection of consumers or patients.[36]

The hypothesis can therefore be that harmonized standards are of a high quality when it comes to preventing harm to consumers or patients, but only if they are accompanied by effective monitoring and enforcement mechanisms. EU law has not developed rules concerning the compensation for harm, if it does occur, and that quality aspect is therefore not covered at the EU level. National private laws can provide frameworks for liability in contract or tort and they may be relied on instead by consumers or patients who have suffered harm. The second hypothesis, however, is that national private laws are likely to lead to compensation in fewer cases than those to which the standard applies, as their individual approach leads to tailor-made solutions whereas standards tend to over-regulate.

To test these hypotheses, the starting point of the comparison is the goal of the Medical Devices Directive, quoted earlier, which states that it aims to ensure a high level of protection for patients, users, and third parties. More specifically, it entails that medical devices should comply with technical standards developed by the European standard-setting organization CEN, and that their quality and safety should be guaranteed through certification by notified bodies.

The relation between the technical standards for the quality and safety of breast implants and the rules of tort and contract law hinges upon a number of open norms: 'defect' or 'defectiveness' in product liability law, '(un)satisfactory quality' in sales law, and 'unsuitable' in relation to the use of equipment. I will discuss each in turn.

[35] European Commission, Scientific Committee on Emerging and Newly Identified Health Risks (SCENIHR), 'Opinion on the Safety of Poly Implant Prothese (PIP) Silicone Breast Implants' (12 May 2014) 5 <https://ec.europa.eu/health/scientific_committees/emerging/docs/scenihr_o_043.pdf>.

[36] The choice between *ex-ante* regulation and *ex-post* compensation through private law can also be approached from a regulatory perspective, taking into account insights from law and economics; see eg L Kaplow, 'Rules versus Standards: An Economic Analysis' (1992) 42 Duke Law Journal 557. In this chapter, however, the focus will be on the interplay between norms. See further pp 200.

The term 'defect' is central to the EU's product liability regime. The Product Liability Directive imposes a regime of strict liability on producers and importers in cases where defective goods causes death or personal injury, or damage to property other than the defective product itself.[37] According to Article 6(1) of the Directive, a product is defective when it does not provide the safety which a person is entitled to expect, taking account of all circumstances, including its presentation, the reasonably envisaged use of the product, and the time when it was put into circulation. The term 'defect' has been subject to debate as the wording of Article 6 makes it subject to varying interpretations.[38] In relation to medical devices, however, an important clarification was added by the CJEU's judgment in *Boston Scientific*. The Court held in that case that

> where it is found that products belonging to the same group or forming part of the same production series, such as pacemakers and implantable cardioverter defibrillators, have a potential defect, such a product may be classified as defective without there being any need to establish that that product had such a defect.[39]

For medical devices such as pacemakers, therefore, the risk of a defect may be sufficient to hold that a product is defective in the sense of the Directive. The Court justifies this by pointing out the severe consequences of a malfunction of this type of product, and the vulnerability of patients in this regard.[40] In the PIP litigation, product liability could have been a ground for liability of the producer. It became irrelevant in practice after the declaration of PIP's bankruptcy in 2010.[41] Regardless of that, it could have been argued that the risk of defects would have been sufficient in this case to follow the CJEU's decision in *Boston Scientific*. PIP's production process involved the large-scale and random use of industrial silicone gel instead of medical silicone gel, which increased the risk of leaking or tearing of the breast implants.[42]

An alternative ground for liability, not against PIP or a notified body but against the doctors or the hospitals who had used the PIP breast implants on patients,

[37] Council Directive 85/374/EEC on the approximation of laws, regulations and administrative provisions of the Member States concerning liability for defective products [1985] OJ L210/29 (Product Liability Directive), Arts 2 and 9.

[38] D Fairgrieve and G Howells, 'Rethinking Product Liability: A Missing Element in the European Commission's Third Review of the European Product Liability Directive' (2007) 70 Modern Law Review 962, 967–70.

[39] Joined cases C-503/13 and C-504/13 *Boston Scientific Medizintechnik GmbH v AOK Sachsen-Anhalt—Die Gesundheitskasse and Betriebskrankenkasse RWE*, ECLI:EU:C:2015:148, at [43].

[40] ibid [39].

[41] PWJ Verbruggen and BJ van Leeuwen, 'Europese regelgeving inzake medische hulpmiddelen. Het PIP-schandaal, de "Nieuwe Aanpak" en consumentenbescherming' [2015] Tijdschrift voor Consumentenrecht 111, 115.

[42] Compare European Commission, Scientific Committee on Emerging and Newly Identified Health Risks (SCENIHR) (n 35). See also PWJ Verbruggen and BJ van Leeuwen, 'Aansprakelijkheid voor gebrekkige medische hulpmiddelen' [2015] Nederlands Tijdschrift voor Burgerlijk Recht (NTBR) 308.

could be pursued on the basis of contract law. Several grounds of liability could be pursued—in particular non-conformity in sale of goods law or unsatisfactory performance of a contract for medical treatment—but each would have to deal with the question whether the breast implants were unsuitable and whether the harm could be attributed to the doctors or hospitals who had used them. Claimants in the United Kingdom have based their claims against clinics and surgeons on non-conformity in sales law.[43] The litigation was conducted through a group action on behalf of 1,000 to 2,000 women. After several delays in the hearing of the case, due to a dispute between one of the private clinics involved and its insurer, many claims have now been settled.[44] There is therefore no clear answer to the questions that were at stake in the case, namely whether the PIP breast implants were of unsatisfactory quality, and what remedies would be open to the claimants if the breast implants were found not be of satisfactory quality.[45]

In the Netherlands, claims have been pursued on the basis of breach of a contract for medical treatment. The classification as sales contracts was rejected by the courts on the ground that patients did not purchase the PIP breast implants, but rather obtained them as part of the treatment that they received.[46] Claims on the basis of breach of a contract for medical treatment, however, were not outright rejected. What needed to be established was whether doctors or hospitals had failed in their duty of care towards patients by using PIP breast implants. That duty of care is expressed in Dutch law as a duty to 'observe the standards of a prudent care provider' (Article 7:453 Dutch Civil Code, henceforth DCC).[47] It encompasses a responsibility for the use of equipment, provided that a non-performance in this regard can be attributed to the care provider (Article 6:77 DCC).

The devil is in the detail of the application of these rules to individual cases. First instance and appeal courts in the Netherlands found it hard to decide whether the risk of harm caused by leaking breast implants should be attributed to doctors or hospitals, and whether the use of industrial silicone gel in itself is sufficient ground for holding that implants were 'unsuitable' equipment. Courts were also in doubt as to which circumstances should be taken into account when answering these

[43] Section 4(2) of the Sale of Goods and Services Act 1982 stipulates that in contracts for the transfer of property in goods there is an implied term that the goods are of satisfactory quality; compare section 9 of the Consumer Rights Act 2015.

[44] BJ van Leeuwen, *European Standardisation of Services and Its Impact on Private Law. Paradoxes of Convergence* (Hart Publishing 2017) 150. See also C Glinski and P Rott, 'Regulating Certification Bodies in the Field of Medical Devices: The PIP Breast Implants Litigation and Beyond' (2019) 27 European Review of Private Law 403, 421; *Travelers Insurance Company Ltd v XYZ* [2018] EWCA Civ 1099.

[45] Van Leeuwen, *European Standardisation of Services and Its Impact on Private Law* (n 44) 150–51. See also the order for the group action of 17 April 2012 at <https://www.gov.uk/guidance/group-litigation-orders#pip-breast-implant>.

[46] See eg Court of Appeal 's-Hertogenbosch 25 November 2014, ECLI:NL:GSHE:2014:4936, para 3.6.2. In some cases the claim failed on factual grounds; see eg District Court Maastricht 19 October 2011, ECLI:NL:RBMAA:2011:2014, para 4.1, where non-conformity might have been a ground for implants produced *after* 2001, but the claimant had undergone surgery in early 2001.

[47] Translation available at <http://www.dutchcivillaw.com/civilcodebook077.htm>.

questions. Is it relevant, for example, that the doctor has greater medical expertise than the patient? At the same time, the doctor trusted the certificate given by TÜV and could not have known that industrial silicone gel was used in the production of the implants. Further, while patients in some cases can rely on their insurance to pay for the costs of replacement of breast implants, hospitals cannot take recourse on the producer, as PIP has been declared bankrupt. Broader societal issues may also come into play: the attribution of non-performance to the care provider can have a stifling effect on the development of new methods of treatment. Altogether, the doubts related to the weighing of these circumstances made it difficult for the courts to decide, and therefore for the affected claimants to obtain compensation for the harm that they suffered as a result of PIP's fraudulent production process.

The Court of Appeal in 's-Hertogenbosch referred the questions concerning attribution and defective equipment to the Dutch Supreme Court in a (domestic) preliminary reference procedure. The Supreme Court held that the damage caused by a faulty implant could not be attributed to the hospital.[48] Interestingly, an earlier judgment from the same court, but with a different composition, had held that the use of industrial silicone gel made a breast implant unsuitable in the meaning of Article 6:77 *Burgerlijk Wetboek* (DCC).[49] That approach would give claimants an advantage in establishing liability and would have given the signal that the loss should be borne by the hospitals who used the implants rather than by the patients. Still, the claimants would in individual cases have to prove that the implants used on them contained industrial gel. Many women did not have this information. The random process by which PIP used medical or industrial silicone gel in its production process moreover makes it unlikely that individual claimants will be able to establish which gel was used in their case.[50]

In sum, these examples show that, while the *ex-post* compensation of harm through private law can take a more nuanced approach to individual cases, it also makes it much harder to ensure a high level of protection for consumers or patients. The precise applicability of rules is unclear, and practically it may be hard to obtain proof needed in support of certain claims. That means that the protection that can be achieved through private law is often under-inclusive, in contrast to the over-inclusiveness of technical standards that already prohibit the use of products if there is only a risk that they may cause harm. Convergence, arguably, could be achieved by holding that compliance with an EU standard should be implied in contract in order to ensure the effectiveness of the New Approach.[51] However, that position has so far not been followed in legislation or case law, meaning that

[48] Court of Appeal 's-Hertogenbosch 27 August 2019, ECLI:NL:GHSHE:2019:3188; Dutch Supreme Court 19 June 2020, ECLI:NL:HR:2020:1090.

[49] Court of Appeal 's-Hertogenbosch 25 November 2014 (n 46), para 3.6.3.2.

[50] Compare Verbruggen and Van Leeuwen, 'Europese regelgeving inzake medische hulpmiddelen' (n 41) 117.

[51] Van Leeuwen, *European Standardisation of Services and Its Impact on Private Law* (n 44) 154–55.

European standards and national contract laws should still be considered as separate routes, employing their own substantive rules. Likewise, the standards used for certification are not one-on-one connected with the standards of care required in tort,[52] which means that also in this respects different levels of protection can apply.

IV. Substantive Deliberation in the Shadow of EU Law's Values and Objectives

Recapitulating, *ex-ante* standards can set a high level of protection, and could be more protective than the *ex-post* compensation of claimants on the basis of national contract or tort law. The instrumental-normative goal of lawmaking in a legal pluralist constellation can therefore, at least in theory, be achieved through the use of harmonized standards. Standards can protect against the occurrence of harm. However, a practical problem is that monitoring and enforcement often fall short of maintaining the objectives set by standards. This is a flaw in the regime of the New Approach and, unless it is remedied by fine-tuning of the regulatory framework for certification and inspection, private law will have to function as an *ex-post* safety net. National contract and tort laws can secure the second element of quality tested in this chapter: the compensation of harm. As was seen, however, hurdles can be encountered in obtaining damages in individual cases. Outcomes depend on whether it can be established that products were 'defective' or 'unsuitable', and whether harm can be attributed to those who have used a product without realizing the risks entailed, such as the doctors who used PIP breast implants on their patients. Where private law falls short of compensating harm, one can again turn to public regulation and aim to fine-tune the process by which harmonized standards are monitored and enforced. In the wake of the PIP scandal, some adjustments have been made to the New Approach. For example, stricter rules for the recognition of notified bodies have been introduced, as well as a requirement for notified bodies to conduct unannounced inspections.[53]

The process of fine-tuning *ex-ante* public regulation and *ex-post* compensation through private law can be regarded through the lens of regulatory theory.[54] However, as it concerns the interplay between norms developed in the framework of EU law and norms developed in national private laws, the case study

[52] ibid 164–65. Van Leeuwen however argues that convergence in tort could be achieved within the framework created by the New Approach.

[53] See Verbruggen and van Leeuwen (n 41) 114.

[54] See for a discussion of regulatory rationales, primarily from economic perspectives, eg C Veljanovski, 'Economic Approaches to Regulation' in R Baldwin, M Cave, and M Lodge (eds), *Oxford Handbook of Regulation* (OUP 2010) 17; JA den Hertog, 'Review of Economic Theories of Regulation' Tjalling C Koopmans Research Institute Discussion Paper Series Nr 10–18 (2010) <https://dspace.library.uu.nl/handle/1874/309815>.

on harmonized standards in EU law also informs the analysis of legal pluralism and lawmaking presented in the earlier chapters of this book. It reveals how the instrumental-normative approach to lawmaking in European private law practically plays out in the creation of norms at the EU level, through standards, and in national private laws. A better understanding of that interplay can be of help in determining how a substantive deliberation between lawmaking actors could be facilitated.

The case study on harmonized standards, and more specifically the PIP litigation, in this respect reveals some insights on how the substantive quality of norms is determined through the involvement of different lawmaking actors. The EU legislature, standard-setting organizations, the CJEU, and national courts work together in the pursuit of the two aspects focused on in this chapter for measuring quality: the prevention of harm and the compensation of harm if it does occur. The PIP case shows that standards cannot always prevent harm from arising, and that EU law as well as national private laws can fall short in providing compensation to individual claimants through tort or contract law. The overall outcome in this case, therefore, does not reach the quality level aimed for. However, while that conclusion reflects the current situation, efforts are being made to improve these outcomes. The public regulatory framework is being adapted—introducing stricter rules for the recognition of notified bodies and for inspections—and in national systems courts are still figuring out whether in some cases harm may be attributed to doctors or hospitals, giving ground to the compensation of harm through payment of damages.

Considering these efforts from a legal pluralist perspective, lawmaking actors at different levels of regulation, it is submitted, are striving to achieve the goals underlying European private law. The norms that are being pursued coincide with the objectives and values laid down in Articles 2 and 3 of the Treaty on European Union.[55] They are expressed more concretely in secondary legislation. The example discussed in the case study in this chapter was the Medical Devices Directive's objective that 'medical devices should provide patients, users and third parties with a high level of protection'.[56] As was seen, the CJEU was unwilling to translate this objective into concrete liability rules relating to notified bodies, leaving that aspect to national tort law. Also, liability of users, for example doctors and hospitals, is left to national tort and contract laws. At the same time, however, the Court's judgment in *Schmitt* can be seen as a step towards the instrumental use of national private laws in the pursuit of EU law's objectives. The Court held that 'the purpose of the notified body's involvement is to protect end users of medical devices' and that liability towards end users may arise under national laws, 'subject to the principles of equivalence and effectiveness'.[57] EU law therefore through this judgment extends

[55] Consolidated version of the Treaty on European Union [2012] OJ C326/01 (TEU).
[56] Medical Devices Directive (n 28), recitals.
[57] *Schmitt* (n 4) [60].

its influence over national tort laws. Some see this as part of a continuing trend of constitutionalization of private law through EU law.[58] In the broader context of EU law's objective to pursue a social market economy, one might indeed see the case as a reflection of social justice aims. As was stated in Chapter 4, it remains to be seen what space such examples will have beside the EU's internal market project, yet recent years have seen continuing trends towards social considerations in European private law.[59] While that entails that private actors, such as notified bodies or standard-setting organizations, may to some extent be drawn into the public regulatory framework of EU law, it also means that individual enforcement of rights following from EU law increases, thereby making private actors partly responsible for ensuring the effectiveness of those rights.

The case study in this chapter therefore illustrates that lawmaking in European private law takes place in a context that involves different lawmaking actors—public and private—at different levels of regulation, yet operating in the shadow of the objectives and values laid down in the EU Treaties. The following chapter will examine in more detail how their actions can be moderated through 'checks and balances' between different actors.

[58] cf Verbruggen and Van Leeuwen, 'Europese regelgeving inzake medische hulpmiddelen' (n 29).

[59] Chapter 4. See also H-W Micklitz, *The Politics of Justice in European Private Law. Social Justice, Access Justice, Societal Justice* (CUP 2018).

9
Managing Pluralism

Which mechanisms can provide 'checks and balances' for the rules created by different lawmakers in a legal pluralist constellation? This question brings together a number of the lines set out in previous chapters. It follows from the finding at the end of the previous chapter that lawmaking by private actors in the platform economy does not per se lead to lower levels of consumer protection but that certain risks are present when lawmaking is in the hands of private companies. Large tech companies, such as Airbnb and Amazon, are primarily driven by the goal of running a profitable enterprise. The protection of consumers, or more broadly users, of their products and services is a corollary to that overarching objective. Monitoring of the substance of norms is therefore required to ensure that the values and objectives of EU law are observed in contracts involving European consumers and businesses. The same is true for consumer markets that are partly governed by standardization.

This chapter examines how monitoring of norms can take place in a strong legal pluralist constellation. To maintain legal pluralism, it is submitted, care should be taken not to immediately revert to public regulation in every situation where norms fail to comply with the values and objectives of EU law, which would entail the imposition of a monist perspective on lawmaking actors. Lawmaking processes occur over time and within the context of what has been called a putative legal order.[1] Instead, therefore, the chapter will examine what opportunities exist for the creation and maintenance of private governance mechanisms based on voluntary participation. These mechanisms are, by definition, an expression of the public and private autonomy of lawmaking actors, in other words of the ability to self-legislate and to choose the design of contractual relations freely. The important mechanisms in European contract law are standardization, optional instruments, and online dispute resolution (ODR). Each depends on the voluntary use, and in some instances creation, of the mechanism by private actors.[2] When private actors are involved at the stage of developing a monitoring mechanism, as is

[1] Following the terminology used by Lindahl; see H Lindahl, *Authority and the Globalisation of Inclusion and Exclusion* (CUP 2018) 34 and in detail Chapter 3, pp 53.

[2] Although it has been recognized that use is not always voluntary, for instance where producers can only enter a particular market by complying with the technical standard set by a national certification body. See Case C-171/11 *Fra.bo SpA v Deutsche Vereinigung des Gas- und Wasserfaches eV (DVGW)—Technisch-Wissenschaftlicher Verein*, ECLI:EU:C:2012:453 (*Fra.bo*); BJ van Leeuwen, 'From Status to Impact, and the Role of National Legislation: The Application of Article 34 TFEU to a Private Certification Organisation in *Fra.bo*' (2013) 4 European Journal of Risk Regulation 405, 406.

Legal Pluralism in European Contract Law. Vanessa Mak, Oxford University Press (2020). © Vanessa Mak.
DOI: 10.1093/oso/9780198854487.001.0001.

the case with standardization of contracts, their involvement can be regarded as an expression of public autonomy. When private actors voluntarily use instruments aimed at safeguarding minimum values and rules—which can be the case for all three mechanisms—that can in turn be an expression of their private autonomy.[3]

Besides mechanisms based on voluntary participation of private actors, co-regulatory mechanisms also exist that involve both public and private actors. That observation raises the question of whether in some instances the opportunity for private governance exists only because it is mandated by public regulation, hence curbing the space for the coexistence of norms in a strong legal pluralist constellation. To define that space, the chapter will also consider where the boundaries of private governance are located. While co-regulation is relevant in consumer markets, it will be argued that its reach is context- or subject-specific, and that there are areas that can be governed almost exclusively through contract and private governance mechanisms.

The structure of the chapter is as follows. First, the mechanisms for monitoring the substance of private lawmaking, in so far as they relate to European contract law, will be mapped. Second, the spaces that exist between private and public regulation in relation to each of these instruments will be examined. The second aspect goes to the core of the problem and I will therefore only briefly introduce the mechanisms for monitoring, and their interrelation (sections I and II), before commencing the more in-depth analysis of the space that private regulation has besides public regulation (sections III and IV). The relevant mechanisms that can be discerned are: standardization of contracts, the use of optional instruments or model rules in contract law, and monitoring through online dispute resolution.

Seeing that these mechanisms actively rely on the participation of private actors, it is submitted that changing views on the responsibilities of private actors may herald an approach that regards private actors as joint guardians of substantive norms of EU law. That is of particular relevance now that consumer markets are increasingly governed by private regulation, as the case study of the platform economy has shown. From this perspective, section III will consider where private governance should be placed in the broader spectrum of governance approaches. While private regulation is becoming an increasingly important form of regulation in consumer markets, in particular those in the platform economy, it may reach its limits in cases where issues are concerned that go beyond contract law, such as consumer safety or access to markets. Section III will consider in which circumstances private regulation goes over into co-regulation, and what this entails for the division of responsibilities between lawmaking actors. The final part, section IV, considers how new forms of governance—in particular experimentalist

[3] For a discussion of these concepts and their position in legal pluralist theory, see Chapter 2, p 39.

governance—could lend support to creating and maintaining spaces for private governance, fitting with a strong legal pluralist approach to lawmaking.

I. Standardization, Optional Instruments, and Dispute Resolution

In monist legal systems governed by the rule of law, checks and balances between lawmakers exist in the legislative process—where proposals for new government legislation tend to be subject to review by parliament—and between the legislator and the judiciary. An independent judiciary, itself bound by rules laid down in a constitutional law, can guarantee that legislators do not overstep the boundaries of their power.[4]

Online platform operators have been hailed as 'new governors',[5] resembling nation states,[6] or as 'private legislators' (*private Gesetzgeber*),[7] suggesting that they independently set the rules that apply between themselves and their users, and in user-to-user transactions. While that perspective, which has also been advocated in the previous chapter, justly gives credit to the freedom that many platform operators enjoy in determining the rules of engagement on their platform, it perhaps pays too little heed to questions of monitoring and enforcement. If one wishes to keep using the metaphor of private legislators, the enquiry needs to be extended from the legislative powers of private lawmakers to ways in which monitoring instruments can curtail those powers, in the same way that governors or legislators of nation states are subject to checks and balances.

Due to their assumption that no formal hierarchies exist between legal sources, legal pluralist perspectives, however, offer less straightforward answers to the way in which checks and balances are maintained between lawmaking actors. For lawmaking in European contract law, in particular as it extends to private regulation, at least three alternatives to the monist, state-centred perspective have emerged in recent decades.

The first is standardization by private entities. Standardization generally serves as an *ex-ante* mechanism for ensuring that private actors comply with certain minimum rules, namely those laid down in the relevant standard. Users of the standard declare that the products or services supplied by them comply with the

[4] This model is prevalent in most EU Member States, although it has come under pressure in Eastern Europe, with for example the Polish government seeking to oust judges from its Supreme Court through controversial changes to the constitution.

[5] K Klonick, 'The New Governors: The People, Rules, and Processes Governing Online Speech' (2018) 131 Harvard Law Review 1598.

[6] M Cantero Gamito, 'Regulation.com. Self-Regulation and Contract Governance in the Platform Economy: A Research Agenda' (2017) 9 European Journal of Legal Studies 53, 56.

[7] H Schweitzer, 'Digitale Plattformen als private Gesetzgeber: Ein Perspektivwechsel für die europäische "Plattform-Regulierung"' (2019) 27 Zeitschrift für Europäisches Privatrecht 1.

standard, which then sets a benchmark for the reasonable expectations that contractual counter-parties may have vis-à-vis the user.[8] Some aspects of standardization have been the subject of research—in particular the transparency, legitimacy, and accountability of private regulators[9]—but only scarce research has been done on the use and quality of standards for services.[10] Empirical research in this field could be of use in further developing theories of lawmaking in European private law, in particular from a legal pluralist perspective in which private regulation is considered a source of law. Standards remain an important source of co-regulation and self-regulation by industry, and they can fill gaps when legislation is slow in forthcoming.

Second, optional instruments and model rules can fulfil a coordinating function in legal pluralist constellations of lawmakers. Optional instruments are sets of rules that parties can choose to apply to their contract. A prominent example is the proposed Common European Sales Law (CESL), which was intended to function as a twenty-ninth regime of contract law in Europe, alongside the national contract laws of the Member States.[11] The CESL proposal was however withdrawn at the end of 2015 and replaced by two proposals for EU directives covering a more limited scope, namely online sales and digital content contracts,[12] adopted in 2019.[13] Model rules function in a similar way to optional instruments, but with one distinction: parties can choose which rules they wish to use and, other than with optional instruments, do not have to adopt the set of rules in total.[14] In the field of European contract law, the Principles of European Contract Law (PECL) were

[8] For a description of the functioning of standard-setting organizations (SSOs) see N Gandal and P Régibeau, 'Standard-setting Organisations. Current Policy Issues and Empirical Evidence' in P Delimatsis (ed), *The Law, Economics and Politics of International Standardisation* (CUP 2015) 394, 398 ff. See also Chapter 8.

[9] C Scott, F Cafaggi, and L Senden (eds), *The Challenge of Transnational Private Regulation: Conceptual and Constitutional Debates* (Wiley-Blackwell 2011). On legitimacy, CANMY Cauffman and M Eliantonio (eds), *The Legitimacy of Standardisation as a Regulatory Technique* (Edward Elgar 2020).

[10] BJ van Leeuwen, *European Standardisation of Services and Its Impact on Private Law. Paradoxes of Convergence* (Hart 2017) on tourism and health; M Mataija, *Private Regulation and the Internal Market: Sports, Legal Services, and Standard Setting in EU Economic Law* (OUP 2016) on sports standards.

[11] See European Commission, 'Proposal for a Regulation of the European Parliament and of the Council on a Common European Sales Law' COM(2011) 635 final (proposed CESL). If Scotland is counted as a separate jurisdiction alongside England and Wales, one might speak of a thirtieth regime.

[12] European Commission, 'Proposal for a Directive of the European Parliament and of the Council on certain aspects concerning contracts for the supply of digital content' COM(2015) 634 final; European Commission, 'Proposal for a Directive of the European Parliament and of the Council on certain aspects concerning contracts for the online and other distance sales of goods' COM(2015) 635 final.

[13] Directive (EU) 2019/770 on certain aspects concerning contracts for the supply of digital content and digital services [2019] OJ L136/1; Directive (EU) 2019/771 on certain aspects concerning contracts for the sale of goods, and repealing Directive 1999/44 [2019] OJ L136/28.

[14] The contractual nature of this route is paramount, therefore. Model rules should be distinguished from model laws, which are uniform sets of rules on specific topics, intended to pursue harmonization of laws through adoption by national legislatures. See R Goode, 'Reflections on the Harmonisation of Commercial Law' (1991) I Uniform Law Review 54, 57.

intended to function in this manner.[15] Parties can, according to Article 1:101 subsection 2 of the PECL, choose to incorporate them, in part or in whole, or stipulate that the Principles govern the contract. The term 'govern' should be understood in a narrow sense here, since the Rome I Regulation only allows a choice of law for state law. If a choice is made for the PECL, it can therefore be overridden by rules of state law.[16] Besides the PECL, a newer set of model rules that are likely to become important for the platform economy are the Model Rules on Online Platforms, developed under the aegis of the European Law Institute (ELI).[17] The substance of these rules was discussed in Chapter 6.[18]

Optional instruments and model rules fit with strong legal pluralism because they depend upon the voluntary use of these rules by private actors. In this respect, they are similar to voluntary standards. They differ from standards, however, in the way in which they are created. Whereas standardization bodies in the process of making new standards include representatives from all relevant stakeholder groups in a more or less hierarchy free setting,[19] the creation of optional instruments and model rules often takes a more legislative approach. The PECL, the Draft Common Frame of Reference (DCFR)[20] and the proposed CESL were all drafted by groups of academics who aimed to draft codification type rules. In case of the latter two, the DCFR and the CESL, the drafting process was instigated and coordinated by the European Commission. In recent years, the European Law Institute (ELI) has become the main platform for the development of model rules in Europe. ELI is a non-profit organization that, modelled after the American Law Institute (ALI), aims to write restatements of laws based on comparative legal research of existing legal systems in Europe.[21] ELI has produced model rules relatively quickly in comparison to the formal legislative route through the European legislature and it is likely to become a significant influence on lawmaking in European law. Seeing that

[15] Principles of European Contract Law (PECL) Parts I and II, Introduction, xxi–xxiii. For an analysis of the PECL's impact on contract law in Europe, see H Beale, 'The Role for European Contract Law: Uniformity or Diversity?' in F de Elizalde (ed), *Uniform Rules for European Contract Law? A Critical Assessment* (Hart Publishing 2018) 9.

[16] Regulation (EC) No 593/2008 on the law applicable to contractual obligations (Rome I) [2008] OJ L177/6, Art 3(1). For a discussion of choice of law in relation to the PECL and the UNIDROIT Principles of International Commercial Contracts see E McKendrick, 'Restatements of Contract Law' in R Goode, H Kronke, and E McKendrick, *Transnational Commercial Law. Text, Cases and Materials* (2nd edn, OUP 2015) 461, 470 ff.

[17] See <https://www.europeanlawinstitute.eu/projects-publications/current-projects-feasibility-studies-and-other-activities/current-projects/online-platforms/> accessed 28 February 2020, as are all websites in this chapter.

[18] See pp 144.

[19] While all groups are represented, it is often presumed that the voice of businesses is stronger in determining the final text of standards. See below, p 209.

[20] Study Group on a European Civil Code and Research Group on the Existing EC Private Law (Acquis Group), *Principles, Definitions and Model Rules of European Private Law: Draft Common Frame of Reference. Full Edition* (Sellier 2009).

[21] For a description and mission statement see <https://www.europeanlawinstitute.eu/about-the-eli/>.

the model rules developed through the Institute are of a non-binding nature, their adoption and use depends on voluntary uptake by private actors. Although rules are developed by academics, or with academics in the lead, rather than through a representation of all stakeholder groups, the success of these types of model rules depends on their acceptance by norm addressees. They therefore fit within a legal pluralist constellation in which private actors can freely decide to follow or not follow rules and, in that sense, can self-legislate.

Third, the regulatory role of alternative dispute resolution (ADR) or online dispute resolution (ODR) has become more important with the rise of the platform economy. Many disputes never reach state courts, for instance because of high costs, the long duration of procedures, and the uncertainty of outcomes.[22] Online dispute resolution, however, has gained a strong foothold in the platform economy, with eBay reporting a number of 60 million cases per year resolved through its dispute resolution centre.[23] ADR bodies, also encompassing ODR, are often free to decide disputes on the basis of broader principles such as 'reasonableness',[24] and therefore play an important role in developing rules in the private sphere.

Taken together, the three strategies for managing pluralism function as monitoring mechanisms for rules developed in the private sphere that can, either *ex ante* or *ex post*, help ensure that minimum values of EU law are being observed and complied with. Strong legal pluralism in an instrumental-normative sense, at the same time, requires that public regulators only intervene if private regulation falls short of complying with the minimum values and objectives of EU law. In that way, legal pluralism may be coordinated without falling back on an ordering leading back to the nation state.[25]

II. Governance without Hierarchies

Can it be said, then, that intervention by public regulators in relation to the three monitoring mechanisms of standardization, supervision, and dispute resolution is an *ultimum remedium* and that otherwise lawmaking actors are free to determine

[22] These factors weigh even more heavily in cross-border situations; compare N Reich, 'Transnational Consumer Law—Reality or Fiction?' (2009) 27 Penn State International Law Review 859.

[23] Recorded in 2014 and said to increase annually; see LF Del Luca, C Rule, and K Rimpfel, 'eBay's De Facto Low Value High Volume Resolution Process: Lessons and Best Practices for ODR Systems Designers' (2014) 6 Yearbook on Arbitration and Mediation 204, 205.

[24] C Hodges, I Benöhr, and N Creutzfeldt, 'Findings and Conclusions' in C Hodges, I Benöhr, and N Creutzfeldt (eds), *Consumer ADR in Europe* (Hart 2012) 413, discussing examples from the United Kingdom and from the Netherlands. For the Netherlands, which has one of the most developed consumer ADR systems in Europe, see also M Knigge and E Verhage, 'The Impact of the ADR Directive on Article 7:904 par. 1 DCC Explored. What is "Unacceptable According to Standards of Reasonableness and Fairness" after the Implementation of the Directive?' in CG Breedveld-de Voogd and others (eds), *BW Krant Jaarboek* (Kluwer 2016) 61, 65.

[25] cf Chapter 2, p 45; Chapter 3, p 69.

rules independently? Each mechanism can plausibly be explained in that light, as will become apparent. I will discuss each in turn.

A. Standardization

The primary feature that establishes standardization as a mechanism fitting a legal pluralist perspective is that it depends on the voluntary creation, adoption, and use of standards by interested parties. Standards therefore, when they are developed through a cross-border network of private actors, are part of the same private legal order from which other rules emanate that are developed beyond the state. Private actors themselves decide upon the rules of interaction that apply to legal relations between them.

One particular problem with standardization is that power relations are often not equal between interested parties. It has been said that standard-setting in regulated sectors reinforces extant interests of producers.[26] That risk is imaginable, as parties with more expertise and lobbying power—often producers—are likely to have more weight in standard-setting organizations than smaller firms or final consumers. Moreover, firms whose performance is strongly affected by the distributive effect of a new standard have a large incentive to get involved in the standard-setting process and to influence the outcome in their direction.[27] At the same time, arguments can be put forward that support the idea that greater effort is spent on promoting the better technology[28] or, by analogy, the better rules. For instance, use of the better technology would result in better products designed around the standard, and hence in higher sales. Further, SSO participants with interests on the user side of the market would prefer the better standard.[29]

Another potential problem in Europe is that the EU institutions have increasingly drawn standardization into the public regulatory sphere. The Court of Justice of the European Union (CJEU) has extended the application of free movement rules to private certification bodies and has held that harmonized technical standards are part of EU law, thereby bringing them into the scope of application of the preliminary reference procedure.[30] These cases have created possibilities for producers and importers to challenge harmonized standards for restricting their

[26] See Gandal and Régibeau, 'Standard-setting Organisations. Current Policy Issues and Empirical Evidence' (n 8) 402.

[27] T Büthe and W Mattli, *The New Global Rulers: The Privatization of Regulation in the World Economy* (Princeton University Press 2011) 12. See also C Brändli, 'Book Review. The New Global Rulers: The Privatization of Regulation in the World Economy' (2012) 18 Swiss Political Science Review 538.

[28] Gandal and Régibeau, 'Standard-setting Organisations. Current Policy Issues and Empirical Evidence' (n 8) 408.

[29] ibid.

[30] *Fra.bo* (n 2); Case C-613/14 *James Elliott Construction Ltd v Irish Asphalt Ltd*, ECLI:EU:C:2016:821.

market position,[31] and potentially also for stakeholders to challenge the validity of standards.[32] Around the same time, the European legislature made the publication of harmonized standards in the EU's official journal susceptible to legality review in direct actions. Regulation 1025/2012 on European standardization implies that the European Commission does not just provide information on the standard by its publication, but makes an *ex-ante* assessment of the harmonized standards compliance with the requirements which it aims to cover in order to give effect to corresponding Union legislation.[33] This provision, clarifying a relation between information and assessment that was unclear before, seems to put it 'beyond doubt that the act of publication of the references is an act that can be challenged in a direct action before the European Courts under Article 263 TFEU'.[34] Standards could be challenged by a broad spectrum of affected parties, including national standard bodies as well as affected manufacturers or importers whose products are excluded from harmonized standards.[35] The repercussions that the case law and the 2012 Regulation have had until now, however, are unknown. It will have to be seen whether the voluntary character of standards will increasingly be circumscribed by judicial review.[36]

Although many empirical questions about their functioning remain unanswered, there is no doubt however that standards can function as drivers for the maintenance of quality of products and services in consumer markets.[37] This is also, gradually, becoming the case for consumer markets in the platform economy, in particular with regard to the services aspect of the market. In this context, several degrees of standardization can be envisaged at the transnational and at the European level. The state of the field is in flux.

To begin with, an International Organization for Standardization (ISO) standard has been crafted for the platform market, relating to online consumer

[31] H Schepel, 'The New Approach to the New Approach: The Juridification of Harmonized Standards in EU Law' (2013) 20 Maastricht Journal of European and Comparative Law 521.

[32] It has however been argued that this is a relatively small risk, since the Court is unlikely to agree to rule on the validity of standards created by private entities, which are non-EU institutions. See A van Waeyenberge and D Restrepo Amariles, 'James Elliott Construction: A "New(ish) Approach" to Judicial Review of Standardisation' (2017) 42 European Law Review 882, 891–92.

[33] Regulation (EU) No 1025/2012 on European standardisation [2012] OJ L316/12, Art 10(6).

[34] Schepel, 'The New Approach to the New Approach' (n 31) 531, with reference to Art 263 of the Consolidated version of the Treaty on the Functioning of the European Union [2012] OJ C326/47 (TFEU).

[35] ibid.

[36] Verbruggen has nonetheless rightly pointed out that harmonized standards seem to be subject to a process of constitutionalization, through which they are increasingly subjected to constitutional principles of EU law such as free movement regulation and effective legal protection. See PWJ Verbruggen, 'Good Governance of Private Standardization and the Role of Tort Law' (2019) 27 European Review of Private Law 319.

[37] On the distinction between technical standards and quality standards, see P Delimatsis, 'Standardisation in Services—European Ambitions and Sectoral Realities' (2016) 41 European Law Review 513, 520.

reviews.[38] The standard lays down detailed requirements for organizations to manage consumer review systems effectively, with the aim of increasing consumer trust and protecting suppliers from exploitation.[39] In order to achieve these goals, the standard identifies as guiding principles: integrity, accuracy, privacy, security, transparency, accessibility, and responsiveness (Article 4.1). Interestingly, the commitment of review authors (ie consumers reviews) to these goals is secured through contractual means, namely through terms and conditions that state the rules and criteria that reviewers have to comply with (Article 4.2.3.1) and that they have to accept before submitting a review (Article 4.2.3.2). This means that there is a voluntary element at the stage of implementation of the standard in the form of a cooperation agreement between the use of the standard (ie the operator of the online review system) and the consumers and suppliers using the review system. Non-compliance with the terms and conditions is sanctioned by rejection or removal of reviews (Article 4.2.3.3).

The ISO standard sets out what one could consider the 'basic requirements' for creating and monitoring reliable online review systems. If a European standard is developed in the future, as has been suggested,[40] it could take inspiration from this standard. Seeing that the European Union has a special position due to its institutional structure and its commitment to the pursuit of common values, a European standard could perhaps go beyond the contractual mechanism laid down in the ISO standard. It should, however, pay heed to data protection concerns.

Considering more advanced possibilities, Busch has suggested that 'techno-legal standards' could be developed, particularly with an eye to ensuring the quality of online review systems,[41] but also for the tailored (or 'granulated') dissemination of information to users.[42] Techno-legal standards are technologies that can be employed in the pursuit of certain legal objectives. For example, when sufficiently developed, algorithms could be used to provide personalized disclosures about product descriptions and quality tailored to the informational needs of individual users based on their user profiles.[43] While these technologies provide novel ways

[38] ISO 20488:2018 on 'Online Consumer Reviews—Principles and Requirements for their Collection, Moderation and Publication'.

[39] C Naden, 'Putting the Trust Back in Online Reviews', ISO news <https://www.iso.org/news/ref2295.html>.

[40] Chapter 6, pp 148.

[41] C Busch, 'Crowdsourcing Consumer Confidence: How to Regulate Online Rating and Review Systems in the Collaborative Economy' in A De Franceschi (ed), *European Contract Law and the Digital Single Market: The Implications of the Digital Revolution* (Intersentia 2016) 223.

[42] C Busch, 'Self-Regulation and Regulatory Intermediation in the Platform Economy' in M Cantero Gamito and H-W Micklitz (eds), *The Role of the EU in Transnational Legal Ordering: Standards, Contracts and Codes* (Edward Elgar 2020) 115; SSRN <https://ssrn.com/abstract=3309293>, 11–12.

[43] ibid 12, and C Busch, 'Implementing Personalized Law: Personalized Disclosures in Consumer Law and Privacy Law' (2019) 86 University of Chicago Law Review 309. See also L Strahilevitz and A Porat, 'Personalizing Default Rules and Disclosures with Big Data' (2014) 112 Michigan Law Review 1417; P Hacker, 'Personalizing EU Private Law: From Disclosures to Nudges and Mandates' (2017) 25 European Review of Private Law 651; C Busch, 'The Future of Pre-contractual Information

for communication and information sharing with consumers, however, regulators should be wary of potential negative effects that they may have. One important effect is that personalized information pre-selects information for consumers and thereby limits their autonomy by steering or 'nudging' them towards certain purchasing choices.[44] The safer option, for now, would be to use techno-legal standards only for quality monitoring.

On an aggregate level, technology could also enable online platforms to share data on compliance with legal norms with other lawmaking actors. Besides regular audits, which entail the risk that some data provided by platforms is inaccurate, it has been suggested that a so-called application programming interface (API) might be used.[45] An API does not provide access to raw data to parties external to the platform, but it enables them to run 'queries' to verify compliance.[46] This technology could be used as a monitoring mechanism in co-regulatory governance structures, where it enables governments to test the compliance levels achieved through self-regulation by online platforms.[47] Whereas that view fits with a more top-down notion of regulation and governance, it could also be envisaged that technologies enable lawmaking actors to engage in discursive practices that would fit a legal pluralist constellation.[48] That may require more detailed data sharing than APIs can provide, which, presumably, will not be problematic from a technological point of view—as other technologies can be developed—-but it could pose challenges in relation to data protection.[49]

Standardization could therefore in several forms be used as an instrument for safeguarding consumer interests in markets governed (primarily) by private regulation. In particular the development of quality standards for services could be relevant for consumer markets governed primarily by private regulation and contracting.

At the same time, the voluntary character of standardization can also be its weak spot. Whether standards will be developed is very much dependent on voluntary action from interested parties. Lacking the factors under which public regulators are sometimes pressured to act—such as public opinion, or the need to protect

Duties: Personalization of Disclosures with Big Data' in C Twigg-Flesner (ed), *Research Handbook on EU Consumer and Contract Law* (Edward Elgar 2016) 221.

[44] C Busch and A De Franceschi, 'Granular Legal Norms: Big Data and the Personalization of Private Law' in V Mak, TFE Tjong Tjin Tai, and A Berlee (eds), *Research Handbook in Data Science and Law* (Edward Elgar 2018) 408.

[45] A Sundararajan, 'The Collaborative Economy: Socioeconomic, Regulatory and Policy Issues' (In-depth Analysis for the IMCO Committee of the European Parliament 2017) 24.

[46] ibid.

[47] This is Sundararajan's view; see Sundararajan, 'The Collaborative Economy: Socioeconomic, Regulatory and Policy Issues' (n 45) 24–25.

[48] On the idea of substantive deliberation through discursive processes, see Chapter 3, pp 64 ff.

[49] The sharing of personal data is very much restricted in Europe on the basis of the General Data Protection Regulation; see Regulation (EU) 2016/679 on the protection of natural persons with regard to the processing of personal data and on the free movement of such data [2016] OJ L119/1.

larger groups in society from harm—the development of standards sometimes does not get off the ground if it is dependent on industry only. In the 'new' consumer markets created by the platform economy this could be a problem. Platform operators are likely to push for standardization only if it is in their interest, for example if the creation of a standard enhances consumer trust. The ISO standard for online consumer reviews can be regarded as an example of that.

Besides private regulation, co-regulation can still be an option for the pursuit of specific EU policy goals. Nonetheless, even after the European Commission's efforts to promote the development of standards for services through co-regulation, processes have been slow. Van Leeuwen points to a perceived rhetoric on the part of the Commission, which lacks the back-up of more specific actions.[50] That is not entirely plausible if one considers that standardization has been on the rise at the EU level as well as in national systems. What could be a problem, however, is that standards are not necessarily being developed in all of the areas where they are most urgently needed.[51] For the example discussed here, online consumer reviews, it is noteworthy that the European Union is lagging behind with the development of a standard, whereas ISO has already developed one. This could be due to differences between CEN—the European Committee for Standardization—and ISO in terms of voting systems and speed of operation, but also to the EU's overall hesitance to pursue regulation or co-regulation in the platform economy.[52] Important to realize is also that the European Union in the field of services only has limited competences, for instance in relation to social and healthcare services,[53] but also in relation to tourism and consumer protection.[54] This limitation means that co-regulation instigated by the European Commission, such as the Commission's mandate for the ESOs to develop horizontal standards for services,[55] will focus on selective areas of EU policy. The future will show whether standardization will be further pursued in relation to quality of services.[56]

[50] Van Leeuwen, *European Standardisation of Services and Its Impact on Private Law* (n 10).

[51] Delimatsis points out that progress in the development of European service standards has been slow. In the period 2005–2009 only 5 per cent of the overall standardization activity in services occurred at the European level, versus 95 per cent at the national level. For goods the number was 20 per cent. See Delimatsis (n 37) 525.

[52] See Chapter 6, p 138.

[53] Delimatsis, 'Standardisation in Services—European Ambitions and Sectoral Realities' (n 37) 521.

[54] Van Leeuwen, *European Standardisation of Services and Its Impact on Private Law* (n 10) 74, 114.

[55] COM(2016) 357 final, 3–4, and COM(2014) 500 final, 3.

[56] Delimatsis, 'Standardisation in Services—European Ambitions and Sectoral Realities' (n 37) 532, with reference to European Commission, 'The annual Union work programme for European standardization for 2015' COM(2014) 500 final, 10.

B. Optional Instruments and Model Rules

A second mechanism for the coordination of lawmaking in a legal pluralist constellation is provided by optional instruments and model rules. For these, also, one can ask the question whether they are instruments of private regulation, created and used on a voluntary basis by norm addressees. Or do they operate within the space mandated by public regulation? The answer would appear to lean towards the private sphere. Whilst public regulators may be involved in the drafting of rules—which was the case for the CESL proposal of the European Commission, but is not the case for the Model Rules on Online Platforms developed by an ELI working group—the use of optional instruments and model rules in practice depends solely on the preferences and choices of private actors. Contracting parties may even be able to add their own imprint to the rules by choosing to what degree they wish to incorporate model rules into their contract, provided that the rules so allow. The PECL, for example, stipulate in Article 1:101 subsection 2 that '[t]hese Principles will apply when the parties have agreed to incorporate them into their contract or that their contract is to be governed by them'. That provision is generally seen as expressing that the PECL can be incorporated into contracts, which is not controversial. However it does not imply that the PECL can be chosen as the governing law of the contract, as Article 3 of the Rome I Regulation does not permit a choice for non-state law.[57] Although the Principles also, in Article 1:102, stipulate that parties may not derogate from the mandatory rules of the PECL, that provision is of limited reach. The term 'mandatory' in this case only means that parties who choose to incorporate the PECL will have to include terms that the Principles themselves say need to be included. By contrast, contractual rules can also be curbed by mandatory rules of the applicable national law or by rules that are considered mandatory regardless of the applicable law.[58] Seeing that there are not many 'mandatory' rules in the PECL—the duty of good faith, the reduction of a grossly excessive stipulated payment for non-performance, and curbs on contractual provisions excluding or limiting liability[59]—the parties' freedom to stipulate their contract in accordance with their preferences is still very broad.

The space that parties have to self-regulate, however, can differ from one optional instrument to another. Both the available options for incorporation and the substantive choices that parties can contractually make in relation to the adopted model rules are open to variation. The proposed CESL, which was the most ambitious attempt at an optional instrument for European contract law to date, may function as an example to illustrate some of the possible alternatives.[60]

57 See McKendrick (n 16).

58 Compare Rome I Regulation (n 16) Art 3. See also R Goode, 'International Restatements of Contract and English Contract Law' (1997) II Uniform Law Review 231, 246.

59 McKendrick, 'Restatements of Contract Law' (n 16) 487.

60 The proposed CESL was withdrawn from the European Commission's legislative agenda at the end of 2014.

One of the main issues that came up in relation to the CESL is what status it should have in relation to other sources of law—in particular national, EU, and international law—for the purposes of private international law.[61] Being envisaged by the European Commission as an 'optional instrument' that contracting parties would be able to choose as a self-standing set of rules governing their contract,[62] the question arose how such a regime could be introduced in accordance with the limitation laid down in Article 3 of the Rome I Regulation, prescribing that only state law can be opted for as the chosen law. Further, a substantive debate arose on the question whether the CESL laid down a regime with a sufficiently high level of consumer protection, and whether consumers might under the rules of private international law be able to invoke the protection of their own national consumer laws in cases where these were more protective. The latter possibility, grounded in Article 6(2) of the Rome I Regulation, would render the idea of the CESL as a self-standing regime meaningless.

The puzzle that arose is a familiar one in the governance discourse in European private law: who should do what at what level of regulation?[63] Should the European legislator be able to introduce the CESL as a self-standing regime, it would erase the fall-back on national law made possible by Article 6(2) of the Rome I Regulation, at least for the part of the 'contract law market' that would start using the CESL for their contracting practices. The prerogative of national legislators to determine the level of consumer protection laid down in their national laws would be curtailed. That could be particularly problematic if the level of consumer protection adopted in the CESL were to be lower than that found in national laws.[64]

Several solutions presented themselves as to how the proposed CESL could be introduced in relation to existing laws.[65] First, the CESL could be regarded as a twenty-eighth regime (now twenty-ninth) for contract law in Europe, beside the twenty-seven (now twenty-eight) national legal systems in the European Union. Contracting parties would in that scenario be able to choose it as the applicable law to their contract in the same way that they would choose a national regime under Article 3 of the Rome I Regulation.[66] The European Commission did not favour

[61] For a comprehensive analysis, see G Dannemann, 'Choice of CESL and Conflict of Laws' in G Dannemann and S Vogenauer (eds), *The Common European Sales Law in Context* (OUP 2013) 21.

[62] Proposed CESL (n 11) 11.

[63] H-W Micklitz, 'The Visible Hand of European Regulatory Private Law—The Transformation of European Private Law from Autonomy to Functionalism in Competition and Regulation' (2009) 28 Yearbook of European Law 3.

[64] It has however been suggested that a higher level of consumer protection in the CESL could have negative consequences for consumers, such as an increase in prices; see eg H Eidenmüller and others, 'The Proposal for a Regulation on a Common European Sales Law: Deficits of the Most Recent Textual Layer of European Contract Law' (2012) 16 Edinburgh Law Review 326.

[65] For an overview, see European Parliament, Directorate-General for Internal Policies, Policy Department C: Citizens' Rights and Constitutional Affairs, 'The Functioning of the CESL within the Framework of the Rome I Regulation' (2012) <http://www.europarl.europa.eu/ document/activities/ cont/201211/20121120ATT55984/20121120ATT55984EN.pdf>.

[66] The CESL would in this case have been considered to be of a state law character in the sense of Art 3 of the Rome I Regulation. See Dannemann, 'Choice of CESL and Conflict of Laws' (n 61) 26.

this option, noting that the instrument would not fully work as a self-standing regime since consumers would still be able to invoke provisions of consumer protection of their own national laws under Article 6(2) of the Rome I Regulation in cases where those laws offer stronger protection than the CESL.

A second option would be to regard the CESL as a uniform regime of international law. In that case, the instrument would not be subject to rules of private international law but it would stipulate its own scope and applicability.[67] That option could have found a basis in recital 14 of the Rome I Regulation, albeit that a basis in a recital only is not very strong, the more so considering the uncertain wording of recital 14.[68] Another concern of the European legislator would be that a uniform law, similar to the Contracts for the International Sale of Goods (CISG), could be supplemented or overridden by mandatory rules of national law. Since the scope of the proposed CESL excludes certain issues—such as legal personality, the invalidity of a contract because of a lack of capacity, the transfer of ownership—it becomes necessary to revert to national law for those.[69]

The third option, and the one preferred by the European Commission, was to introduce the CESL as part of national laws. In this scenario it would function as a second regime beside the existing rules of national contract law, to be applicable if the parties to a contract chose it.[70] The European Commission has expressed its preference for this option because it can ensure the application of the CESL as a self-standing regime: being part of national law and of equal application throughout the EU it becomes impossible to invoke other national consumer protection rules under Article 6(2) of the Rome I Regulation.

In the light of the perceived need for a coordinated legal pluralism, this third model would appear quite appealing. It can enhance legal certainty for contracting parties since, if they were to opt for the CESL as the applicable law to their contract, the only set of rules they would have to deal with are those of the CESL. Unlike in the existing legal framework or the two other suggested scenarios, a trader would not have to reckon with the (potentially twenty-eight) different regimes of consumer protection that he may encounter in the EU Member States in which his customers reside. That could make the instrument attractive from a viewpoint of legal certainty—knowing which rules apply and to some extent being able to predict the outcome of potential disputes—and it could also decrease transaction costs

[67] Giesela Rühl made a plea for this option, calling it a '1st regime'; see G Rühl, 'The Common European Sales Law: 28th Regime, 2nd Regime or 1st Regime?' (2012) 19 Maastricht Journal of European and Comparative Law 148.

[68] European Parliament, 'The Functioning of the CESL within the Framework of the Rome I Regulation' (n 65) 12.

[69] N Kornet, 'The Common European Sales Law and the CISG. Complicating or Simplifying the Legal Environment?' (2012) 19 Maastricht Journal of European and Comparative Law 164.

[70] Proposed CESL (n 11), explanatory memorandum (4, 6, 8, and 9) and proposed recital 9.

since traders would not need to perform a check of various national consumer laws before being able to enter a foreign market.[71]

The question whether this third model would also result in a desirable level of consumer protection is perhaps not as straightforward. On the one hand, the drafters of the CESL could ensure that the instrument adopts a high level of consumer protection—which appeared to be the case in the final version of the proposal before it was withdrawn.[72] In any event, as it was envisaged to become part of national laws, the instrument would have had to give at least the protection prescribed by EU Directives aiming for minimum harmonization, as well as comply with consumer protection rules laid down in Directives aimed at full harmonization.[73] On the other hand, however, the text of the CESL would have fixed the level of consumer protection across a wide area of European contract law—sales contracts make up roughly 70–75 per cent of cross-border transactions in the EU[74]—with little chance of resetting or renegotiating that level. Apart from contracting parties' freedom to either opt for the CESL or for another (national) law, there would have been very little space for deliberation on the chosen level of protection. One wonders if an exclusion of the possibility for consumers to invoke their national laws on the basis of Article 6(2) of the Rome I Regulation, so categorically, would have been the wisest solution. By enabling recourse to national rules, albeit at the cost of legal certainty, at least a space is preserved in which the conditions for consumer protection that a national context might require are given an outlet. Although such local preferences could in the long term be phased out by national laws' adaptation to the EU framework or to other national laws, that kind of incremental, bottom-up process can often be preferable to the top-down imposition of a regime.[75]

Even if an instrument like the CESL could perform a coordinating function in a legal pluralist framework, this example should make clear that the balancing of various interests remains a delicate process. The enhancement of legal certainty must on occasion give way to local interests regarding consumer protection.

[71] See eg F Chirico, 'The Function of European Contract Law: An Economic Analysis', in P Larouche and F Chirico (eds), *Economic Analysis of the DCFR. The Work of the Economic Impact Group within the CoPECL Network of Excellence* (Sellier 2010) 9.

[72] European Parliament, Directorate-General for Internal Policies, Policy Department C: Citizens' Rights and Constitutional Affairs, 'Consumer Protection under the Proposal for a Common European Sales Law' (2012) <http://www.europarl.europa.eu/RegData/etudes/note/join/2012/462507/IPOL-JURI_NT(2012)462507_EN.pdf>.

[73] European Parliament, 'The Functioning of the CESL within the Framework of the Rome I Regulation' (n 65) 14.

[74] Services make up approximately 28 per cent of the export of goods and services in the EU, and 23 per cent of imports. The most recent data from the OECD (July 2014) are available at <http://ec.europa.eu/eurostat/statistics-explained/index.php/International_trade_in_services>.

[75] For example because top-down harmonization leaves many differences between national laws in place. Also, harmonization may be resisted on the ground that it cannot sufficiently take account of local economic preferences or of cultural factors; for an analysis in European private law, see G Comparato, *Nationalism and Private Law in Europe* (Hart Publishing 2014).

Further, the position of the EU legislator in the lawmaking process should not, as might be thought, be above the Member States' legislators but rather besides them, in a context of substantive deliberation.

An interesting point to note is that this deliberation is not only—as submitted—desirable from the legal pluralist view in which legal norms coexist in a non-hierarchical relationship but that it is also already partly reflected in the legal construction through which the CESL was supposed to be introduced (albeit with the restriction that the EU legislator is the one who decides on the final text). The EU legislator opted for a Regulation in which the text of the CESL was included in an annex. According to the reading of the European Parliament, this construction means that the Regulation (including the text of the annex) would be part of EU secondary law and could therefore be subject to autonomous EU interpretation, monitored by the CJEU.[76] Since the instrument would have been introduced as part of national law, it would also have had to comply with the levels of consumer protection set by existing EU Directives. In that guise, it could be envisaged that some cross-fertilization between the CESL and national laws might have occurred. The drafters of the CESL would have had to make sure that their text did indeed comply with existing rules. That would have required a compatibility check with the texts of existing Directives, but it also would have invited a comparison with national implementations of those Directives, which on occasion have given local colour to the way in which minimum harmonization rules are implemented. For example, the proposed remedies of the CESL could themselves have been the result of such deliberation. Where EU Directive 1999/44/EC laid down a hierarchy of remedies with repair and replacement coming before termination, thereby effectively giving the seller a 'right to cure' a defective performance, the CESL proposed a different solution. Article 106 (in particular subsections 1 and 3) would have given the buyer a free choice of remedies. In addition, Article 114(2) of the CESL would have permitted termination for all non-conformity in a consumer sales contract and a consumer contract for the supply of digital content, unless the lack of conformity was insignificant.[77] A consumer would therefore be free, if purchased goods turn out to be non-conforming, to immediately terminate the contract and ask for his money back. That solution is likely to have been inspired by similar rights in English and Irish law, which allow the buyer to reject the goods and claim his money back.[78]

Deliberation between lawmakers is therefore, in some instances, already encompassed in current governance structures. One should nonetheless be cautious to infer from this example concerning the CESL that the lawmaking process in EU

[76] European Parliament, 'The Functioning of the CESL within the Framework of the Rome I Regulation' (n 65) 15.

[77] For an analysis, see M Chen-Wishart and U Magnus, 'Termination, Price Reduction, and Damages' in G Dannemann and S Vogenauer (eds), *The Common European Sales Law in Context* (OUP 2013) 647, 658.

[78] Compare the analysis by Schulte-Nölke in a position paper for the European Parliament (n 72) 15.

law always provides a space for substantive deliberation between lawmakers. As was highlighted in Chapter 3, other governance models may be superimposed on the same constellation of lawmakers, for example intergovernmental lawmaking, parliamentary lawmaking, regulatory lawmaking, or judicial lawmaking.[79] Hence, with regard to optional instruments and model rules, the space for deliberation in the creation of the instruments may differ. At the same time, a second space for deliberation exists between the drafters and the users of optional instruments and model rules. Users can decide whether and to what degree to use the rules when designing their legal relations with other parties. The process brings optional instruments and model rules into the private sphere where they become part of the lawmaking process through individual choices of contracting parties. Although that lawmaking process cannot overall be characterized as a process of regulatory competition, it has been argued that the informed choice of rules by a small but sophisticated group of users can have effects on the substance of regulation.[80] The promotion of a high level of consumer protection in an optional instruments such as the proposed CESL could therefore, if parties recognize this as the preferred outcome, lead to the adoption of rules that comply with the EU's minimum level of consumer protection.

C. Online Dispute Resolution

The third mechanism, ODR, provides a space for resolving disputes between businesses and consumers that is largely designed through private regulation. Private actors, such as platform operators like eBay and Airbnb, can create dispute resolution platforms as a service for their customers. The availability of efficient, low-cost, and fast dispute resolution can be a factor contributing to the trust building that platforms need to engage in in order to attract users. If we apply the premise of voluntary creation and use of norms to this mechanism, how well does it fit the idea of a legal pluralist constellation of lawmakers in European contract law?

As a starting point, the substantive norms that arbitrators use to decide disputes are often phrased in an open manner, referring to reasonableness and fairness.[81] This would indicate that the space for substantive deliberation and choices between norms is significant. At the same time, a legality requirement applies, meaning that the decisions of ADR bodies may not fall below the level of consumer protection that a consumer would have had under mandatory rules of national law.[82] Those mandatory rules of national law inherently also include harmonized rules of EU

[79] See Chapter 3, p 68.
[80] Chapter 5, p 122.
[81] Above, n 24.
[82] Directive 2013/11/EU on alternative dispute resolution for consumer disputes [2013] OJ L165/63, Art 11.

consumer law that have been implemented into national private laws. The minimum values of EU law that are central to the instrumental-normative approach advocated in this book are therefore included in this provision, as a floor for protection that consumers can count on across the European Union. In their countries of residence, consumers may enjoy even higher levels of consumer protection if the Member State in which they have residence has 'gold plated' the minimum rules laid down in a given consumer law directive, that is that is has introduced or maintained rules that offer more protection to consumers than the minimum level prescribed by the directive. Generally, also outside the ADR context, consumers can invoke stronger protection provided by national contract law against professional counter-parties on the basis of Article 6(2) of the Rome I Regulation. There is, therefore, a framework of minimum values and objectives that applies to disputes resolved through ODR, but it is embedded in a context that accommodates legal pluralism.

Of the three mechanisms for managing pluralism identified here, ODR is nonetheless the most complex to reconcile with a strong legal pluralist perspective. Where standardization and the use of optional instruments and model rules operate *ex ante*, in the lawmaking process when rules and contracts are designed, ODR operates *ex post*, namely after a dispute has arisen. In that circumstance, differences between legal orders may actually lead to conflicts, for example if an ODR regime uses practical solutions that are completely different from the default rules of general contract or consumer law. Such practical solutions could for instance take the form of an automatic return of money paid in case goods delivered to a consumer are defective.[83] In the *ex-ante* phase, by comparison, the differentiation between legal orders does not hinder their coexistence and does not require an answer to the question which lawmaker has ultimate authority.[84]

Also for ODR, however, the argument in favour of strong legal pluralism can be upheld if one considers the space that it maintains for norm creation through substantive deliberation. ODR, as well as ADR, regimes allow arbitrators to decide disputes on the basis of norms established by the provider of the dispute resolution platform, such as reasonableness and fairness. In many legal systems, further, the decisions of ODR and ADR bodies are considered binding between the parties and can only be challenged in court on the grounds of a marginal assessment. That means that parties can challenge procedural shortcomings, but that the substance of the ODR or ADR procedure is generally not put to the test. In the European

[83] This solution has a practical advantage over other solutions, such as replacement, that require further communication between seller and buyer. In practice, eBay gives buyers a money back guarantee in many cases of non-delivery or non-compliance with the seller's description of goods; see Del Luca, Rule, and Rimpfel, 'eBay's De Facto Low Value High Volume Resolution Process: Lessons and Best Practices for ODR Systems Designers' (n 23) 207–08. See also G-P Calliess, 'Online Dispute Resolution: Consumer Redress in a Global Market Place' (2006) 7 German Law Journal 647.

[84] This question goes back to the second aspect of legal pluralist theories, discussed in Chapter 2, ie toleration. See p 41.

Union, the substantive outcome will have to comply with the level of consumer protection prescribed by mandatory rules of national consumer law—as per the legality requirement laid down in Article 11 of the ADR Directive—but that requirement is of an open nature.[85] It does not prescribe which rule or remedy needs to be applied, and in practice most ADR decisions appear to comply with this requirement.[86] Therefore, ODR may operate in a space that is legitimized by public regulation, but a space that leaves much room for the application of varying substantive norms. As such, it fits with the idea of a substantive deliberation between lawmaking actors.[87]

III. Private Governance vs Co-Regulation

The three mechanisms described in the previous section are examples of governance mechanisms that leave room for self-legislation by private actors who are addressees of rules. These mechanisms appear to fit well with consumer markets that are largely governed by contract, such as the platform economy. To what extent they can adequately provide coordinating mechanisms for lawmaking in a legal pluralist constellation is however dependent on another factor: namely, on how far-reaching contractual regulation can be in these markets. In some instances, co-regulation may be required to achieve certain policy goals. By way of illustration, I will explore what type of goals may require co-regulation in the platform economy (section III.A). In that context, potential issues for co-regulation seem to be concentrated on two specific areas only, namely product safety (section III.B) and market access (section III.C).

A. Beyond Private Governance

This book has taken the rise of the platform economy as a reason to explore lawmaking from a legal pluralist perspective in which private regulation, in terms of substance, is regarded as a source of valid norms alongside public regulation. The rapid growth of the platform economy and the hesitance of public regulators to subject platforms to regulation, often with the argument that they do not wish to stifle innovation, have meant that lawmaking in consumer markets has indeed shifted towards the private sphere. In that light, the governance mechanisms

[85] See above, n 82.

[86] Compare M Knigge and CMDS Pavillon, 'The Legality Requirement of the ADR Directive: Just Another Paper Tiger?' (2016) 5 Journal of European Consumer and Market Law 155.

[87] The norms developed through ODR can also be seen as social norms that become 'law' through their function of 'stabilizing normative expectations'. See G-P Calliess and M Renner, 'Between Law and Social Norms: The Evolution of Global Governance' (2009) 22 Ratio Juris 260

discussed in section II are relevant. Moreover, they are likely to remain so for a while longer, as public regulators are seeking to define their position vis-à-vis large tech companies. Whilst the balancing of regulation and innovation continues to be a relevant theme, the lobbying powers of large companies also mean that public regulation is often delayed, and that the real lawmaking powers lie with private actors through private regulation and contracting.

That picture, nevertheless, requires more nuance when it concerns issues going beyond contracting between platforms and users. The relevance of competition law has already been hinted at,[88] and likewise public authorities have picked up on data protection and privacy. The CJEU and the European Commission have engaged with such questions in relation to Google, Airbnb, and Uber. The Commission has on three occasions fined Google. It has sought to limit the company's hold on competition in the advertising market,[89] and to sanction unfair competition with shopping sites that appear in its search results and with the pre-instalment of its own search engine on rival browsers using the Android operating system.[90] The Commission, in cooperation with national competition authorities, has also pressured Airbnb to comply with transparency rules of EU consumer law.[91] The CJEU, in turn, through its preliminary reference procedure has given rulings that require Uber to comply with national—in this case Spanish—taxi service regulations and that require Google to apply the 'right to be forgotten' if users request their information to be removed from search results.[92]

It would appear, therefore, that private governance encounters limitations when it goes beyond contractual issues.[93] That is perhaps not very surprising, as the issues at stake in the cases discussed here concern collective interests and fundamental rights—competition, data protection—and generally require supervision and, if need be, regulation by public regulators. It is however a relevant observation

[88] Chapter 4, pp 79; Chapter 7, pp 185.

[89] European Commission, 'Antitrust: Commission fines Google €1.49 billion for abusive practices in online advertising' (Press release, 20 March 2019) <http://europa.eu/rapid/press-release_IP-19-1770_en.htm>.

[90] European Commission, 'Antitrust: Commission fines Google €2.42 billion for abusing dominance as search engine by giving illegal advantage to own comparison shopping service' (Press release, 27 July 2017) <http://europa.eu/rapid/press-release_IP-17-1784_en.htm>; European Commission, 'Antitrust: Commission fines Google €4.34 billion for illegal practices regarding Android mobile devices to strengthen dominance of Google's search engine' (Press release, 18 July 2018) <http://europa.eu/rapid/press-release_IP-18-4581_en.htm>.

[91] European Commission, 'EU Consumer Rules: The European Commission and EU Consumer Authorities Push Airbnb to Comply' (Press release, 16 July 2018), available at <europa.eu/rapid/press-release_IP-18-4453_en.htm>.

[92] Case C-131/12 *Google Spain v Mario Costeja González*, ECLI:EU:C:2014:317; Case C-434/15 *Asociación Profesional Elite Taxi v Uber Systems Spain, SL*, ECLI:EU:C:2017:981.

[93] That conclusion finds support in Michèle Finck's comparison of regulatory alternatives, which assesses how well regulatory strategies are able to deal with information asymmetries, externalities, rapidly changing contexts, and enforcement. My argument nonetheless is more favourable towards self-regulation. Compare M Finck, 'Digital Co-regulation: Designing a Supranational Legal Framework for the Platform Economy' (2018) 43 European Law Review 43.

in the light of the question to what extent private governance mechanisms can accommodate lawmaking in a legal pluralist constellation. One question that requires examination is whether contractual relations between platforms and users also concern interests that cannot be monitored or regulated through private governance mechanisms alone.

The answer to that question, arguably, is that private governance in the platform economy in some instances is not sufficient. It encounters limitations in at least two respects: the monitoring of product safety and the regulation of access to platforms.[94]

B. Product Safety

The first, product safety, is a concern because producers outside Europe do not always use the same, high safety standards for consumer products as are required in the European Union. Products sold through the Chinese trading platform Alibaba are often cheaply manufactured and of dubious safety. That applies for example to toys and electronics, such as fake Apple plugs. When consumers in Europe buy them, they may not realize that they are taking a safety risk when using these products.[95] Second, market access can be impaired, in particular for third-party traders who wish to offer goods through platforms, because users are dependent on the platform operator for the continued use of the platform. As was seen in Chapter 7, platform operators can impose strict targets on third-party traders, and suspend their accounts if those are not met.[96] The contractual rights of third-party traders are poorly balanced with those of the platform in these cases and their access to markets can relatively easily be lost.

In relation to these issues, a co-regulatory approach is likely to be more suitable than an approach solely based on private governance mechanisms. Co-regulation means that a public regulator works together with private actors to achieve certain policy goals. For product safety in Europe, one step towards co-regulation has already been taken. The European Commission signed a Product Safety Pledge with four leading online marketplaces in 2018.[97] While this is a promising development,

[94] These are also identified as the main issues in consumer markets by Hatzopoulos. See V Hatzopoulos, *The Collaborative Economy and EU Law* (Hart Publishing 2018), chapter 2 (on market access and consumer protection). See also chapter 3 (on data), and chapter 4 (on competition).

[95] S Hickey, 'Is buying online from China a good idea?' *The Guardian* (London, 3 September 2017) <https://www.theguardian.com/money/2017/sep/03/buying-online-china-aliexpress-beware-pitfalls>.

[96] Chapter 7, pp 181.

[97] The signatories are Alibaba, Amazon, eBay, and the French platform Rakuten. For the full text of the pledge, see European Commission, 'Product Safety Pledge. Voluntary commitment of online marketplaces with respect to the safety of non-food consumer products sold online by third party sellers' <https://ec.europa.eu/info/sites/info/files/voluntary_commitment_document_4signatures3-web.pdf>.

it is relatively light touch, as it relies on national authorities and on users to report safety concerns to the platform operator. The platform operator itself, besides being obliged to respond to requests from authorities and users to remove dangerous content, is not under a duty actively to monitor the safety of goods sold through the platform. Platform operators are however obliged to take measures aimed at preventing the reappearance of dangerous product listing already removed, and to provide information and to train sellers on compliance with EU product safety rules.[98] Still, this set of obligations does not prevent dangerous products from being sold on the European market. It cannot be compared, for example, to a certification regime. Perhaps in the future stricter measures will be needed, albeit that it is difficult to decide in what form. It would be impracticable, for instance, to introduce a mandatory safety check at customs for all low value products bought through Alibaba.

For comparison, existing co-regulatory regimes based on certification may provide inspiration, although monitoring and enforcement will have to be ensured. The PIP scandal can be seen as a cautionary tale, but also as a step towards making private actors jointly responsible for securing public goals such as the protection of health.[99]

C. Market Access

Another area in which co-regulation may be the best approach is in the pursuit of the protection of market access, for example in the form of mandatory requirements that platform operators need to fulfil before they can suspend a supplier's account. In 2019, the European Commission adopted a Regulation on transparency in platform-to-business relationships.[100] The Regulation contains a provision on the suspension of platform-supplier contracts stipulating that the platform must, if it decides to partly or wholly suspend or terminate the contract, 'provide the business user concerned, prior to or at the time of the restriction or suspension taking effect, with a statement of reasons for that decision on a durable medium'.[101] That statement of reasons should include reference to the specific facts or circumstances that led to the decision to suspend the supplier's account, as well as reference to the applicable grounds for that decision.[102] Notably, the Regulation is concerned with information provision to the supplier, but it does not affect the substantive grounds

[98] For an overview, see European Commission, 'European Commission and four online marketplaces sign a Product Safety Pledge to remove dangerous products' (Press release, 25 June 2018) <http://europa.eu/rapid/press-release_IP-18-4247_en.htm>.

[99] See Chapter 8, pp 197–199.

[100] Regulation (EU) 2019/1150 on promoting fairness and transparency for business users of online intermediation services [2019] OJ L186/57 (P2B Regulation).

[101] P2B Regulation (n 100), Art 4(1) and recital 23.

[102] P2B Regulation (n 100), Art 4(5) and Art 3(1)(c).

on which suspension or termination would be allowed, besides identifying a limited set of circumstances in which the platform may terminate without giving notice.[103] That is potentially problematic, as the rules would probably not tackle cases in which third-party suppliers are unjustly suspended from a platform, even if they have complied with performance requests within a given notice period.[104]

In addition to the proposed Regulation, private governance mechanisms perhaps can function as a fall back option. Model rules are already in the making. The ELI Working Group for Draft Model Rules on Online Intermediary Platforms has in the course of 2018 added a provision to its draft dealing with termination of the contract between the platform operator and a third-party supplier.[105] The draft provision suggests that platform operators will have to obey minimum notice periods, or that the contract can be terminated with immediate effect if there is good cause for doing so. In the latter case, before suspension of the supplier's contract can take effect, the supplier must have been given a fixed time period for remedial action which has expired to no avail, or the supplier's account must already have been temporarily suspended. These stipulations, although they go beyond the Platform to Business (P2B) Regulation, still focus primarily on formal requirements. If the Model Rules in their final version do not stipulate what counts as 'a good cause' for immediate termination, or wording to that effect, they also cannot protect third-party suppliers in Amazon-type situations. One alternative fall back option may then be the use of codes of conduct, developed for specific sectors of industry. The Regulation explicitly encourages the use of such codes of conduct.[106] That approach is exemplary of co-regulation: the proposed Regulation sets the framework and it encourages private actors to develop more detailed rules.

As an aside, alternative solutions to dealing with market access have been suggested in the literature. Schweitzer has made a plea for the application of the law of associations to online platforms which would regulate who is included in, or excluded from, the use of the platform.[107] Somewhat comparable is Sundararajan's suggestion of self-regulatory collectives, similar to professional organizations for law or medicine.[108] These are interesting suggestions but for now they are indicative only of ad hoc solutions in specific sectors. The European Commission's proposed P2B Regulation, which appears to reflect an overall approach that is

[103] For example, if the platform operator is subject to a legal or regulatory obligation with requires it to terminate the provision of the whole of its online intermediation services to a given business user in a manner which does not allow it to respect that notice period. See P2B Regulation (n 100), Art 4(4).

[104] See the case study on Amazon in Chapter 7, p 177 ff.

[105] Working document for the ELI Working Group's 2018 meeting in Aalborg; on file with author. The final version of the Model Rules available in August 2019 speaks of 'a compelling reason'.

[106] P2B Regulation (n 100), Art 17 and recital 48.

[107] See Schweitzer, 'Digitale Plattformen als private Gesetzgeber' (n 7).

[108] Sundararajan, 'The Collaborative Economy: Socioeconomic, Regulatory and Policy Issues' (n 45) 23–24, with reference to a California initiative concerning ride-sharing services.

coherent with other legislation in the field of European contract law, steers towards a co-regulatory approach based on contract law and information requirements.[109]

Co-regulation, in various forms, can therefore respond to issues concerning the contractual relationships between platforms and users that cannot be solved through private governance mechanisms alone. Such issues are product safety and market access for third-party suppliers. It is noteworthy that not more aspects have come to the fore in the examination of the platform economy.[110] That suggests that most aspects relating to the contractual relationships between platforms and users can be dealt with through contract law and private governance mechanisms. Platform operators, therefore, come close to being *private Gesetzgeber* ('private legislators').[111]

IV. Experimentalism

One final question, then, is how the process of substantive deliberation could be designed in the form of a governance strategy. Each of the mechanisms discussed above—standardization, model rules, ODR—requires the active involvement of private actors. Co-regulation, although instigated and controlled by public regulators, requires the same.[112] In a strong legal pluralist context, however, there is no obvious governance structure that brings together all lawmaking actors in a discursive process, as most governance approaches regard the coordination of lawmaking as part of a hierarchically steered process.

The suggestion has been put forward in scholarship that experimentalist governance could provide a useful governance framework for European private law.[113] Experimentalist governance has been developed in political theory as a mechanism by which policy goals can be pursued through an interaction of various entities. Although it was designed for dealing with policy issues, and is open as to how policies may be pursued, the basic elements of its framework can be superimposed on lawmaking processes in European private law.

Considering those basic elements first, in general terms experimentalist governance 'describes a set of practices involving open participation by a variety of entities (public or private), lack of formal hierarchy within governance arrangements, and

[109] cf C Twigg-Flesner, 'The EU's Proposals for Regulating B2B Relationships on Online Platforms—Transparency, Fairness and Beyond' (2018) 7 Journal of European Consumer and Market Law 222.

[110] Not in the research conducted for this book, but also not in policy documents or other literature.

[111] cf Schweitzer, 'Digitale Plattformen als private Gesetzgeber' (n 7). By contrast, Busch regards platforms as providers of private ordering services or as regulatory intermediaries implementing public ordering. See Busch, 'Self-Regulation and Regulatory Intermediation in the Platform Economy' (n 42). Also in favour of a co-regulatory approach, Finck, 'Digital Co-regulation: Designing a Supranational Legal Framework for the Platform Economy' (n 93).

[112] Compare Chapter 8, pp 190.

[113] Y Svetiev, 'The EU's Private Law in the Regulated Sectors: Competitive Market Handmaiden or Institutional Platform?' (2016) 22 European Law Journal 659.

extensive deliberation throughout the process of decision making and implementation'.[114] It therefore implies that lawmaking actors at different levels of regulation and implementation work together to achieve common goals through a recursive review process. There is therefore a continuous feedback from other levels, in which 'outcomes are subject to peer review, and goals and practices are periodically and routinely evaluated and reconsidered in the light of the data gathered, the results of the peer review, and the shared purposes'.[115] Experimentalist governance can be a useful framework under four conditions:[116] (i) governments are unable to formulate a comprehensive set of rules and efficiently and effectively monitor compliance with them; (ii) governments must not be stymied by a lack of agreement on basic principles (ie experimentalist governance can no more work if there is too little agreement than if there is too much, this is called the 'Goldilocks Zone'); (iii) civil society actors must be deeply involved in the politics in issue; and (iv) the issue must not be a matter of high politics.

The application of experimentalist governance to lawmaking in European private law appears at first glance to have sufficient bearings, albeit that it might require modifications to fit the needs of European market regulation through private law. The four conditions for its application appear roughly to be fulfilled. While there is agreement in the European Union that markets should be regulated to ensure the economic and social inclusion of consumers,[117] the diversification of lawmaking across formal and informal (or public and private) actors creates a complex picture within which it is uncertain that responsibility will be taken for ensuring consumer protection, and by whom. Therefore, while there is sufficient agreement on the goal—that is in the so-called Goldilocks Zone—lawmaking is not coordinated between actors in a way that enables that goal to be reached. The third and fourth condition are also met, seeing that civil society actors (such as businesses, consumers, and their representative organizations) are deeply involved in debates about market regulation and in actual lawmaking (eg through standards for services). The issue, arguably, is also not one of high politics; rather, it concerns the way in which regulation can contribute to the basic conditions under which markets can function at EU and national levels. This is primarily a question of policy, rather than politics, with the EU Treaties providing the framework within which specific policy questions are moderated.

There are nevertheless further questions that will need to be addressed if experimentalist governance is to be adopted as—at least the basis of—a governance

[114] G de Búrca, RO Keohane, and C Sabel, 'New Modes of Pluralist Global Governance' (2013) 45 NYU Journal of International Law and Politics 723, 738.
[115] ibid 739.
[116] ibid 781–83.
[117] See *Strategy 2020* and the consumer protection policy laid down in Art 38 of the EU Charter of Fundamental Rights [2000] OJ C364/1, and in Arts 114 and 169 of the Consolidated version of the Treaty on the Functioning of the European Union [2012] OJ C326/47 (TFEU).

framework for European private law. Some questions are whether the theory fits with lawmaking processes in the field, in terms of the participating lawmaking entities and the procedures of interaction and deliberation between them, and whether the goal of achieving a 'high level of consumer protection' is achieved through these strategies. To obtain answers to these questions, the theory will need to be tested on the existing strategies for lawmaking in European private law that have emerged, or that are emerging, as the role of private actors in lawmaking increases. Strategies that would merit investigation are the ones discussed in section II, in particular standardization of services, and rulemaking ADR and ODR by private actors. Of potential interest could also be the emergence of new norms through direct participation of consumers in market regulation, for example through online review systems.[118] Online review systems draw in another group of private actors as lawmakers: consumers themselves, who through their reviews can impart to businesses which rules *they* would like to apply. These mechanisms have all in recent years come to the fore as instances in which the role of private actors as rule-makers is of increasing importance. All in all, to verify whether an experimentalist approach can work in European private law, an empirical study of these emerging strategies would be helpful in order to determine who makes rules, at what level (national, EU, transnational), and whether the result of the process is that a high level of consumer protection is achieved.

Although the application of experimentalist governance to European private law may therefore open up new avenues for research, it is important to bear in mind the criticism that has been raised by critical legal scholars in relation to the theory. Their criticism of experimentalism to the EU internal market is that the theory lacks its own normative content, thereby creating the risk that extant inequalities are reinforced as the most powerful lawmaking actors have the final say on the substance of rules.[119] Others have defended experimentalism as a mechanism that allows for mutual adjustment and hybridization of EU and local policy goals. In that view, experimentalism actually provides a strategy that enables a deliberation of market and social goals between lawmaking actors at different levels of regulation in a problem-solving, work-in-progress manner.[120] Applied to lawmaking in private law in the EU consumer market, the latter view seems defendable, perhaps with the explicit addition that if experimentalism only provides the institutional framework, the actors involved in lawmaking will provide normative substance to the debate. While there is perhaps always a risk of market values overruling social values, as the EU market is based on neoliberal ideology, or of regulatory capture of lawmaking actors, the built-in review and feedback mechanisms enable checks and

[118] For an exploration of the question whether online review systems require regulation, see C Busch, 'Crowdsourcing Consumer Confidence' (n 41).

[119] Compare M Bartl, 'Internal Market Rationality, Private Law and the Direction of the Union: Resuscitating the Market as the Object of the Political' (2015) 21 European Law Journal 572.

[120] See Svetiev, 'The EU's Private Law in the Regulated Sectors' (n 113).

balances on the outcomes of lawmaking. These should guarantee that envisaged normative goals are met.

V. Conclusions

This chapter has considered the mechanisms for 'managing pluralism' in European contract law. The rise of the platform economy has led to a shift from public to private governance in consumer markets. Similar developments can be observed in other areas where lawmaking takes place beyond the state, such as in international trade and in sectors of consumer markets where standardization of services has become increasingly important. That shift towards private governance fits with the idea of a strong legal pluralist constellation of lawmakers, in which private regulation is considered a source of rules (or even of law) that is hierarchically on par with public regulation. The substance of rules is considered relevant, not their pedigree.

Whether, and to what extent, this idea can be upheld has been put to the test through an analysis of three mechanisms for managing pluralism in European contract law: standardization, model rules, and ODR. These mechanisms are primarily driven by private actors. The question, from a legal pluralist perspective, is whether they create a space for lawmaking by private actors in European contract law, separate from the hierarchy imposed by state law or public regulation that has been paradigmatic since the creation of the Westphalian nation state. This chapter reveals that this space indeed exists and that overall private governance seems to have the upper hand when lawmaking takes place beyond the state.

Standardization is driven by actors from industry and depends on voluntary involvement in its creation, adoption, and use. Even if standards are also developed as part of co-regulation—where standards are created at the instigation of a public regulator, such as the European Commission—the voluntary involvement of private actors is crucial to their success. The downside of standardization is however that it is perhaps not used often enough. In the platform economy, the until now only standard for services is ISO standard 20488:2018 on online consumer reviews. European standards have yet to be adopted.

Optional instruments and model rules also reside primarily in the private sphere. While they can be created by various actors—public regulators, legal scholars—their uptake depends solely on voluntary use by private actors. In that context, variation can still exist in the freedom that instruments leave for private actors to exercise their freedom of contract. In some instances, it may not be possible to contract out of certain provisions once the optional instrument or set of model rules is chosen to apply to the contract. Where that is the case, drafters can have an influence on the substance of norms, for example on the level of consumer protection. Various forms of interaction between public regulators (as drafters) and private actors (as users, or also as drafters) are possible. With its emphasis on private governance, however, this mechanism fits well with a strong legal pluralist perspective.

Third, ODR is the mechanism that is the most circumscribed by public regulation. In Europe, it is subject to the legality requirement laid down in the ADR Directive, which prescribes that consumers are entitled to the level of consumer protection set by mandatory rules of the national law of their country of residence. In addition, ODR and ADR are generally subject to marginal assessment by state courts if parties' choose to challenge a decision. Within that delimited space, however, there is still significant space for the substantive development of rules. The legality requirement does not prescribe what form remedies in contract should take, leaving it to the ODR committee to decide which solution is preferable in the given circumstances of a case. Furthermore, a marginal assessment touches upon procedural aspects but leaves substance alone. ODR can therefore also be a relevant source of norm creation in a legal pluralist constellation. In the platform economy, it can for example provide data on which remedies consumers prefer if a good or service does not live up to their expectations. More insights may in this way be procured on transparency and fairness in contracting in the platform economy.

While these three mechanisms driven by private actors can monitor lawmaking beyond the state for many aspects of European contract law, limitations to private governance nonetheless exist. These are likely to occur when collective interests or fundamental rights are at stake; hence, issues that go beyond contractual relations between private actors. In the platform economy issues that require input from public regulators are product safety and market access. Neither, until now, appear to be adequately protected by private regulation alone. Co-regulation can however provide solutions, and is being pursued as a strategy for lawmaking.

Finally, that leaves the question how lawmaking can be coordinated so that it includes all relevant lawmaking actors. This is an extremely difficult question and no governance theory for European contract law has succeeded in providing a definitive answer. This chapter has explored experimentalist governance as a potential coordinating structure that can fit a legal pluralist constellation. Its main feature is that it would enable deliberation through discursive practices between lawmaking actors. Given the rudimentary nature of the theory, only a few pointers can be provided as to how it would function, but these are promising and they invite further investigation. As with every mechanism based (partly) on private regulation, however, checks and balances will have to be maintained to prevent the reinforcement of extant interests of powerful players. The novelty in this case is that they are being sought beyond the state.

10
Realizing the EU Social Market Economy through Law

Long-term trends in society, economics, and science often appear as waves. Perspectives change over time, in many cases in response to societal or market disruptions, crises,[1] or in science through sudden breakthroughs. Perhaps the same can be said of perspectives on lawmaking in private law. After a wave of positivist codifications at the beginning of the twentieth century, followed by a turn to general theories of legal pluralism in the socio-legal scholarship of the 1960s and 1970s, and neo-formalism again in the emergence of European private law in the 1990s and early 2000s, private law returns to legal pluralism. Transnational legal scholarship has grappled with 'new' legal pluralism as a lens through which to examine lawmaking process beyond the state,[2] and more or less simultaneously debates on the monist or pluralist nature of European private law have been conducted.[3]

This book has taken stock of legal pluralist debates on private law beyond the state with a view to identifying how the rise of private regulation and, to some extent, judicial lawmaking can be accommodated in lawmaking processes in European private law. Those questions have become relevant as the use of private regulation continues to increase not only for business transactions but also, with the rise of the platform economy, in consumer markets. At the same time, the Court of Justice of the European Union (CJEU) has broadened the scope for the pursuit of social goals of the Union through its interpretations of consumer contract law.[4]

[1] Famous in economic theory are Kuznet waves, which are Milanovic's extrapolation of Kuznet curves to explain alternating increases and decreases in inequality. See B Milanovic, *Global Inequality. A New Approach for the Age of Globalization* (Belknap/Harvard University Press 2016) 50 ff. On processes of rising and stagnating welfare in factor markets (ie markets for land, lease, labour, and capital), see B van Bavel, *The Invisible Hand? How Market Economies have Emerged and Declined Since AD 500* (OUP 2016).

[2] cf N Walker, *The Intimations of Global Law* (CUP 2015) 114; P Schiff Berman, *Global Legal Pluralism. A Jurisprudence of Law Beyond Borders* (CUP 2012); N Krisch, *Beyond Constitutionalism: The Pluralist Structure of Postnational Law* (OUP 2010) 296; R Michaels, 'Global Legal Pluralism' (2009) 5 Annual Review of Law and Social Sciences 243. See in detail Chapter 2.

[3] L Niglia (ed), *Pluralism and European Private Law* (Hart Publishing 2013); JM Smits, 'Plurality of Sources in European Private Law, or: How to Live With Legal Diversity?' in R Brownsword and others (eds), *The Foundations of European Private Law* (Hart Publishing 2011) 323; H-W Micklitz, 'The Visible Hand of European Regulatory Private Law—The Transformation of European Private Law from Autonomy to Functionalism in Competition and Regulation' (2009) 28 Yearbook of European Law 3. See in detail Chapter 5.

[4] Case C-415/11 *Mohamed Aziz v Caixa d'Estalvis de Catalunya, Tarragona i Manresa (Catalunyacaixa)*, EU:C:2013:164 is regarded as a landmark case in this respect. See Chapter 4, pp 85.

Legal Pluralism in European Contract Law. Vanessa Mak, Oxford University Press (2020). © Vanessa Mak.
DOI: 10.1093/oso/9780198854487.001.0001.

In the responses to his book on general legal pluralism, Schiff Berman has observed the recognition of legal pluralism as an accepted descriptive framework,[5] however the conclusions on European private law are more nuanced and, in some respects, they are still in flux. The theoretical foundations of a descriptive and normative case for strong legal pluralism in European private law can be developed, as earlier chapters have shown.[6] The theory, moreover, can find support in cases studies of lawmaking in the platform economy and through standardization.[7] Still, however, the relation between the juridical rationality of national private laws and the market rationality of EU law—both ideal types—tends to be viewed in scholarship and practice either from a monist, state-centred basis or through the prism of 'ordered' legal pluralism.[8] The view presented in this book is therefore in many respects pushing the boundaries of existing perspectives, and it is meant to generate further discussion on the future of lawmaking in European private law. As lawmaking continues to evolve, and private actors are both in size and in influence rivalling state power,[9] the questions discussed in this book are likely to remain relevant until well into the future.

This chapter presents the main findings of the enquiry into lawmaking in European private law (section I). It also discusses the reach of the proposed perspective on lawmaking and reflects upon avenues for further research (section II).

I. Findings

Drawing together the lines developed in the previous chapters, a legal pluralist perspective appears to have become a better fit for lawmaking beyond the state than the monist, state-centred model. Applied to European private law, the theory can be further elaborated. The EU's shared values and objectives can provide the basis for an instrumental-normative approach to lawmaking that ensures that minimum values and objectives of EU law are safeguarded. Several arguments have come to the fore to support that conclusion.

First, strong legal pluralism is both descriptively and normatively preferable over a monist, state-centred approach to lawmaking in transnational private law and, by the same token, European private law. Descriptively, it acknowledges the decreasing relevance of a hierarchy between lawmaking actors and shifts emphasis towards the substance of norms. Normatively, strong legal pluralism is preferable since it gives space to multiple viewpoints and values, and thereby supports

[5] P Schiff Berman, 'How Legal Pluralism Is and Is Not Distinct from Liberalism: A Response to Dennis Patterson and Alexis Galán' (2013) 11 International Journal of Constitutional Law 801, 802.

[6] In particular Chapters 2, 3, 4, and 5.

[7] Chapters 6, 7, and 8.

[8] Chapter 5, pp 94.

[9] Large tech companies' assets have outgrown some state's gross domestic product in some cases.

the public autonomy—that is, the power to self-legislate—of actors. In support of this argument of recognition, there is a supplementary role for toleration through which differences and norm conflicts between legal orders can be moderated.

Second, concerns about the normative substance of rules—which is a different type of normativity than the one discussed before, concerning the normative case for a strong legal pluralist perspective—may arise due to the greater space for lawmaking granted to private actors, who engage in processes of self-regulation and co-regulation. The shift from public to private regulation entails a risk that insufficient heed will be paid to public interests, such as consumer protection and the observance of general values of contract law. To safeguard these interests, however, it is submitted that European private law has an advantage over transnational private law in a broader sense of the word: norm conflicts are moderated within the EU legal order, which sets minimum normative standards due to European private law's commitment to common objectives and values laid down in the EU Treaties. Applied to lawmaking in European private law, a strong legal pluralist perspective translates into what I have called a substantive deliberation between lawmaking actors. That approach prescribes that norms should be developed through a recursive process between lawmaking actors in which their substance is examined and can be adjusted in response to the norms developed by other, public or private, actors. This substantive deliberation can be embedded in an approach that preserves strong legal pluralism, namely an instrumental-normative model for lawmaking. The model is instrumental because it assumes that certain goals can be pursued through law, and normative in the sense that the envisaged goal is to safeguard the minimum values and objectives of EU law.

Third, the framework set by the values and objectives of EU law, as laid down in Articles 2 and 3 of the Treaty on European Union (TEU)[10] and elaborated in other clauses of the Treaties as well as in secondary legislation, may at first glance seem at odds with a strong legal pluralist theory. Strong legal pluralism supposes that norms co-exist without a formal hierarchy, and it seems counterintuitive to hold that lawmaking must adhere to minimum values and objectives. There are nonetheless arguments that reconcile the two viewpoints. In Europe an overlapping consensus exists on the categorical protection of weaker parties, and value pluralism can exist in the shadow of this moral principle.[11] Further, if legal orders are understood, as they are in socio-legal scholarship, on a space-time dimension, it is possible to conceive of the European Union as a putative legal order aimed at the pursuit of 'an ever closer union'.[12] The pursuit of common values is part of this

[10] Consolidated version of the Treaty on European Union [2012] OJ C326/01 (TEU).

[11] The principle of overlapping consensus developed by Rawls is moral in the sense that it presupposes a morally significant core of commitments between otherwise incommensurable doctrines, and is more than a strategic agreement of a pragmatic nature. cf J Rawls, 'The Domain of the Political and Overlapping Consensus' (1989) 64 New York University Law Review 233; J Rawls, *Justice as Fairness: A Restatement* (Harvard University Press 2001) 32–33.

[12] See Chapter 3, p 52 ff.

putative legal order rather than a goal that is hierarchically imposed on lawmaking actors. Finally, private governance mechanisms in European private law are based on voluntary participation, hence fitting with strong legal pluralism's element of public autonomy.

Fourth, the practical applicability of this model is tested in the book through two case studies of lawmaking in contract and consumer law. The first case study relates to the platform economy, focusing on transparency at the stage of contract formation. That study shows that the objectives and values of European contract and consumer law in this respect appear to have been met by lawmakers. The case study on standardization, in a different context, confirms that lawmaking in European private law, when it involves public and private regulators, operates in the shadow of the objectives and values of EU law.

Finally, however, the acceptance of a broad space for private regulation entails risks. In practice, more powerful market actors are likely to have the main say in determining the substance of norms that are created and applied to private law relationships. In the platform economy, that lawmaking power rests with large tech companies such as Airbnb, Amazon, Alibaba, and Uber. While consumer protection levels may be high, as Chapter 7 reveals, one trade-off that is made to maintain high levels of customer satisfaction is that the terms and conditions imposed on third-party suppliers are very burdensome. Left to market forces, the balance of interests is unlikely to be corrected. Mechanisms will therefore have to be developed to ensure that the values of EU law concerning consumer protection and contractual values are safeguarded in practice. The book considers several mechanisms that might fulfil this function: standardization, model rules, and optional instruments, and online dispute resolution. Each of these mechanisms can serve to strengthen the position of other private actors—for example, smaller businesses, consumers, and consumer organizations—in the process of lawmaking in the private sphere.

II. Discussion

Having developed a theory of lawmaking based on strong legal pluralism and tested it on three case studies in European private law, questions remain. One important question for legal theory, but also for legal practice, is how far the theory reaches. Can it be applied to all aspects of consumer markets or is the changing hierarchy between lawmaking actors specific to online markets? Technological developments are also having effects on offline markets and a re-evaluation of monist, state-centred approaches to lawmaking may in that context equally be required.

Other challenges lie in the vulnerability of Europe as a guardian of the social market economy within which consumers and businesses operate. It has been argued that legal pluralism in Europe is moderated by the objectives and values laid down in the EU Treaties, which directly or indirectly influence the substance of norms developed by public and private lawmakers. Can political risks to the European Union destabilize the suggested approach by upsetting the Union's objectives and values?

Finally, lawmaking in European contract and consumer law is concerned with only one or two aspects of citizens' lives—their economic participation and, as a corollary, their social inclusion—yet it fits within a broader framework of citizens' rights in EU law. Policy-making in labour law or environmental law, for example, are related to consumer law as they also impact upon the economic and social position of citizens. Yet, EU law tends to treat these areas as separate fields, both from an institutional perspective as in legislation. One wonders whether more could be done with the integration objectives laid down in the EU Treaties, in particular in the light of pursuing a social market economy.

The following sections present some reflections on each of these questions, without aiming to provide an exhaustive answer to them. Rather, they can be seen as starting points for further research.

A. Generalization of Conclusions

The book has dealt with European contract and consumer law, with specific focus on the challenges of the platform economy and of standardization in consumer markets. To what extent are the findings of the previous chapters applicable for the broader field of European private law? That question entails a reflection on the distinction between online and offline transactions.

While this book has focused for a large part on online transactions in the platform economy, the majority of consumer contracts are still concluded in offline, brick-and-mortar shops and with local service providers.[13] Those transactions are governed by the national law of the country in which the contract is concluded, which in Europe will be influenced by harmonized rules of consumer contract law. For those types of transactions some of the issues discussed in this book could be of lesser relevance, as consumer protection interests are monitored by the national legislator who can ensure that minimum values and objectives are determined, and the courts and dispute resolution bodies, who can ensure that these values and objectives are met. That includes the rules of European consumer law, which for sale of goods will soon prescribe new harmonized rules on conformity and remedies for all online and offline sales in business-to-consumer (B2C) contracts.[14]

[13] The percentage of e-commerce sales as part of global retail sales is expected to reach 17.5 per cent in 2021; see <https://www.statista.com/statistics/534123/e-commerce-share-of-retail-sales-worldwide/> accessed 28 February 2020, as are all websites in this chapter. E-commerce in Europe amounted to €621 billion in 2019; see <https://ecommercenews.eu/ecommerce-in-europe-e621-billion-in-2019/>.

[14] Directive (EU) 2019/771 on certain aspects concerning contracts for the sale of goods, and repealing Directive 1999/44 [2019] OJ L136/28.

Nevertheless, also in this context a plurality of norms can exist. Offline transactions can be regulated through private regulation and contracting too, if traders decide to stipulate terms and conditions and codes of conduct. Perhaps the main distinction in comparison to online platforms is that in the offline environment most transactions are B2C contracts. Therefore, consumer protection will apply as a minimum, and the focus will be on enforcement of consumer protection rules rather than on questions of validity of norms.[15]

At the same time, even in the offline environment technological changes are taking place that potentially require a fundamental revision of the regulatory framework for consumer contract law, with greater attention to the private sphere. Examples are the use of smart contracts, that through programming are largely self-executing,[16] and the rise of the Internet of Things (IoT), which connects (consumer) goods to the Internet and implies that software and algorithms largely determine the expectations that consumers may have from these goods. In both cases, subjective conformity requirements are likely to be of greater relevance than objective requirements. That means that suppliers are able to stipulate through their terms and conditions which reasonable expectations users may have from their products and services. Objective quality standards laid down in legislation can in these circumstances provide only limited protection to consumers.

Lawmakers' struggle with objective and subjective conformity standards can be observed in the drafting process of the Directive on contracts for the supply of digital content, the final text of which was adopted in April 2019.[17] The first proposal gave preference to subjective conformity requirements.[18] While the final version of the Directive, after amendments by the European Parliament, imposes objective conformity requirements on suppliers in B2C contracts, the protection that consumers can derive from these may for now still be limited. Article 8(1)(a) of the Directive refers to technical standards and sector-specific industry codes of conduct. Until these have been developed for a broad range of products and services, however, that provision will be of little use to consumers. Further, Article 8(1)(b) refers to 'the qualities and performance features, including in relation to functionality, compatibility, accessibility, continuity and security, normal for digital content or digital services of the same type and which the consumer may reasonably expect'. What is 'normal' and what the consumer may 'reasonably' expect are open norms for which at this stage it is difficult to say what they entail in specific

[15] See by contrast the discussion on online platforms, where many relationships are not of a B2C nature and therefore not subject to rules of consumer protection; Chapter 7, p 165.

[16] M Raskin, 'The Law and Legality of Smart Contracts' (2017) 1 Georgetown Law Technology Review 305, 309.

[17] Directive (EU) 2019/770 on certain aspects concerning contracts for the supply of digital content and digital services [2019] OJ L136/1.

[18] Proposal for a Directive of the European Parliament and of the Council on certain aspects concerning contracts for the supply of digital content, COM(2015) 634 final, Art 6(2) ('To the extent that the contract does not stipulate').

situations. The same reservation applies to the updates, including security updates, that the consumer may reasonably expect (see Article 8(2)(b)).

Other challenges to consumer law in offline contexts are created by the so-called servitization of markets. Servitization refers to a shift from transactions in which ownership of goods is obtained to contracts that give access to goods, often in combination with services. An example is the provision of light by Philips at Schiphol Airport. The agreement in this case is not for the sale of lamps but rather for the provision of light through luminaries chosen by Philips, and retained in ownership by them. The agreement also includes service provisions, for example for maintenance and the replacement of lamps.[19] While the Philips agreement concerns a B2B arrangement, similar types of transactions are increasingly concluded in consumer markets. Popular examples are lease contracts for cars or bicycles, or for the lease of clothing.[20] Seeing that services contracts are less influenced by European harmonization than consumer sales contracts, and in many national laws not governed by specific consumer contract rules but by general contract law, consumer protection may be diminished by these types of arrangements. Also here, private regulation and contracting will become more important sources of norms.

Altogether, changes in consumer markets due to the emergence of new technologies and new business models have an impact not only on online but also on offline transactions. While the degree to which markets are influenced by such developments may differ, one characteristic that is shared is the greater relevance of private regulation and contracting, resulting in an absence of clear consumer protection rules. In that respect, a legal pluralist perspective on lawmaking becomes relevant also for offline transactions, at least until a (national or European) legislator introduces new regulation that can subsequently be enforced through the state's institutional structures.

B. Objectives and Values in Flux

Besides the scope of application of the theory, another aspect that may be open to change is the basis of the theory in objectives and values of EU law. Chapter 4 revealed that there is a minimum set of common values in European contract and consumer law. It is found primarily in the EU Treaties, with Article 3(3) TEU's commitment to the pursuit of a social market economy finding support in the specific consumer law provisions of Articles 12, 114(3), and 169(1) TFEU[21] and in the

[19] See <http://www.lighting.philips.com/main/cases/cases/airports/schiphol-airport>.

[20] For a discussion see V Mak and E Terryn, 'Circular Economy and Consumer Protection. The Consumer as a Citizen and the Limits of Empowerment through Consumer Law' (2020) 43 Journal of Consumer Policy 227.

[21] Consolidated version of the Treaty on the Functioning of the European Union [2012] OJ C326/47 (TFEU).

EU Charter of Fundamental Rights.[22] Similar objectives and values can be identified in the EU's social *acquis*, for example in Articles 153 and 155 TFEU.

The robustness of this normative basis is however not a given. To give hands and feet to consumer, social, and environmental policies, the European Union is primarily dependent on the development of secondary legislation and flanking initiatives, of which the Social Pillar is an example. The CJEU may also contribute to developments in these areas through 'activist' decisions in its case law,[23] albeit that the Court operates within a system of checks and balances that contains its space for policy-making.[24] However, the pursuit of values and objectives through more specific measures presupposed that there is agreement about the substance of such values and objectives. As the European Union in recent years has struggled to agree on high-profile political issues—for example in relation to the Greek debt crisis, immigration, Poland's judicial reforms, and Brexit—a poignant question is whether the Union can actually maintain common values and objectives. If not, the basis of its normative legal order is precarious.

There is no straightforward answer to this question. On the one hand, it might be said that the Treaties will not soon change, and that therefore some minimum set of common values and objectives is guaranteed. The legal framework endorsing common values and objectives exists, in other words, and it can frame political and economic decision making. Nonetheless, that legal framework cannot ultimately guarantee the observance of values and objectives. First, to give effect to them, further policy-making and legislation will have to give hands and feet to the values and objectives laid down in the EU Treaties. As has been observed, the degree of action taken in different fields at which values and objectives of the EU are directed—non-discrimination, work, environment, the pursuit of a social market economy—varies quite significantly.[25] That could be explained by the limited legislative competences of the European Union in each of these fields, as well as the difficulty sometimes to harness the political will required for the adoption of new legislation. The failure of more comprehensive harmonization projects in the field of European private law, such as the adoption of a Common European Sales Law, can be attributed to this factor.[26] Further, the Treaties are open to varying socio-economic readings.[27] To some degree, therefore, where the balance is struck

[22] EU Charter of Fundamental Rights [2000] OJ C364/1.

[23] Compare M Dawson, B De Witte, and E Muir (eds), *Judicial Activism at the European Court of Justice* (Edward Elgar 2013).

[24] L Conant, *Justice Contained. Law and Politics in the European Union* (Cornell University Press 2002).

[25] cfS Weatherill, *Law and Values in the European Union* (OUP 2016) 137–38, who nonetheless observes that 'the Court has actively concerned itself to adopt an interpretative approach which seeks to make real the Treaty's policy priorities'.

[26] On the failure of the proposed CESL, H Beale, 'The Role for European Contract Law: Uniformity or Diversity?' in F de Elizalde (ed), *Uniform Rules for European Contract Law? A Critical Assessment* (Hart Publishing 2018) 14.

[27] C Kaupa, *The Pluralist Character of the European Economic Constitution* (Hart Publishing 2016) 6.

between economic and social interests is variable. That is reflected in the case law of the CJEU in consumer law and labour law.[28]

At the same time, even if the legal framework provided by the Treaties cannot in itself guarantee in which ways common values and objectives will continue to inspire and demarcate lawmaking choices in European private law, an underlying philosophical argument is still at play. As was argued in Chapter 3, the European Union can be regarded as a putative legal order. The Treaty of Rome's preamble expresses the determination to lay the foundations of an 'ever closer union between the peoples of Europe'. Who the 'peoples of Europe' are may change, for example with expansion of the Union or with the exit of Member States. However, the sentiment does not change. The European Union is above all a regional cooperation aimed at structuring multi-level governance and the performance of defined tasks.[29] Its structure and definition are inspired and guided by the values and objective laid down in the Treaties, which go beyond the interests of individual Member States or their citizens. In that sense, Europe distinguishes itself from state structures in which governance is in the hands of a political majority. The Union, having a more demarcated purpose focused on market integration and an increasing number of social and political goals in which cooperation between Member States is desired, has no 'popular or populist sheen' and should not have it.[30] Perhaps that makes its values and objectives resistant to change.

Whether the proclaimed common values and objectives laid down in Articles 2 and 3 TEU are sufficient ground for keeping the European project together, nonetheless, remains an object of scrutiny. The putative order that was envisaged in the Treaty of Rome could, at least in theory, collapse. Even if that does not happen, Eurosceptic views are likely to highlight the EU's market-orientated purpose and downplay its role in social policy or intergovernmental cooperation with regard to security and migration.[31] The balance between economic policy and social objectives will therefore have to be assessed continuously.

For the object of study of this book—European private law, in particular consumer and contract law—nonetheless, the EU appears to provide a solid framework at least of common values and objectives. Lawmaking in this field is grounded in internal market policy, complemented with social goals. The latter part, social policy, is in flux but it is gaining ground in legislation and case law in the field of consumer and contract law. Examples are the protection of consumers against over-indebtedness through consumer credit regulation, and the protection of the right to housing through unfair terms regulation in consumer contract law. Such

[28] See Chapter 4, p 89 ff.
[29] Weatherill, *Law and Values in the European Union* (n 25) 396.
[30] ibid.
[31] Weatherill (n 25) 406–09.

examples could be seen as glimmers of social justice, contributing to achieving an EU social market economy.[32]

C. EU Consumer Law, Labour Law, Environmental Law—Separate but Connected

Another issue is how lawmaking in European private law, focused on contract and consumer law, compares to other areas in which the European Union has committed itself to the pursuit of common values and objectives, in particular through legislative action. Examples are labour law and environmental law. These fields are considered separate areas in the institutional and legal framework of the Union,[33] yet they can have direct ramifications for consumers' lives. Employment, simply said, provides people with an income and thereby enables them to act as consumers. Environmental protection overlaps with consumer law in sustainability policies aimed at achieving a circular economy.[34]

I focus here on the legislative action of the European Union, although private regulation has also become important in these fields of law. As in consumer markets, the position of lawmaking actors is changing in relation to the regulation of employment relations and environmental protection. Private actors are increasingly involved in the development of rules and practices. In the platform economy or gig economy, the terms and conditions applicable to workers are primarily determined through contracts, including standard terms, and private regulation in the form of, for example, codes of conduct. Environmental protection, for instance through the pursuit of a circular economy, is also for a large part dependent on voluntary adoption of sustainability policies by suppliers and manufacturers. The theory of lawmaking based on substantive deliberation could therefore, perhaps with modifications, be applied to these fields too. What is unclear, however, is which objectives and values in EU law would provide a framework for lawmaking. That question would merit further research, in particular to determine the extent to which social rights have gained a place besides market rights (comparable to the analysis of consumer law in Chapter 4). Some observations can be made as a stepping stone for further research.

32 Chapter 4.

33 SA de Vries, 'General Reflections on the Exercise of Economic Rights by EU Citizens' in SA de Vries and others (eds), *EU Citizens' Economic Rights in Action. Re-thinking Legal and Factual Barriers in the Internal Market* (Edward Elgar 2018) 2, 11, noting that EU citizenship includes expressions of economic (consumer) rights as well as worker rights, but that the two fields are not connected in EU law. Compare also H-W Micklitz, *The Politics of Justice in European Private Law. Social Justice, Access Justice, Societal Justice* (CUP 2018) 196 ff.

34 The relation between the two is explored in more detail in Mak and Terryn, 'Circular economy and Consumer Protection' (n 20) 234–35. See also C Kye, 'Environmental Law and the Consumer in the European Union' (1995) 7 Journal of Environmental Law 31, 32 ff; J Karsten and LA Reisch, 'Sustainability Policy and the Law' (2008) 4 German Policy Studies 45.

First, the right to access to work, laid down in Article 15 of the EU Charter of Fundamental Rights could be considered a social right that is relevant for consumers. How this provision fits into the broader framework of rights, principles, and policies in EU law, in relation to the laws of the Member States, is however less straightforward than in the field of consumer law. Whereas consumer contract law is to a very large degree harmonized through EU law, labour law is still primarily governed by the national laws of the Member States, despite harmonizing measures for specific issues, such as the posting of workers.[35] An explanation for that difference is not so much that competences are shared between the Union and the Member States—that is also the case for consumer law—but rather that labour law touches upon broader socio-legal policies that have been developed at Member State level and that there is therefore less space to develop new policies. Whereas the EU's competences do not allow it to intervene in labour law related issues such as social security, collective bargaining, minimum wages, and unemployment policy, national consumer law was not at rest in the Member States when the European Union took on a leading policy role.[36] The EU's involvement in the field of labour law has hence been restricted to establishing the role and function of trade unions in the making and enforcement of self-standing rules,[37] and the individualization of employees and workers through subjective enforceable 'rights'.[38] Overall, in EU labour law policy, the social dimension seems to lose out to economic interests.[39]

Environmental policy in relation to consumer markets is less developed, not only at the national level but also in EU law. Although Member States have to varying degrees introduced recycling regimes for waste and repair policies for defective goods, sustainability and climate change concerns have only recently gained ground on economic policy. The Netherlands is one of the few countries that has set out a strategy in which a self-standing commitment to the implementation of a circular economy is included in a holistic and long-term strategic way. This means that the implementation of a circular economy is regarded as an autonomous goal, not per se embedded in a long-term economic strategy, and that it encompasses the

[35] The EU's posted workers Directive of 1996 has recently been revised. See Directive (EU) 2018/957 amending Directive 96/71/EC concerning the posting of workers in the framework of the provision of services [2018] OJ L173/16, which Member States should have implemented by 30 July 2020.

[36] Micklitz, *The Politics of Justice in European Private Law* (n 33) 8–9.

[37] cf Case C-438/05 *International Transport Workers' Federation and Finnish Seamen's Union v Viking Line ABP and OÜ Viking Line Eesti* [2007] ECR I-10779, ECLI:EU:C:2007:772 and Case C-341/05 *Laval un Partneri Ltd v Svenska Byggnadsarbetareförbundet* [2007] ECR I-11767, ECLI:EU:C:2007:809.

[38] Micklitz, *The Politics of Justice in European Private Law* (n 33) 8. Other than Micklitz implies, the individualization approach would seem to apply not only to employees but in a broader sense to workers. Compare Chapter IV of the EU Charter of Fundamental Rights, albeit that the status of the provisions of the Chapter as rights or principles remains unclear. See below, p 244.

[39] The social market economy is only directly referred to in Case C-201/15 *AGET Iraklis*, ECLI:EU:C:2016:972, at [76], which notably is a case that supports the *Viking* and *Laval* judgments that have often been criticized for preferring the market over the social. See C Barnard and SA de Vries, 'The "Social Market Economy" in a (Heterogeneous) Social Europe: Does it Make a Difference?' (2019) 15 Utrecht Law Review 47.

entire value chain for production.[40] At EU level, legislative action is not driven by a consistent policy framework but until now has been focused on a number of specific actions on the supply and demand sides of the market. On the supply side, the Union has introduced legislation to reduce the use of plastics, such as lightweight carrier bags and packaging,[41] and for the reduction of waste.[42] Further, in 2018 agreement was reached on new EU-wide rules aimed at banning certain single-use plastics, such as straws, plastic plates, plastic utensils, and cotton swabs with plastic stems.[43] On the demand side of the market, EU policy has primarily focused on 'light touch' regimes that appeal to EU citizens to endorse sustainable lifestyles.[44] It has been suggested that further measures could be taken to promote a circular economy in consumer markets, for example by strengthening consumer rights in relation to repair of goods and in the promotion of servitization as a new business model.[45]

The framework of EU law nevertheless suggests that further integration of consumer and labour law, and potentially also environmental policy, would be possible

[40] See Dutch Council for the Environment and Infrastructure (Rli), 'Europe Goes Circular. Outlining the Implementation of a Circular Economy in the European Area', 9–10 <https:// www.rli.nl/sites/default/files/rli_eu_goes_circular_-_eeac_working_group_on_circular_economy_def_1.pdf>. See also Government of the Netherlands, 'A Circular Economy in the Netherlands by 2050. Government-wide Programme for a Circular Economy' https://www.government.nl/documents/policy-notes/2016/09/14/a-circu- lar-economy-in-the-netherlands-by-2050. For an analysis, V Mak and E Lujinovic, 'Towards a Circular Economy in EU Consumer Markets—Legal Possibilities and Legal Challenges and the Dutch Example' (2019) 8 Journal of European Consumer and Market Law 4, 5.

[41] The latest revision of the Packaging and Packaging Waste Directive occurred in 2015 with the adoption of Directive (EU) 2015/720 amending Directive 94/62/EC as regards reducing the consumption of lightweight plastic carrier bags [2015] OJ L115/11.

[42] The range of measures adopted and proposed aims at the whole production cycle from the use of raw materials, the design, production, delivery, distribution, and consumption of products and services as well as the disposal and recycling of materials and the use of secondary raw materials. See HM Schally, 'The Circular Economy Action Plan: An Agenda for Change!' in B Keirsbilck and E Terryn (eds), *Circular Economy and Consumer Protection* (Intersentia 2019) 3, and see Communication from the Commission to the European Parliament, the Council, the European Economic and Social Committee and the Committee of the Regions, 'Closing the Loop—An EU Action Plan for the Circular Economy' COM(2015) 614 final; European Commission, 'Proposal for a Directive of the European Parliament and of the Council amending Directive 2008/98/EC on waste' COM(2015) 595 final; European Commission, 'Proposal for a Directive of the European Parliament and of the Council amending Directive 94/62/EC on packaging and packaging waste' COM(2015) 596 final; European Commission, 'Proposal for a Directive of the European Parliament and of the Council amending Directive 1999/31/EC on the landfill of waste' COM(2015) 594 final; European Commission, 'Proposal for a Directive of the European Parliament and of the Council amending Directives 2000/53/EC on end-of-life vehicles, 2006/66/EC on batteries and accumulators and waste batteries and accumulators, and 2012/19/EU on waste electrical and electronic equipment' COM(2015) 593 final.

[43] 'EU reaches agreement on single-use plastic ban' <https://www.dw.com/en/eu-reaches-agreement-on-single-use-plastic-ban/a-46797494>. The European Commission proposed a directive to this effect in May 2018; see European Commission, 'Proposal for a Directive of the European Parliament and of the Council on the reduction of the impact of certain plastic products on the environment' COM(2018) 340 final.

[44] Karsten and Reisch, 'Sustainability Policy and the Law' (n 34) 48; O Mont and C Dalhammar, 'Sustainable Consumption: At the Crossroads of Environmental and Consumer Policies' (2005) 8 International Journal of Sustainable Development 258.

[45] Mak and Terryn, 'Circular Economy and Consumer Protection' (n 20) 235 ff, and 239 ff.

in the future. Moreover, greater emphasis could be placed on the social dimension of EU law, besides economic policy. The values and objectives of EU law laid down in Articles 2 and 3 TEU point in that direction, with their emphasis on the pursuit of a social market economy. Further, Articles 9, 11, and 12 TFEU oblige the European Union to take account of requirements linked to the promotion of a high level of employment, consumer protection requirements, and environmental protection requirements in the development of Union policies and activities. These provisions therefore oblige the EU institutions to integrate these requirements into broader policy-making and legislative action.

The difficult question is how further integration can be given shape within the framework of EU law, taking account of the division of competences between the European Union and the Member States, and the direct appeal that citizens can make for the enforcement of individual rights based on EU law. Several pathways are open and may be pursued to a greater extent than they have been until now in the light of the EU's social market economy.[46] In the following, I will focus particularly on labour law, which is gaining new momentum with the implementation of the European Social Pillar (ESP).[47]

At the EU level, integration may pursued through harmonization of laws, the regulation of the free movement of persons and of services, and through policies and legislation developed under the Social Pillar. Until now, as was seen, harmonization has occurred only in limited areas of labour and environmental law. Also in free movement case law, the emphasis has been on market goals rather than social objectives.[48] The ESP may give new momentum to a move towards greater social protection in policy making. While it could be seen as window dressing, in a less cynical view the ESP has the capacity to make a difference, for instance by boosting the mainstreaming of social protection.[49] Its political endorsement gives justification to the EU's Directorates General to act, and a 'social scoreboard' will monitor the implementation of the Pillar, with results on trends and performance being fed into the European Semester of economic policy coordination.[50] Member States could also be encouraged by the ESP to take account of the social consequences of their actions. Overall, the ESP could stimulate the mainstreaming of social policy at a macro level, whereas harmonization could focus on the micro level.[51]

[46] These overlap to some extent with the pathways for the enforcement of civil rights identified by De Vries; see SA de Vries, 'Securing Private Actors' Respect for Civil Rights within the EU: Actual and Potential Horizontal Effects of Instruments' in SA de Vries, H de Waele, and M-P Granger (eds), *Civil Rights and EU Citizenship. Challenges at the Crossroads of the European, National and Private Spheres* (Edward Elgar 2018) 43.

[47] For information on the European Social Pillar, see <https://ec.europa.eu/commission/priorities/deeper-and-fairer-economic-and-monetary-union/european-pillar-social-rights_en>.

[48] See above, pp 241.

[49] Barnard and de Vries, 'The "Social Market Economy" in a (Heterogeneous) Social Europe' (n 39) 57.

[50] ibid.

[51] ibid.

Besides EU and Member State action, in some cases citizens can pursue the protection of fundamental rights through EU free movement regulation. Private actors can for instance rely on protection where civil rights go hand in hand with economic rights but there is also space, according to the Court's judgment in *Schmidberger*, for the protection of civil rights under the free movement scheme where civil rights clash with the Treaty freedoms.[52] Further, in some, albeit limited, circumstances they may directly invoke rights laid down in the EU Charter of Fundamental Rights. Such direct effect has until now however only been recognized in limited circumstances. The CJEU's case law restricts it to situations in which the Charter phrases entitlements as 'rights', and not mere 'principles', in accordance with the distinction made by Article 52(5) of the Charter. The status of individual Charter provisions as rights or principles, however, is not clear. In its 2014 judgment in *AMS* the CJEU denied horizontal effect to Article 27 of the Charter, concerning workers' representation.[53] Moreover, in the same case Advocate General Cruz Villalon develops an argument favouring the assumption that social and employment rights generally belong to the category of principles.[54] More recently, in its 2018 judgment in *Bauer*, the CJEU held that the right to annual leave following from this provision of the Charter has direct effect in horizontal relations between private parties, here between an employer and the widow of one of its employees.[55] The case is seen as confirmation that Charter provisions can only have horizontal direct effect if they stipulate rights. *Bauer* at the same time seems to provide an opening for a broader understanding of social rights laid down in the Charter, and for their enforcement in horizontal relationships. That could have ramifications for other 'rights' laid down in the Charter. For example, Article 31 of the Charter stipulates that '[e]very worker has the right to working conditions which respect his or her health, safety and dignity' and '[e]very worker has the right to limitation of maximum working hours, to daily and weekly rest periods and to an annual period of leave'.[56]

Therefore, several pathways can be distinguished for the pursuit of social goals in the field of labour law, fitting with the EU's objective to pursue a social market economy. The pursuit of social rights protection through labour law could therefore go hand in hand with its protection through consumer law. Both fields of law

[52] Case C-112/00 *Schmidberger* [2003] ECR I-5659, ECLI:EU:C:2003:333, where the exercise of the right to freedom of speech and assembly obstructed the free movement of goods. De Vries, 'Securing Private Actors' Respect for Civil Rights within the EU' (n 46) 53–57.

[53] Case C-176/12 *Association de médiation sociale (AMS)*, ECLI:EU:C:2014:2. See De Vries, 'Securing Private Actors' Respect for Civil Rights within the EU' (n 46) 60–61.

[54] Opinion of Advocate-General Cruz Villalón, Case C-176/12 *Association de médiation sociale v Union locale des syndicats CGT and others*, ECLI:EU:C:2013:491, at [49] and [55].

[55] Joined Cases C-569/16 and C-570/16 *Stadt Wuppertal v Maria Elisabeth Bauer* and *Volker Willmeroth v Martina Broßonn*, ECLI:EU:C:2018:871.

[56] It has been argued that Article 31 of the Charter should be considered a 'right' rather than a 'principle'; A Bogg, 'Article 31—Fair and Just Working Conditions' in S Peers and others (eds), *The EU Charter of Fundamental Rights: A Commentary* (Hart Publishing 2014) para 31.34.

could contribute to the promotion of social inclusion—for which economic inclusion would be a prerequisite—and the protection of EU citizens from a 'fall into poverty'.[57] Future research and policy initiatives could focus on pathways in law, beyond the state but also beyond consumer contract law, that can contribute to these goals.

[57] Compare J Biemans and AG Castermans, *Barmhartigheid in het burgerlijk recht. Preadvies voor de Vereniging voor Burgerlijk Recht* (Uitgeverij Paris 2017), who focus in particular on consumer credit regulation as an instrument of poverty protection.

Bibliography

Abernethy S, 'Building Large-Scale Online Dispute Resolution and Trustmark Systems' (paper presented at the UNECE Forum on ODR 2003 by the President/CEO of SquareTrade) <https://www.mediate.com/Integrating/docs/Abernethy.pdf>

Aboulafia M (ed), *Habermas and Pragmatism* (Routledge 2002)

Akman P, 'Searching for the Long-Lost Soul of Article 82 EC' (2009) 29 Oxford Journal of Legal Studies 276

Albors-Llorens A and Jones A, 'The Images of the "Consumer" in EU Competition Law' in D Leczykiewicz and S Weatherill (eds), *The Images of the Consumer in EU Law. Legislation, Free Movement and Competition Law* (Hart Publishing 2016) 43

Alemanno A and Sibony A-L (eds), *Nudge and the Law: A European Perspective* (Hart Publishing 2015)

Bagchi A, 'The Political Economy of Regulating Contract' (2014) 62 American Journal of Comparative Law 687

Barnard C and Vries SA de, 'The "Social Market Economy" in a (Heterogeneous) Social Europe: Does it Make a Difference?' (2019) 15 Utrecht Law Review 47

Bartl M, *Legitimacy and European Private Law* (doctoral thesis, EUI 2012) <http://cadmus.eui.eu/bitstream/handle/1814/22455/2012_Bartl.pdf?sequence=2>

Bartl M, 'Internal Market Rationality, Private Law and the Direction of the Union: Resuscitating the Market as the Object of the Political' (2015) 21 European Law Journal 572

Bartl M, 'Socio-Economic Imaginaries and European Private Law' in PF Kjær (ed), *The Law of Political Economy: Transformations in the Function of Law* (CUP, 2020); SSRN: https://ssrn.com/abstract=3317374

Bavel B van, *The Invisible Hand? How Market Economies have Emerged and Declined Since AD 500* (OUP 2016)

Beale,H, and others, *Cases, Materials and Text on Contract Law* (2nd edn, Hart Publishing 2010)

Beale H, 'European Contract Law: the Common Frame of Reference and Beyond' in C Twigg-Flessner (ed), *Cambridge Companion to European Union Private Law* (CUP 2010) 116Beale H, 'The Role for European Contract Law: Uniformity or Diversity?' in F de Elizalde (ed), *Uniform Rules for European Contract Law? A Critical Assessment* (Hart Publishing 2018) 9

Bederman DJ, *Custom as a Source of Law* (CUP 2010)

Beitz CR, 'Rawls's Law of Peoples' (2000) 110 Ethics 669

Benton L, 'Historical Perspectives on Legal Pluralism' (2011) 3 Hague Journal on the Rule of Law 57

Biemans J and Castermans AG, *Barmhartigheid in het burgerlijk recht. Preadvies voor de Vereniging voor Burgerlijk Recht* (Uitgeverij Paris 2017)

Black J, 'Proceduralizing Regulation: Part I' (2000) 20 Oxford Journal of Legal Studies 597

Bogg A, 'Article 31—Fair and Just Working Conditions' in S Peers and others (eds), *The EU Charter of Fundamental Rights: A Commentary* (Hart Publishing 2014)

Bohman J and Rehg W, 'Jürgen Habermas' in EN Zalta (ed), *The Stanford Encyclopedia of Philosophy* (Fall 2017 edition) <https://plato.stanford.edu/archives/fall2017/entries/habermas/>

Bolton G, Greiner B, and Ockenfels A, 'Engineering Trust: Reciprocity in the Production of Reputation Information' (2013) 59 Management Science 265

Bozdoganoglu B, 'Tax Issues Arise from a New Economic Model: Sharing Economy' (2017) 8 International Journal of Business and Social Science 119

Brändli C, 'Book Review. The New Global Rulers: The Privatization of Regulation in the World Economy' (2012) 18 Swiss Political Science Review 538

Braucher J, 'New Basics: Twelve Principles for Fair Commerce in Mass-Market Software and Other Digital Products' in JK Winn (ed), *Consumer Protection in the Age of the 'Information Economy'* (Ashgate 2006)

Brown I and Marsden CT, *Regulating Code: Good Governance and Better Regulation in the Information Age* (MIT Press 2013)

Brownsword R, 'The Theoretical Foundations of European Private Law' in R Brownsword and others (eds), *The Foundations of European Private Law* (Hart Publishing 2011) 159

Brugger W, 'Communitarianism as the Social and Legal Theory behind the German Constitution' (2004) 2 International Journal of Constitutional Law 431

Buijze A, *The Principle of Transparency in EU Law* (dissertation, Utrecht University 2013) <https://dspace.library.uu.nl/handle/1874/269787>

Buijze A, 'The Six Faces of Transparency' (2013) 9 Utrecht Law Review 3

Búrca G de, Keohane RO, and Sabel C, 'New Modes of Pluralist Global Governance' (2013) 45 NYU Journal of International Law and Politics 723

Busch C, 'DIN-Normen für Dienstleistungen—Das Europäische Normungskomitee produziert Musterverträge' [2010] Neue Juristische Wochenschrift 3061

Busch C, 'Crowdsourcing Consumer Confidence. How to Regulate Online Rating and Review Systems in the Collaborative Economy' in A De Franceschi (ed), *European Contract Law and the Digital Single Market. The Implications of the Digital Revolution* (Intersentia 2016) 223

Busch C, 'The Future of Pre-contractual Information Duties: Personalization of Disclosures with Big Data' in C Twigg-Flesner (ed), *Research Handbook on EU Consumer and Contract Law* (Edward Elgar 2016) 221

Busch C, 'Verbraucherschutz in der Platformökonomie', WISO Diskurs 15/2018 (Friedrich Ebert Stiftung 2018) <http://library.fes.de/pdf-files/wiso/14618.pdf>

Busch C, 'Article 8: Reputational Feedback Systems' in C Busch and others (eds), *Model Rules on Online Intermediary Platforms* (Jagiellonian University Press 2019) 77–83

Busch C, 'Implementing Personalized Law: Personalized Disclosures in Consumer Law and Privacy Law' (2019) 86 University of Chicago Law Review 309

Busch C, 'Self-Regulation and Regulatory Intermediation in the Platform Economy' in M Cantero Gamito and H-W Micklitz (eds), *The Role of the EU in Transnational Legal Ordering: Standards, Contracts and Codes* (Edward Elgar 2020) 115; SSRN: <https://ssrn.com/abstract=3309293>

Busch C and De Franceschi A, 'Granular Legal Norms: Big Data and the Personalization of Private Law' in V Mak, TFE Tjong Tjin Tai, and A Berlee (eds), *Research Handbook in Data Science and Law* (Edward Elgar 2018) 408

Busch C and others, 'Discussion Draft of a Directive on Online Intermediary Platforms' (2016) 5 Journal of European Consumer and Market Law 164

Butenko A and Cseres K, 'The Regulatory Consumer: Prosumer-Driven Local Energy Production Initiatives', Amsterdam Law School Research Paper No 2015-31, Amsterdam

Centre for European Law and Governance Research Paper No 2015-03 < https://ssrn.com/abstract=2631990>

Butenko A and Larouche P, 'Regulation for Innovativeness or Regulation of Innovation?' (2015) 7 Law, Innovation and Technology 52

Büthe T and Mattli W, *The New Global Rulers: The Privatization of Regulation in the World Economy* (Princeton University Press 2011)

Cafaggi F, 'The Many Features of Transnational Private Rule-Making: Unexplored Relationships Between Custom, Jura Mercatorum and Global Private Regulation' (2015) 36 University of Pennsylvania Journal of International Law 101

Calliess G-P, 'Online Dispute Resolution: Consumer Redress in a Global Market Place' (2006) 7 German Law Journal 647

Calliess G-P, 'Transnational Consumer Law: Co-Regulation of B2C-E-Commerce' in O Dilling, M Herberg, and G Winter (eds), *Responsible Business. Self-Governance and Law in Transnational Economic Transactions* (Hart Publishing 2008)

Calliess G-P and Renner M, 'Between Law and Social Norms: The Evolution of Global Governance' (2009) 22 Ratio Juris 260

Calliess G-P and Zumbansen P, *Rough Consensus and Running Code* (Hart Publishing 2010)

Cantero Gamito M, 'The Transformation in the Making of Private Law via Telecommunications Regulation' in H-W Micklitz and Y Svetiev (eds), 'A Self-Sufficient European Private Law—A Viable Concept?', EUI Working Papers LAW 2012/31

Cantero Gamito M, 'Regulation.com. Self-Regulation and Contract Governance in the Platform Economy: A Research Agenda' (2017) 9 European Journal of Legal Studies 53

Capps P and Machin D, 'The Problem of Global Law' (2011) 74 Modern Law Review 794

Castells M, *The Rise of the Network Society* (2nd edn, OUP 2010)

Cauffman CANMY and Eliantonio M (eds), *The Legitimacy of Standardization as a Regulatory Technique* (Edward Elgar 2020, forthcoming)

Cecot C, and others, 'An Evaluation of the Quality of Impact Assessment in the European Union with Lessons for the US and the EU', AEI-Brookings Joint Center for Regulatory Studies Working Paper 2007 No 07-09 <https://ssrn.com/abstract=984473>

Chen-Wishart M and Magnus U, 'Termination, Price Reduction, and Damages' in G Dannemann and S Vogenauer (eds), *The Common European Sales Law in Context* (OUP 2013) 647

Cherednychenko OO, 'The Impact of Fundamental Rights' in C Twigg-Flesner (ed), *Research Handbook on EU Contract Law and Consumer Law* (Edward Elgar 2016) 109

Chirico F, 'The Function of European Contract Law: An Economic Analysis', in P Larouche and F Chirico (eds), *Economic Analysis of the DCFR. The Work of the Economic Impact Group within the CoPECL Network of Excellence* (Sellier 2010)

Chirico F and Larouche P, 'Conceptual Divergence, Functionalism and the Economics of Convergence' in S Prechal and B van Roermund (eds), *The Coherence of EU Law: The Search for Unity in Divergent Concepts* (OUP 2008) 463

Christensen CM, Raynor ME, and McDonald R, 'What is Disruptive Innovation?', Harvard Business Review 2015 <https://hbr.org/2015/12/what-is-disruptive-innovation>

Cohen M and Sundararajan A, 'Self-Regulation and Innovation in the Peer-to-Peer Sharing Economy' (2015) 82 The University of Chicago Law Review Dialogue 116

Collins H, *The European Civil Code. The Way Forward* (CUP 2008)

Collins H, 'The Revolutionary Trajectory of EU Contract Law towards Post-national Law' (paper presented at the Final Workshop: European Regulatory Private Law. 'A European Advantage in Transnational Lawyering?', EUI, Florence, 26–27 May 2016)

Collins H, 'Building European Contract Law on Charter Rights' in H Collins (ed), *European Contract Law and the Charter of Fundamental Rights* (Intersentia 2017) 1

Commission on European Contract Law, *Principles of European Contract Law. Parts I and II* (partly revised edn, Kluwer 1999) and *Part III* (Kluwer 2002)

Comparato G, *Nationalism and Private Law in Europe* (Hart Publishing 2014)

Comparato G, *The Financialization of the Citizen. Social and Financial Inclusion through European Private Law* (Hart Publishing 2018)

Conant L, *Justice Contained. Law and Politics in the European Union* (Cornell University Press 2002).

Cortés P, *Online Dispute Resolution for Consumers in the European Union* (Routledge 2011)

Cortés P, *The Law of Consumer Redress in an Evolving Digital Market* (CUP 2018)

Cui R, Li J, and Zhang DJ, 'Reducing Discrimination with Reviews in the Sharing Economy: Evidence from Field Experiments on Airbnb', SSRN: <https://ssrn.com/abstract=2882982>

Cutler CA, *Private Power and Global Authority* (CUP 2003)

Dagan H, 'Between Regulatory and Autonomy-Based Private Law' (2016) 22 European Law Journal 644

Dannemann G, 'Choice of CESL and Conflict of Laws' in G Dannemann and S Vogenauer (eds), *The Common European Sales Law in Context* (OUP 2013) 21

Darian-Smith E, *Law and Societies in Global Contexts* (CUP 2013)

Däubler-Gmelin H, 'Die Entscheidung für die so genannte Große Lösung bei der Schuldrechtsreform—Zum Entwurf Eines Gesetzes zur Modernisierung des Schuldrechts' (2001) Neue Juristische Wochenschrift 2281

Davies G, 'The European Union Legislature as an Agent of the European Court of Justice' (2016) 54 Journal of Common Market Studies 846

Davies G and Avbelj M (eds), *Research Handbook on Legal Pluralism and EU Law* (Edward Elgar 2018)

Deakin S, 'The Lisbon Treaty, the Viking and Laval Judgments and the Financial Crisis: in Search of New Foundations for Europe's "Social Market Economy"' in N Bruun, K Lörcher, and I Schömann (eds), *The Lisbon Treaty and Social Europe* (Hart Publishing 2012) 19

Delimatsis P, 'Standardisation in Services—European Ambitions and Sectoral Realities' (2016) 41 European Law Review 513

Delimatsis P, 'Standard-Setting in Services: New Frontiers in Rule-Making and the Role of the EU' in P Sauvé and M Roy (ed), *Research Handbook on Trade in Services* (Edward Elgar 2016) 268

Del Luca LF, Rule C, and Rimpfel K, 'eBay's De Facto Low Value High Volume Resolution Process: Lessons and Best Practices for ODR Systems Designers' (2014) 6 Yearbook on Arbitration and Mediation 204

Delmas-Marty M, *Ordering Pluralism. A Conceptual Framework for Understanding the Transnational Legal World* (N Norberg tr, Hart Publishing 2009)

Devenney J, 'Private Redress Mechanisms in England and Wales for Unfair Commercial Practices' (2016) 5 Journal of European Consumer and Market Law 100

Domurath I, *Consumer Vulnerability and Welfare in Mortgage Contracts* (Hart Publishing 2017)

Dorssemont F, 'Values and Objectives' in N Bruun, K Lörcher, and I Schömann (eds), *The Lisbon Treaty and Social Europe* (Hart Publishing 2012) 47

Drexl J, *Die wirtschaftliche Selbstbestimmung des Verbrauchers* (Mohr Siebeck 1998)

Drobnig U, 'Ein Vertragsrecht für Europa' in JF Baur, KJ Hopt, and KP Mailänder (eds), *Festschrift für Ersnt Steindorff zum 70. Geburtstag am 13 März 1990* (De Gruyter 1990) 1141

Duin A van, 'Metamorphosis? The Role of Article 47 of the EU Charter of Fundamental Rights in Cases Concerning National Remedies and Procedures under Directive 1993/13/EEC' (2017) 6 Journal of European Consumer and Market Law 190

Edelman B, Luca M, and Svirsky D, 'Racial Discrimination in the Sharing Economy: Evidence from a Field Experiment' (2017) 9 American Economic Journal: Applied Economics 1

Eidenmüller H, 'Recht als Produkt' (2009) 64 JuristenZeitung 641

Eidenmüller H and others, 'The Proposal for a Regulation on a Common European Sales Law: Deficits of the Most Recent Textual Layer of European Contract Law' (2012) 16 Edinburgh Law Review 326

Elshout M and others, 'Study on Consumers' Attitudes towards Terms and Conditions (T&Cs). Final Report' (European Commission 2016) <https://ec.europa.eu/info/sites/info/files/terms_and_conditions_final_report_en.pdf>

Engle Merry S, 'Legal Pluralism' (1988) 22 Law and Society Review 869

Etzioni A, 'The EU: the Communitarian Deficit' (2013) 15 European Societies 312European Research Group on the Existing EC Private Law (Acquis Group), *Contract I: Pre-contractual Obligations, Conclusion of Contract, Unfair Terms* (Sellier 2007)

European Research Group on the Existing EC Private Law (Acquis Group), *Contract II: General Provisions, Delivery of Goods, Package Travel and Payment Services* (Sellier 2009)

Fabre C, 'Social Rights in European Constitutions' in G de Búrca, B De Witte, and L Ogertschnig (eds), *Social Rights in Europe* (OUP 2005) 15.

Fairgrieve D and Howells G, 'Rethinking Product Liability: A Missing Element in the European Commission's Third Review of the European Product Liability Directive' (2007) 70 Modern Law Review 962

Falk Moore S, 'Law and Social Change: the Semi-Autonomous Social Field as an Appropriate Object of Study' (1973) 7 Law and Society Review 719

Faure MG, 'Economic Analysis of Tort Law and the European Civil Code' in A Hartkamp and others (eds), *Towards a European Civil Code* (4th and expanded edn, Kluwer Law International 2011) 985

Fejős A, 'Mortgage Credit in Hungary' (2017) 6 Journal of European Consumer and Market Law 139

Ferguson N, *The Tower and the Square* (Penguin Books 2017)

Ferri D and Cortese F (eds), *The EU Social Market Economy and the Law. Theoretical Perspectives and Practical Challenges for the EU* (Routledge 2018)

Finck M, 'Digital Co-regulation: Designing a Supranational Legal Framework for the Platform Economy' (2018) 43 European Law Review 43

Fischer J, 'Consumer Protection in the United States and European Union: Are Protections Most Effective Before or After a Sale?' (2014) 32 Wisconsin International Law Journal 308

Fischer-Lescano A and Teubner G, *Regime-Kollisionen: Zur Fragmentierung des globalen Rechts* (Suhrkamp Verlag 2006)

Fuller LL, *The Morality of Law* (9th edn, Yale University Press 1973)

Galán A and Patterson D, 'The Limits of Normative Legal Pluralism: Review of Paul Schiff Berman, *Global Legal Pluralism: A Jurisprudence of Law beyond Borders*' (2013) 11 International Journal of Constitutional Law 783

Gandal N and Régibeau P, 'Standard-Setting Organisations. Current Policy Issues and Empirical Evidence' in P Delimatsis (ed), *The Law, Economics and Politics of International Standardisation* (CUP 2015) 394

Gerber D, 'Constitutionalising the Economy: German Neo-liberalism, Competition Law and the "New" Europe' (1994) 42 American Journal of Comparative Law 25

Gerven W van and Lierman S, *Algemeen Deel. 40 jaar later. Privaat- en publiekrecht in een meergelaagd kader van regelgeving, rechtsvorming en rechtstoepassing* (Kluwer 2010)

Gierke O von, *Die soziale Aufgabe des Privatrechts* (Springer 1889)

Giesen I, *Alternatieve Regelgeving en Privaatrecht* (Kluwer 2007)

Giliker P, 'The Consumer Rights Act 2015—a Bastion of European Consumer Rights?' (2016) 37 Legal Studies 78

Glinski C and Rott P, 'Regulating Certification Bodies in the Field of Medical Devices: The PIP Breast Implants Litigation and Beyond' (2019) 27 European Review of Private Law 403

Goode R, 'Reflections on the Harmonisation of Commercial Law' (1991) I Uniform Law Review 54

Goode R, 'International Restatements of Contract and English Contract Law' (1997) II Uniform Law Review 231

Goode R, Kronke H, and McKendrick E, *Transnational Commercial Law. Text, Cases and Materials* (2nd edn, OUP 2015)

Gordley J, *The Philosophical Origins of Modern Contract Doctrine* (OUP 1991)

Griffiths J, 'What is Legal Pluralism?' (1986) 24 Journal of Legal Pluralism and Unofficial Law 1

Grifoni and others P, 'Sharing Economy: Business Models and Regulatory Landscape in the Mediterranean Areas' (2018) 11 International Business Research 62

Gutman K, 'The Development of Consumer Law in the US: Comparisons with the EU Experience' (2012) 4 Journal of European Consumer and Market Law 212

Gutman K, *The Constitutional Foundations of European Contract Law: A Comparative Analysis* (OUP 2014)

Haas PM, 'Policy Knowledge: Epistemic Communities' in NJ Smelser and PB Baltes (eds), *International Encyclopedia of the Social and Behavioral Sciences* (Elsevier 2001) 11578

Habermas J, 'Replik auf Einwände' in J Habermas, *Vorstudien und Ergänzungen zur Theorie des kommunikativen Handelns* (Suhrkamp 1995) 553

Habermas J, *Between Facts and Norms* (W Rehg tr, MIT Press 1998)

Habermas J, *Wahrheit und Rechtfertigung. Beiträge zur Diskurstheorie des Rechts und des demokratischen Rechtsstaats* (Suhrkamp 1999)

Habermas J, *The Postnational Constellation. Political Essays* (M Pensky tr, Polity Press 2001)

Hacker P, 'Personalizing EU Private Law: From Disclosures to Nudges and Mandates' (2017) 25 European Review of Private Law 651

Hart HLA, *The Concept of Law* (3rd edn, OUP 2012)

Hartkamp AS, Sieburgh C, and Devroe W (eds), *Cases, Materials and Text on European Law and Private Law* (Hart Publishing 2017)

Hatzopoulos V, *The Collaborative Economy and EU Law* (Hart Publishing 2018)

Heinemann A, 'Social Considerations in EU Competition Law' in D Ferri and F Cortese (eds), *The EU Social Market Economy and the Law. Theoretical Perspectives and Practical Challenges for the EU* (Routledge 2018) 123

Held D, 'Democratic Accountability and Political Effectiveness from a Cosmopolitan Perspective' (2004) 39 Government and Opposition 364

Held, D and others, *Global Transformations: Politics, Economics, and Culture* (Stanford 1999) 14
Helfand MA (ed), *Negotiating State and Non-State Law. The Challenge of Global and Local Legal Pluralism* (CUP 2015)
Helleringer G, 'The Potential for Contract Clauses to Build a European Legal Culture' in G Helleringer and K Purnhagen (eds), *Towards a European Legal Culture* (Beck/Hart Publishing/Nomos 2014)
Hendry J, 'Legal Pluralism and Normative Transfer' in G Frankenberg (ed), *Order from Transfer. Comparative Constitutional Design and Legal Culture* (Edward Elgar 2013) 153
Hesselink MW, 'Five Political Ideas of European Contract Law' (2011) 7 European Review of Contract Law 295
Hesselink MW, 'Unfair Terms in Contracts Between Businesses' in J Stuyck and R Schulze (eds), *Towards a European Contract Law* (Sellier 2011) 131
Hesselink MW, 'The Case for a Common European Sales Law in an Age of Rising Nationalism' (2012) 8 European Review of Contract Law 342
Hesselink MW, 'How Many Systems of Private Law are there in Europe? On Plural Legal Sources, Multiple Identities and the Unity of Law' in L Niglia (ed), *Pluralism and European Private Law* (Hart Publishing 2013) 199
Hesselink MW, 'The New European Legal Culture—Ten Years On' in G Helleringer and K Purnhagen (eds), *Towards a European Legal Culture* (Beck/Hart Publishing/Nomos 2014) 17
Hesselink MW, 'Democratic Contract Law' (2015) 11 European Review of Contract Law 123
Hesselink MW, 'Private Law, Regulation, and Justice' (2016) 22 European Law Journal 681
Hesselink MW, 'Unjust Conduct in the Internal Market. On the Role of European Private Law in the Division of Moral Responsibility between the EU, its Member States and Their Citizens' (2016) 35 Yearbook of European Law 410
Hodges C, 'The Consumer as Regulator' in D Leczykiewicz and S Weatherill (eds), *The Images of the Consumer in EU Law. Legislation, Free Movement and Competition Law* (Hart Publishing 2016) 245
Hodges C, Benöhr I, and Creutzfeldt-Banda N (eds), *Consumer ADR in Europe* (Hart Publishing 2012)
Hodges C, Benöhr I, and Creuztfeldt-Banda N, 'Consumer-to-Business Dispute Resolution: the Power of CADR' (2012) 13 ERA Forum 199
Hoek AAH van, 'Managing Legal Diversity—New Challenges for Private International Law' (2012) 30 Nederlands Internationaal Privaatrecht 362
Hondius EH, 'The Notion of Consumer: European Union versus Member States' (2006) 28 Sydney Law Review 89
Hooker MB, *Legal Pluralism: An Introduction to Colonial and Neo-Colonial Laws* (Clarendon Press 1975)
Howells G, Twigg-Flesner C, and Wilhelmsson T, *Rethinking EU Consumer Law* (Routledge 2018)
Jessup PC, *Transnational Law* (Yale University Press 1956)
Joerges C, 'What is Left of the European Economic Constitution?' (2005) 30 European Law Review 461, 474
Jull Sørensen M, 'Private Law Perspectives on Platform Services: Uber. A Business Model in Search of a New Contractual Legal Frame?' (2016) 5 Journal of European Consumer and Market Law 15

Junuzović M, 'Transparency of (Pre-)Contractual Information in Consumer Credit Agreements: Is Consistency the Missing Key?' (2018) 14 Croatian Yearbook of European Law & Policy 69

Kalouta G, 'The Draft Common Frame of Reference in the Courts' in M Andenas and D Fairgrieve (eds), *Courts and Comparative Law* (OUP 2015) 696

Kaplow L, 'Rules versus Standards: An Economic Analysis' (1992) 42 Duke Law Journal 557

Karsten J and Reisch LA, 'Sustainability Policy and the Law' (2008) 4 German Policy Studies 45

Kaupa C, *The Pluralist Character of the European Economic Constitution* (Hart Publishing 2016)

Keirsbilck B, *The New European Law of Unfair Commercial Practices and Competition Law* (Hart Publishing 2011)

Kelsen H, *Pure Theory of Law* (M Knight tr, University of California Press 1967)

Király M, 'The Rise and Fall of Common European Sales Law' (2015) 2 ELTE Law Journal 31

Klonick K, 'The New Governors: The People, Rules, and Processes Governing Online Speech' (2018) 131 Harvard Law Review 1598

Knigge M and Pavillon CMDS, 'The Legality Requirement of the ADR Directive: Just Another Paper Tiger?' (2016) 5 Journal of European Consumer and Market Law 155

Knigge M and Verhage E, 'The Impact of the ADR Directive on Article 7:904 par. 1 DCC Explored. What is "Unacceptable According to Standards of Reasonableness and Fairness" after the Implementation of the Directive?' in CG Breedveld-de Voogd and others (eds), *BW Krant Jaarboek* (Kluwer 2016) 61

Komesar N, *Imperfect Alternatives: Choosing Institutions in Law, Economics and Public Policy* (University of Chicago Press 1997)

Koop C and Lodge M, 'What is Regulation? An Interdisciplinary Concept Analysis' (2017) 11 Regulation and Governance 95

Kornet N, 'The Common European Sales Law and the CISG. Complicating or Simplifying the Legal Environment?' (2012) 19 Maastricht Journal of European and Comparative Law 164

Krehoff B, 'Legitimate Political Authority and Sovereignty: Why States Cannot be the Whole Story' (2008) 14 Res Publica 283

Kreide R, 'The Ambivalence of Juridification. On Legitimate Governance in the International Context' (2009) 2 Global Justice: Theory Practice Rhetoric 18

Krisch N, *Beyond Constitutionalism: The Pluralist Structure of Postnational Law* (OUP 2010)

Krommendijk J and Loth MA, *Europese rechters in gesprek. Verhalende annotaties* (Boom Juridisch 2018)

Kronman AT, 'Contract Law and Distributive Justice' (1980) 89 Yale Law Journal 472

Kumm M, 'The Cosmopolitan Turn in Constitutionalism: on the Relationship between Constitutionalism in and beyond the State' in JL Dunoff and JP Trachtman (eds), *Ruling the World? Constitutionalism, International Law and Global Governance* (CUP 2009) 258

Kye C, 'Environmental Law and the Consumer in the European Union' (1995) 7 Journal of Environmental Law 31

Kymlicka W, *Multicultural Citizenship. A Liberal Theory of Minority Rights* (OUP 1995)

Lasser M de SOl'E, *Judicial Deliberations: A Comparative Analysis of Transparency and Legitimacy* (OUP 2009)

Leal-Arcas R, Lesniewska F, and Proedrou F, 'Prosumers: New Actors in EU Energy Security', Queen Mary School of Law Legal Studies Research Paper No 257/2017 <https://ssrn.com/abstract=3010714>

Leczykiewicz D, '"Where Angels Fear to Tread": The EU Law of Remedies and Codification of European Private Law' (2012) 8 European Review of Contract Law 47

Leeuwen BJ van, 'From Status to Impact, and the Role of National Legislation: The Application of Article 34 TFEU to a Private Certification Organisation in *Fra.bo*' (2013) 4 European Journal of Risk Regulation 405

Leeuwen BJ van, 'PIP Breast Implants, the EU's New Approach for Goods and Market Surveillance by Notified Bodies' (2014) 5 European Journal of Risk Regulation 338

Leeuwen BJ van, *European Standardisation of Services and Its Impact on Private Law. Paradoxes of Convergence* (Hart Publishing 2017)

Legrand P, 'Against a European Civil Code' (1997) 60 Modern Law Review 44

Leskinen C and Elizalde F de, 'The Control of Terms that Define the Essential Obligations of the Parties under the Unfair Contract Terms Directive: *Gutiérrez Naranjo*' (2018) 55 Common Market Law Review 1595

Liebman L, 'The American Law Institute: a Model for the New Europe?' in F Cafaggi and H Muir-Watt, *Making European Private Law. Governance Design* (Edward Elgar 2008) 209

Linarelli J, 'Global Legal Pluralism and Commercial Law' in P Schiff Berman (ed), *Oxford Handbook on Global Legal Pluralism* (OUP) <https://www.researchgate.net/publication/329024616_GLOBAL_LEGAL_PLURALISM_AND_COMMERCIAL_LAW>

Lindahl H, *Fault Lines of Globalization* (OUP 2013)

Lindahl H, *Authority and the Globalisation of Inclusion and Exclusion* (CUP 2018)

Lindseth P, 'The Eurozone Crisis, Institutional Change, and "Political Union"' in F Allan, E Carletti, and J Gray (eds), *Political, Fiscal, and Banking Union in the Eurozone?* (Wharton Financial Institutions Center Press 2013), SSRN: <https://ssrn.com/abstract=2495818>

Lobel O, 'The Law of the Platform' (2016) 101 Minnesota Law Review 87

Loos MBM, and others, 'Digital Content Contracts for Consumers. Analysis of the Applicable Legal Frameworks and Suggestions for the Contours of a Model System of Consumer Protection in Relation to Digital Content Contracts, Final Report: Comparative Analysis, Law & Economics Analysis, Assessment and Development of Recommendations for Possible Future Rules on Digital Content Contracts. With an Executive Summary of the Main Points' (study performed for the European Commission 2011) <ec.europa.eu/justice/consumer-marketing/files/legal_report_final_30_august_2011.pdf>

Loos MBM, 'Transparency of Standard Terms under the Unfair Contract Terms Directive and the Proposal for a Common European Sales Law' (2015) 23 European Review of Private Law 179

Loos MBM, *Algemene voorwaarden* (Boom juridische uitgevers 2018)

Loos MBM, 'Transparency Under the UCTD: Could You Please Explain what these Terms are Supposed to Mean?' (2020) 9 Journal of European Consumer and Market Law 25

Loos MBM and Samoy I (eds), *The Position of Small and Medium-Sized Enterprises in European Contract Law* (Intersentia 2014)

Lörcher K, 'Social Competences' in N Bruun, K Lörcher, and I Schömann (eds), *The Lisbon Treaty and Social Europe* (Hart Publishing 2012) 165

Low G, 'The (Ir)relevance of Harmonisation and Legal Diversity to European Contract Law: A Perspective from Psychology' (2010) 18 European Review of Contract Law 285

Lucy W, 'What's Private about Private Law?' in A Robertson and HW Tang (eds), *The Goals of Private Law* (Hart Publishing 2009) 47

Lurger B, 'A Radical View of Pluralism? Comments on Jan Smits' in L Niglia, *Pluralism and European Private Law* (Hart Publishing 2013) 173

Luzak JA and Junuzović M, 'Blurred Lines: Between Formal and Substantive Transparency in Consumer Credit Contracts' (2019) 8 Journal of European Consumer and Market Law 97

Luzak JA and Mak V, 'The Consumer Rights Directive' in AS Hartkamp and others (eds), *De invloed van het Europese recht op het Nederlandse privaatrecht* (Kluwer 2014) 67

MacCormick N, 'Beyond the Sovereign State' (1993) 56 Modern Law Review 1

MacCormick N, 'Risking Constitutional Collision in Europe' (1998) 18 Oxford Journal of Legal Studies 517

Majone G, 'The Rise of the Regulatory State in Europe' (1994) 17 West European Politics 77

Mak C, 'The One and the Many: Translating Insights from Constitutional Pluralism to European Contract Law Theory' (2013) 21 European Review of Private Law 1189

Mak C, 'Rights and Remedies: Article 47 EUCFR and Effective Judicial Protection in European Private Law Matters' in H-W Micklitz (ed), *Constitutionalization of European Private Law* (OUP 2014) 236

Mak V, 'Specific Performance in English Consumer Sales Law' in JM Smits, D Haas, and G Hesen (eds), *Specific Performance in Contract Law: National and Other Perspectives* (Intersentia 2008) 121

Mak V, *Performance-Oriented Remedies in European Sale of Goods Law* (Hart Publishing 2009)

Mak V, 'Full Harmonization in European Private Law: A Two-Tracked Concept' (2012) 20 European Review of Private Law 213

Mak V, 'The "Average Consumer" of EU Law in Domestic and European Litigation' in D Leczykiewicz and S Weatherill (eds), *The Involvement of EU Law in Private Law Relationships* (Hart Publishing 2013) 33

Mak V, 'According to Custom … ? The Role of "Trade Usage" in the Proposed Common European Sales Law (CESL)' (2014) 10 European Review of Contract Law 64

Mak V, 'Globalization, Private Law and New Legal Pluralism', NYU Jean Monnet Working Paper Series, JMWP 14/15 <http://jeanmonnetprogram.org/wp-content/uploads/JMWP-14-Mak.pdf>

Mak V, *The Character of European Private Law* (inaugural lecture, Tilburg University 2015)

Mak V, 'Unfair Commercial Practices and Dutch Private Law' (2015) 4 Journal of European Consumer and Market Law 246

Mak V, 'Private Actors as Norm-Setters through Choice-of-Law': The Limits of Regulatory Competition' in C Cauffman and JM Smits (eds), *The Citizen in European Private Law: Norm-Setting, Enforcement and Choice* (Intersentia 2016) 99

Mak V, 'Private Law Perspectives on Platform Services. Airbnb: Home Rentals between AYOR and NIMBY' (2016) 5 Journal of European Consumer and Market Law 19Mak V, 'Pluralism in European Private Law' (2018) 20 Cambridge Yearbook of European Legal Studies 202

Mak V, 'Social Considerations in EU Consumer Law: the Legislator, the Court and a Rhapsody in Blue' in D Ferri and F Cortese (eds), *The EU Social Market Economy and the Law. Theoretical Perspectives and Practical Challenges for the EU* (Routledge 2018) 213

Mak V and Lujinovic E, 'Towards a Circular Economy in EU Consumer Markets—Legal Possibilities and Legal Challenges and the Dutch Example' (2019) 8 Journal of European Consumer and Market Law 4

Mak V and Terryn E, 'Circular economy and Consumer Protection. The Consumer as a Citizen and the Limits of Empowerment through Consumer Law' (2020) 43 Journal of Consumer Policy 227

Mak V, Tjong Tjin Tai TFE, and Berlee A (eds), *Research Handbook on Data Science and Law* (Edward Elgar 2018)

Mataija M, *Private Regulation and the Internal Market: Sports, Legal Services, and Standard Setting in EU Economic Law* (OUP 2016)

Mayer-Schönberger V and Ramge T, *Reinventing Capitalism in the Age of Big Data* (Basic Books 2018)

McKendrick E, 'Restatements of Contract Law' in R Goode, H Kronke, and E McKendrick, *Transnational Commercial Law. Text, Cases and Materials* (2nd edn, OUP 2015) 461

Menting M-C, *Industry Codes of Conduct in a Multi-Layered Dutch Private Law* (dissertation, Tilburg University 2016, unpublished), <https://pure.uvt.nl/ws/portalfiles/portal/23090135/Menting_Industry_07_12_2016_emb.pdf>

Meuwese ACM, *Impact Assessment in EU Lawmaking* (dissertation, Leiden University 2008) 42, <https://openaccess.leidenuniv.nl/bitstream/handle/1887/12589/Thesis.pdf>

Michaels R, 'Global Legal Pluralism' (2009) 5 Annual Review of Law and Social Sciences 243

Michaels R, 'Of Islands and the Ocean: The Two Rationalities of European Private Law' in R Brownsword and others (eds), *The Foundations of European Private Law* (Hart Publishing 2011) 139

Michaels R, 'Globalization and Law: Law Beyond the State' in R Banakar and M Travers (eds), *Law and Social Theory* (Hart Publishing 2013) 287

Michaels R, 'Why We Have No Theory of European Private Law Pluralism' in L Niglia (ed), *Pluralism and European Private Law* (Hart Publishing 2013) 139

Michaels R, 'What is Non-State Law? A Primer' in MA Helfand, *Negotiating State and Non-State Law. The Challenge of Global and Local Legal Pluralism* (CUP 2015) 41

Michaels R, 'A Symmetry of Asymmetries? A Private-International-Law Reconstruction of Lindahl's Work on Boundaries' (2019) 29 Duke Journal of Comparative & International Law 405

Michaels R, 'The Functional Method of Comparative Law' in M Reimann and R Zimmermann (eds), *The Oxford Handbook of Comparative Law* (OUP 2019) 345

Michaels R and Jansen N, 'Private Law Beyond the State? Europeanization, Privatization, Globalization' (2006) 54 American Journal of Comparative Law 843

Micklitz H-W, 'Perspektiven des europäischen Privatrechts—Ius commune praeter legem?' (1998) 6 Zeitschrift für europäisches Privatrecht 253

Micklitz H-W, 'The Visible Hand of European Regulatory Private Law—The Transformation of European Private Law from Autonomy to Functionalism in Competition and Regulation' (2009) 28 (1) Yearbook of European Law 3

Micklitz H-W, 'Failure or Ideological Preconceptions? Thoughts on Two Grand Projects: the European Constitution and the European Civil Code' in K Tuori and S Sankari (eds), *The Many Constitutions of Europe* (Ashgate 2010) 109

Micklitz H-W (ed), *The Many Concepts of Social Justice in European Private Law* (Edward Elgar 2011)

Micklitz H-W, 'Social Justice and Access Justice in Private Law', EUI Working Papers LAW 2011/02

Micklitz H-W, *Brauchen Konsumenten und Unternehmen eine neue Architektur des Verbraucherrechts? Gutachten A zum 69. Deutschen Juristentag* (CH Beck 2012)

Micklitz H-W, 'The ECJ between the Individual Citizen and the Member States—A Plea for a Judge Made European Law on Remedies' in H-W Micklitz and B De Witte (eds), *The European Court of Justice and the Autonomy of the Member States* (Intersentia 2012) 349Micklitz, H-W, 'The Expulsion of the Concept of Protection from the Consumer Law and the Return of Social Elements in the Civil Law: A Bittersweet Polemic' (2012) 35 Journal of Consumer Policy 283

Micklitz H-W, 'Monistic Ideology versus Pluralistic Reality—Towards a Normative Design for European Private Law' in L Niglia (ed), *Pluralism and European Private Law* (Hart Publishing 2013) 29

Micklitz H-W, 'The Forgotten Dimension of European Private Law' in L Azoulai, *The Question of Competence in the European Union* (OUP 2014) 125

Micklitz H-W, *The Politics of Justice in European Private Law. Social Justice, Access Justice, Societal Justice* (CUP 2018)

Micklitz H-W and Domurath I (eds), *Consumer Debt and Social Exclusion in the EU* (Ashgate 2015)

Micklitz H-W and Patterson D, 'From the Nation State to the Market: The Evolution of EU Private Law as Regulation of the Economy Beyond the Boundaries of the Union?' in B Van Vooren, S Blockmans, and J Wouters, *The EU's Role in Global Governance. The Legal Dimension* (OUP 2013) 59

Micklitz H-W and Reich N, 'The Court and Sleeping Beauty: the Revival of the Unfair Contract Terms Directive (UCTD)' (2014) 71 Common Market Law Review 771

Micklitz H-W and Sieburgh C, 'Primary EU Law and Private Law Concepts' in H-W Micklitz and C Sieburgh (eds), *Primary EU Law and Private Law Concepts* (Intersentia 2017) 1

Micklitz H-W and Svetiev Y (eds), 'A Self-Sufficient European Private Law—A Viable Concept?', EUI Working Papers LAW 2012/31

Milanovic B, *Global Inequality. A New Approach for the Age of Globalization* (Belknap/Harvard University Press 2016)

Mišćenić E, 'Croatian Case "Franak": Effective or "Defective" Protection of Consumer Rights?' (2016) 5 Harmonius Journal of Legal and Social Studies in South East Europe 184

Möller H, 'Liberalismus' (1950) 62 Jahrbücher für Nationalökonomie 24

Mont O and Dalhammar C, 'Sustainable Consumption: At the Crossroads of Environmental and Consumer Policies' (2005) 8 International Journal of Sustainable Development 258

Monti G, *EC Competition Law* (CUP 2007)

Muir Watt H, 'Conflicts of Law Unbounded: The Case for a Legal-Pluralist Revival' (2016) 7 Transnational Legal Theory 313

Nebbia P, *Unfair Contract Terms in European Law. A Study in Comparative and EC Law* (Hart Publishing 2007)

Niglia L, 'Prologue: Of Pluralism and European Private Law' in L Niglia (ed), *Pluralism and European Private Law* (Hart Publishing 2013) 1

Niglia L, 'The Double Life of Pluralism in Europe: Between Constitutionalism and Private Law—Arguments for a Post-Formalist Paradigm' in L Niglia (ed), *Pluralism and European Private Law* (Hart Publishing 2013) 13

Nolan D, 'Causation and the Goals of Tort Law' in A Robertson and HW Tang (eds), *The Goals of Private Law* (Hart Publishing 2009) 165

O'Brien C, *Unity in Adversity: EU Citizenship, Social Justice and the Cautionary Tale of the UK* (Hart Publishing 2017)

O'Hara EA and Ribstein LE, *The Law Market* (OUP 2009)

Ogus A, 'Rethinking Self-Regulation' (1995) 15 Oxford Journal of Legal Studies 97

Ogus A, 'Competition between National Legal Systems: A Contribution of Economic Analysis of Comparative Law' (1999) 48 International and Comparative Law Quarterly 405

Podszun R and Kreifels S, 'Digital Platforms and Competition Law' (2016) 5 Journal of European Consumer and Market Law 33

Prassl J, *Humans as a Service. The Promise and Perils of Work in the Gig Economy* (OUP 2018)

Prechal S, 'Competence Creep and General Principles of Law' (2010) 3 Review of European Administrative Law 5

Prechal S and Leeuw M de, 'Dimensions of Transparency: The Building Blocks for a New Legal Principle?' (2007) 0 Review of European Administrative Law 51

Prüfer JO and Schottmüller C, 'Competing with Big Data', Tilburg Law School Legal Studies Research Paper Series No 06/2017, SSRN: <https://ssrn.com/abstract=2918726>

Purnhagen K and Rott P (eds), *Varieties of European Economic Law and Regulation. Liber Amicorum for Hans Micklitz* (Springer 2014)

Raiser L, 'Vertragsfunktion und Vertragsfreiheit' (1960) part IV, reprinted and online <http://www.european-law-school.eu/media/ReaderGrundmann.pdf>

Ramsay I, 'Consumer Redress and Access to Justice' in CEF Rickett and TGW Telfer (eds), *International Perspectives on Consumers' Access to Justice* (CUP 2003) 17

Ramsay I, *Consumer Law and Policy* (3rd edn, Hart Publishing 2012)

Ranchordás SH, 'Online Reputation and the Regulation of Information Asymmetries in the Platform Economy' (2018) 5 Critical Analysis of Law 127

Raskin M, 'The Law and Legality of Smart Contracts' (2017) 1 Georgetown Law Technology Review 305

Rawls J, *A Theory of Justice* (Belknap 1971)

Rawls J, 'The Domain of the Political and Overlapping Consensus' (1989) 64 New York University Law Review 233

Rawls J, *Justice as Fairness: A Restatement* (Harvard University Press 2001)

Reich N, 'Competition Between Legal Orders: A New Paradigm of EC Law?' (1992) 29 Common Market Law Review 861

Reich N, 'A European Contract Law, or an EU Contract Law Regulation for Consumers?' (2005) 28 Journal of Consumer Policy 383

Reich N, 'Horizontal Liability in EC Law: Hybridization of Remedies for Compensation in Case of Breaches of EC Rights' (2007) 44 Common Market Law Review 705

Reich N, 'Transnational Consumer Law—Reality or Fiction?' (2009) 27 Penn State International Law Review 859

Reich N, *General Principles of EU Civil Law* (Intersentia 2013)

Reich N, 'The Principle of Effectiveness and EU Contract Law' (2013) Osservatorio del diritto civile e commerciale 337

Reich N, 'Product Liability and Beyond: An Exercise in Gap-Filling' (2016) 24 European Review of Private Law 619

Renda A, and others, 'Study on the Legal Framework Covering Business-to-Business Unfair Trading Practices in the Retail Supply Chain. Final Report' (European Union 2014) <http://ec.europa.eu/internal_market/retail/docs/140711-study-utp-legal-framework_en.pdf>

Riefa C, 'The Reform of Electronic Consumer Contracts in Europe: Towards an Effective Legal Framework?' (2009) 14 Lex Electron 17

Riefa C, *Consumer Protection and Online Auction Platforms. Towards a Safer Legal Framework* (Ashgate 2015)

Risse T, '"Let's Argue!": Communicative Action in World Politics' (2000) 54 International Organization 1

Robertson A and Tang HW (eds), *The Goals of Private Law* (Hart Publishing 2009)

Rühl G, 'The Common European Sales Law: 28th Regime, 2nd Regime or 1st Regime?' (2012) 19 Maastricht Journal of European and Comparative Law 148

Rühl G, 'Regulatory Competition in Contract Law: Empirical Evidence and Normative Implications' (2013) 9 European Review of Contract Law 61

Rutgers JW, 'The DCFR and the EC-Treaty' in MW Hesselink, C Mak, and JW Rutgers, 'Constitutional Aspects of European Private Law' (2009) 5 Centre for the Study of European Contract Law Working Paper Series 62, <http://ssrn.com/abstract=1413089>

Rutgers JW, 'Case Note: Court of Justice of the European Union 28 July 2016, Case C-191/15 *Verein für Konsumenteninformation v Amazon EU Sàrl*, ECLI:EU:C:2016:612' (2017) 64 Netherlands International Law Review 163

Sandel M, *Liberalism and the Limits of Justice* (2nd edn, CUP 1998)

Sassen S, *A Sociology of Globalization* (WW Norton 2007)

Scammell M, 'The Internet and Civic Engagement: The Age of the Citizen-Consumer' (2000) 17 Political Communication 351

Schagen EAG van, *The Development of European Private Law in a Multilevel Legal Order* (dissertation, Tilburg University 2013, unpublished)

Schagen EAG van, 'The Hidden Potential of Regulatory Impact Assessments (RIAs) in the Private Law *Acquis*' (2014) 22 European Review of Private Law 69

Schally HM 'The Circular Economy Action Plan: An Agenda for Change!' in B Keirsbilck and E Terryn (eds), *Circular Economy and Consumer Protection* (Intersentia 2019) 3

Scharpf FW, 'The European Social Model: Coping with the Challenges of Diversity' (2002) 40 Journal of Common Market Studies 645

Scharpf FW, 'Legitimacy in the Multilevel European Polity' (2009) 1 European Political Science Review 173

Schaub M, 'Wie is consument?' (2017) Tijdschrift voor Consumentenrecht 30

Schepel H, *The Constitution of Private Governance: Product Standards in the Regulation of Integrating Markets* (Hart Publishing 2005)

Schepel H, 'The New Approach to the New Approach: The Juridification of Harmonized Standards in EU Law' (2013) 20 Maastricht Journal of European and Comparative Law 521

Schiff Berman P, *Global Legal Pluralism. A Jurisprudence of Law Beyond Borders* (CUP 2012)

Schiff Berman P, 'How legal pluralism is and is not distinct from liberalism: A response to Galán and Patterson' (2013) 11 International Journal of Constitutional Law 801

Schiff Berman P, 'Non-State Lawmaking through the Lens of Global Legal Pluralism' in MA Helfand (ed), *Negotiating State and Non-State Law. The Challenge of Global and Local Legal Pluralism* (CUP 2015) 15

Schmid CU, 'The Instrumentalist Conception of the Acquis Communautaire in Consumer Law and its Implications on a European Contract Law Code' (2005) 1 European Review of Contract Law 211

Schulte-Nölke H, 'The Brave New World of EU Consumer Law—Without Consumers, or Even Without Law?' (2015) 4 Journal of European Consumer and Market Law 135

Schwartz A and Wilde LL, 'Imperfect Information in Markets for Contract Terms: The Examples of Warranties and Securities Interests' (1983) 69 Virginia Law Review 1387

Schwartz A and Wilde LL, 'Product Quality and Imperfect Information' (1985) 52 The Review of Economic Studies 251

Schweitzer H, 'Digitale Plattformen als private Gesetzgeber: Ein Perspektivwechsel für die europäische "Plattform-Regulierung"' (2019) 27 Zeitschrift für Europäisches Privatrecht 1

Scott C, Cafaggi, F, and Senden, L (eds), *The Challenge of Transnational Private Regulation: Conceptual and Constitutional Debates* (Wiley-Blackwell 2011)

Shalin DN, 'Introduction: Habermas, Pragmatism, Interactionism' (1992) 15 Symbolic Interaction 251

Sieburgh C, 'A Method to Substantively Guide the Involvement of EU Law in Private Law Matters' (2013) 21 European Review of Private Law 1156
Smith SA, 'In Defence of Substantive Fairness' (1996) 112 Law Quarterly Review 138
Smits JM, *The Making of European Private Law* (Intersentia 2002)
Smits JM, 'Plurality of Sources in European Private Law, or: How to Live with Legal Diversity?' in R Brownsword and others (eds), *The Foundations of European Private Law* (Hart Publishing 2011) 323
Smits JM, 'A Radical View of Legal Pluralism' in L Niglia, *Pluralism and European Private Law* (Hart Publishing 2013) 161
Smits JM, 'Het privaatrecht van de toekomst' (2015) 52 (2) *Tijdschrift voor Privaatrecht* 517
Sokol DD, 'Troubled Waters Between US and European Antitrust' (2017) 115 Michigan Law Review 955
Sousa Santos B de, *Toward a New Legal Common Sense* (2nd edn, CUP 2002)
Stanford J, *A Short Guide to the Economics of Capitalism* (2nd edn, Pluto Press 2015)
Steennot R, 'Belgium: Private Law Remedies for Breach of the Prohibition of Unfair Commercial Practices' (2015) 4 Journal of European Consumer and Market Law 188
Strahilevitz L and Porat A, 'Personalizing Default Rules and Disclosures with Big Data' (2014) 112 Michigan Law Review 1417
Strawson PF, *Individuals* (1959, reprint Routledge 1991)
Study Group on a European Civil Code, Research Group on the Existing EC Private Law (Acquis Group), *Draft Common Frame of Reference (DCFR). Principles, Definitions and Model Rules of European Private Law. Full Edition* (Sellier 2009)
Study Group on Social Justice in European Private Law, 'Social Justice in European Contract Law: A Manifesto' (2004) 10 European Law Journal 653
Sundararajan A, *The Sharing Economy* (MIT Press 2016)
Sundararajan A, 'The Collaborative Economy: Socioeconomic, Regulatory and Policy Issues' (In-depth Analysis for the IMCO Committee of the European Parliament 2017)
Svetiev Y, 'The EU's Private Law in the Regulated Sectors: Competitive Market Handmaiden or Institutional Platform?' (2016) 22 European Law Journal 659
Swire PP, 'When Should "Consumers-as-Producers" Have to Comply with Consumer Protection Laws?' (2008) 31 Journal of Consumer Policy 473
Tamanaha B, 'Understanding Legal Pluralism: Past to Present, Local to Global' (2008) 30 Sydney Law Review 375
Tamanaha B, *The Perils of Pervasive Legal Instrumentalism* (Wolf Legal Publishing 2008)
Taylor C, *Sources of the Self* (Harvard University Press 1989)
Teubner G, 'Global Bukowina: Legal Pluralism in the World Society' in G Teubner (ed), *Global Law without a State* (Dartmouth 1997) 3
Teubner G, *Constitutional Fragments: Societal Constitutionalism and Globalization* (OUP 2012)
Tiebout C, 'A Pure Theory of Local Expenditure' (1956) 64 Journal of Political Economy 416
Toffler A, *The Third Wave* (Bantam Books 1980)
Trentmann F, *Empire of Things. How We Became a World of Consumers, from the Fifteenth Century to the Twenty-first* (Allen Lane 2016)
Tridimas T, 'The ECJ and the National Courts: Dialogue, Cooperation, and Instability' in A Arnull and D Chalmers (eds), *The Oxford Handbook of European Union Law* (OUP 2015) 403
Twigg-Flesner C, 'Bad Hand? The "New Deal" for EU Consumers' (2018) 15 Zeitschrift für das Privatrecht der Europäischen Union 166

Twigg-Flesner C, 'The EU's Proposals for Regulating B2B Relationships on Online Platforms—Transparency, Fairness and Beyond' (2018) 7 Journal of European Consumer and Market Law 222

Twining W, *General Jurisprudence* (CUP 2009)

Twining W, 'Normative and Legal Pluralism: A Global Perspective' (2010) 20 Duke Journal of International and Comparative Law 473

Unberath H and Johnston A, 'The Double-Headed Approach of the ECJ Concerning Consumer Protection' (2007) 44 Common Market Law Review 1237

d'Usseaux F, 'Formal and Substantive Aspects of the Transparency Principle in European Private Law' [1998] Consumer Law Journal 320

Verbruggen PWJ, 'Private Regulation in EU Better Regulation. Past Performance and Future Promises' (2017) 19 European Journal of Law Reform 121

Verbruggen PWJ, 'Good Governance of Private Standardization and the Role of Tort Law' (2019) 27 European Review of Private Law 319

Verbruggen PWJ and Leeuwen BJ van, 'Aansprakelijkheid voor gebrekkige medische hulpmiddelen' [2015] Nederlands Tijdschrift voor Burgerlijk Recht (NTBR) 308

Verbruggen PWJ and Leeuwen BJ van, 'Europese regelgeving inzake medische hulpmiddelen. Het PIP-schandaal, de "Nieuwe Aanpak" en consumentenbescherming' [2015] Tijdschrift voor Consumentenrecht 111

Verbruggen PWJ and Leeuwen BJ van, 'The Liability of Notified Bodies under the EU's New Approach: The Implications of the PIP Breast Implants Case' (2018) 43 European Law Review 394

Vogenauer S, 'Regulatory Competition through Choice of Law and Choice of Forum in Europe: Theory and Evidence' (2013) 21 European Review of Private Law 13

Vries SA de, 'General Reflections on the Exercise of Economic Rights by EU Citizens' in SA de Vries and others (eds), *EU Citizens' Economic Rights in Action. Re-thinking Legal and Factual Barriers in the Internal Market* (Edward Elgar 2018) 2

Vries SA de, 'Securing Private Actors' Respect for Civil Rights within the EU: Actual and Potential Horizontal Effects of Instruments' in SA de Vries, H de Waele, and M-P Granger (eds), *Civil Rights and EU Citizenship. Challenges at the Crossroads of the European, National and Private Spheres* (Edward Elgar 2018) 43

Waeyenberge A van and Restrepo Amariles D, 'James Elliott Construction: A "New(ish) Approach" to Judicial Review of Standardisation' (2017) 42 European Law Review 882

Walker N, *The Intimations of Global Law* (CUP 2015)

Weatherill S, 'Competence Creep and Competence Control' (2004) 23 Yearbook of European Law 1

Weatherill S, *EU Consumer Law and Policy* (2nd edn, Edward Elgar 2013)

Weatherill S, 'Article 38—Consumer Protection' in S Peers and others (eds), *The EU Charter of Fundamental Rights: A Commentary* (Hart Publishing 2014)

Weatherill S, *Contract Law of the Internal Market* (Intersentia 2016)

Weatherill S, *Law and Values in the European Union* (OUP 2016)

Weitzenboeck EM, 'Looking Back to See Ahead: The Changing Face of Users in European E-Commerce Law' (2015) 23 Artificial Intelligence Law 201

Wendehorst C, 'Platform Intermediary Services and Duties under the E-Commerce Directive and the Consumer Rights Directive' (2016) 5 Journal of European Consumer and Market Law 30

Whittaker S and Zimmermann R, *Good Faith in European Contract Law* (CUP 2000)

Wilhelmsson T, *Social Contract Law and European Integration* (Dartmouth 1995)Wilhelmsson T, 'Varieties of Welfarism in European Contract Law' (2004) 10 European Law Journal 712

Willett C, *Fairness in Consumer Contracts: The Case of Unfair Terms* (Ashgate 2007)

Winn JK, 'The Secession of the Successful: The Rise of Amazon as Private Global Consumer Protection Regulator' (2016) 58 Arizona Law Review 193

Winn JK and Webber M, 'The Impact of EU Unfair Contract Terms Law on US Business-to-Consumer Internet Merchants (2006) 62 Business Law 209

Witte F De, 'The Architecture of a Social Market Economy' in P Koutrakos and J Snell (eds), *Research Handbook on the EU's Internal Market* (Edward Elgar 2016) 117

Woodman GR, 'Ideological Combat and Social Observation. Recent Debate about Legal Pluralism' (1998) 42 Journal of Legal Pluralism 21

Zumbansen P, 'Defining the Space of Transnational Law: Legal Theory, Global Governance and Legal Pluralism', Comparative Research in Law & Political Economy, Research Paper No 21/2011 <http://digitalcommons.osgoode.yorku.ca/clpe/59>

Zumbansen P, 'The Constitutional Itch: Transnational Private Regulatory Governance and the Woes of Legitimacy' in MA Helfand, *Negotiating State and Non-State Law. The Challenge of Global and Local Legal Pluralism* (CUP 2015) 83

Index

For the benefit of digital users, indexed terms that span two pages (e.g., 52–53) may, on occasion, appear on only one of those pages